Semantics

The study of meaning in language has developed dramatically over the last fifty years. *Semantics* is distinctive as it not only presents a general introduction to the topic, including the most recent developments, but it also provides a unique perspective for addressing current issues. It opens by introducing readers to the study of logic (natural deduction) as the background against which developments have taken place. This demonstrates the link between semantics and the study of reasoning and how this view can provide new solutions to the puzzles that have plagued the approaches presented in other textbooks. The major subject areas of semantics are discussed, including quantification, anaphora and discourse, tense and aspect, ellipsis and context and word meaning. The book also presents state-of-the-art research in topics at the forefront of semantics.

RONNIE CANN is a Reader in the Department of Linguistics and English Language at the University of Edinburgh.

RUTH KEMPSON is a Professor of Linguistics in the Department of Philosophy at King's College London.

ELENI GREGOROMICHELAKI is a Research Fellow in the Department of Philosophy at King's College London.

CAMBRIDGE TEXTBOOKS IN LINGUISTICS

General editors: P. AUSTIN, J. BRESNAN, B. COMRIE, S. CRAIN, W. DRESSLER, C. EWEN, R. LASS, D. LIGHTFOOT, K. RICE, I. ROBERTS, S. ROMAINE, N. V. SMITH

Semantics

An Introduction to Meaning in Language

Semantics
An Introduction to Meaning in Language

RONNIE CANN

University of Edinburgh

RUTH KEMPSON

King's College London

ELENI GREGOROMICHELAKI

King's College London

CAMBRIDGE
UNIVERSITY PRESS

CAMBRIDGE UNIVERSITY PRESS

Cambridge, New York, Melbourne, Madrid, Cape Town, Singapore, São Paulo, Delhi

Cambridge University Press
The Edinburgh Building, Cambridge CB2 8RU, UK

Published in the United States of America by Cambridge University Press, New York

www.cambridge.org
Information on this title: www.cambridge.org/9780521525664

First published 2009

Printed in the United Kingdom at the University Press, Cambridge

A catalogue record for this publication is available from the British Library

ISBN 978-0-521-81962-6 hardback
ISBN 978-0-521-52566-4 paperback

Contents

Figures

Preface

Semantics, broadly construed, is the study of meaning in language; but don't be fooled into thinking that such a characterisation is nothing more than a definition: a lot hangs on the word **in**. The theoretical study of semantics is the attempt to get to grips with what the expressions of a natural language contribute to some over-all process of interpretation that the language makes possible. The challenge of understanding such a central aspect of human behaviour has gripped the greatest thinkers for many centuries and within many philosophical traditions.

The development of semantics, more narrowly, over the last half-century within linguistics, provides an almost textbook illustration of the way scientific theorising progresses. Intellectual argumentation feeds the sociology of academic custom; the successful view then squeezes out the rejected view so that it becomes first derided and then unthinkable; over time, this rejected stance emerges again, yet in a variant so transformed by the methodology of the successful view that new questions can be raised and new insights achieved that simply couldn't in principle have been articulated at the earlier stage of debate.

In the current state of play in semantics, the view which has held total sway for nearly half a century is now the invariable stance of all semantics textbooks: *semantics* is the articulation of the relation between natural language expressions and the world around which language enables humans to talk about. Yet, in the research that has been developing over the last twenty years, the assumptions on which semantics has been grounded have been progressively shifting; and, in consequence, earlier disputes over the relation between semantics and the cognitive enterprise in general can be seen in an entirely different light, with new insights into natural-language understanding emerging in the light of the way the formal tools developed in semantic theorising have evolved.

This textbook is novel in aiming to introduce its readers to semantics in a way that will enable them not merely to appreciate the way the discipline of semantics has evolved over the last thirty years, but also to see the significance of the various shifts that are continuing to take place. Readers are provided with sufficient background in logic to see how formal investigation of natural language is grounded in the concept of formal language defined in logic. From this, they are introduced to the dispute over the status of semantic representations within the explanation of natural language, with consequent total abandonment of any form of cognitive representation within semantic explanation. They are then introduced in depth to some of the major areas of formal semantic research: quantification, anaphora, tense/aspect, ellipsis and lexical meaning. Through the detailed characterisation of research in these areas, we have tried to give a sense both of why formal semantics has been so justly pre-eminent in semantic research, and yet how development of formal-semantic tools have led to the re-exploration of semantic representations within semantic explanation, albeit in a totally transformed way. Finally, in conclusion, we have suggested that new work in some of these areas promises to provide a drawing together of cognitive and semantic approaches to natural language.

At the most broad level, our aim has been to give readers a sense of how formal tools transform the nature of theoretical debate by sharpening the focus of intellectual ideas and thereby create new questions and hence new insights. If the reader comes to see that the developments in formal semantics over the last half-century are indeed an illustration of why it is that, in fruitful theoretical research, there is so often the push-me pull-you relation between foundational insights and formal methodologies, then we will deem it to have succeeded in its aims.

This book has benefited from a number of different influences. It has been written since the second author's shift to the Philosophy Department at King's College London, and she is happy to thank the department for the entirely convivial intellectual atmosphere within which exploration of some of these ideas has taken place. It brings together different teaching experiences of semantics by all three authors severally teaching at both undergraduate and postgraduate levels; and, reflecting these, the book is aimed at senior undergraduates, and master's level students. Though the book combines introduction to semantics with introduction to logic, it has been quite explicitly written for linguistics students, and respecting that objective, we decided, after extended discussion, to write the logic sections ourselves, rather than turning to any one of a number of logicians who might well have been happy to contribute. Our view was that, in areas such as logic with tightly articulated formal content, it may sometimes be better to have an introduction written by authors somewhat outside the working core of the discipline, as only they can have a sense of what those coming from the other discipline need to know, and only they will be so crass as to try and extract just those relevant subparts.

So, in thanking those who have given us such support, we include first and foremost Dov Gabbay and Wilfried Meyer-Viol, from whom we have learnt an enormous amount over the years. There are however a lot of other people to thank, who have given us intellectual stimulation, friendship and collegiality over the years. Of the colleagues of the first author, special thanks go to Dan Wedgwood, who provided valuable input from the experience of teaching some of the material of this book, to Nik Gisborne for introducing him to the mysteries of lexical semantics, to Caroline Heycock, Bob Ladd, Heinz Giegerich and other colleagues at the University of Edinburgh whose friendship and collegiality have been a constant source of (critical) support over the last few decades. Then there are colleagues from elsewhere in London University who have contributed to the development of these ideas either by their own work or by the influence their ideas have had on our own: Lutz Marten, Shalom Lappin, Jonathan Ginzburg. Thanks are also due to the two research teams at Edinburgh and London and other affiliated folk: David Adger, Stavros Assimakopoulos, Miriam Bouzouita, Stelios Chatzikyriakidis, Andrew Gargett, Patrick Healey, Christine Howes, Jieun Joe Kiaer, Akiko Kurosawa, Merilin Miljan, Greg J. Mills, Matt Purver, Yo Sato, Ian Underwood, Virve Vihman, Graham White, Yi-Cheng Wu, and Aiko Yamanaka. We thank Alexander Davies and Timothy Pritchard for valuable feedback on Chapter 8, Duilio d'Alfonso for very helpful discussions concerning the material in Chapters 2–3, and to members of the Philosophy Department and in particular Mark Textor, Richard Samuels and David Papineau for illuminating discussions. Of all the friends and colleagues with whom we have argued over the years about the issues raised in this book, whether in agreement or disagreement, we would like to thank in particular: Nicholas Asher, Emmon Bach, Holly Branigan, Robyn Carston, Wynn Chao, Robin Cooper, Annabel Cormack, Arash Eshghi, Raquel Fernández-Rovira, Tim Fernando, Justin Fitzpatrick, Chris Frauenberger, Asli Göksel, Jennifer Kane, Hans Kamp, Udo Klein, Nathan Klinedinst, Miltiadis Kokkonidis, Ivona Kucerova, Nancy Kula, Yuki Kuroda, Staffan Larsson, Trevor Marchand, Greg J. Mills, Glyn Morrill, Ad Neeleman, Stanley Peters, Martin Pickering, Paul Piwek, Devyani Sharma, Horst Simon, Mark Steedman, Graham Stewart, Matthew Stone, Elizabeth Traugott, Stavroula Tsiplakou, Hiroyuki Uchida, Hans van der Koot, Klaus von Heusinger Reiko Vermeulen and Deirdre Wilson, all of whom have contributed in one way or another to the crystallisation of our views. We thank Helen Barton, Andrew Winnard and their production team at Cambridge University Press for getting us cheerfully through the book-preparation process. The first-named author is grateful for support in the final stages of preparing this book from the Leverhulme Trust (Major Research Fellowship F00158BF). The second and third authors are grateful for support from both the Leverhulme Trust for its support of the Dialogue Matters research network (F07 04OU), during which crystallisation of the ideas about word meaning and ellipsis modelling have evolved, and to the ESRC for its support of the Dynamics of Conversational Dialogue project during the final stages of preparation (ESRC RES-062-23-0962).

Finally we thank Ruth's mother for still remaining healthy and well at such an advanced age throughout the final stages of preparing this manuscript. We dedicate this book to her in testament to her fortitude, her ability to combine a strong sense of philosophical enquiry with an equally strong sense of humour, and her Quaker training in never giving in when times get hard. The model she has provided for her family has, indirectly, been a model to us all.

1   Preliminaries for model building

1.1   Introduction

Talking about language and meaning should, surely, be easy: the fact that we use language to pass on information to each other, to describe what we see around us, to reflect on our thoughts about ourselves, each other and the future, to confide in others about those thoughts and anxieties must mean that the concept of meaning for language is the heart and soul of what languages are about. Yet, as soon as we start probing what concept of meaning we should articulate, the phenomenon threatens to slip away under our fingers in a morass of open-endedness. So, for example, we can use words to mean the opposite of what the words themselves seem to mean, as in the first part of speaker B's reply to speaker A:

(1.1)   A. How are things?
           B. Everything's perfect. My computer's seized up for the second time in
              three days.

We can also use words loosely, but nevertheless successfully, as when one might say:

(1.2)   I am shaking with fear.

And we can use words to convey something really rather different from what the words normally mean, as when one of us utters *She's an angel* to refer to a sister. Metaphorical use of words and phrases fades into ambiguity, along a cline of intermediate cases, as in (1.3), where neither *spend* nor *driven* relate to more familiar concrete interpretations associated with money or cars:

(1.3)   I spend my life driven by terror.

Then, less conventionally, language can be used to convey meaning quite indirectly, as when, instead of greeting people as one joins them for lunch, one signally fails to greet them in any conventionalised way, starting immediately with:

(1.4)   Don't ask me to construct a research proposal ever again. It's been a
           nightmare.

with a clear underlying message that the speaker is over-stressed, flustered and in need of calming down. (Notice in passing the use of *nightmare* to describe an event with no implication whatever that one had slept through it.) Indirect use of language is common and pervasive; witness also the effectiveness of B's reply to A in the following exchange clearly implying that she doesn't like him:

(1.5)   A: Are you inviting me to your party?
          B: I'm only inviting people I like.

Through all this Pandora's box of data, certain aspects of language and its construal nevertheless stand out. First, despite all the problems of characterising the various uses to which language can be put, in using a language we have a clear capacity to combine words together to yield an interpretation for a sentence as a whole:

(1.6)   No man I ever met kissed me when we were first introduced.

In processing (1.6), the individual words *no, man, I, ever, met, kissed, me, when, we, were, first, introduced* are parsed in turn, each adding to the information that has been established up to that point in the parse, progressively building up the meaning of the whole from those individual parts. Even without a time-linear parsing perspective, it is clear that the individual words combine with neighbouring words in a systematic way to determine some composite whole. This is known as the *principle of compositionality*, which takes it to be a universal property of natural languages that the meanings of complex expressions are constructed from the meanings of the words they contain and the way those words are put together by the syntax of a language. In other words, the meanings we ascribe to strings of words are not random, but determined, at least to a large part, by building blocks of meanings given by the words and modes of combination, including word order and grammatical processes such as passivisation, question formation etc.

Second, running somewhat counter to this idea, on almost every occasion of use of a sentence, its construal may depend on the immediate context in which the sentence is uttered. For example, in answers to questions, the answer in some sense completes the structure which the question, as its context, provides:

(1.7)   A: What shall I give Eliot?
          B: A teddy bear.

The string uttered may be just one word referring to some activity going on in the discourse situation, as when a parent shouts to a child reaching up to a saucepan full of boiling water:

(1.8)   Don't.

or when a parent of a teenager looking at the waves beside their son holding his surfboard in his hand less dictatorially says:

(1.9)   I wouldn't, if I were you.

This is part of a much more general phenomenon of *context-dependence*, which is in part conventionalised within a language. Some words have as their intrinsic content the signalling of the need to find a semantic value from the surrounding context of utterance. These are pronouns and other so-called anaphoric expressions such as the determiner *the*, and VP (verb phrase) pro-predicate forms, like *do, do so* or *did, did so* below:

(1.10)   John came in. He was sick.

(1.11)   John came in. The poor dear was sick.

(1.12)   John saw Mary and so did Sue.

These anaphoric expressions may even act as place-holders for getting their value from some subsequent part of the utterance:

(1.13)   It is possible that I am wrong.

(1.14)   She's an angel, my sister.

(1.15)   If you want me to do so, I will come with you.

But such signals, which direct the hearer to context to establish their interpretation, are, apparently, not necessary. We may deliberately leave out portions of sentences, knowing that our hearer will be able to recover the intended interpretation from the surrounding context. This is the phenomenon called *ellipsis*:

(1.16)   John has finished his homework, but Sue hasn't.

(1.17)   I am seeing someone today, but I don't know who.

(1.18)   John will be interviewing the President, Harry the Vice-President.

(1.19)   I persuaded Tom to visit Mary in hospital, and Sue did Harry.

(1.20)   If you want me to, I will come with you.

These various ellipsis phenomena have been analysed as heterogeneous, not subject to a single form of explanation; but what underlies them all is the fact that the context, in some sense, provides the meaning for the elliptical expression.

   However, the reliance of meaning on context can go further even than this, with speakers and hearers switching roles midway through an utterance:

(1.21)   A: What shall I give
             B: Eliot? A teddy bear.
             A: Or a dinosaur?

What A says in (1.21) can be taken as a context which provides enough information for B to take over as though he had been the speaker – he doesn't have to start from the beginning and say everything silently before providing the continuation. Equally, A is able to switch into being a hearer as though she had been listening throughout that utterance. Just like B, she doesn't have to parse everything from scratch again. To the contrary, she just picks up as hearer from where she leaves off as speaker: the context is sufficient for her to parse from that point. As this example shows, this switching can happen successively. This is not just a random performance error or sloppiness. It is something we can all do fluently, and from very early on in child language acquisition. Universally children love the kind of game where you sing to them:

(1.22)   A: Old MacDonald had a farm. And on that farm he had a
           B (child): Dog.

So it appears that, though we can use words to successively build up a composite whole, this process has also to be sensitive to how the context contributes to such a process.

The concept of compositionality is made more problematic by the third aspect of language: the variation in how much meaning a word may have, and, accordingly, how essential words are to the point being made. Some are critical, as is each word in (1.6) and the only word in (1.8), others barely make any difference. The first word in (1.13) seems purely a prop required by English word order; and yet others, like the *that* in (1.23) and *there* in (1.25), make no difference at all as can be seen by the paraphrases in (1.24) and (1.26) which omit *that* and *there* and still seem to mean the same thing:

(1.23)   No man that I ever met kissed me when we were first introduced.

(1.24)   No man I ever met kissed me when we were first introduced.

(1.25)   There is something I must tell you.

(1.26)   I must tell you something.

So we have to articulate the precise nature of structural and meaning properties of natural language, in order to determine the precise role that words in a language play in this process of establishing interpretations for sentences. With (1.25)–(1.26), we stumble on a different puzzle. Though there is a difference in the order of the words, and clearly some structural relation between what is expressed by *there is* and the remainder, the resulting meaning is the same. But this might suggest, perhaps, that the structural properties of sentences have to be seen as something different from just the provision of a basis for interpretation, as there can be strings with different structure and yet the same interpretation.

1.2   Explaining semantics: starting from words?

In making a first stab at the problem of compositionality, one might assume that one should first look at word meanings, and then define a process of combining those meanings together. So, let us suppose, one should be able to turn to a dictionary and take definitions from there as a starting point. It might come as a surprise to someone coming to the study of semantics for the first time, but any such move turns out to be a complete failure. Despite long and very rich traditions of dictionary-making, there are really very few words for which we can successfully provide definitions at all. There are verbs of causation such as *kill, blacken, paint*, there are kinship terms such as *bachelor, mother*. But the list stops almost at that point. But it's worse than that; for, even within this list, such verbs have their interpretation very largely determined by context. As Jerry Fodor vividly spells out in detail (Fodor 1998), the concepts of painting the Sistine Chapel, painting one's sitting-room wall, painting one's signature on the painting and painting one's face red do not all involve 'causing some surface to be covered with paint' as a dictionary definition might lead us to expect: paint factories that explode and totally cover some road with paint have not thereby painted the road. To get even remotely close to a reasonable definition one has to shift into a definition such as 'cover a surface with paint having the primary intention so to do'. Now this might be closer to what, upon reflection across a reasonably broad range of usages, an analyst might think had to be specified as the meaning of the word. But is this what the child has to learn in order to use the word *paint*? When the child says in tears, *Mummy, you've painted my dinosaur*, have they not used the word correctly unless they have some complex intention-attribution on the part of the mother in mind? And it won't do to say the word is simply ambiguous according as these different concepts are invoked, as otherwise, by that criterion, every word of the language will be ambiguous. And, though indeed we might conclude that there is much more ambiguity than might be considered at first sight, we certainly should not trivialise this as applying to every single word in the language.

Unless we are content to invoke lexical ambiguity for a word each time its interpretation in some use is at all distinct from that of previous uses, this flexibility of use suggests that there is something else going on between words themselves and the actions/events/objects in the world which they describe, a topic which we shall return to in Chapter 8. In the mean time, even in the vanishingly few cases which can be given some superficially appropriate definition, it seems that we have to invoke different *concepts* for what it is that the word *paint* can be used to express; and these are arguably indefinitely rich and variable, complex and highly context-dependent. So, in all cases, the idea that there might be a unique correlation between words and some meaning that they express on the basis of which composite phrasal/sentential meanings can be explained turns out to be a non-starter.

This difficulty was recognised early in the systematic study of language, and some argued in consequence that the energies of the linguist should be directed to capturing the various *sense relations* which a word enters into, as the basis for capturing a more restricted sense of word meaning. This would be at least a step forward, since one would be expressing sense-relations between words, hence at least indicating the web of meanings into which a word can be seen to fit. In fact, this is what regular dictionaries do in practice: they define the meaning of a word by giving some other expression(s) of the language to which it might be said to correspond. We can indeed identify a number of sense relations that hold between words (and phrases); and a large body of work has been put into this enterprise. In particular, such work flourishes in computer science language-directed research, where it plays an important role in developing more intelligent search strategies than just blind pattern-matching.

It is generally assumed that there are at least three basic types of sense relations:

(1.27)   *Synonymy*: sameness of sense (pullover/sweater).

(1.28)   *Hyponymy*: sense inclusion (cat/animal, house/dwelling).

(1.29)   *Antonymy*: oppositeness in sense (cold/hot, dead/alive, big/small).

From these basic relations we can derive a web of connections among words in a language that permit a wide range of inferences over the sentences that contain them. So from (1.30) we can infer (1.31) (among many others):

(1.30)   Joan's pullover is yellow.

(1.31)   Joan's sweater is yellow.

from (1.32) we can infer (1.33):

(1.32)   I do not like animals.

(1.33)   I do not like cats.

and from (1.34) we can infer (1.35):

(1.34)   This water is cold.

(1.35)   This water is not hot.

There are many extensions to these basic relations that we will not go into here, including complex and non-traditional approaches to lexical relations that try to derive the intuitive inference from (1.36) to (1.37):

(1.36)   John wants a hamburger.

(1.37)   John wants to eat a hamburger.

There are very interesting challenges here as to how to distinguish what each word contributes; and giving classificatory lists of what is synonymous with what, what is an antonym of what, etc. may seem like a first step in meaning analysis – part of the gathering of data that is an essential prerequisite of theory construction. Certainly, discussion of such issues is always incorporated in basic linguistic semantics textbooks, but it quickly becomes apparent that these are little more than a distraction from the task of defining a general characterisation of what the meaning of a word consists in. Far from providing any such explanation, they simply presuppose that this question has been answered, and the classifications of uses of these words merely constitute a basis for gathering together those words that have the same or related meaning. All these lists are doing is indicating relations between words, not providing explanations of why these relations hold and how. At most, then, they set out the problems to be explained; but merely looking through them, however assiduously, never in and of itself leads to the explanation that has to be constructed. That has to come from some external reflection of what it is that brings words together into these various classes.

Indeed, the discipline of collecting up appropriate databases of semantic relations provides a good illustration of an *inductive* approach to meaning. *Inductivism* is a term for the methodology which presumes that classifying data, facts under some description, is a necessary step in establishing theoretical explanations of phenomena, and, if done properly, can constitute a base from which theoretical explanations emerge. Moreover, as the argument would have it, the bonus of the inductivist methodology is that researchers are not imposing their own world-view or preconceptions about the data on the data themselves, for these are analysed prior to any such theory construction. However, this view of theory construction, and more particularly of linguistic theorising, is doomed to failure. Theories come from having an idea and then formulating a theory sufficiently precisely around it so that we can evaluate whether that idea is fruitful. It never comes just from making lists of data, as there are just too many data to know what to look for. As the philosopher Karl Popper notably pointed out to students, the instruction 'Observe!' is impossible to conform to, even in informal situations (Popper 1965), let alone when in search of a theory. One needs to have a hypothesis about what it is one is hoping to find, as driven by some background theory. Only then can the search be sufficiently focused to yield fruitful results, either to confirm one's current theoretical hypothesis or, through negative results, to lead one to modify one's theory and, that way, to gradually improve it. We need to know what it is that we are looking for. Observation alone, so Popper claimed, will never yield theoretical results. This was, at the time of Popper writing in the mid-1930s, a controversial stance, when an inductivist methodology of solemnly collecting supposed facts held sway. But now, in a modified form, this is a standard enough view of scientific practice. With inductivism never in principle able to lead to conclusions, but merely to confirmations of hypotheses, we need to state our theories about some phenomenon, in this case linguistic meaning, in terms that are sufficiently precise: in particular, they must either be falsifiable or at least sufficiently precise so that they can lead to other falsifiable hypotheses, each to be tested in their due turn.

For the particular challenge we face in linguistics, what we need in explaining meaning is some basis for formulating a model from which to start to explore a **formal** account of the basis of meaning for natural language; and then, having constructed such models, we evaluate them by assessing their ability to withstand constant attempts at refutation. This is of course just standard methodology for science as applied to semantic theorising. But it is pressing nonetheless. For if we want an explicit characterisation of the nature of language, and more particularly of interpretation of the lexical and phrasal expressions within that, we cannot fail to take up the challenge of constructing formal models to reflect the insights about language that we want to express.

1.2.1   Constructing a semantic theory

So what do we do to construct a theory of semantics? First, we have to set out the criteria that we expect minimally to be met by any part-way reasonable explication of interpretation for natural language expressions. And then we turn to putative models of language to see how well they can meet the target of satisfying those criteria. We have already touched on such minimal criteria. In the first place is the problem of the compositionality of meaning: the meaning of sentences and the phrases that make them up are dependent on the contribution made by the words they contain and the way such sentences are constructed – word order, voice alternations, and so on. An adequate semantic theory must provide an account of how the meanings assigned to words are put together in a systematic way by the syntactic constructions of a language to yield interpretations. And this process, whatever it is, must allow for recursive complexity in order to account for the multiple-embedding properties of natural languages.

Howsoever we characterise this relationship between a sentence as a form and its interpretation(s), there must be appropriate characterisation of the syntax–semantics relation, for there is, as we've seen, a systematic relation between the way the words are structured into units and the way in which they themselves contribute to the whole process of interpretation, however small a slice of meaning any individual word provides. Prediction of semantic relations such as *synonymy*, *hyponymy*, *entailment*, etc., must also be expected to be included in this list of criteria by which a putative semantic theory might be judged. Again, whatever the basis upon which interpretations of expressions are constructed, both simple and complex, there are systematic relations between expressions in virtue of such interpretations; and these a semantic theory should surely be able to characterise, much like a syntactic theory is expected to characterise which strings of a language constitute wellformed sentences.

Now a test of whether we are getting the right semantics for sentences is whether this specification will yield appropriate relations between sentences, said to hold in virtue of their meaning. As we saw above, certain inferential relations hold between sentences simply by virtue of the lexical relations that hold between the words they contain. But there are relations that hold between sentences by virtue, if you like, of their structure and of the grammatical expressions they contain. As with *homonymy*, *synonymy* and *antonymy*, we might thus recognise three primary relations that hold between sentences ($\models$ is the notational symbol for 'derivability in virtue of semantic content'):

(1.38)   a. *Entailment*: a sentence S_1 entails ($\models$) sentence S_2 if and only if the propositional content of S_1 includes that of S_2.
   King's College is on the Strand and is very noisy. $\models$
   King's College is very noisy.
   King's College is on the Strand. $\models$
   There is a building on the Strand.

   b. *Paraphrase*: a sentence S_1 paraphrases sentence S_2 if and only if the propositional content of S_1 is identical to that of S_2 (mutual entailment).

Mary fed the cat. $\models$
The cat was fed by Mary. $\models$
It was the cat that Mary fed.

   c. *Contradiction*: a sentence S_1 contradicts sentence S_2 if and only if the propositional content of S_1 necessarily excludes that of S_2 (S_1 entails the negation of S_2).

Mary likes dogs, but hates cats.
Mary does not like dogs.

Being able to predict these relations, presumed to hold among sentences, is one of the primary driving factors behind theoretical approaches to semantics, capturing entailments in particular. As we shall see as the book progresses, there are a number of different ways of going about this task with differing levels of success and with different implications for the nature of natural-language semantics and the way human beings understand what is said.

1.3   Breaking out of the language circle

In the search for a genuine basis for explaining what the intrinsic content of expressions of language consists in, and how they induce entailment relations, there are two alternative approaches that have been put forward, both serious contenders for success: one is a *representationalist* view that involves assuming representations of content as part of the explanation, the other involves only a mapping from words onto so-called *denotations*, that is, what the words can be used to make assertions about.

1.3.1   The language-of-thought hypothesis

On the first, psychologically based view, we use language to express concepts, and it is the concepts that we have constructed from words with which we reason about the world around us, not the words themselves. The words do no more than provide procedures to enable us to construct such concepts; and it is these which are systematically combined to form complex composite concepts, propositions, with which we reason. On this view, language is just one type of *input system* on a par with vision and other vehicles for retrieving the information that the world around us provides. With language and vision alike, the stimuli which these input systems process enable us to construct concepts with which we reason about the world around us. A systematic property of such input systems is, however, that the information which the particular stimulus intrinsically carries systematically under-determines the interpretations imposed upon it – indeed an input system must have this property to be economical and flexible. So the input stimuli we manipulate depend on context for the way in which they are interpreted. In the language case, too, it is the concepts that we use words to construct which denote the objects we use our words to refer to, not the words themselves. So, on this view, all cognition – vision, language-processing, hearing, processing smells – involves analysing input stimuli from which we construct concepts that we take to be the content of the input information. This may seem a far-fetched view of language, and worse of vision, but in fact such a perspective is becoming a mainstream view of vision. As Francis Crick put it:

> It is difficult for many people to accept that what they see is a symbolic interpretation of the world – it all seems so like the 'the real thing'. But in fact we have no direct knowledge of objects in the world.   (Crick 1994: 33)

On this view, there is ample room for incorporating theories of context. The concepts that we construct from words may naturally be said to be determined by context in one of two ways: either in interaction with those concepts that have just been constructed out of words uttered just previously, or from information independently constructed from other input, such as vision. The *underspecification* of language and its dependence on context is then seen to be a systematic part of what it means to be a sub-system of a cognitive system, clearly an advantage as an explanation of the psychological basis of semantic interpretation. On this view, input stimuli constrain but do not fully determine their interpretation, and this underspecification interacts with information provided by the immediate cognitive context to determine the concepts that we take to be the content of what it is that we see, hear, understand, and so on. This is a mind-internal process, hence computational and, in this sense, syntactic, a mapping from one form of mind-internal representation to another. Essential to this form of explanation is an internal system of conceptual representations – the so-called *language of thought*.

The instigator of this language-of-thought view, Jerry Fodor, puts it thus:

> It's entirely natural to run a computational story about the attitudes [beliefs, intentions and other kinds of thought] together with a translation story about language comprehension; and there's no reason to doubt, so far at least, that the sort of translation that is required is an exhaustively syntactic operation. . . Syntax is about what's in your head, but semantics is about how your head is connected to the world. Syntax is part of the story about the mental representations of sentences, but semantics isn't.   (Fodor 1989: 419)

From a general viewpoint, as a programmatic statement, this perspective might seem surprisingly common sense, if you like it at all, despite the more abstract view of word meaning that it imposes. For the words, on this view, serve to provide constraints on the concepts that, in context, they are taken to express. It has to be said, however, that for a long time this perspective has mainly been articulated in the form of programmatic statements with little or no attempt to give formal substance to them. And, remember, we have committed ourselves to the working assumption that providing formal models that substantiate such programmatic statements is an essential prerequisite for any serious contender for an account of the nature of interpretation of a linguistic signal; and formal models involving such representations are only now being explored in detail.

When this representationalist programme was first put forward, it is arguable that it was not formulated tightly enough. Certainly, it was met with outright derision by those that hold the alternative view in which meaning as expressed in language inheres in a language–world relation defined directly from words onto objects/events, etc. Nevertheless, as we shall see, if it can be given a robust enough grounding in formal understanding of the phenomenon in question, such a programme has the attraction of bringing together natural-language semantics with research programmes of psychology. Indeed, we might add as a desideratum that any putative model of semantics for a language should be evaluated by how good an interface it allows with general cognitive processing, since the greater the remove from processing, the less plausible it will be as a basis for modelling natural-language interpretation.

1.3.2   Language and the world

On the alternative view, to give the semantics of a given natural-language expression is to articulate the relation between it and the objects/events, etc. which it can be used to describe. This view gets very solid backing from formal-language systems in which this is the concept of semantics by definition. It has been presumed by so many people for the last thirty years that it is worth considering how this view came to be so universally accepted. On this received view, no explanation is complete without an explication of the language–world relation as part of the grammar of natural languages, a move which has the supposed advantage of bypassing any need to construct such dangerous constructs as concepts. The following quotation fixed people's views at the time when the alternative language-of-thought position was first being put forward (with advocacy of so-called *semantic markers* by Katz as part of such an internalised system of semantic representations, see Chapter 8):

> Semantic Markers are symbols: items in the vocabulary of an artificial language we may call Semantic Markerese. Semantic interpretation by means of them amounts merely to a translation algorithm from the object language to the auxiliary language Markerese. But we can know the Markerese translation without knowing the first thing about the meaning of the English sentence: namely the conditions under which it would be true. Semantics with no treatment of truth conditions is not semantics. Translation into Markerese is at best a substitute for real semantics, relying either on our tacit competence (at some future date) as speakers of Markerese or on our ability to do real semantics at least for the one language Markerese. Translation into Latin might serve as well, except in so far as the designers of Markerese may choose to build into it useful features – freedom from ambiguity, grammar based on symbolic logic – that might make it easier to do real semantics for Markerese than for Latin.   (Lewis 1970: 18–19)

This was taken as a devastating critique, so much so that pretty much without exception, all semanticists turned their back on the challenge of articulating serious conceptualist methodologies, and adopted instead the semantics-as-truth-conditions view, a perspective which, with its impressive formal backing, has been the only seriously entertained view for nearly half a century. Indeed, for a long time, representationalist stances were dismissed as unthinkably informal, and not a contender for serious debate.

As things will turn out, re-addressing this debate is the heart of what this book is about; and in due course we shall get back to subsequent attempts to meet the challenge of articulating a formal representationalist view of natural-language content. But we shall get there only through the state of the art which the field has provided, that is, via exploration of the influential meaning-as-truth-conditions route, considering its various manifestations and how successful they are and where they fail, and, finally, through attempts to address the problems that this view faces, finding ourselves knocking at the door of the long-rejected but now re-emergent alternative. As we shall hope to show, it is clear in retrospect why this was the only possible route to have taken. It is only in the light of these various attempts to articulate a more direct view of the language–world correlation that our formal vocabulary has got refined to a point where, ironically, it is the previously derided representationalist views which now seem to many to be the weightier competitor. At the time that Lewis was writing in the early seventies, the tools simply weren't available to make this a serious candidate.

According to the view in which sentence meaning comprises truth conditions which must be met if any utterance of the sentence is said to be true in the world, it is the concept of what **a sentence** denotes which is taken as basic, and words are seen merely as suitable abstractions from some established set of truth conditions holding of sentences – merely the individuable elementary parts of the jigsaw that contribute to such truth conditions. Sentences are seen as vehicles for asserting true descriptions. Note in passing that this view of semantics is not completely eschewed in the Fodorian view described in the previous section. The Fodor quotation in section 1.3.1 recognises that representations of content that can be internally manipulated nevertheless map onto the world, with a presumed distinction between 'what's in your head' and 'how your head is connected to the world'. The main difference is where one considers the explanation of semantic phenomena to lie: in the head or in the world. One way of putting the underlying questions in the debate is to ask: are mental representations (internal concepts) necessary for explaining such phenomena, or not? If they are, are they all that is necessary for the purposes of explanation and, if not, can the language–world relation provide the requisite basis of explanation?

1.4   Truth-conditional semantics

The truth-conditional view of semantics has a long tradition. Two central figures in the development of this view at the turn of the twentieth century were Ferdinand de Saussure and Gottlob Frege. Both took the relation between the word or expression of a language and the entity it picks out to be basic, but both recognised that there was more to be said than simply giving a word–object correspondence. De Saussure claimed that a *sign* consists of a *signifier* (*signifiant*) and *signified* (*signifié*); Frege set out the notion *Bedeutung* (reference), the thing in the world a sign picks out or *denotes*. We might take, as the starting point for such a view, that the meaning of the term is the thing it denotes. In some cases, the relation between the word in the language and the object(s) it picks out in the world may seem straightforward. Suppose we agree that one way of giving content to the word *cat* is to define a correspondence between the word and the set of all cats, these objects being the set of entities that the word can serve to pick out (i.e. of which we can truthfully say *That is a cat*). More abstractly, but nonetheless conceivably, the meaning of *kick*, too, might similarly be said to be the set of all events where one thing kicks another.

But there are very real problems to confront, almost right from the start. There is the property of identity of referent for expressions which arguably do not mean the same. On this view, if two words (or phrases) pick out the same things, then they will mean the same. So, for example, if the phrase *the students in this room* happens to pick out exactly the same set of people as *the current honours students in linguistics*, on this denotational account of meaning the two descriptions mean the same thing. A more traditional illustration concerns the trio of referring expressions: *Venus*, *the Morning Star* and *the Evening Star*. These all denote the same object (the planet Venus), but, of course, they do not mean the same thing. If it is true that John believes that Venus is a planet, this does not imply that John believes that the Morning Star is a planet, for John may not know that they are one and the same object. Another illustration of the problem concerns expressions that fail to denote anything at all in the real world. *Phoenix* and *unicorn* both fail to denote (they denote the empty set of things) but 'phoenix-hood' is not the same as 'unicorn-hood' and *Mary dreamt about a phoenix* does not imply *Mary dreamt about a unicorn*.

So we need something more than just denotation, meaning 'things in the world': we need a concept that allows us to talk about 'unicorn-hood' (or 'unicorn-ness') not just unicorns (i.e. the property that identifies that an object is an instance of a unicorn). So, although the concepts 'phoenix' and 'unicorn' both fail to denote in the real world, they can be semantically differentiated. Indeed, we know that they must be, because the properties that unicorns would have if they existed are different from the properties that phoenixes would have if they existed. Phoenixes are long-lived birds with fantastic plumage that regenerate through fire. Unicorns are horse-like creatures that have a single horn growing from their forehead. We know in any case that distinct sentences, with distinct meanings indeed may nevertheless describe the same event, as in the two sentences taken as assertions by Ronnie about Ruth's husband:

(1.39)   Michael read today's *Guardian*.

(1.40)   Your husband read yesterday's paper.

Despite the possible equivalence of this pair of sentences in context, we would not want to say that, as sentences, they have the same meaning. Hence, we cannot directly equate the meaning of a sentence with some event that it denotes. Instead, we need to consider what information a sentence contains that enables it to be used in this way. The essential point here is that, even if we want to take the relation between language and objects in the world to form the basis of our theory of linguistic meaning, we nevertheless have to recognise that this cannot be a direct correlation. The relationship must be more abstract. This was recognised by Frege, among others, who distinguished between *Bedeutung*, 'reference' – the sort of denotation discussed above – and *Sinn*, 'sense', the property that enables the reference of an expression to be identified (or the way of presentation of the reference). These days, this distinction is typically referred to using Rudolph Carnap's terminology: the *extension* of an expression refers to the objects it picks out (reference) and its *intension* is the property that determines the extension.

Each of these difficulties constitutes a big research area in articulating the mapping between the natural-language expression and what it is taken to correspond to. A first answer to the question 'What is the meaning of a sentence?' is taken to be that sentence-meaning is more abstract than a description of some event. Rather it constitutes a set of *truth conditions*, constraints which must hold of the world in which the sentence is uttered if it is to be true in that world. Words are then characterised as contributing to such constraints to determine the entities that can be picked out in any given use of a sentence. Bringing back into the picture the criteria of success which we take theories of meaning to have to provide, an explanation of compositionality might be given by defining words as contributing to sentence-meanings in a systematic way. Given the methodology of trying to define sentence meaning and the correspondence with true/false, and seeing words as systematically contributing to these, this is definitional. The meaning of a sentence is determined in a regular and predictable way from the words (and phrases) that it contains.

There is indeed a systematic correlation between the way words are ordered, arranged into units, and the way they are understood. The basic building blocks of sentence meaning are given by the denotations of its component words. However, even leaving out the problem of context, this is invariably mediated by syntax, and nontrivially, so that the order of words and the structural configurations in which they appear to be arranged interact to determine how a sentence is to be understood. A basic fact of English is that the two sentences (1.41) and (1.42), though they contain the same words, do not have the same meaning:

(1.41)   Mary buried the dog.

(1.42)   The dog buried Mary.

Now in identifying what is different about these, we need to be able to articulate the various relations involved – the syntax identifies the subject, the object, the indirect object, and so on. But there is much, much more to it than this. Consider the following sentence:

(1.43)   John saw the man with the telescope.

Depending on whether the phrase *with the telescope* is taken to be associated with *the man* or with *saw*, different interpretations arise, not merely of the sentence, but of the words themselves. Very generally, words contribute to the building up of appropriate semantic constructs relative to systematic principles, and these principles are in some sense determined by some structural analysis for the sentence (for example to disambiguate (1.43)) and the syntactic category into which a word falls; but the interaction between these is often subtle and complex. So prepositions may either contribute information about location (space or time), or identify participants in an event other than those identified by subjects and objects. Determiners may specify quantities of things or connect things to the preceding discourse. Specialised verbs (such as the modal auxiliaries in English) may provide information about whether some described event is possible or necessary or is desirable or within the ability of the individual presented as subject. And, of course, it is not just individual words which contribute to meaning, but also morphology or even phonology. Thus, in English, tense is morphologically encoded (unlike, for example, Chinese) and adds information about when an event occurs. Although the basic function of tense is to relate events temporally to each other and the time of utterance (past, present, future), there are nevertheless idiosyncratic aspects of tense systems that vary cross-linguistically. For example, the English present tense (as in other Germanic languages) may express present or future time (as in *I am seeing my sister tomorrow*) (this is a matter to which we return in detail in Chapter 6). From a phonological perspective, prosody may also add meaning, as found with the possibility of forming questions in English from apparent declarative statements by altering the prosodic contour, as in *You're coming?* where the intonation is indicated by the question mark in the orthography. And there are many more such properties that may be more or less grammaticalised that contribute to the way a sentence is understood. But nevertheless, we must retain some concept of compositionality: these various inputs that the words provide do all systematically combine to determine the propositions conveyed by utterances of the sentence in which they are contained.

To give you a sense of the intricacies involved in characterising truth conditions for even very simple sentences, we take what may seem a completely banal example – without a modal, and without any aspectual complexity as to how an event can be seen as extending across a span of time (or relating to other induced times). For (1.44), we duly just straightforwardly list the contribution to truth conditions of the containing sentence made by each word and phrase, mediated by the syntax.

(1.44)   Mary buried a cat in the garden.

Mary (syntactic subject)
    an entity that is conventionally referred to as 'Mary' and acting as initiator of the described action.

a cat (syntactic object)

  'a': an entity not previously in the discourse context.

  'cat': an entity that has the property of being a cat.

the garden (syntactic adjunct)

  'the': an entity unique and previously given in the discourse context.

  'garden': an entity (a place) that has the property of being a garden.

buried (main verb)

  an activity event that involves one entity (the *agent* = subject) putting a second entity (the *theme* = object) into a hole (*location* = adjunct) in the ground and covering it over with earth (or other debris).

PAST an event that occurred before the time of utterance.

Putting these together, in order for the sentence *Mary buried a cat in the garden* to be true, it has to be the case that:

> There is an entity conventionally referred to as 'Mary'; there is an entity not previously identified in the discourse that has the property of being a cat; there is a garden that has been identified already in the discourse; and the first entity is engaged in the activity of burying the second at a location identified by the third.

So, as the proponent of the meaning-as-truth-conditions view would have it, to articulate the conditions which have to hold in the world if propositions expressed by the sentence are to be true is both necessary and sufficient as an explanation of the concept of meaning for sentences of natural language. More abstractly, we might express the task for the meaning-as-truth-conditions programme as one of constructing a formal model of meaning that fulfils the following schema for each and every one of the infinite set of sentences that constitutes an individual language:

(1.45)   *Snow is white* if and only if snow is white.

Such sentences have been dubbed *T-sentences*: the theoretical task they impose is very far from trivial. Understanding their significance necessitates the distinction between *object language* and *metalanguage*, a distinction which is critical in modelling natural languages, as we shall see throughout what follows.

(1.46)   a. The *object language* is the language under investigation.
            b. The *metalanguage* is the language selected to express statements about the object language.

In the so-called T-sentences, English is the object language: hence the use of italics in the T-sentence referring to the string *Snow is white* in (1.45). Yet it is also the metalanguage used to talk about that language. And, as the metalanguage statement puts it, what has to be characterised to yield a theory of meaning for natural language is the correspondence between each one of the arbitrary sentences of the language and the object/event/property-attribution, etc. which it is used to make an assertion about. An appropriate such correspondence holds only if the sentence so listed is true just in case the object/event/property-attribution itemised in the T-sentence is also true. The objective for truth-conditional semantics, accordingly, is to define pairings between structured phonological sequences of the language (sentences) and some characterisation of the conditions that must hold if that string of the language is to be taken as a true assertion.

There are two major tasks implicit in this. First the specification to be given has to be defined by a recursive mechanism applying to sentence-parts, since the number of sentences is indefinitely large and any sentence may be indefinitely long. To provide a complete characterisation for even one natural language accordingly **has** to involve a formal recursive specification. Because we have to account for any arbitrary string of, say, English, a mere listing of appropriate correlations for a string and its truth conditions cannot in principle provide a complete specification. Second, in providing a formal mechanism for capturing such T-sentences, there has to be an appropriate extension to account for the *indexical* elements associated with utterance interpretation along lines such as:

> If u is an utterance of *she is happy* and the speaker of u refers with *she* to x, and x is female, then u is true if and only if x is happy.

That is, the linguistic meaning of the context-dependent elements and the mechanism for resolving this relative to arbitrary contexts has to apply as part of the conditions that must be fulfilled for the T-sentence to hold (a problem we return to in Chapters 6–8). So whatever reference is made to context, it has to feed into the compositional process of determining interpretation in a systematic way. Furthermore if semantics is to be taken to be a component of grammar, then it would seem that the rules that determine such pairings must constitute rules of grammar for the language in question.

1.5   Logic, meaning and context

The question is: how to go about characterising truth conditions? And here is where linguists have turned to logic, the formal study of inference. Logics are so-called *formal languages*: they were defined to provide the basic pattern for studying any arbitrary sequences of inferences independent of subject-matter. The very fact that they constitute a study of inference would in itself be illuminating for linguists setting out on the task of modelling inferential relations as expressed in natural languages. But there is a further reason to study such formal languages. They provide the clearest pattern we know of what it means to model an in principle open-ended phenomenon in an appropriately formal way. A finite set of rules is defined that induces infinitely long and infinitely many expressions, and then procedures are also defined for associating each one of these expressions with interpretations, as a result of which all appropriate patterns of inference are correctly characterised. By defining a system of rules that determines exactly the right set of expressions in some object language (no more and no less), and then attributing to them interpretations that determine exactly the right set of inferential relations between sentences, the system so defined constitutes an explanation of the phenomenon of inference itself, for we have a procedure which recursively applies to capture exactly the right set of objects. This is just the pattern we also want for natural languages. We want a system of rules which determines all and only the wellformed sentences of the language, and for each such string determines an interpretation for it such that exactly the right set of meaning-relations between sentences can be seen to hold. If we can do this, then, following the pattern of logic, we may be able with some confidence to determine that we have a minimally acceptable explanation of the phenomenon itself, of what constitutes a natural language.

So we are going to be looking at logic not simply as a basis for doing semantics, but as a point of departure for correlating the syntax of expressions with their interpretation in a principled and formal way. Whether we like what we have got when we have done it is another matter, and this we shall come to in due course. But the need to go formal is inescapable; and logic forms an excellent, indeed, arguably, the only possible point of departure. For those readers who know any logic at all, the shift from our having pointed out initially the extensive dependency of natural-language interpretation on the context in which expressions are uttered to the statement that we will be turning to logic as a basis for modelling the rich array of effects displayed in language may seem at best perplexing. For those readers who don't know any logic, the switch into the study of logic may seem just baffling. When we get into the details of the propositional logic system, its highly abstract nature and absolutely minimalist internal structure will certainly seem a million miles away from what we can use language for: we will find, at least initially, no internal structure to the individual propositions at all, and we will be manipulating letters as standing for such sentence-sized objects as though their internal structure doesn't even matter; and there won't be **any** reference to concepts of context. So, you would be entirely justified in asking, how could such a system be appropriate for modelling natural language? Indeed, in one real sense, you would be right – in the end, it will turn out not to be **directly** appropriate, and precisely because of the phenomenon of context-dependence and what that means in understanding language.

It is, however, generally assumed that context-dependence in natural-language use should be left for some theory of *pragmatics* to account for. It is certainly the case that any theory of semantics has to be associated with a theory of pragmatics (explaining **how** languages are used in context to convey a far richer range of information than is encoded in the expressions themselves) in order to come anywhere close to an adequate theory of natural-language meaning. The big question, however, concerns the independence of semantics from pragmatics. In a pragmatic theory such as that associated with Paul Grice, pragmatic inference operates only after the construction of some propositional form provided by semantics. But, as we have already seen, there are situations in which it is impossible to construct the appropriate semantic representation (and there-fore identify its *truth-theoretic*, denotational, content) without making pragmatic choices.

(1.47)   Every student was told that their marks were bad.

(1.48)   Some students of mine are pretty miserable. Their marks were bad.

(1.49)   John and Mary were miserable. Their marks were bad.

(1.50)   If their marks were bad, every student was miserable.

In (1.47), the clause *their marks were bad* cannot be assigned denotational con-tent until a pragmatic choice is made about the reference of the pronoun. Such assignment of reference may involve extended inference over real-world knowl-edge as in (1.51)–(1.52), where it is knowledge of what constitutes 'newlyweds' (i.e. one male and one female) and 'cars' (that they have doors and one can be inside them) that enables one to assign a referent to *his* or *the door* respectively.

(1.51)   The newlyweds were miserable. His marks were bad.

(1.52)   I couldn't get out of the car. The door was jammed.

The extent of contextual interaction with semantic processing indicates the importance of inference in deriving the meaning of an utterance and the impos-sibility that interpretation is strictly linear. The standard semiotic view of the grammar shown below therefore cannot be correct, and it is this order of dependence which we shall be querying in due course:

Instead we must look to having a system in which context interacts with processing to derive appropriate propositional structures.

Although we will not be discussing pragmatics in any great detail in this book, nevertheless we assume as background to our discussion of contextual effects the post-Gricean theory of *relevance* put forward by Deirdre Wilson and Dan Sperber (Sperber and Wilson 1995). This theory is robustly cognitive (rather than normative or rational, as in other theories of pragmatics), taking the *cognitive principle of relevance* as something that we, as humans, necessarily follow and that it is against this background that inferential communication takes place:

(1.53)   *Cognitive principle of relevance*: human cognition tends to be geared to the maximisation of relevance.

In communication, Relevance Theory assumes that ostensive stimuli (those that are intentionally made to communicate) carry a presumption of their own optimal relevance:

(1.54)   *Optimal relevance*: an ostensive stimulus is optimally relevant to an audience if and only if:
           a. It is relevant enough to be worth the audience's processing effort.

  b. It is the most relevant one compatible with the communicator's abilities
     and preferences.

Relevance itself is defined in terms of a trade-off between the effort needed to
process some input such as the utterance of some string of words and the infor-
mational benefit gained from undertaking that inferential processing. Sperber
and Wilson define *relevance* in the following broad terms:

  Relevance of an input to an individual
  a. Other things being equal, the greater the positive cognitive effects
     achieved by processing an input, the greater the relevance of the input
     to the individual at that time.
  b. Other things being equal, the greater the processing effort expended, the
     lower the relevance of the input to the individual at that time.   (Wilson
     and Sperber 2004: 609)

Whatever the details to be substantiated in this claim, this view of pragmatics is
an explicit commitment to providing an explanation of the context-dependence
of all interpretation of incoming signals by the human processor in terms of interaction between what the input encodes and general cognitive constraints. In the
case of language, this involves interaction between what is encoded within the
grammar and this principle of optimal relevance. By linking effort and gain in
this way, Relevance Theory provides a powerful and useful means of accounting for contextual effects of interpretation, on which we can depend to flesh
out what will at times seem like very impoverished systems for accounting for
meaning in natural language. Yet, despite their central emphasis on how signals
get enriched in context as driven by such general cognitive principles, relevance
theorists have agreed with semanticists that semantics as encoded in natural-
language expressions should be articulated within the semantic component of
grammar (though they disagree with them as to the form such an encoding might
take), with information from the output of semantics feeding into the pragmatic
process of *enrichment* that determines how utterances are understood in context.
This process of enriching what the grammar provides to determine full utterance content is taken to be a rich inferential process that involves interaction
between sentence meanings as the output from the grammar and additional information that the particular context may make available. In due course, we shall
be querying this assumed order of dependence, but, initially, we shall respect the
orthodoxy and assume provisionally that the dependence of utterance content on
context can be resolved without threatening the general correspondence between
the meaning of a sentence string and sets of truth conditions to be associated with
that string.

There is one point in particular to be emphasised at this stage. The study of
logic is essential for the study of semantics both in order to understand the modelling of inference on the one hand, which is the core semantic relation, and, on
the other hand, to understand the mind-set of linguists as they have approached

the problem of formally modelling natural language. Our introduction to basic principles of logic is given with these two assumptions at the forefront. Accordingly, as we proceed through the introduction of the syntax, semantics and proof system for predicate logic, and from there on to the characterisation of inference in language more generally, we will always be alert to the need to point out the significance of the tools we are introducing, not merely for understanding the particular phenomenon itself but also for using these logic tools in the task of designing an appropriate formal semantics for natural language. And the goal in such a task is the modelling of our ability to understand natural-language expressions as uttered in context.

1.6   Further reading

Essential background to any formal modelling is the debate in the middle of the last century between Thomas Kuhn and Karl Popper on the nature of scientific paradigms and the role of falsification in science (Kuhn 1962; Popper 1965) with the compromise stance held by Lakatos and Musgrave: a core text in this area is Lakatos and Musgrave (1972). Lexical field theories of word meaning have a long history predating the Chomskian revolution in linguistic theorising, for example Lyons (1981); Cruse (1986). Chomsky (1965) was the originator of the *competence/performance* distinction: see Larson and Segal (1995) for a view of semantics as a component of competence. All basic semantics textbooks set out criteria for evaluating semantic theories (Kempson 1977; Cann 1993; de Swart 1998; Chierchia and McConnell-Ginet 2000). Fodor's language-of-thought hypothesis and the attendant claims that language constitutes an innate, modular input system (Fodor 1981, 1983, 1990, 1998) have been the subject of much debate within philosophy of psychology; see Stainton (2006) for a representative sample of current debates. A general programme for truth-theoretic semantics, following definitions by Montague, was set out in Lewis (1970) and reprinted many times since (e.g. Davidson and Harman 1972). Articulating T-sentences as the basis for a theory of meaning constitutes the Davidsonian programme: see Lepore and Ludwig (2005). Pragmatics as a field is broadly split between normative approaches, following Grice's papers published as Grice (1989), and cognitive approaches, following Sperber and Wilson (1995; second edition), see also Carston (2002) and Wilson and Sperber (2004). Useful reader collections are Davis (1991); Burton-Roberts (2007). Many of the issues introduced in this book are addressed by contributions in Lepore and Smith (2006).

2   The syntax of logical inference

We have seen in Chapter 1 that we want to be able to get some clearer understanding of what we take meaning in natural languages to consist in. As a test of such an account, we want to be able to pinpoint what it means for expressions to have the same meaning, whether these expressions are simple, one-word expressions or complex sentence sequences. We want to be able to understand how it is that, as speakers of the language, we can put together words or groups of words and from them recursively compose more and more complex expressions, in each case being able to rely on the fact that the way each complex expression is understood depends on what it's made up of and the way the words are put together. And from this, we then want to be able to explain the various patterns of inference: we want, that is, an explanation of what it might mean to say that a given sentence follows from some other sentence in virtue of its meaning. To add to the challenge, we have set our sights on meeting the requirement of providing a formal model of meaning in natural language, which means that we will be providing a formal basis for the mapping of strings of a given language onto some assigned content in a way that reflects the general principles within the language for mapping the meaning of the individual words onto the meaning of all more complex expressions that can be formed from them. To this general goal, we have added the further desideratum that a successful account should be one which is at least compatible with general psychological considerations of how people can be said to use language.

2.1   Language and logic

As we stated in the last chapter, we begin our quest to understand the meaning of natural-language utterances by turning to *logic*, the formal study of inference. Inference, as we saw in Chapter 1, is the phenomenon of some piece of information following from another in virtue of the content which, in some sense, they share. We can **infer** from the fact that John admires Mary and Mary is Hungarian, that John admires Mary. In this case the inference can be reflected in natural language, as the sentence *John admires Mary* is contained within the sentence *John admires Mary and Mary is Hungarian*: all we have to do is to define what we take to be contributed by the meaning of the single word *and*. We can also infer from the fact that John admires Mary and Mary can read Akkadian, that John admires someone who can read Akkadian. Again this time, the step of inference has a reflection in the meaning of the sentence *John admires someone who can read Akkadian* and its relation to the meaning conveyed by the sentence *John admires Mary and Mary can read Akkadian*. However, to ensure reflection of this form of inference through natural-language sentences, we will have to establish what correspondence there is between relative clause sequences and coordinate sentences, and the relation also between referring to someone named Mary and conveying the information that they are a person suitably described by the term *someone*. Finally, we can also infer from the fact that Mary is admired by John that John admires Mary. As a result, the natural-language sentences *Mary is admired by John* and *John admires Mary* express the same content. In order to explain how a natural language like English successfully reflects this inference we shall need to have established some analysis of the correspondence between the active and passive constructions.

In this respect, what all these examples demonstrate is that inference patterns which individual languages express may depend on analyses of items and constructions of the particular language in question. To get at the concept of inference itself, independent of its language-specific expression, we need to move one step back from any one natural language. We want an account of inference that is not particular to any one language but is in some sense more general, applying no matter what individual language the inference step might be expressed in. Accordingly, logical so-called *formal* languages were devised that, by definition, provided the basis for modelling a given set of inference patterns, in particular those that hold independent of, hence across all types of, either subject-matter or the specifics of the natural language in which the inference patterns might be displayed. The goal was to capture all and only the types of inference under study across a full, in principle infinite, set of such inferences, in this sense providing a formal model of inference itself.

The first step in such a formal analysis is to define a language with expressive power that is appropriate for the type of inference being studied, and then to define some minimal, basic set of patterns in such a way that all and only the valid inferences expressible by the language defined could be captured. If this task can be achieved, providing a complete characterisation of a given type of inference, then the task is said to be successful – successful because it encompasses all the right types of inference and excludes anything that is not a valid step of inference. There are two types of inference which standard logic is set up to express resulting in two systems of inference or *logics*. One is composed just of forms of inference involving relations between sentences, the so-called *propositional logic*. This covers sentential connections as might be expressed by the logical counterparts of the English connectives *and*, *or*, *if* and negation. For example, in such a system, the conclusion expressible by the sentence *John admires someone who can decipher Akkadian* can be shown to follow logically from the joint assumptions expressible by the pair of sentences *Mary can decipher Akkadian* and *If Mary can decipher Akkadian, then John admires someone who can decipher Akkadian.* (Notice how this inference does not depend on analysing the relative clause itself.) The second system of inference, involving an enrichment of propositional logic, *predicate logic*, covers in addition forms of inference which involve analysis below the level of sentence. This involves quantified forms of reasoning involving (a) reasoning from general statements to particular statements, e.g. from *Mary can decipher every known cuneiform script* to *Mary can decipher Akkadian* via the knowledge that Akkadian is written in a cuneiform script and (b), in the inverse direction, from particular statements to general, e.g., from *Mary can decipher Akkadian* to *Mary can decipher at least one known cuneiform script*. In these latter two cases, the validity of the reasoning **does** involve essential reference to the subparts of the sentences: one has to have rules for licensing the shift from expressions involving every member of some set of individuals to some particular individual, here from *every known cuneiform script* to *Akkadian*; and conversely for the shift from expressions involving some particular individual to general assertions about some set of individuals, here from *Akkadian* to *at least one cuneiform script*.

2.2   Proof theory and model theory: syntax vs. semantics?

The very fact that predicate and propositional logic together constitute a study of inference would in itself be illuminating for linguists setting out on the task of modelling inferential relations as expressed in natural languages. Over and above this, there is, however, an entirely independent reason for being interested in studying logic, which relates to the representationalist vs. denotational debate about the nature of language interpretation. Within the study of logical inference itself, there are two modes of explanation of the phenomenon. On the one hand there is the syntactic, proof-theoretic, route in which the concept of inference is defined in terms of rules mapping one assertion onto another in virtue of form, that is, in terms of internal structural properties of the system itself. This is particularly suggestive for modelling cognitive steps of inference in that the characterisation of inference is totally system-internal: no reference is made to anything external to that system. However, there is the alternative denotational characterisation of inference, to which the proof-theoretic method is systematically correlated. According to that other form of explanation, the same concept of inference is formally modelled in terms of ascribed correspondences between the one assertion and what it denotes and the other inferred assertion and what, given the former assertion, it **has** to denote. The explanation, that is, is in essentially denotational terms. Both of these forms of explanation meet minimal conditions of adequacy on our criterion of success for a formal explanation of inference. As we shall see, both provide characterisations of *synonymy*, *entailment* and other major semantic relations for the formal languages which logic defines.

Back in the 1970s, when the dispute between whether natural-language semantics should involve essential invocation of semantic representations or, conversely, should solely involve mappings from natural-language strings onto denotational contents was at its height, one reason why formal semanticists argued that the denotational–semantic route had to be the right basis for capturing natural-language semantics is that there are lots of proof systems of inference, each defined with somewhat different rule formulations but yet coinciding on some agreed denotational interpretation. So, according to the argument, it is **only** a characterisation in terms of the denotational semantic properties of the expressions which constitutes a unique explanation of the phenomenon of inference itself. However, the debate might properly have involved reference to the criterion of providing a basis for explaining inference as a cognitive activity in which the human system engages. This narrows down the number of proof systems dramatically. There is just one type of proof system which, uniquely among proof systems, has properties redolent of human reasoning processes. This system is aptly termed *natural deduction*. Natural-deduction systems are defined in terms of individual steps in sequence needed to move from input assumptions as given to some conclusion to be demonstrably derived by the proof rules alone. There are several such systems, and they may differ in slight variations of rule formulation, and in addition as to how explicit the level of accompanying annotations on those proof steps has to be. However, they share important properties, and they are informally recognised to be the type of proof system which most closely corresponds to how humans reason, in having a pronounced procedural step-by-step flavour. As we shall eventually argue, this procedural flavour can be used to provide the basis for modelling the processing of natural-language structure as that unfolds in utterance interpretation. We shall come to this in due course (Chapter 7). In the mean time, it is sufficient to bear in mind that while a number of proof systems may have been devised for the study of inference, natural deduction is uniquely well adapted as a formal basis from which to explore formal properties of natural language.

First in this chapter, we are going to set out a system of natural deduction for the propositional calculus. With only a minimal sketch of the appropriate formal language, we introduce the rules of inference one by one, since it is these rules which correspond, in some cases very closely indeed, to processes humans naturally and constructively reason with. Having introduced the proof rules in some detail, we then set out the formal language of the propositional logic. We go on to extend the language and the rules of deduction to cover quantificational reasoning as expressed in predicate logic (predicate and propositional logic together constitute the so-called *classical logic*). We then show how, even without any access to a denotational-semantic characterisation, we can characterise concepts of *inference* (= *entailment*) and *equivalence* (= *synonymy*). In Chapter 3, we will then set out a system of semantics for propositional and predicate logic so that we can see both syntactic and semantic properties of the language in tandem. Both proof-theoretic and denotational characterisations of inference in classical logic provide a basis from which all and only the valid inferences of the logic are expressible. Proof systems do so by making available proof rules which allow the deduction of all and only the valid forms of inference, in which the inferred formula is a conclusion from the inferring formula taken as the sole basic assumption in a proof. Denotational–semantic systems do so by characterising patterns of inference between two formulae in terms of their being true in all and only the same models (at least for finite models). Jointly, these give us a rich dual starting point for the modelling of natural-language semantics and human-reasoning processes. So study of classical logic is an essential starting point for the study of how meaning in natural languages should be modelled.

2.3   Logic, inference and natural-language semantics

Inference is arguably the central notion in any semantic theory. From the fact that John's dog came to the UK with him from China, and the background fact that any dog which comes to the UK from any other country must go into quarantine for six months in order to be in this country legally, we can infer that either John's dog went into quarantine for six months after their arrival in the UK or his dog is here illegally. Equally, given the general knowledge that any language which is verb-final must have a case-rich system in order to be incrementally interpretable, we can infer, once having discovered that Japanese is a verb-final language, that either Japanese has a case-rich system or it is not interpretable incrementally. These examples provide further illustration of how the phenomenon of inference is independent of the particular subject-matter. One might dispute the supposed 'facts' on which these particular steps of reasoning depend, but the validity of the step of reasoning is in each case unimpeachable. One might, for example, legitimately dispute the animal-import restriction as so far worded, as the restriction in fact only holds of countries that have rabies endemically – there is no such ban on animals entering the UK from Japan, for example, as Japan has had no reported instances of rabies in its animal population. Equally, one might choose to dispute the causal correlation of case specifications and incremental interpretability on the grounds that Japanese is unlike languages in which incremental interpretability is well established.[1] But neither of these disputes would affect the logical validity of the underlying argument. With such general background facts taken as **presumed** to be true, the pattern of reasoning in our two illustrative cases is identical, and not in doubt. Indeed they constitute two illustrations of the same argument. Nevertheless, despite the variation across the different subject-matters, the inference patterns set up here in some sense depend on the words used, for they depend on what is involved in joining two assertions by *and*, and on what is involved in making the inferential step from a general statement about sets of individuals as expressed through *any* in English to a statement about a particular individual.

---

[1] Actually, this would be a mistake since there is a great deal of evidence that processing of Japanese is just as sensitive to on-line processing constraints as any other language.

So there is clearly some correlation between logics and the structured inferences which they reflect and expressions of natural language from which they are an abstraction.

The logics to be defined take a tiny subset of the patterns of inference expressible in natural language, ones that hold universally across all languages. These formal languages abstract out of the natural-language patterns of inference a formal model of patterns of inference, defining a language with connectives ∧ (*conjunction*, 'and'), ∨ (*disjunction*, 'or'), ¬ (*negation*, 'not'), → (*material implication*, approximately 'if ... then ...') and quantifiers ∀ and ∃. The criterion of success for such systems is that they both license exactly the right set of wellformed strings of the languages so defined and, in addition, license all and only the valid inferences expressible by such systems. Of the two sub-systems of classical logic, propositional logic is the simplest possible system in which a syntactic system of inference is defined. And to get the full power of predicate logic, all that is needed is the addition of two more operators, the universal (∀) and existential (∃) quantifiers and their *Elimination* and *Introduction* rules.

2.3.1   Natural deduction: a syntactic mode of inference

Among logicians, *natural deduction* is well known to be the proof system that is closest to on-line human reasoning. It models reasoning through essentially local individual steps, with the context of what assertions or interim conclusions have already been made determining whether some inference step is or is not applicable. So in setting out an account of the system of natural deduction with enough detail to see how these rules interact, we hope to give the reader a practical sense of the dynamics of natural deduction, as a preliminary to exploring the significance of such formal systems for natural language (this account will merely be sufficient for linguistic purposes, see the Further reading section for further references, which are an essential counterpart to the over-slim characterisation to be provided here). Where a choice has to be made between equivalent variants, we adopt forms of the rules which correspond in some intuitive way to the form of rules which the human reasoner adopts.

As input to this sketch, we start from the observation that humans are, as we might put it, inference engines. Given some premises to reason with, we can go on and on and on, as, for example, in the following parody of routine night-time anxieties:

(2.1)   I haven't paid the electricity bill and the deadline is tomorrow. If I don't pay the bill tomorrow, they will cut off our supply. If they cut off our supply, my computer battery will fail. If my computer battery fails, I won't get my thesis finished on time. If I don't get my thesis finished on time, I will get the department into trouble. If I get the department into trouble, they won't hire me or recommend me for any other job. If they don't hire me and I can't get another job, we won't be able to afford the rent. If we can't afford the rent, we shall lose our flat. If we lose our flat, we will become homeless.

At this point, you might spring out of bed and start pacing up and down, totally robbed of sleep for the rest of the night, worrying that you're going to be homeless. Or, more rationally, you reason to yourself: 'It is not true that we will be homeless; all I can conclude, in the worst scenario, is that **if** I don't pay the electricity bill tomorrow, we will become homeless; so I'd better remember to pay the electricity bill tomorrow' (the caveat of 'in the worst scenario' is because of the subtleties of temporal reasoning in natural language, which we are setting aside here). Reasoning, that is, is something we do in our heads day in, day out. Moreover, there is quite generally little or no checking as to whether the premises that spring to mind are true or not; and no such checking is essential to any such reasoning. To the contrary, one simply assumes some proposition is true and deduces something that follows from it, then adopts that, and deduces something from it, and so on. If, then, the mode of reasoning to be selected for linguistic purposes is one that reflects the dynamics of the psychological processes of reasoning that we humans engage in much of the time, the mode of representation will have to be that which involves a structural mode of reasoning, one that licenses a shift from assumptions of one sort or another to their conclusion in virtue of their form, and not one that involves having established and checked out the denotational contents of such assumptions via a mapping onto entities and events in the world. As Fodor put it (see Chapter 1), syntax is what is in the head, semantics is the relation between what's in the head and the world around that is outside it. And it is this syntactic mode of reasoning which natural-deduction methods directly reflect.

2.4   Natural deduction for propositional logic

We start with the propositional calculus, which models only suprasentential relations, and has no sub-sentential structure at all. The lexicon of the language has merely capital letters, P, Q, R, S, and these are taken to be names of propositions (here taken to be what declarative clauses express when uttered as statements and basic truth-denoting constructs),[2] with rules of combination involving three connectives and a negation operator. The reason for use of letters as propositional names is that sentence-internal structure is irrelevant in this initial, minimal, system. (We come to predicate logic, where sentence-internal structure is introduced, later.) Since the reasoning steps define transitions between strings with distinct connectives, for each connective there has to be a rule introducing it, an *Introduction* rule which creates more complex structure, and a rule removing the connective, an *Elimination* rule, licensing the transition from a composite structure to a simpler one. As we shall see immediately, the system is a web of proof rules that interact to yield an indefinitely large set of

---

[2] The definition of what propositions exactly are, is fraught with difficulty. We will avoid the issue here for simplicity, taking a simple stance on what philosophically is a complex issue.

inferences, each one of which is a valid inference. Seen as a set of procedures, the system is rather like a child's rail-track building system: the parts can click together in different ways to yield different results and then be taken apart to be used again to different effect. An individual *proof* of inference is just one way of clicking together the procedures licensed.

The goal in any individual proof is to establish some given conclusion from just the premises given as assumptions, by only the rules of inference defined. To see any one such derivation in the manner of a game, the instruction for any one such game (the construction of a proof) is to get from some set of *Basic Assumptions* to a given conclusion as goal. Schematically, for every valid inference step, there must be a proof of the following form:

$$\phi_i, \ldots, \phi_j \vdash \psi_k$$

where $\phi_i, \ldots, \phi_j$ are basic assumptions, ψ_k is the conclusion, $\vdash$ is the sometimes-called 'assertion sign' asserting the validity of the presented proof (it can be read as *therefore*). The only steps allowed in any proof are those provided by the deduction rules defined. Such sequences of assumptions leading to a conclusion are called *sequents*. In natural-deduction systems, additional assumptions may be constructed (this the is the *rule of Assumptions*), but these must always be discharged and removed from the set of assumptions before the final step of the proof is derived, as we shall shortly see.

2.4.1 Conditional Elimination: *Modus Ponens* ▰▰▰▰▰▰▰▰

The primary rule of *natural deduction* is colloquially referred to as *Modus Ponens*, or, more transparently, $\rightarrow$ *Elimination*, read as *Conditional Elimination*. The full Latin term is *Modus Ponendo Ponens*, usually translated as 'mode of affirming by affirming', i.e. by affirming the first proposition (the *antecedent*), the second (the *consequent*), is automatically affirmed. This rule, which eliminates the conditional connective $\rightarrow$, is arguably the most central rule in logic, this and its converse so-called *Conditional Introduction* rule. This is a rule on which the middle-of-the-night reasoning turns, and its applicability to human reasoning is not in doubt, even though the structure on which it depends with no sub-clausal structure looks very abstract as compared to its natural-language counterparts. This might be sketched as:

$$\frac{\phi \rightarrow \psi, \phi}{\psi}$$

where ϕ, ψ are variables that range over any propositions whatever. The rule will apply, for example, to a pair of formulae as follows:

$$\frac{P, P \rightarrow S}{S}$$

This proof can be illustrated by the following simple argument which substitutes words from English for the logical form, yielding a self-evidently valid deduction:

> If it is raining, then I will take my umbrella.
>
> It is raining.
>
> So, I will take my umbrella.

But substitutions for ϕ and ψ need not be simple, single propositions, but complex formulae:

$$\frac{(P \rightarrow (Q \wedge R)) \rightarrow S, P \rightarrow (Q \wedge R)}{S}$$

The only difference is that previously ϕ is instantiated as P, whereas here ϕ is instantiated as $P \rightarrow (Q \wedge R)$ (in both cases ψ is instantiated as S).

$\rightarrow$ *Elimination* is a two-premise rule: the top line of the rule sets out two premises which constitute the input to the rule, one a compound premise with a $\rightarrow$ connecting the two parts, the other a simpler one corresponding to the part to the left of the $\rightarrow$ (the antecedent of the conditional). What the bottom line sets out is the result of applying the rule, viz. the assertion of the formula to the right of the $\rightarrow$ on its own (the consequent of the conditional). What this rule expresses is that if a formula of the form $\phi \rightarrow \psi$ and a formula of the form ϕ can both be independently derived at arbitrary steps of the proof, then relative to the assumptions on which those formulae themselves depend, ψ can be derived. There is one important point of terminology to note here: a *premise* is any formula of propositional logic serving as input to some step of inference within a proof; an *assumption* is a premise which is taken as true within a proof. To bring out the difference between assumptions and premises, a premise may be the result of some previous step of inference, at this later stage serving as input to a further inferential step. An assumption is a premise which is not derived from anything else in that proof.

Application of this rule alone enables us to prove the validity of an inference of the form:

$$P \rightarrow Q, \quad P \vdash Q$$

The proof involves first setting out the basic assumptions, with each basic assumption given a separate line in the proof, recording it as indeed a basic assumption, and then showing which rule can be used to manipulate these assumptions, in this particular case, this being just the one step of $\rightarrow$ *Elimination*:

(2.2)

Assumption made	Proof Line	Formula	Rule with Lines used
1	1	$P \rightarrow Q$	Basic Assumption
2	2	P	Basic Assumption
1, 2	3	Q	$\rightarrow$ Elim, 1, 2

To take the columns in turn from the right and back across the page, we start from the fourth column, which shows what rule is applied and to what lines in the proof. The first two steps in the proof involve listing the basic assumptions, here listed as a rule. Indeed natural-deduction systems allow construction of any assumptions as one such rule (this is the *rule of Assumptions*). Basic assumptions are retained throughout the proof, other assumptions are discharged. The third column gives the formula licensed at that particular proof step, the second enumerates the number of the lines in the proof, and the first column records the assumptions on which the step depends. The proof is successful if the assumptions of the last line of the proof are no more than the basic assumptions. In the one-step proof-derivation above, the numbering is all but identical, and so apparently trivial, but as we shall very shortly see, this is by no means invariably the case.

In defining the rule itself, we have to allow that it can occur at any point in a proof. In addition, to be certain of what assumptions the overall proof depends on, we need at each stage to keep track of the assumptions on which the input to the rule depends. Accordingly, we shall need a general form of definition in which this record of how assumptions accumulate is made explicit:

$\rightarrow$ **Elimination, Conditional Elimination (*Modus Ponens*)**

$$X \quad i \quad \phi \rightarrow \psi$$
$$\cdots$$
$$\cdots$$
$$Y \quad j \quad \phi$$
$$\cdots$$
$$\cdots$$
$$X, Y \quad m \quad \psi \qquad \rightarrow \text{Elim}, i, j$$

The information on the left gives X, Y as variables over any number of assumptions, the variables i, j, m refer to distinct steps in the proof. The listing of X,Y at step m shows that the proof step is dependent on the assumptions of both premises which form the input to the rule. The listing of i, j with the acronym form of the rule indicates the lines of the proof for the two premises used.

What we are now seeing is the manipulation also of the distinction between *metalanguage* and *object language*. The rules themselves are meta-level statements that express generalisations over proofs of the language. They are schemas for a valid step of inference: substitute the Greek-letter metavariables with some formula as value, and the result will be a valid inference, a minimal proof.[3] Any application of the rule, once these substitutions are made, involves a transition from one or more object-level formulae to some further object-level formula.

---

[3] We shall adopt as a general convention that Greek letters are used for logic metavariables. *Metavariables* are expressions in the metalanguage used to refer generally to expressions of the object language.

Hence the simplest form of proof, that containing just the rule of → *Elimination*, is a proof, as in (2.2): this is a proof which is solely made up of one instantiation of the rule of → *Elimination*.

For a further and less trivial example, let's assume we want to formally model the step of inference that reflects the neurotic English reasoner:

(2.3)   If I am anxious, I can't sleep.
             If I can't sleep, I cannot function properly.
             If I cannot function properly, I am likely to make bad decisions.
             I am anxious.
             Therefore, I am likely to make bad decisions.

As is standard in modelling propositional reasoning, we abstract away from the particular words, and focus on the structure of the argument. We assign propositional letters to each of the sentences:

P I am anxious.
Q I can't sleep.
R I cannot function properly.
S I am likely to make bad decisions.

and apply the rules from there in a proof of the form:

$$P \to Q, Q \to R, R \to S, P \vdash S$$

In the format already indicated in the statement of the rule, we have all the information we need to enable us to keep track of individual steps in the proof:

Assumption made	Proof Line	Formula	Rule with Lines used
1	1	$P \to Q$	Basic Assumption
2	2	$Q \to R$	Basic Assumption
3	3	$R \to S$	Basic Assumption
4	4	P	Basic Assumption
1, 4	5	Q	→ Elim, 1, 4
1, 4, 2	6	R	→ Elim, 2, 5
1, 4, 2, 3	7	S	→ Elim, 3, 6

Again taking the rightmost column first, this fourth column displays the rule that has been used to reach the particular step, and the lines which provide the input to the proof step. The first column, on the other hand, keeps track of the assumptions. This is crucial in natural-deduction proofs, as the nature of the exercise is to make sure that in any successful proof, the conclusion line is reached based only on the formulae provided as assumptions for the proof as a whole (and not any extra assumptions that might get constructed along the way). The second column is the line of the proof, which is a simple vertical numbered listing. The third column is the proof step itself.

Notice that the listed assumptions, the line of the proof and the lines cited as input to the proof step do not necessarily coincide. At line 5, the numbers recorded in the assumptions column happen to match, as in this particular case, the lines used, i.e. lines 1 and 4, happen themselves to be assumptions. However, at line 6 this isn't so. At line 6, the step of → *Elimination* used lines 2 and 5 of the proof: but though line 2 is an assumption, line 5 is not; it depends on assumptions 1 and 4. And so on. Finally, we see displayed at the last line of the proof that we have indeed established the conclusion S from the four formulae given initially as basic assumptions.

In this proof, assumptions have been written as though given by a rule, and this is correct as it is a rule of natural deduction that anything can be assumed at any stage in a natural-deduction proof (this is the *rule of Assumptions*). The challenge for natural-deduction proofs is indeed to establish that the conclusion can be derived only from the assumptions given as input, no matter what additional assumptions might get made in proceeding to that conclusion.[4] Valid inference of a conclusion from some set of formulae is by definition deducibility of the conclusion based solely on these formulae as assumptions: so at the last line of the proof, the set of assumptions in the assumption list must not include formulae other than those formulae given initially as basic assumptions.

Notice how the proofs themselves, just like the rules, display the difference between meta-level and object-level statements. The object-level formulae are the strings of propositional calculus (in the third column above) which constitute the substance of the proof lines and the phenomenon of inference which the individual proof steps set out. The meta-level statements are the proof annotations which provide indication about how and why each proof step is licensed, enabling the display and explanation of the example of a valid inference that the propositional formulae display. This may seem a trivial reflection at this stage, with so little of the detail of the system to hand, but we shall be arguing later that sensitivity to the **process** by which information unfolds is central to explaining properties of language. This means that natural-deduction proof systems, being explicitly defined to bring out the fine structure of how some valid inference is step-wise defined, give us the closest congener to the use of natural languages for human reasoning. So being alert to natural deduction's simultaneous display of object-level reasoning and meta-level reflections on such a step will be important in what follows (see Chapters 3, 7, 8).

2.4.2 Conditional Introduction: Conditional Proof

So far we have had only two rules, the rules of *Assumptions* and → *Elimination*. Introducing conditional propositions is as natural to human

---

[4] This free use of additional assumptions is what makes natural deduction distinctive as a proof system, and what makes it so close to natural human reasoning.

reasoning as → *Elimination*. Indeed this is the form of the more rational middle-of-the-night reasoning where the reasoner happily gets back to sleep having concluded 'If I don't pay the bill tomorrow, we will be homeless.' The conclusion takes the form of a conditional, and for this we define a rule that introduces the connective →. The rule of → *Introduction* (to be read as 'Conditional Introduction'), which is often known as *Conditional Proof*, is a rule which in the face of some conclusion based on some assumption enables the assumption to be retracted, not so much by withdrawing it from the proof altogether as by absorbing it into the conclusion, drawing a weaker conditional conclusion in which the assumption is nested inside a conditional:

$$P \rightarrow Q, Q \rightarrow R \vdash P \rightarrow R$$

1	1	$P \rightarrow Q$	Basic Assumption
2	2	$Q \rightarrow R$	Basic Assumption
3	3	P	Assumption
1, 3	4	Q	→ Elim, 1, 3
1, 2, 3	5	R	→ Elim, 2, 5
1, 2	6	$P \rightarrow R$	→ Intr, 3, 5

A natural-language analogue would be:

(2.4)   If I don't pay the bill tomorrow, then we risk being made homeless.
           If we risk being made homeless, then my anxiety will increase fourfold.
           Therefore, if I don't pay the bill tomorrow, my anxiety will increase
           fourfold.

Notice that both assumptions and conclusion take the form of a conditional. In this proof, it isn't possible to move directly from the two assumptions that are given to the conclusion, because the structural condition for → *Elimination* isn't met: this needs, strictly, a pair of formulae of the form $\phi \rightarrow \psi$ and ϕ. However, the goal is nevertheless to demonstrate the conditional conclusion $P \rightarrow R$. The move made is to take the antecedent of that conditional, adding P as an additional assumption – here we see the nontrivial use of the *rule of Assumptions*. Then, having once used this assumption as the trigger for two steps of → *Elimination* to derive R (which is the consequent of the conditional conclusion to be established), we can by → *Introduction* obtain the required conditional conclusion. By definition, → *Introduction* is the step which licenses shifting of some additional assumption made, here P, out of the list of assumptions and into the body of the proof, here deriving $P \rightarrow R$. A proof containing an application of → *Introduction* thus characteristically involves a sub-proof, here lines 3–5. In this sub-proof an additional assumption is made and a stronger, interim conclusion is derived, in order, subsequently, in the main proof, to draw the weaker conclusion while dropping the additional assumption. To keep track of which assumptions are given and which are constructed, we call the former *Basic Assumptions* – these are ones which are given as statements from which the required conclusion is to be drawn. *Assumptions* are used as additional assumed statements that need somehow to be discharged in the course of the proof. The form of the rule is as follows:

→ Introduction, Conditional Introduction

$$
\begin{array}{lll}
i & i & \phi & \text{Assumption} \\
& & \cdots & \\
& & \cdots & \\
X, i & j & \psi & \\
X & k & \phi \to \psi & \to \text{Intr}, i, j
\end{array}
$$

For a further example, consider:

$$P \vdash (P \to Q) \to Q$$

$$
\begin{array}{llll}
1 & 1 & P & \text{Basic Assumption} \\
2 & 2 & P \to Q & \text{Assumption} \\
1,2 & 3 & Q & \to \text{Elim}, 1, 2 \\
1 & 4 & (P \to Q) \to Q & \to \text{Intr}, 2, 3
\end{array}
$$

As we shall see in due course in Chapter 4, the significance of this particular proof is its demonstration of the validity of what is called in type theory *type-lifting*, a process much discussed in accounts of natural-language quantification with lifting from some simple individual-type e term to a higher (generalised quantifier) type $(e \to t) \to t$ term, a move we shall return to (Chapter 4). This inference is valid in this direction only: there is no proof from an assumption of $(P \to Q) \to Q$ to P.

Exercise 2.1

Construct English analogues to the following and construct rules showing how the conclusion follows from the assumptions given, using the rules of derivation introduced so far:

a. $P \to (P \to Q), P \vdash Q$
b. $P \to Q, Q \to R \vdash P \to R$
c. $P \to (Q \to R) \vdash (P \to Q) \to (P \to R)$
d. $P \to (Q \to (R \to S)) \vdash R \to (P \to (Q \to S))$
e. $P \to Q \vdash (Q \to R) \to (P \to R)$

2.4.3   Negation and extending the set of conditional rules

Double Negation

In all inference systems, the manipulation of negation – the assertion that some state of affairs does not hold – introduces complications. All that we know for sure is that if we assert that it is false that some proposition is false, it has to be the case that that proposition is true: two negatives make a positive. If it is not the case that it is not the case that there is a Queen of

England then we are licensed to deduce that there is a Queen of England. The double negative form of the assertion entails the simple non-negative assertion; and vice versa. Accordingly in natural deduction, a rule referred to as *Double Negation*, (DN), is defined, or, more strictly a pair of rules comprising ¬ *Elimination* and ¬ *Introduction* respectively. This licenses both the elimination of two negation signs in front of any proposition whatever, and, equally, the introduction of two negation signs in front of any proposition. Like → *Elimination* and → *Introduction*, no sub-propositional structure is needed. We give it here in its most general form with both the *Elimination* and *Introduction* variant:

Double Negation

$$X \quad i \quad \neg\neg\phi \qquad\qquad X \quad i \quad \phi$$
$$\ldots \qquad\qquad\qquad \ldots$$
$$\ldots \qquad\qquad\qquad \ldots$$
$$X \quad j \quad \phi \quad \text{DN}, i \qquad X \quad j \quad \neg\neg\phi \quad \text{DN}, i$$

Notice that this is a single-premise rule, with just one premise as the input assumption, matching the one formula as output. The assumptions remain the same, as being a two-way rule, the content remains unaltered.

Reasoning with negation and conditionals

With *Double Negation* to hand, one further rule is defined that enables the **antecedent** in a conditional formula to be isolated by deriving an assertion of the falsity of this antecedent. This is a rule which enables a step of reasoning to go from some assertion about the **consequent** (the right-hand side formula in a conditional statement) to some assertion about the **antecedent** (the left-hand side formula) via interaction with negation.

Let's start again from natural language as an informal pattern. Supposing that we agree that the following sentence is true: *If John is a classicist, he reads Latin*. It then turns out: *He doesn't read Latin*. From this we are licensed to conclude *John isn't a classicist*. This is called *Modus Tollens* (MT; the full term is *Modus Tollendo Tollens*, roughly translated as 'the way of denying by denying', since by denying the truth of the consequent you conclude the denial of the antecedent):

Modus Tollens

$$X \quad i \quad \phi \to \psi$$
$$\ldots$$
$$\ldots$$
$$Y \quad j \quad \neg\psi$$
$$\ldots$$
$$\ldots$$
$$X, Y \quad m \quad \neg\phi \qquad \text{MT}, i, j$$

Like → *Elimination*, this is a two-premise rule, and like → *Elimination*, it removes the conditional connective, licensing the assertion in our English form of reasoning that John isn't a classicist from the combined assumption of the conditional assertion and the assertion of the negation of its consequent.

If we now put this together with a negative form of the consequent, we can reveal a positive form of the antecedent, this time through combination with the rule of *Double Negation*. Suppose that we agree that if John isn't good at languages he won't be able to speak Georgian, and it turns out that he is able to speak Georgian. We then are justified in concluding relative to these assumptions that John is good at languages.[5]

By using the rules as given, we can see the step of inference above as an interaction between *Modus Tollens* and *Double Negation*. Shifting into variables for our simple propositions, the form of the proof is:

$$\neg P \to \neg Q, Q \vdash P$$

1	1	$\neg P \to \neg Q$	Basic Assumption
2	2	Q	Basic Assumption
2	3	$\neg\neg Q$	DN, 2
1, 2	4	$\neg\neg P$	MT, 1, 3
1, 2	5	P	DN, 4

Notice here the step from line 3 to line 4. The structural condition which is the input to *Modus Tollens* demands that the formula takes the form $\neg\psi$, and the formula at line 3 meets this condition if we analyse ψ as $\neg Q$. The result of any application of *Modus Tollens* is $\neg\phi$, and applying this rule to lines 1, 3 requires that ϕ be $\neg P$ which yields at line 4 $\neg\neg P$. Hence by *Double Negation* the conclusion P.

Exercise 2.2

Find proofs for the following sequents, using the rules of derivation introduced so far:

a. $Q \to (P \to R), \neg R, Q \vdash \neg P$
b. $P \to \neg\neg Q, P \vdash Q$
c. $\neg\neg Q \to P, \neg P \vdash \neg Q$
d. $\neg P \to \neg Q, Q \vdash P$
e. $P \to \neg Q \vdash Q \to \neg P$
f. $\neg P \to Q \vdash \neg Q \to P$

---

[5] Georgian is an extremely hard language, notoriously providing exceptions to many phenomena thought by linguists to be general properties of language.

2.4.4   The Elimination and Introduction rules for ∧ ▬▬▬▬▬▬

With the rules for the connective corresponding to *and* as a sentence coordinator, ∧, the situation is much simpler. If two propositions are independently established then the compound proposition joining them together in a coordinate propositional formula can equally be taken as established. Conversely, if the coordinate propositional formula is an established proof step, then each of the two formulae that make up that coordinate propositional formula can be separately derived. These two rules are so obvious, it may seem hard even to see them as needing explicit rule formulation. If we know that John is a classicist and he reads Latin, then we can certainly infer that John is a classicist. Conversely, if we separately establish that John is a classicist and that he reads Latin, then it is a simple step of inference to deduce that John is a classicist **and** he reads Latin. This is the proof-theoretic analogue of the truth-table information (familiar in all textbooks: see 3.2): if both propositions are independently true, then their conjunction is entailed. If some conjunction of propositions is true, then independently each is entailed. In either direction, the output of the rule depends on exactly the same assumptions as the input to the rule. In effect, neither the elimination of the connective nor its introduction changes anything.

We now give the two rules together.

∧ Introduction

$$
\begin{array}{llll}
X & i & \phi \\
& \cdots \\
& \cdots \\
Y & j & \psi \\
& \cdots \\
& \cdots \\
X, Y & m & \phi \wedge \psi & \wedge \, \text{Intr}, i, j
\end{array}
$$

This rule (read as 'And Introduction') will enable us at any stage to take two independently derived formulae and conjoin them to form a compound formula.

∧ Elimination

$$
\begin{array}{llll}
X & i & \phi \wedge \psi \\
& \cdots \\
& \cdots \\
X & m & \phi/\psi & \wedge \, \text{Elim}, i
\end{array}
$$

∧ *Elimination* (read as 'And Elimination') is the inverse. If at any stage of a proof one has established a compound formula joined by ∧, either one of the conjuncts can be established as a derived line in the proof.

We now set out proofs which involve interaction between the rules we have introduced. To see ∧ *Introduction* in action in combination with → *Introduction*, we go through the following:

$$(P \land Q) \to R \vdash P \to (Q \to R)$$

The English analogue of this would be:

(2.5)   If John is studying at Oxford and he can read Latin, then he can probably
           read classical Greek.

(2.6)   If John is studying at Oxford, then if he can read Latin, he can probably
           read classical Greek.

Notice in passing how pronouns are used when information has to be carried over identically from the construal of one clause or sentence into the construal of another, an issue we return to in depth in Chapter 5. In the mean time, we rely on tacit understanding of this mechanism in order to achieve reasonably natural English counterparts to the logical formulae under discussion.

Returning to technical details, notice the bracketing in the formal display, which makes unambiguous that the $\to$ between P and $(Q \to R)$ is the primary connective of the conclusion (taking scope over both P and $Q \to R$), and also that the $\to$ between $(P \land Q)$ and R is the primary connective in the single basic assumption. Recall that a conditional conclusion can, very generally, be derived by taking as an additional assumption the antecedent formula of that conclusion, here P. So in the goal of proving the conditional conclusion $P \to (Q \to R)$, we may choose to assume P. But having once assumed P and anticipating what it is that from this extra assumption needs to be derived, we see that the conclusion to be derived is itself conditional: $(Q \to R)$. Accordingly, we start the proof itself by adding **two** additional assumptions to the formula given as basic assumption, namely P and Q; and from these we seek to establish R as an intermediate conclusion, since this is the nested consequent in the overall conclusion. These extra assumptions then can be coordinated together by $\land$ *Introduction*. Why do we want to do this? The answer to this is that we shall need to derive $(P \land Q)$ in order to apply $\to$ *Elimination*. So once having done this, applying $\to$ *Elimination* to get R, we can use **two** steps of $\to$ *Introduction* to drive the conclusion which is the overall goal:

$$(P \land Q) \to R \vdash P \to (Q \to R)$$

1	1	$(P \land Q) \to R$	Basic Assumption
2	2	P	Assumption
3	3	Q	Assumption
2, 3	4	$P \land Q$	$\land$ Intr, 2, 3
1, 2, 3	5	R	$\to$ Elim, 1, 4
1, 2	6	$Q \to R$	$\to$ Intr, 3, 5
1	7	$P \to (Q \to R)$	$\to$ Intr, 2, 6

This proof is pretty much self-explanatory: just note that the fact that P and Q in this proof happen to be assumptions isn't relevant to the application of

∧ *Introduction*. There have to be two applications of → *Introduction*: this is because → *Introduction* requires one assumption at a time to be absorbed into the body of the proof. There is accordingly no possibility of getting rid of the two assumptions P and Q by a single step of → *Introduction*. If more than one assumption needs to be shifted from the assumption-set into the body of the proof, this has to be done by successive steps of → *Introduction*. With these two steps of → *Introduction* in this proof, by the time the conclusion is reached, only the basic assumption given will remain, as is required in the assigned goal of proving this inference by the rules. Hence the two last steps of the proof at lines 6–7.

The manipulation of ∧ *Elimination* is just as simple as ∧ *Introduction*. We see it in the derivation of a very well-known equivalence: that a composite conditional proposition involving two conditional connectives is equivalent to a conditional proposition in which two of these are taken as a compound coordinate antecedent:

$$P \rightarrow (Q \rightarrow R) \vdash (P \wedge Q) \rightarrow R$$

In other words our inference goes in both directions, and our English analogues (2.5)–(2.6) are predicted to be equivalent.

The reverse direction of proof is as follows:

1	1	$P \rightarrow (Q \rightarrow R)$	Basic Assumption
2	2	$P \wedge Q$	Assumption
2	3	P	∧ Elim, 2
2	4	Q	∧ Elim, 2
1, 2	5	$Q \rightarrow R$	→ Elim, 1, 3
1, 2	6	R	→ Elim, 4, 5
1	7	$(P \wedge Q) \rightarrow R$	→ Intr, 2, 6

Notice here at lines 3 and 4, that the derivation of P and then separately Q doesn't change the assumption at all; the assumption remains the compound coordinated formula. What this means is that, unlike in the previous proof, there is only **one** assumption to be got rid of, that is the coordinated formula which constitutes the assumption made at line 2, so in this proof there is indeed only one application of → *Introduction*, which, in one step, brings in the assumption both of P and of Q but in the form of the single compound formula $P \wedge Q$, now as the antecedent to the conditional conclusion.

Exercise 2.3

Provide English analogues to the following, and demonstrate that they are valid proofs:

a. $P \vdash Q \rightarrow (P \wedge Q)$
b. $P \wedge (Q \wedge R) \vdash Q \wedge (P \wedge R)$
c. $(P \rightarrow Q) \wedge (P \rightarrow R) \vdash P \rightarrow (Q \wedge R)$

2.4.5   ∨ **Introduction and ∨ Elimination** ▬▬▬▬▬▬▬▬▬

The rules of ∨ *Introduction* and ∨ *Elimination* (read as 'Or Introduction' and 'Or Elimination' respectively) are not so straightforward, though for very different reasons. ∨ *Introduction* is **very** straightforward formally; but it is just generally counter-intuitive that anyone would ever want to draw such a conclusion. This is the step of inference that from any established proposition, you can join it to any proposition whatsoever across the ∨ connective (corresponding to the English word *or*) and the result will be a valid step of inference. However, the intuition behind the applicability of this rule might be illustrated by looking at what it means to be an administrative peace-maker. Consider a context of two people arguing about the next move to make after a rather ill-tempered meeting where all that matters is that they report what the meeting achieved. Suppose also that one of them is a peace-maker and wants a compromise. The peace-maker might seek a form of resolution by supposedly shifting from the assumption that 'We submit a summary document' to 'Either we submit a summary document or we submit notes on the meeting' while still privately holding to the view that they will submit a summary document. If indeed it is the case that they submit a summary document, then it will certainly be the case that either they submitted a summary document or they submitted notes on the meeting. What they have agreed will still hold: so no one will lose face or need to retract anything, for the first nondisjunctive statement is stronger than the second disjunctive one. Quite generally, disjunction $P \vee Q$ is true if **at least one** of its disjuncts is true, so that the rule ∨ *Introduction* cannot lead from a true premise to a false conclusion, though in leading to a weaker one, it may fail to be informative.

∨ **Introduction**

$$X \quad i \quad \phi$$
$$\ldots$$
$$\ldots$$
$$X \quad m \quad \phi \vee \psi \quad \vee \text{Intr}, i$$

∨ *Elimination* is formally harder to manipulate, but actually conceptually much more natural. Supposing you confront the issue of whether to get travel insurance. As you reflect, you might reason:

(2.7)   Either I'm going to worry about my health while abroad or I'm going to worry about losing my luggage.
If I am going to worry about my health while abroad, then I should get travel insurance.
If I am going to worry about losing my luggage, then I should get travel insurance.

Faced with these three assumptions, despite being a professional worrier, there is one decision that you do **not** have to worry over: it is the decision as to whether or not to get travel insurance. You should get travel insurance. This is already in some sense decided for you, for this conclusion follows without having to be reflected on independently. That you should get travel insurance is a logical consequence of your other three worries: whichever of the two putative sources of worry holds, the conclusion that you should get travel insurance will follow. This is the inference step of ∨ *Elimination*; and it has a real functional purpose. It enables some complex step of reasoning to proceed from a disjunctive premise to a conclusion, even though a disjunction is a relatively weak form of commitment, relative to the caveat that this conclusion must be deducible from each of its parts taken separately.

As in the case of → *Elimination*, the simplest type of proof is one that matches the making of these assumptions and the immediate deduction of the conclusion. Since the rule is complex to set out, we give this application of the rule directly, before presenting a full definition.

$$P \rightarrow R, Q \rightarrow R, P \vee Q \vdash R$$

The essential property of any proof involving ∨ *Elimination* involves two subproofs, one from each of the disjuncts in the disjunction, deriving the conclusion being sought.

1	1	$P \rightarrow R$	Basic Assumption
2	2	$Q \rightarrow R$	Basic Assumption
3	3	$P \vee Q$	Basic Assumption
4	4	P	Assumption
1, 4	5	R	→ Elim, 1, 4
6	6	Q	Assumption
2, 6	7	R	→ Elim, 2, 6
3, 1, 2	8	R	∨ Elim, 1, 2, 3, 4, 5, 6, 7

We list the basic assumptions, one of which is a disjunction. Then at line 4 a further assumption is constructed, in recognition of the basic assumption at line 3. This is the assumption of the first half of the disjunction (listed not as a *Basic Assumption* but as an *Assumption*), from which some conclusion has to be derived, as a sub-proof. Such a conclusion is derived at line 5 by → *Elimination*. The list of assumptions for this step thus contains the extra constructed assumption at line 4 and the *Basic Assumption* that is used in establishing this line, viz. the assumption made at line 1. The second half of the proof involves constructing a further assumption, the second part of the disjunction, at line 6, initiating a second sub-proof. Again, the same conclusion is derived, but this time from this new additional assumption and the second basic assumption made at line 2. So the rule used is again → *Elimination* yielding line 7, but the assumptions are those of line 6 and line 2. This proof, with its two sub-proofs, now fulfils the conditions needed as input to the line of ∨ *Elimination*. We have a disjunction and some one conclusion derived from both parts of that disjunction. ∨ *Elimination* can now apply, to deduce that very same conclusion, but now to be taken from the disjunction itself. The set of assumptions made at the final line of the proof involves dropping both the assumption made at line 4 and the assumption

made at line 6, replacing these two assumptions with the assumption made at
line 3 – that is, the disjunction itself. What has to be listed with this proof step
of ∨ *Elimination* is the line at which the disjunction occurs in the proof, here
line 3, the line of the proof at which the first half of that disjunction is assumed,
here line 4, the line at which some conclusion was drawn, here line 5, the line
at which the second half of the disjunction is assumed, here line 6, and the line
at which the very same conclusion was drawn from that assumption, here line 7.
The proof step has thus used five lines of proof to get some conclusion already
drawn at two other steps in the proof. This may look repetitive, but in this step, it
is the assumptions that are shifted to something weaker than had been assumed
at either of the two earlier occurrences of that very same formula.

   As with all other rules, the rule itself has to be defined to apply at any stage of
the proof, and the formulation that makes this possible is as follows (notice the
characterisation of the two added assumptions as *Assumption*):

∨ **Elimination**

$$
\begin{array}{llll}
X & i & \phi \vee \psi & \\
 & & \cdots & \\
 & & \cdots & \\
j & j & \phi & \text{Assumption} \\
 & & \cdots & \\
 & & \cdots & \\
j, Y & k & \gamma & \\
m & m & \psi & \text{Assumption} \\
 & & \cdots & \\
 & & \cdots & \\
m, Z & n & \gamma & \\
X, Y, Z & p & \gamma & \vee \text{Elim}, i, j, k, m, n
\end{array}
$$

In this rule, in place of some disjunction $\phi \vee \psi$, first ϕ is assumed and then some
conclusion derived, and then ψ is assumed and the same conclusion derived. If
that is so, the conclusion is said to be derived from the disjunction $\phi \vee \psi$, in that
step dropping the two intermediate additional assumptions. X, Y, Z, as before,
range over sets of assumptions. X is the set of assumptions on which the original disjunction depended. Y is the set of assumptions on which the conclusion
derived from ϕ may have depended, in addition to the assumption ϕ itself; Z is,
similarly, the set of assumptions on which the conclusion derived from ψ may
have depended in addition to the assumption specific to that disjunct. So, to recapitulate: in concluding that some conclusion γ is derivable from the disjunction,
we conclude it from each of the disjuncts, ϕ and ψ, using whatever assumptions
are necessary in addition to assuming these in their own right. We then move to
the same conclusion γ again, this time replacing the assumptions of ϕ and ψ
themselves with whatever assumptions the disjunction depended on. The record
of the lines used involves five lines: the disjunction, the assumption of each of
the disjuncts and the conclusions derived from each.

Exercise 2.4

Find proofs for the following:

a. $Q \vdash P \vee Q$
b. $P \wedge Q \vdash P \vee Q$
c. $(P \rightarrow R) \wedge (Q \rightarrow R) \vdash (P \vee Q) \rightarrow R$
d. $P \rightarrow Q, R \rightarrow S \vdash (P \wedge R) \rightarrow (Q \wedge S)$
e. $P \rightarrow Q, R \rightarrow S \vdash (P \vee R) \rightarrow (Q \vee S)$

2.4.6   *Reductio ad Absurdum*: a constrained variant

With just one more rule, the set of rules for propositional logic will be complete. This last rule is invariably known by its Latin name *Reductio ad Absurdum (RAA)* ('reduction to absurdity'). This is a rule which, in the face of a derived contradiction, allows an assumption to be altogether abandoned and replaced by the assertion of its negation. So it is, by definition, a rule of ¬ *Introduction*. This form of reasoning has played a very large role in theory development across the years. To construct a theoretical model of some phenomenon, a number of hypotheses are formulated, which we take as premises to which the theory is committed, either by assumption or by deduction from other assumptions. If in the process of testing that theory, a contradiction is derived, then one knows for sure that the full set of premises constituting the proposed model cannot be correct: at least one assumption to which that theory is committed must be at fault. *Reductio ad Absurdum*, known by its acronym *RAA*, is the step of inference which allows such an assumption to be dropped, with its negation replacing it in the set of premises constitutive of the theory under development. To give an anecdotal example, consider a scenario in which watching a nature programme on TV, two of us might debate the basis of what we are slumped in front of:

(2.8)   If this is a UK beaver, the film was made in Scotland.

(2.9)   If this is a Canada beaver, the film was not made in Scotland.

We are in agreement that if we can establish the film was made in Scotland and that the film was not made in Scotland, we will between us have an inconsistent set of premises, and one of us will have to drop at least one assumption. Characteristically however, the one that retracts their assumption will probably not simply say, 'OK I was wrong', but simply shift into constructing some more complex assumption such as:

(2.10)   If this is a Canada beaver, then the film was not made in Scotland, unless the beaver is one that has just been introduced into Scotland from Canada.

This is the stuff of which theories are made. This involves the construction of premises that in principle are testable. However, when faced with internal inconsistency, human nature being what it is, the proponents of the theory are not led to abandon the hypothesis under investigation. Rather, in order to yield compatibility with the facts, they accept the cost of constructing a more complex auxiliary assumption to protect the simpler, stronger, assumption from falsification. Another example might be:

(2.11)   If Latin is a verb-final language, then whatever occurs after the verb can't be part of the same clause.

(2.12)   If Latin is a verb-medial language, then whatever occurs after the verb can be part of the same clause.

In this case, the issue remains in dispute. Some people argue that Latin is a verb-final language and explain away the difficult cases as not part of the same clause (rather contrary to the apparent evidence); others argue that whatever occurs after the verb is indeed able to function as an intrinsic part of the clause. But what they are agreed on is that one cannot hold to a theory in which whatever occurs after the verb in Latin both is and is not part of the same clause as the verb itself. One of the assumptions on which these two assertions depend has to be abandoned or modified.

In defining the rule syntactically, the first step is to define what constitutes a *contradiction*. In this strictly syntactic perspective, this can be defined to be invariably a formula of the form:

$$\phi \wedge \neg\phi$$

The rule then states that if from some assumption ϕ plus possibly other assumptions, some **other** formula ψ and its negation $\neg\psi$ can both be derived, yielding $\psi \wedge \neg\psi$, then the assumption ϕ can be removed from the assumptions on which that line depends, deriving $\neg\phi$ on the basis of any other assumptions on which $\psi \wedge \neg\psi$ depended:

RAA (*Reductio ad Absurdum*) $\neg$ **Introduction**

i	i	ϕ	Assumption
		$\ldots$	
		$\ldots$	
i, X	j	ψ	
		$\ldots$	
		$\ldots$	
i, Y	k	$\neg\psi$	
		$\ldots$	
		$\ldots$	
i, X, Y	m	$\psi \wedge \neg\psi$	
X, Y	n	$\neg\phi$	RAA, i, m

As with the other rules, let's see this in action. We wish to establish the validity of:

$$P \rightarrow Q, P \rightarrow \neg Q \vdash \neg P$$

The proof is simple and direct. We start with two assumptions as given, add a third which is the opposite of what we wish to conclude, derive a contradiction and derive the required (negative) conclusion.

1	1	$P \rightarrow Q$	Basic Assumption
2	2	$P \rightarrow \neg Q$	Basic Assumption
3	3	P	Assumption
1, 3	4	Q	$\rightarrow$ Elim, 1, 3
2, 3	5	$\neg Q$	$\rightarrow$ Elim, 2, 3
1, 2, 3	6	$Q \wedge \neg Q$	$\wedge$ Intr, 4, 5
1, 2	7	$\neg P$	RAA, 3, 6

$\wedge$ *Introduction* in the construction of the contradiction is an almost invariant step, since it enables the two conjuncts of a coordinated contradiction to be put together to yield the right form of input for *RAA*. Then with *RAA*, out of the assumptions on which that contradiction depends, we can abandon any one assumption. In the event, in the particular proof here, it is the assumption made at line 3 specific to the goal of establishing a contradiction that is rejected, deriving the required conclusion $\neg P$ on the basis of the two formulae provided as input assumptions.

RAA has a property not shared by other rules: it involves retraction of some assumption, which may have been independently derived. As a consequence of this, it is a rule which demonstrates that though humans are what we called earlier inference-drawing mechanisms, they are not blind inference engines, for other factors may get in the way. As happens to most of us at least once a week, we often mis-hear what others say to us. In such circumstances, a common mistake is to take some absurd interpretation which the speaker couldn't possibly have intended and, rather than recognising the looming inconsistency this absurd interpretation will give rise to and so abandon our first attempt at processing what is said, we simply query what is said, sometimes with rising irritation that our interlocutor could have been so stupid as to intend the interpretation which we, in our haste, have recovered. Take for example a long-married couple preparing to go out to a party together at a friend's house close by in north London. The conversation goes as follows (Surrey is a county outside Greater London on the south side):

(2.13)   A: Are you going to hurry?
           B (mishearing). Surrey? Of course not. I'm coming with you.

B's interpretation of A's question, though a logically possible interpretation for some utterance, is not a possible one in the circumstances, and a more reflective interlocutor might bother to reason on from their first interpretation to the reflection that what A had said risks deriving an inconsistency, namely that B is both coming to the party with A, and yet not coming to the party with A (the party is in north London in the opposite direction from Surrey). Because such interpretation has to be rejected, one might surely expect that B would go on from this to reason that he had made a mistake, and so establish a more plausible and correct interpretation of the stimulus he was offered. But, at this point, unfortunately, relevance constraints get in the way. The cognitive system, according to relevance-theoretic assumptions, is constrained to maximise relevance by engaging in minimum cognitive effort for adequate inferential effects. Since understanding A's question as whether B is going to Surrey has yielded inferential effects, albeit thoroughly implausible ones, B rests content with thinking that A has said something idiotic rather than engaging in the very considerable increase in effort needed to reject the derived interpretation, start again and establish some alternative interpretation. The problem, seen relevance-theoretically, is that such a more sensible interpretation is made automatically less relevant because of the cost of effort involved in making the needed revision on top of the unsuccessful first parse. So, however much we may individually hope that we are considerate, kindly members of the social group within which we live, optimising for relevance on the basis of taking into account what our speaker could reasonably have intended, by far the majority of us inevitably maximise relevance for ourselves at the cost of coming to uncharitable judgements about others. This should not however be taken to have consequences for *RAA* as a logical step of inference. To the contrary, *RAA* has an important inferential function in the more reflective business of theory construction where time constraints are not as pressing as getting off to a party!

2.4.7   Commentary: propositional logic for linguists

Even though learning about natural-deduction systems of inference is unquestionably a mind-stretching activity, it might nevertheless seem as though simply enumerating proof rules of inference is hardly a top priority for linguists – why put so much emphasis on a coarse-grained system of inference, when the complexity of natural languages clearly requires something more fine-grained? But as we shall now see, this system can be extended seamlessly to include *Elimination* and *Introduction* rules for the two predicate logic quantifiers and then we shall have to hand a complete, very small syntactic system – just four connectives and two operators, with twelve associated rules in total – which will then, without any more stipulation at all, express exactly the full, infinite set of valid inferences of classical logic. And, as we shall see in due course, the dynamics of natural-deduction processes are of interest in their own right, echoing the on-line and essentially local process of how interpretation can be incrementally built up.

Before turning to the extension provided by predicate logic rules, it will be useful to have made explicit what has so far been assumed – the syntactic rules of propositional logic:

R1 If ϕ is a wellformed formula, then $\neg\phi$ is a wellformed formula.
R2 If ϕ, ψ are wellformed formulae, then $(\phi \wedge \psi)$ is a wellformed formula.
R3 If ϕ, ψ are wellformed formulae, then $(\phi \vee \psi)$ is a wellformed formula.

R4 If ϕ, ψ are wellformed formulae, then $(\phi \rightarrow \psi)$ is a wellformed formula.
R5 Nothing else is a wellformed formula.

As before, Greek letters are metavariables to be instantiated by particular expressions of the language, so the rules are schemata for inducing wellformed strings of propositional logic. In all cases, the *scope* of the connective, what it applies to, is the minimal propositional formula in which the connective itself occurs, as indicated by the brackets introduced in the definition of the rules R2–R4 (brackets are omitted in rule R1, for simplicity).

We might also note in passing that, even without any mention of quantification, we have established a basis for grounding concepts of *entailment* and *synonymy*. *Entailment* between two sentences is nothing other than *inference*, which in proof-theoretic systems is defined to be the deduction of a conclusion within a proof containing one basic assumption. All our one-premise rules illustrate this, but so also do all the proofs containing one basic assumption and their conclusion. Hence, by definition, *John admires someone who reads Latin and Mary reads Latin* entails *Mary reads Latin*. In passing, we also noted a concept of *equivalence*, or, as we might now call it, *synonymy*. Any proof from one assumption to conclusion, and, in reverse, from that one conclusion as assumption to the other as conclusion is an instance of synonymy. (2.5)–(2.6) were illustrations of this:

(2.5)   If John is studying at Oxford and he can read Latin, then he can probably read classical Greek.

(2.6)   If John is studying at Oxford, then if he can read Latin, he can probably read classical Greek.

So, with concepts of inference and synonymy now formally defined, we are well on the way to establishing the core semantic relations which are a core part of any formal semantic model.

As we shall now see, predicate logic takes these core notions and extends the range of inferences expressible to a sub-sentential level. But the core concept of inference is already set up by the assumptions underpinning propositional logic.

Exercise 2.5

Find proofs for the following sequents:

a. $P \wedge (Q \vee R) \vdash (P \wedge Q) \vee (P \wedge R)$
b. $P \vee (Q \wedge R) \vdash (P \vee Q) \wedge (P \vee R)$
c. $P \wedge Q \vdash \neg(P \rightarrow \neg Q)$
d. $\neg(P \vee Q) \vdash \neg P \wedge \neg Q$
e. $\neg(P \wedge Q) \vdash \neg P \vee \neg Q$
f. $P \wedge Q \vdash \neg(\neg P \vee \neg Q)$
g. $P \rightarrow Q \vdash \neg P \vee Q$
h. $\neg P \rightarrow Q \vdash P \vee Q$

2.5 Predicate logic

Predicate logic defines an articulation of fine structure below the level of proposition; so what had been treated in the propositional system by simply stipulating primitive propositional variables P, Q, etc. gets replaced in the extended system by rules defining how predicate expressions combine with argument expressions to yield wellformed formulae of propositional type. As part of this, quantification over individuals is defined at this sub-sentential level, while nevertheless allowing quantifiers to bind over propositional formulae of arbitrary complexity. To see the full relevance of predicate logic for linguists, we have to turn first to issues of translation from one language, say English, into predicate logic formulae.

Three basic types of vocabulary items are added in the extension from propositional to predicate logic. First, there are predicate-letters which are taken as primitive vocabulary items in much the same way as propositional-letters stand for propositions in the propositional calculus. Here we only use predicate-letters are of two sorts. There are one-place predicates and two-place predicates. Second, there are name-like devices for picking out individuals, also of two types, the *variables* whose interpretation is given in conjunction with the quantifiers to which we return, and the naming devices, so-called *individual constants* or *terms*. With just these we can formally model the internal structure of assertions of the type *Tom smokes, John ignored Bill, Tom died, Tom married Sue* as involving a predicate and a number of individual constants as arguments:

$$\text{Tom smokes.} \quad S(a)$$
$$\text{Tom married Sue.} \quad M(a, b)$$

Here a, b are individual constants; S is a one-place predicate that combines with a to form a propositional formula, $S(a)$. M is a two-place predicate that combines with a pair of argument expressions to yield a propositional formula. In virtue of the restriction to a restricted set of semantic types, there is in the assumption of translatability of natural language onto predicate logic a certain looseness: nouns, adjectives and verbs are all translated onto predicates. For example, *Tom is a man* characteristically gets a translation no different in category from *Tom smokes*. A nominal *a man* which occurs as a complement to the verb *be* is treated as a predicate, hence translating *Tom is a man* as 'Man(Tom)'. And so too are adjectives. *Tom is anxious* is represented as 'Anxious(Tom)'. In both cases, the copula verb is simply suppressed. Since our concern at this juncture is with predicate logic itself, we will not pursue this further at this stage. But there is a point of methodology to notice in passing, that there is call for intelligent guesswork in translating natural-language sentences into putative analogues of predicate logic. All predicate-logic formulae are interpretable relative to arbitrary domains of discourse. The challenge in translation is then to select a predicate-logic formula that sufficiently brings out the truth-conditional content specific to the individual natural-language expression.

2.5.1   Predicate logic syntax

Turning now to the syntax of predicate logic itself, the system has two syntactic rules articulating sub-propositional structure, which we add to the rules of propositional logic in section 2.4.6, excluding the final clause (**R5**) which explicitly excludes everything else from being a wellformed formula:

R5 If α is a term, and γ is a one-place predicate, then $\gamma(\alpha)$ is a wellformed formula (wff).
R6 If α, β are terms, and γ is a two-place predicate, then $\gamma(\alpha, \beta)$ is a wellformed formula.

These are add-ons to the syntactic rules of the propositional logic system, enabling the construction of arbitrarily complex formulae, each one of which contains internal predicate-argument structure. So one can construct such formulae as:

$$S(a) \wedge M(a, b)$$

or

$$M(a, b) \rightarrow S(b)$$

and so on.

Third, and most important, there are the quantifying operators. Quantifiers constitute the major addition to propositional calculus, the two additional operators whose use is essentially twinned with variables. The two operators are both propositional operators: they apply to propositional formulae to give back a propositional formula. There is the quantifier $\forall$ corresponding to 'For all x it is the case that ...', and the quantifier $\exists$ corresponding to 'There exists at least one x of which it is the case that ...' (Notice how, even in the paraphrase, we need to use such variables to set out the form of interpretation which these impose.) As in mathematics, the variable itself is unrestricted, ranging over any individual in some domain. In the syntax, these variables behave just like individual constants in occurring as arguments of a predicate: within some minimal predicate-argument structure these are so-called *free* variables. However, that same variable is *bound* by the associated quantifier immediately adjoined to that predicate-argument structure within which the variable occurs, and this quantifier dictates the interpretation of all the occurrences of that variable within the given domain, as may be indicated by the pairing of an opening bracket immediately following the quantifying operator and some corresponding closing bracket. This propositional formula constitutes the *scope* of that quantifier.

For example, we might model (2.14), as (2.14'):

(2.14)   Every doctor is well paid. Every doctor works too hard. Therefore every doctor works too hard and is well paid.

(2.14') $\forall x(P(x) \rightarrow Q(x)), \forall x(P(x) \rightarrow R(x)) \vdash \forall x(P(x) \rightarrow (Q(x) \wedge R(x)))$

Notice how the nouns of (2.14) in the suggested translation (2.14′) are assigned the same type, that of predicate type, as adjectives, verbs or indeed whole verb phrases. Here *doctor, is well paid, works too hard* are all assigned the same predicate type. Furthermore quantifiers are not defined as constituents that combine directly with nouns or adjectives. They bind variables across the propositional domain which constitutes their scope, with the construal of all occurrences of that variable totally dictated by the operator with which it is twinned. The syntactic definition of the universal quantifier, which makes the concept of scope explicit, is:

R7 If u is an individual variable and ϕ is a wellformed formula, then $\forall u(\phi)$ is a wellformed formula.

As with propositional logic, the scope of the quantifier is the minimal propositional formula containing the quantifier and its associated variable. Hence, the scope of the quantifier $\forall$ is the minimal string containing it, its associated variable and the immediately following expression ϕ. Sometimes brackets indicating the scope of the quantifier will be used, as needed for clarity.

The syntax of a predicate-logic quantifying expression is worth noting, with its difference from natural-language quantification. On the one hand, quantifiers are propositional operators, not term-creating operators, so that they operate at the propositional level. Reflecting this in Rule R7, $\forall$ is a function applying to a propositional formula as input to yield a propositional formula as output. An associated difference between predicate logic and natural language is that the variables in predicate logic are unrestricted, they range over any element in the domain. In natural language, this is never so. We don't make assertions about all objects whatsoever, but only over objects falling into some set, as in (2.14) about doctors. So in translating into predicate logic as in (2.14′), the restriction on the variable which the quantifier is to bind has to be built into the formula itself, as the first component in a compound formula. So *every doctor* doesn't translate as a unit in predicate logic: indeed it doesn't even correspond to a constituent of a predicate-logic formula. Rather it corresponds to the first part of a compound formula, plus the quantifying operator. Moreover, because the assertion now corresponds on a crude translation to 'For all x, if x is a doctor, then . . .' the connective selected for the English universal quantifying expression has to be the conditional. This is **not** a property of the universal quantifier of the logic itself. $\forall x F(x)$ is a wellformed formula of predicate logic, as is $\forall x(F(x) \wedge G(x))$. The correspondence of the universal quantifier and a conditional as the main connective of the formula that it has scope over is merely a problem for linguists concerned about the relation between natural languages and logic, quite external to the system itself. As indicated earlier, this is merely the methodological question of selecting the predicate-logic formula closest in denotational content to the English quantifying expression *every*.

With the existential quantifier, we face an analogous problem. Syntactically, the existential quantifier is a propositional, variable-binding operator, and accordingly is defined by a rule of syntax essentially like that for the universal quantifier:

R8 If u is an individual variable and ϕ is a wellformed formula, then $\exists u(\phi)$ is a wellformed formula.

Again, there is no defined correlation between the existential quantifier itself and any particular connective. The apparent correlation between *A man is happy* and some propositional conjunction $\exists x(Man(x) \wedge Happy(x))$ is an artefact of the lack of correspondence between predicate logic and natural language, which does not display propositional quantifiers, but which does provide a commitment in the existential case to there being at least one such individual, expressible only via translation onto a conjunction. Again, this issue has no consequences for the logical system itself. But notice here how the use of brackets serves to make explicit the scope of the existential quantifier as ranging over the two open propositional formulae, joined by the connective $\wedge$.

In sum, we now give the full set of syntactic rules for predicate logic.

R1 If ϕ is a wellformed formula, then $\neg\phi$ is a wellformed formula (wff).

R2 If ϕ, ψ are wellformed formulae, then $(\phi \wedge \psi)$ is a wellformed formula.

R3 If ϕ, ψ are wellformed formulae, then $(\phi \vee \psi)$ is a wellformed formula.

R4 If ϕ, ψ are wellformed formulae, then $(\phi \rightarrow \psi)$ is a wellformed formula.

R5 If α is a term, and γ is a one-place predicate, then $\gamma(\alpha)$ is a wellformed formula.

R6 If α, β are terms, and γ is a two-place predicate, then $\gamma(\alpha, \beta)$ is a wellformed formula.

R7 If u is an individual variable and ϕ is a wellformed formula, then $\forall u\phi$ is a wellformed formula.

R8 If u is an individual variable and ϕ is a wellformed formula, then $\exists u\phi$ is a wellformed formula.

R9 Nothing else is a wellformed formula.

2.5.2   Proof rules of predicate logic

With just this reminder of basic syntactic properties of predicate logic, we can now see how proof rules for the two quantifying operators can be defined in such a way as to enable systematic interaction with the elimination and introduction rules for the propositional connectives. As in propositional calculus, there are two rules for each quantifier: one eliminating the quantifier and so moving to a simpler structure (with a name in place of the variable bound by the quantifier), the other introducing the quantifier to derive quantified conclusions.

Universal Elimination and Introduction

The elimination of the universal quantifier is very straightforward, as even a cursory view of its semantics would lead us to expect. If some predicate holds of every member of some set, then it holds of each member of that set. So if for example, of some groups of students comprising Tom, Dick and Harry, we know that every student is shy, then we can deduce that Tom is shy, that Dick is shy and that Harry is shy. If we have any name occurring within a proof, in the presence of a universally quantified formula, we can substitute that name, as we can be certain that it will hold of that named individual: whatever assumptions that universally quantified formula depended on will be carried over to the formula with the name, as the inferred formula is a direct consequence of those assumptions in conjunction with the quantified formula. So for the following, for which we give an English analogue, we have a very straightforward proof:

$$\forall x(F(x) \rightarrow G(x)), F(j) \vdash G(j)$$

(2.15)   Every fractious person grumbles. John is fractious. Therefore John grumbles.

We list first the premises given as assumptions, and then with one step of $\forall$ *Elimination*, a step of $\rightarrow$ *Elimination* will lead us directly to the conclusion:

1	1	$\forall x(F(x) \rightarrow G(x))$	Basic Assumption
2	2	$F(j)$	Basic Assumption
1	3	$F(j) \rightarrow G(j)$	$\forall$ Elim, 1, 2
1	4	$G(j)$	$\rightarrow$ Elim, 2, 3

Notice first here the use of the quantifier $\forall$ to bind two occurrences of the variable x, one in the antecedent (the first clause) of the conditional, one in the consequent (the second clause of the conditional). The quantifier and its additional structure in the formula is eliminated by substituting the given name for each occurrence of the variable: the step of $\rightarrow$ *Elimination* will then duly apply exactly as in propositional calculus. However, we really don't need to have a name independently itemised in the proof. If the universally quantified statement holds of any entity whatever, then we can simply construct a name, an *arbitrary name*, and presume that this will be true, no matter what the substituend. Note that $\phi[x]$ means 'ϕ contains at least one free occurrence of the variable x'; $\phi[a/x]$ then means 'the formula you get from replacing every occurrence of x in ϕ with an occurrence of a'.

$\forall$ **Elimination** (Universal Elimination)

$$X \quad i \quad \forall\phi[x]$$
$$\cdots$$
$$\cdots$$
$$X \quad j \quad \phi[a/x] \quad \forall \text{Elim}, i$$

What the rule states is that from a universally quantified formula, there is a licensed transition to a formula dropping that quantifier and substituting all occurrences of the variable which that quantifier binds by some substituend a. There are no restrictions on what that choice of a might be.

This becomes very useful in chains of inference, as we shall shortly see, though when it comes to reintroducing the quantifier, we have to be extremely careful if we are to avoid gross fallacies. Under what circumstances can we deduce $\forall x F(x)$ from some particularised assertion $F(a)$? Well, the best way to see what kind of control has to be imposed is to see a totally fallacious mode of reasoning. Suppose you have a friend Angela who is being hopelessly disorganised – she is being dreadfully late – and she is an artist. Since she is being on this occasion dreadfully late, you are possibly right to conclude that on this occasion she is being disorganised; but you have no right to generalise from this one occasion to the conclusion that she is always hopelessly disorganised, and worse, you have no right to generalise still further that all artists are hopelessly disorganised. Let's see what the fallacy depends on. We have a premise about a named entity. If we take this as assumption, and move to a general conclusion, then we are purporting to move to a general conclusion based on some particular assumption about an individual. So what constraint do we have to impose to prevent this clearly fallacious move? The answer is to check the assumption-set. As long as the assumptions on which the proof step used as the input premise to the step of $\forall$ *Introduction* do **not** contain the name in question, so that only the input premise itself contains that name, then $\forall$ *Introduction* is licensed, and the name in question can be replaced by a variable duly bound by the universal quantifier. This indeed matches the concept of scope for the quantifier, since there must be no assumptions about the term remaining in reintroducing the quantifier to replace that name.

With this in mind we now define $\forall$ *Introduction*. Remember, as above, here again $\psi[x/a]$ means 'the result of replacing every occurrence of a in ψ with an occurrence of x':

$\forall$ **Introduction** (Universal Introduction)

$$X \quad i \quad \psi[a]$$
$$\cdots$$
$$\cdots$$
$$X \quad j \quad \forall x \psi[x/a] \quad \forall \text{Intr}, i$$

> For X a set of assumptions, no assumptions in X may contain any occurrence of a.

Let's see this in action, with a putative translation of what is clearly a valid argument, given that the premises are assumed to be true (as in propositional calculus, the interest is in what follows from certain assumptions, not whether those assumptions themselves are or are not true):

(2.16)   All professors are clever. All professors are arrogant. Therefore all professors are clever and arrogant.

$$\forall x(P(x) \rightarrow Q(x)), \forall y(P(y) \rightarrow R(y)) \vdash \forall z(P(z) \rightarrow (Q(z) \wedge R(z)))$$

In this sequent, we have two premises to be taken as assumptions, and as conclusion a formula which is quantified and contains within it a conditional. (We are here using distinct variables for the distinct quantifiers, but nothing whatever turns on this.) As in propositional calculus, we first list as basic assumptions the premises given:

$$1 \quad 1 \quad \forall x(P(x) \rightarrow Q(x)) \quad \text{Basic Assumption}$$
$$2 \quad 2 \quad \forall y(P(y) \rightarrow R(y)) \quad \text{Basic Assumption}$$

At this point, immediately, $\forall$ *Elimination* can take place, and can be applied twice:

$$1 \quad 3 \quad P(a) \rightarrow Q(a) \quad \forall \text{Elim, 1}$$
$$2 \quad 4 \quad P(a) \rightarrow R(a) \quad \forall \text{Elim, 2}$$

Here the name is constructed, but, since these are universally quantified formulae, true of all individuals, it doesn't matter what name we choose. Furthermore, for the same reason, it doesn't matter that we choose the same name a second time over. At this point, we might take stock. What next? Well, by looking at the conclusion, we might hazard a guess that **if** we make an additional assumption in anticipation of doing a step of $\rightarrow$ *Introduction*, then we will be able to apply $\rightarrow$ *Elimination* more than once. So, let us assume at line 5 $P(a)$, as a straight assumption, something that at some later point, we might wish to withdraw:

$$5 \quad 5 \quad P(a) \quad \text{Assumption}$$
$$5,1 \quad 6 \quad Q(a) \quad \rightarrow \text{Elim, 3, 5}$$
$$5,2 \quad 7 \quad R(a) \quad \rightarrow \text{Elim, 4, 5}$$

Now we look again at the conclusion and see that what we need is a coordinate consequent to the conditional conclusion, so we apply $\wedge$ *Introduction*:

$$1,2,5 \quad 8 \quad Q(a) \wedge R(a) \quad \wedge \text{Intr, 6, 7}$$

Now at this point, we can carry out a step of $\rightarrow$ *Introduction* and incorporate the one additional constructed assumption into the body of the proof, and deduce:

$$1,2 \quad 9 \quad P(a) \rightarrow (Q(a) \wedge R(a)) \quad \rightarrow \text{Intr, 5, 8}$$

Now, check out the assumption list and you will find that the advantage of having done the step of $\rightarrow$ *Introduction* is that, in consequence, neither of the assumptions remaining in the assumptions list makes any mention of the named construct a. That now only occurs in the proof line itself. So $\forall$ *Introduction* is indeed licensed, and we can move to the desired conclusion:

$$1,2 \quad 10 \quad \forall z(P(z) \rightarrow (Q(z) \wedge R(z))) \quad \forall \text{Intr, 9}$$

There is a very standard pattern in this proof, which shouldn't be missed; and we list the proof in sequence now, to bring the pattern out:

$$\forall x(P(x) \rightarrow Q(x)), \forall y(P(y) \rightarrow R(y)) \vdash \forall z(P(z) \rightarrow (Q(z) \wedge R(z)))$$

1	1	$\forall x(P(x) \rightarrow Q(x))$	Basic Assumption
2	2	$\forall y(P(y) \rightarrow R(y))$	Basic Assumption
1	3	$P(a) \rightarrow Q(a)$	$\forall$ Elim, 1
2	4	$P(a) \rightarrow R(a)$	$\forall$ Elim, 2
5	5	$P(a)$	Assumption
5, 1	6	$Q(a)$	$\rightarrow$ Elim, 3, 5
5, 2	7	$R(a)$	$\rightarrow$ Elim, 4, 5
1, 2, 5	8	$Q(a) \wedge R(a)$	$\wedge$ Intr, 6,7
1, 2	9	$P(a) \rightarrow (Q(a) \wedge R(a))$	$\rightarrow$ Intr, 5, 8
1, 2	10	$\forall x(P(x) \rightarrow (Q(x) \wedge R(x)))$	$\forall$ Intr, 9

The pattern is to get rid of the quantifiers at early steps in the proof, then do regular propositional-calculus reasoning in the central body of the proof, then re-introduce the quantificational structure in the closing steps of the proof. It is with this property of natural-deduction proofs that we can return to seeing parallelisms between natural-language expressions and logical expressions. Once the predicate-logic quantifiers are eliminated, we have a simple predicate-argument structure with the structural counterpart to the quantifying expression being exactly the type of all individual argument expressions. Strikingly in this move, the type of term standing in for the quantifier plus its variable is exactly the same type as the variable itself: both are individual types. And this is directly paralleled in human languages. In natural languages, quantifying expressions are invariably simple noun phrases,[6] syntactically of the same constituent-type as the names they provide generalisations over. This strongly suggests that with natural-language reasoning, humans reason with constructed name terms exactly as though these were simple noun phrases: the complexity lies solely in the semantics of these. This proof, recall, was the pattern for (2.16), where, indeed we have repetition of the same expression three times over, exactly as some composite form of name:

(2.16)   All professors are clever. All professors are arrogant. Therefore all professors are clever and arrogant.

If natural languages offer us a glimpse into human psychology, from the cognitive point of view such inference steps are wholly natural; and, arguably, this provides room for analysing natural-language quantifying expressions as mapping onto such constructed names directly. Indeed, in recent times, a number of people have been advocating such a move (as we shall see in Chapters 5 and 7). For the present, we simply note that the lack of parallelism between predicate-logic formulae incorporating quantifiers and their natural-language congeners is

---

[6] Linguists differ in terminology as to whether the syntactic category of a noun phrase is referred to as *NP* or *DP*; in this book for consistency we use the term *NP*.

removed in the individual proof steps that are constructed from such predicate-logic formulae. In the central body of the proof, the expressions corresponding to the natural-language quantified expressions are behaving like these natural-language congeners, exactly as though a specialised form of name. So it is predicate-logic syntax which is unlike natural-language syntax, not its associated proof steps.

Exercise 2.6

Provide as many idiomatic translations as you can for the following, and demonstrate their validity using the rules provided.

a. $\forall x(F(x) \rightarrow G(x)), \forall x(G(x) \rightarrow \neg H(x)) \vdash \forall x(F(x) \rightarrow \neg H(x))$
b. $\forall x(F(x) \rightarrow \neg G(x)), \forall x(H(x) \rightarrow G(x)) \vdash \forall x(F(x) \rightarrow \neg H(x))$
c. $\forall x(F(x) \rightarrow G(x)) \vdash \forall x F(x) \rightarrow \forall x G(x)$

Existential Elimination and Introduction

Exactly the same pattern of reasoning with names in the central body of the proof will apply with existential quantification, with rules of elimination opening a proof and subsequent rules of introduction. However, in the move from existentially quantified formulae to formulae with names, things are more complicated. This is because a claim of existence of at least one individual having some property is a commitment to the claim that out of some domain of individuals, say Tom, Dick and Harry, some one of them has that property, and this means that either Tom has the property, or Dick does or Harry. In other words, an existential claim is equivalent to a disjunction. With the pair of rules *Existential Elimination* and *Existential Introduction*, it is thus *Existential Elimination* which has to reflect ∨ *Elimination*. *Existential Introduction* is much more straightforward.

Existential Introduction (or rather ∃ *Introduction*) is simply the inference from an attribution of a property to some fixed individual to the conclusion that there must be at least one individual that has that property, with the assumptions of the input premise preserved in the output. As before, $\phi[x/a]$ is the result of replacing every instance of a in ϕ with an instance of x.

∃ Introduction (Existential Introduction)

$$X \quad i \quad \phi[a]$$
$$\cdots$$
$$\cdots$$
$$X \quad j \quad \exists x \phi[x/a] \qquad \exists \text{Intr}, i$$

This rule corresponds to the valid inference from asserting that John is sick to the conclusion that someone is sick. This is highly intuitive. If we know that John is sick, we certainly know that someone is sick, quite independent of any specific context-setting. Indeed we need to use this rule to make explicit the validity of reasoning from a stronger universal claim to its weaker counterpart as we can see in the proof below:

(2.17)   Everyone is fair-headed. ⊢ At least one person is fair-headed.

$$\forall x\, F(x) \vdash \exists x\, F(x)$$

1	1	$\forall x F(x)$	Basic Assumption
1	2	$F(a)$	∀ Elim, 1
1	3	$\exists x F(x)$	∃ Intr, 2

This is the reasoning from a general, universally held statement to some weaker existential form of statement, for example from *All extant natural languages are for the purpose of communication* to *Some extant natural languages are for the purpose of communication*. We note in passing that this simple proof demonstrates that in quantificational reasoning as modelled in predicate logic, the domain is non-empty. **Any** universally quantified formula taken as assumption will yield its corresponding existential congener as consequence.[7] As with universally quantified formulae (as indeed all propositional calculus rules), the rule applies to formulae of arbitrary complexity, so equally valid is:

(2.18)   Everyone is fair-headed and will go grey in their forties. ⊢
                At least one person is fair-headed and will go grey in their forties.
$$\forall x (F(x) \wedge G(x)) \vdash \exists x (F(x) \wedge G(x))$$

To complete the picture, we have just one more rule, that of Existential Elimination (∃ *Elimination*). This, as noted, displays the same kind of complexity as ∨ *Elimination*, and is defined in similar terms. Before getting into the complexity of the rule definition, we should note that, like ∨ *Elimination*, ∃ *Elimination* is really very intuitive, and much of our quantificational reasoning depends on it. For example, the validity of the following step of inference is not in doubt:

(2.19)   Everything on this stall that is free is worth having.
                There is something on this stall that is free.
                Therefore, there is something on this stall that is worth having.

This is modelled by the following predicate-logic proof involving two basic assumptions, one of which involves existential quantification. The domain of discourse is the things on the stall; *F* stands for 'free', *H* stands for 'worth having':

$$\forall x (F(x) \rightarrow H(x)), \exists x\, F(x) \vdash \exists x\, H(x)$$

In order to derive some conclusion from the assumption of an existential formula in a proof, it has to be certain that no matter what choice of name is made,

---

[7] There is a big debate in the philosophy of logic literature about the status of quantificational reasoning over empty domains. Here we merely observe that modelling any such reasoning involves a departure from classical predicate logic. We are grateful to Wilfried Meyer-Viol for discussion of this point.

the conclusion would follow. In applying ∃ *Elimination*, as with ∀ *Elimination*, we eliminate the quantifier by moving to a name, an *arbitrary name*, but this time it is by assumption only, which means that before the end of the proof, this assumption must be got rid of. It can indeed be got rid of as long as no assumption whatever is made about what name is chosen. This means the name mustn't occur **anywhere** either in the assumptions made (other than that one created assumption) **or** in the conclusion so far reached. So we are in effect establishing a conclusion from a disjunction of all possible values for the name. The proof is as follows:

$$\forall x (F(x) \rightarrow H(x)), \exists x F(x) \vdash \exists x H(x)$$

As in all proofs, we list the premises given as assumptions:

1	1	$\forall x (F(x) \rightarrow H(x))$	Basic Assumption
2	2	$\exists x F(x)$	Basic Assumption

At line 3, we make the assumption $F(a)$, choosing arbitrarily an assumed name a. Then at line 4, because ∀ *Elimination* is valid for any name whatever, we can eliminate the quantifier from line 1 unproblematically, and with these two premises together we can deduce $H(a)$ by → *Elimination*:

3	3	$F(a)$	Assumption
1	4	$F(a) \rightarrow H(a)$	∀ Elim, 1
1, 3	5	$H(a)$	→ Elim, 3, 4

At this point, ∃ *Introduction* is applicable, as this comes for free. At any point with an assertion about a name this rule can be applied, retaining all the assumptions of the line to which it is applying, so we establish:

1, 3	6	$\exists x H(x)$	∃ Intr, 5

At this point, we have a general conclusion, and of the assumptions on which that conclusion depends, **only** the assumption specific to setting up that name, a, makes any reference to that name. This is equivalent to having demonstrated a general conclusion from a disjunction of assumed arbitrary names either a **or** b **or** c, etc., because the choice of which name was used, made at line 3 in the proof, is irrelevant to the conclusion reached. The pattern of reasoning at this juncture is formally identical to that of ∨ *Elimination*. We can now deduce that the very same conclusion is derivable from the same set of assumptions **except** that the assumption about the name is replaced by the existentially quantified formula, for which this constructed assumption was set up. So at line 7, we finally derive the conclusion we wish, from purely general assumptions, that is, assumptions 1 and 2:

1, 2	7	$\exists x H(x)$	∃ Elim, 2, 3, 6

In line 7, that is, the proof line itself (as in ∨ *Elimination*) remains constant. What changes are two things – the assumption-set, and the record of which rule was used. Assumption 2 replaces assumption 3, and the rule applied, which is ∃ *Elimination*, records the lines used. These are the line at which the existential formula is assumed, line 2, the line at which the additional assumption was made, line 3, and the line at which the conclusion to which this rule is applying was derived, and that is line 6. The pattern is like that of ∨ *Elimination*, except that since there isn't a specific list of disjuncts, there is only one extra assumption and only one assumption-specific conclusion; so there are only three lines to be listed, rather than five, as in ∨ *Elimination*.

We now define the rule, and then list the proof as a whole:

∃ Elimination (Existential Elimination)

$$
\begin{array}{lll}
Y & i & \exists x \phi \\
 & & \cdots \\
 & & \cdots \\
j & j & \phi[a/x] \quad \text{Assumption} \\
 & & \cdots \\
 & & \cdots \\
Y, j & k & \psi \\
Y, i & m & \psi \qquad \exists\,\text{Elim}, i, j, k
\end{array}
$$

For Y a set of assumptions, no assumption in Y, or ψ itself, may contain any occurrence of a.

The proof as a whole:

$$\forall x (F(x) \rightarrow H(x)), \exists x F(x) \vdash \exists x H(x)$$

$$
\begin{array}{lll}
1 & 1 & \forall x (F(x) \rightarrow H(x)) \quad \text{Basic Assumption} \\
2 & 2 & \exists x F(x) \quad\quad\quad\quad\;\; \text{Basic Assumption} \\
3 & 3 & F(a) \quad\quad\quad\quad\quad\;\;\; \text{Assumption} \\
1 & 4 & F(a) \rightarrow H(a) \quad\quad \forall\,\text{Elim}, 1 \\
1,3 & 5 & H(a) \quad\quad\quad\quad\quad \rightarrow \text{Elim}, 3, 4 \\
1,3 & 6 & \exists x H(x) \quad\quad\quad\;\; \exists\,\text{Intr}, 5 \\
1,2 & 7 & \exists x H(x) \quad\quad\quad\;\; \exists\,\text{Elim}, 2, 3, 6
\end{array}
$$

It shouldn't be forgotten that this is an entirely natural form of human reasoning. Another related example is:

(2.20)   Every politician is worrying about re-election. There is at least one politician.
Therefore there is at least one politician that is worrying about re-election.

As with ∀ *Introduction*, the restriction on the rule that there be no assumption made about such a named entity whatever – even in the conclusion itself – is critical to restricting the rules of inference to yield only valid conclusions. Without such a restriction, there would be wild over-generalisation, as one could be able to deduce a universal conclusion from the much weaker existential assumption:

$$
\begin{array}{llll}
1 & 1 & \exists x\, F(x) & \text{Basic Assumption} \\
2 & 2 & F(a) & \text{Assumption} \\
1 & 3 & F(a) & \exists\,\text{Elim} 1, 2, 2 \\
1 & 4 & \forall x\, F(x) & \forall\,\text{Intr}, 3
\end{array}
$$

Yet under no circumstances do we wish to license the conclusion that everyone worries too much from the fact at least one poor soul worries too much! This move is unfortunately commonly made: people regularly, and fallaciously, go from weaker statements to stronger statements, despite the lack of justification. Indeed group-excluding statements commonly take this form:

(2.21)   Some women are annoying. All women are annoying.

(2.22)   Some men are bad at cooking. All men are bad at cooking.

We know such arguments are invalid, but it is important to know why they are invalid. The mistake here is solely in the existence of the assumption about the named entity a in the conclusion, as the assumption itself is freely available; then application of $\forall$ *Introduction* is also licensed as the premise at line 3 is based on a perfectly general assumption.

So, to recap, $\forall$ *Introduction* requires a check that the **assumptions** on which the line to which the rule applies must be perfectly general: so, though that line will characteristically contain a mention of the name under substitution, none of those other assumptions must contain any mention of the selected name being replaced. $\exists$ *Elimination* requires a stricter check: the **line** to which the rule applies must be perfectly general, as must all assumptions **other** than the one made in virtue of the presence of the existential assumption. So, neither the assumptions on which the line depends (except the one starting the chain of inference) nor the line to which the rule applies may contain any mention of the constructed name being replaced.

Though much remains to be said, this now completes the full set of rules of classical logic. In principle the reader has all the tools they need to recreate the proof of **any** arbitrary predicate-logic inference.

Exercise 2.7

Provide as many idiomatic English translations of the following as you can, then demonstrate their validity.

a. $\forall x(F(x) \rightarrow G(x)), \forall x\, F(x) \vdash \exists x(F(x) \wedge G(x))$
b. $\forall x(F(x) \wedge G(x)) \vdash \exists x\, G(x)$
c. $\forall x(F(x) \wedge G(x)) \vdash \exists x\, F(x) \vee \exists x\, G(x)$
d. $\forall x(G(x) \rightarrow \neg H(x)), \exists x(F(x) \wedge G(x)) \vdash \exists x(F(x) \wedge \neg H(x))$
e. $\exists x(G(x) \wedge H(x)), \forall x(G(x) \rightarrow F(x)) \vdash \exists x(F(x) \wedge H(x))$

2.6   Defining inference proof-theoretically

With these proof rules to hand, we are now in a position to evaluate a major result which this composite propositional- plus predicate-logic formalism makes available; and it is a result which may come as a surprise to linguists brought up solely with a model-theoretic tradition. **All** the major semantic relations which linguists require of formal semantic models of natural language have their analogue in logic, and **all** can be expressed in exclusively proof-theoretic, that is syntactic, terms. This is what we now turn to showing, in somewhat more detail.

By definition, *entailment* is a relation between a set of assumptions in a proof, and the conclusion deducible from that set. The latter is truth-dependent on the presumed truth of the former, and demonstrably derivable from that set as the sole assumptions. Entailment between two formulae ϕ and ψ holds if ψ is deducible by the proof rules from ϕ as the sole assumption. Entailments, that is, are among the valid sequents. We have seen examples of these from both propositional- and predicate-logic proofs. We take synonymy here to be proof-theoretic equivalence: this is the strict syntactic analogue of two formulae having identical truth conditions. Two propositions are synonymous if they mutually entail each other; and given the concept of entailment as defined, this means mutually inter-deducible. We give the two-way proofs for two particularly significant semantic results.

2.6.1   The proof-theoretic force of the logical conditional

The first is the demonstration bringing out the intrinsic content of the conditional connective:[8]

$$P \rightarrow Q \dashv\vdash \neg(P \wedge \neg Q)$$

We might give as an English analogue:

(2.23)   If John is fair-headed then he will go grey in his forties. $\dashv\vdash$
            It is not the case both that John is fair-headed and that he will not go grey in his forties.

This particular illustrative example can also be expressed in predicate logic:

$$F(j) \rightarrow G(j) \dashv\vdash \neg(F(j) \wedge \neg G(j))$$

but this merely shows how predicate logic is an extension of propositional logic. All the valid proofs of the propositional calculus carry over into predicate logic, with these formulae conforming to the patterns dictated by the propositional language connectives. So the proof of this sequent would follow exactly the same

---

[8] $\dashv\vdash$ indicates deducibility both from left to right, and from right to left.

pattern as its simpler propositional language counterpart. The pattern in both cases is as follows. In the first left–right direction, we establish:

$$P \to Q \vdash \neg(P \land \neg Q)$$

This is a familiar application of *RAA*, assuming the opposite of what one wants to derive, in order to drop that assumption:

1	1	$P \to Q$	Basic Assumption
2	2	$P \land \neg Q$	Assumption
2	3	P	$\land$ Elim, 2
1, 2	4	Q	$\to$ Elim, 1, 3
2	5	$\neg Q$	$\land$ Elim, 2
1, 2	6	$Q \land \neg Q$	$\land$ Intr, 4, 5
1	7	$\neg(P \land \neg Q)$	$RAA, 2, 6$

In the reverse direction we need to establish:

$$\neg(P \land \neg Q) \vdash P \to Q$$

Because the conclusion is conditional, the first move is to add P as an extra assumption. In order to proceed, we have to bear in mind what we are trying to establish. Given P we want to establish Q. This suggests that if we assume $\neg Q$, maybe this will yield the contradiction that will enable us to derive its opposite. This hunch is indeed justified. Here is the proof.

$$\neg(P \land \neg Q) \vdash P \to Q$$

1	1	$\neg(P \land \neg Q)$	Basic Assumption
2	2	P	Assumption
3	3	$\neg Q$	Assumption
2, 3	4	$P \land \neg Q$	$\land$ Intr, 2, 3
1, 2, 3	5	$\neg(P \land \neg Q) \land (P \land \neg Q)$	$\land$ Intr, 1, 3
1, 2	6	$\neg\neg Q$	$RAA, 3, 5$
1, 2	7	Q	$DN, 6$
1	8	$P \to Q$	$\to$ Intr, 2, 7

What is notable here is that there is no necessary dependence between assumption and formulae that constitute the contradiction other than that the contradiction is derivable from the assumption. Remembering the methodology of theory construction, this isn't surprising. In setting out to devise explanations, we very generally aren't able to anticipate where the inconsistencies in our reasoning will arise. Yet it is remarkably tempting, nevertheless, to think that having made some assumption in anticipation of abandoning it by *RAA*, that one attempts, wrongly, to construct a contradiction made up of that assumption plus its opposite. No such tight a correlation is expected. Furthermore, notice that there is no restriction on such equivalent propositions that the proof procedure to derive one of a pair of propositions be identical to deriving the other. Indeed this could not be the case, as the proof procedure is responsible for simplifying down the internal composite propositional structure, and then reintroducing connectives to yield the other. By definition such equivalent propositions will involve distinct proof steps to yield the same result: the equivalence resides in the output, not in the proof steps themselves. *Equivalence*, that is, is the proof-theoretic analogue of *synonymy*; and *synonymy* is identity of content, not identity in procedures whereby such content might be built up.

2.6.2   The de Morgan equivalences

The second illustration of logical synonymy, or rather its proof-theoretic analogue, logical equivalence, is proof of the derivability of the so-called de Morgan equivalences (see Further reading). Among these is:

$$\forall x F(x) \dashv\vdash \neg \exists x \neg F(x)$$

(2.24)   Everyone is fretful. $\dashv\vdash$ There isn't even one person who isn't fretful.

This is one of the most challenging two-way inferences to characterise in predicate logic, for there are no (two-place) connectives and so it might seem that none of the regular inference rules can be applied. However, it is at this juncture that *RAA* comes into its own, able to be used more than once within an individual proof, thereby giving rise to individual formulae that can then be joined together by $\wedge$ *Introduction* to form a contradiction. Here we assume the opposite of the goal to be achieved, and so make an existential assumption, at line 2. Because of this, we add a further assumption at line 3 which replaces the existential quantifier and its variable by a name. Because the primary assumption at line 1 is a universal quantifier, at line 4, we can eliminate it without any change in assumptions, and this leads at line 5 to a contradiction. From this contradiction we choose provisionally to drop assumption 1. This may seem a surprising move, but, since it is an assumption that we wish in the end to retain, it will set us up with a second step of *RAA*, as immediately unfolds in lines 6–8. What we have at line 6 is a generally quantified formula which depends solely on the assumption made in line 3, because we had an existentially quantified formula in line 2. So by $\exists$ *Elimination*, at line 7, we can now introduce as the assumption on which the general formula depends the existentially quantified assumption at line 2. Having done that, we set up the necessary contradiction which will then enable us to drop this existentially quantified assumption, which had been assumed in order to yield a contradiction. So finally, at line 9 we get the negative conclusion we had set out to derive:

$$\forall x F(x) \vdash \neg \exists x \neg F(x)$$

1	1	$\forall x F(x)$	Basic Assumption
2	2	$\exists x \neg F(x)$	Assumption
3	3	$\neg F(a)$	Assumption

1	4	$F(a)$	$\forall$ Elim, 1
1, 3	5	$F(a) \wedge \neg F(a)$	$\wedge$ Intr, 3, 4
3	6	$\neg \forall x F(x)$	RAA, 1, 5
2	7	$\neg \forall x F(x)$	$\exists$ Elim, 2, 3, 6
1, 2	8	$\forall x F(x) \wedge \neg \forall x F(x)$	$\wedge$ Intr, 1, 7
1	9	$\neg \exists x \neg F(x)$	RAA, 2, 8

The reverse form of inference is notably easier, as we are not trying to derive a negative conclusion. We simply assume the negation of what we want to derive, but with a constructed name, deriving from that an existentially quantified formula. This leads directly to a contradiction at line 4, and we can drop the extra assumption, deriving at line 6, the premise $F(a)$. Since this depends only on the assumption made at line 1, which is a general form of assumption with no assumptions made about any itemised name, we can use $\forall$ *Introduction* to derive the conclusion, as desired:

$$\neg \exists x \neg F(x) \vdash \forall x F(x)$$

1	1	$\neg \exists x \neg F(x)$	Basic Assumpton
2	2	$\neg F(a)$	Assumption
2	3	$\exists x \neg F(x)$	$\exists$ Intr, 2
1, 2	4	$\exists x \neg F(x) \wedge \neg \exists x \neg F(x)$	$\wedge$ Intr1, 3
1	5	$\neg \neg F(a)$	RAA, 2, 4
1	6	$F(a)$	DN, 5
1	7	$\forall x F(x)$	$\forall$ Intr, 6

Notice a general property of these proofs, in exact parallel with propositional calculus. *Entailment* between formulae holds if and only if there is a proof in which there is just one basic assumption. *Synonymy* in this system is logical equivalence – demonstrable deducibility in both directions.

Exercise 2.8

Prove the two-way validity of the following:

a. $P \wedge (Q \vee P) \dashv\vdash (P \vee Q) \wedge P$
b. $\forall x (F(x) \rightarrow (G(x) \rightarrow H(x))) \dashv\vdash \forall x ((F(x) \wedge G(x)) \rightarrow H(x))$

2.6.3   Commentary: theoretical implications

A number of points are worth emphasising here, as it is easy to be fooled by the apparent lack of content of the sentential units into thinking that such systems cannot in principle have any bearing on natural languages. But to the contrary, first, we have in these logics the basic grounds for motivating a fully representationalist account of inference. With just twelve rules, we have a complete characterisation of an infinite set of inferences. This is because the system of rules is recursively applicable and it generates all and only the valid inferences which capture properties of phenomena set out as a condition of success; and, in so doing, it provides a precise formal pattern for scientific modelling of entirely general applicability. Second, natural deduction displays a remarkable degree of parallelism with reasoning as humans use it in the evolved systems of natural language, making available systems of reasoning for generalisations about individuals and about sets of individuals, in essential interaction with compound forms of reasoning. Third, it is of special significance for evaluating what we should take inference to be grounded in. In all that we have set out so far, the selected patterns of reasoning and the semantic relations of entailment and synonymy have been characterised entirely system-internally. Indeed, of the various semantic properties successfully characterised, concepts such as reference and denotation have signally **not** been part of the list. We have accordingly a complete strictly syntactic account of inference: all and only these inferences will be generatable without having to perform any external check on the validity of the assumptions made, and in each case, the rules will be seen to interact purely in terms of form to determine the validity of the inference – a genuinely 'representationalist' account of inference. It is to this property that philosophers such as Fodor refer to when they invoke a syntactic theory of mind. What this means is that we have a basis for expressing core semantic relations without invoking denotational constructs at all. Moreover the system of inference we have taken as central is one that displays at least interesting parallels with natural-language processing. So one might argue that in giving a semantics for natural languages in terms of defining a mapping onto logical formulae, one could then presume on a proof-theoretic characterisation of inference defined over those formulae to determine the necessary entailment relations displayed in natural language. In order to evaluate any such hypothesis, even in a preliminary way, we have to turn to the semantics of this system. And in these formal systems, the link between syntax and semantics is so tight that they constitute two sides of the same coin.

2.7   Further reading

As a preliminary to this chapter, readers could usefully read Guttenplan (1997), an excellent book for a beginner at logic, as is Hodges (2001). The two-volume Gamut (1991) is essential reading for a logic-based introduction to formal semantics. However, a word of caution for a first-time reader of introductory logic books. Proof systems vary; and this leads to minor variation in both the way the rule is defined and conventions on meta-level annotations accompanying the proof steps. In this book, we have followed the natural-deduction account of Lemmon (1965) (an introductory textbook modelled on Fitch-style natural deduction); this is fully compatible with Barwise and Etchemendy (1992), which is an excellent introduction to logic (with *Tarski's World 4.0* electronic exercises to accompany the book). The variation in proof notation, which may, but doesn't always, affect the fine structure of individual proof steps is confusing for someone without a reasonably strong logic background; we would suggest that the reader read in sequence: Guttenplan (1997); Barwise and Etchemendy (1992); and from there branch out to other alternatives as set out in Gamut (1991).

3 The semantics of logical inference: models and semantic types

3.1 Model-theoretic evaluation

It is the semantics of classical logic which has to date been so influential in natural-language semantics, and for good reason. The semantics of classical logic defines a mapping from strings defined by the language onto an interpretation, and this, together with the syntactic rules, provides the basis for syntactic and semantic definitions of inference. Standardly, this interpretation is defined in denotational terms, with every expression assigned some *denotation* or *extension* out of the domain of discourse (see below). This has been taken to be a good starting point for natural languages also, as a reflection of the fact that natural languages enable us to make assertions about the world we inhabit. This being so, the content of expressions in some sense must involve mappings from expressions of the language onto individuals, sets of individuals that share the same properties and more abstract things like the values *true* and *false* as the constructs which the expressions severally denote. Furthermore, as we shall see, there is by definition in classical logic a tight correspondence between syntax and semantics. In consequence, the overall system has a defined syntax, a defined semantics, and a formally articulated syntax–semantics relation. This combined result means that classical logic provides a well-understood system for formal modelling of natural language to use as a starting point. On this denotational view of meaning, semantics just **is** the definition of a mapping from expressions of a language onto what the expressions are taken to denote. If we put a realist spin on this relationship, then this constitutes a formal statement of the language–world relation reflecting the way in which the language as given can express assertions about that world so described.

The basic concept of model-theoretic semantics is that of *extension*, or *denotation*, defined with respect to the *domain of discourse*, which is an arbitrary set of entities, stipulated as part of the *model* with respect to which some formula is evaluated as either *true* or *false* (hence the term *model-theoretic semantics*). This concept of *model* is central, as it is relative to such stipulated models that elementary expressions of the language are assigned an interpretation, and then, relative to that, all compound expressions of the language can have their denotation computed by rule. For each expression of the language, simple or complex, there is a corresponding value, its *extension*, which is some combination of entities provided by the domain of discourse. For the composite terms, the interpretation is given by general rule, but these rules have to operate on some input as determined by the syntax of the system. Furthermore, even the simple, primitive terms have to be given a value so that, in tandem with the rules of syntax, the semantic rules will determine a content for expressions on the basis of interpretation assigned to their parts and the mode of combination which the syntax determines. And because, from the perspective of syntax, the elementary terms (the lexicon of the language from a linguistic perspective) are primitive, unanalysed terms, their value is a stipulation, determined by a *denotation assignment function* which together with the *domain of discourse* is what makes up the *model*. In the case of propositional logic, it is the propositional names P, Q, etc., which are assigned a stipulated value, either the value *true* or the value *false*, by the assignment function. For predicate logic, the concept of a *model* is extended: it includes both a set of individuals constituting the domain of discourse **plus** some denotation assignment function which maps each primitive term of the language onto some construct out of that set. For individual constants (the basic naming devices of the language), this value is an assigned individual, for one-place predicates it is a set of individuals, for two-place predicates a set of ordered pairs of individuals.

3.2   Models for propositional logic

In the case of propositional logic, the concept of *model* is relatively slim, for all that is required are rules for computing the truth or falsity of complex propositional formulae, given the truth or falsity of their input formulae. These rules are often presented as *truth-tables* which define a function from all possible inputs to a specified value. For example, associated with the syntactic rule licensing all strings of the form of the conjunction, of the form $\phi \wedge \psi$, there is the associated truth-table rule: if both ϕ and ψ are true for arbitrary values of ϕ and ψ, then the conjunction is true, and false otherwise, with the four lines of the truth-table spelling out the four alternatives. Each line of the truth-table corresponds to one possible type of contingency, in short, a possible model (here we shift to the standard model-theoretic notation of taking the value *true* as the number 1, and taking the value *false* as the number 0):

	ϕ	ψ	$\phi \wedge \psi$
Line 1	1	1	1
Line 2	0	1	0
Line 3	1	0	0
Line 4	0	0	0

Thus line 1 specifies a contingent circumstance in which both ϕ and ψ are true, line 2 specifies a scenario in which ϕ is false and ψ true, and so on. For each of these stipulated inputs, the truth-table is an algorithm that determines the value of the compound formula. In propositional-logic semantics, the concept of a model is nothing more than a stipulated assignment of truth values to the individual propositional-letters, with the truth-table being an algorithm for determining compound values no matter what the input values are. This can apply to any set of values assigned to the basic expressions and to compound expressions alike.

Similarly with negation and the other connectives – each truth-table is an algorithm for determining values for any formula containing the appropriate connective. For negation, there are only two lines in the table as there is only one input formula. The output value, of course, is the opposite to that of the input:

$$
\begin{array}{c||c}
\phi & \neg\phi \\
1 & 0 \\
0 & 1
\end{array}
$$

The truth-table for $\vee$ (*or*) again has four lines and returns truth for every input of truth values except when both input formulae are false:

$$
\begin{array}{cc||c}
\phi & \psi & \phi \vee \psi \\
1 & 1 & 1 \\
1 & 0 & 1 \\
0 & 1 & 1 \\
0 & 0 & 0
\end{array}
$$

Finally we have the truth-table for the implication connective $\rightarrow$ (often called *material implication*). This is slightly less intuitively appealing than the other tables. It gives true for all input values except when the antecedent is true and the consequent false, which is line 2 of the truth-table. This particular line **is** intuitively correct: if $P \rightarrow Q$ is true then it cannot be the case that P is true but Q is not. The first line of the truth-table is also intuitively reasonable for it states that the conditional is true when P is true Q is also true. The other two lines may be slightly less obvious, however, but note that this is only when we try to relate the uses of natural-language conditional sentences (like the *if … then* construction) and the truth-preserving quality of material implication. For natural-language conditionals there are pragmatic considerations such as the relatedness between antecedent and consequent that determine people's judgements about conditional sentences (see Further reading). In logic, however, the important issue is not to be led to any logical contradiction when manipulating conditionals and this is what the definition below achieves. So the truth-table definition for $\rightarrow$ is:

$$
\begin{array}{cc||c}
\phi & \psi & \phi \rightarrow \psi \\
1 & 1 & 1 \\
1 & 0 & 0 \\
0 & 1 & 1 \\
0 & 0 & 1
\end{array}
$$

We will not go further into the use of truth-tables here, but note that this display method gives an easy way to compute the truth conditions for complex formulae by breaking them down into their component parts. For example, the formula:

$$(P \rightarrow Q) \wedge \neg S$$

can be shown to be true in just three situations: where P and Q are true and S is false; where Q is true and P and S are false; and where all three propositions are false:

P	Q	S	$P \rightarrow Q$	$\neg S$	$(P \rightarrow Q) \wedge \neg S$
1	1	1	1	0	0
1	1	0	1	1	1
1	0	1	0	0	0
0	1	1	1	0	0
0	0	1	1	0	0
0	1	0	1	1	1
1	0	0	0	1	0
0	0	0	1	1	1

We can also display the semantics for the propositional connectives more formally as rules that specify truth conditions of complex formulae in a fashion parallel to the syntactic rules for constructing them. In the rules below, $[[\phi]]$ by definition refers to the truth value that ϕ carries in the relevant situation (more on this in the next section). Note that these semantic rules parallel the first four syntactic rules of propositional logic given in section 2.4.6.

S1 If $[[\phi]]$ is false, then $[[\neg\phi]]$ is true. $[[\neg\phi]]$ is false otherwise.
S2 If $[[\phi]]$ is true and $[[\psi]]$ is true, then $[[\phi \wedge \psi]]$ is true. $[[\phi \wedge \psi]]$ is false otherwise.
S3 If $[[\phi]]$ is true or $[[\psi]]$ is true then $[[\phi \vee \psi]]$ is true. $[[\phi \vee \psi]]$ is false otherwise.
S4 If $[[\phi]]$ is false, or $[[\psi]]$ is true, then $[[\phi \rightarrow \psi]]$ is true. $[[\phi \rightarrow \psi]]$ is false otherwise.

Exercise 3.1

Construct truth-tables for the following complex propositions. (Take care to notice the bracketing.)

a. $(P \wedge Q) \rightarrow (P \vee Q)$
b. $(P \vee Q) \wedge \neg R$
c. $(P \vee \neg Q) \rightarrow (Q \rightarrow P)$
d. $\neg(P \rightarrow \neg Q)$

3.3   Model theory for predicate logic

In predicate logic, where interpretations have to be provided for sub-sentential units, the model is a richer construct, and somewhat closer to what we might intuitively think of as providing a domain of individuals about whom assertions are made. To follow up on our previous informal characterisation, the model is an ordered pair made up of a stipulated set of individuals, often referred to as the *ontology* of the model as it defines what exists within it, and a function assigning some value to each elementary expression of the language out of that set. All values that are computed over the various syntactically complex expressions relative to that model are then no more than some set-theoretic construct out of those individuals. To capture the primary semantic relations of entailment, synonymy, etc., definitions are provided that generalise these model-theoretic characterisations to generalisations over extensions in all possible models. In consequence, this semantics, despite this level of abstraction, provides no formal reconstruction of any notion of *concept* that individual expressions might provide, on the basis of which recursively complex concepts might be expressible. The account is, so the jargon goes, 'rigidly extensional'. The only intrinsic property an expression has is the logical type assigned to it by the syntax: individual type for individual constants (type *e* terms), truth-value-denoting type for propositional formulae (type *t* terms), predicate type for one-place predicates. This is an impoverished concept of content from a linguistic perspective but nevertheless, as we shall see, one that is sufficient for predicting inferential relations within predicate logic.

Bearing this in mind, consider as a first illustration some predicate-logic system interpreted relative to a domain of discourse made up of what in 2008 constituted the Highgrove Royals: these are Prince Charles, Camilla the Duchess of Cornwall, and the two sons, Prince William and Prince Harry.[1] In due course, the membership of this family may change, but for present purposes we can take this as fixed, indeed fixed by stipulation (the correspondence with facts of the matter is purely for purposes of exegesis). The denotation of names in the language, the individual constants and the assignment of values to variables can all be defined relative to this arbitrary model, which we label *M* (*M* for model), for the first step in any model-theoretic semantics is to stipulate some set of individuals relative to which the individual denoting expressions are interpreted. An individual constant, e.g. m_2, may for example, relative to this itemised domain of discourse, be mapped onto the individual Prince Charles. The denotation of one-place predicates is taken to be *sets* of such individuals, written enclosed in {...} (see section 3.3.2). For example, a one-place predicate-letter *J* (a predicate that takes one argument) might be assigned as denotation the set made up of Charles, Harry and William, analogous to the predicate expressed by the English word *male*, i.e. {Charles, Harry, William}. In this connection, remember our caveat: it is **not** the case that the predicate, here *J*, expresses the concept of 'male', even relative to this small domain of discourse – its content is given

---

[1] For those to whom this tiny parochial slice of British history is not available, Prince Charles (the putative future King of England in 2008) and his second wife, Camilla (the Duchess of Cornwall) have as their primary residence at this point in time a mansion at a place called Highgrove where in principle at least Prince Charles's two sons, Prince William and Prince Harry, also live, the former being the elder.

solely by its mapping onto the set of individuals {Charles, William, Harry} with no ordering to that set. In like manner, but now to reflect the extensional analogue of relations between individuals, the denotation of two-place predicates is an arbitrary (possibly empty) set of *ordered pairs*, indicated by ⟨...⟩ (see section 3.3.2). So the interpretation assigned to some two-place predicate-letter M, let us suppose, approximating to the relation *married to*, would be the set of ordered pairs {⟨Charles, Camilla⟩, ⟨Camilla, Charles⟩}. Note the importance of the notion of order in these pairs: it separates out the arguments so that one (conventionally the first member of the pair) is associated with the 'marrier' and the second the 'married'. With verbs like *marry* this separation is not so crucial because the predicate is symmetric. However, with other verbs, like *like*, no symmetry is necessarily involved and so the 'liker' (the first member of the pair) must be kept separate from the 'liked' (the second member). As before, there is no concept of 'married' expressed in this assignment: the assignment is simply an arbitrary set of ordered pairs constructed from the domain of discourse. The point of such stipulations is to provide the basis for a concept of compositionality of content for the full set of constructed expressions. Indeed this is **the** central notion that the formal apparatus is set up to express. For example, the simple predicate-logic string $J(m_2)$ is a wellformed formula according to rules of predicate-logic syntax and true in the model as defined.

The important thing about models, to be borne in mind throughout, is that they are no more than simple stipulations, the point of departure from which characterisation of semantic relations can be given. The domain of discourse defined to be part of a model is an arbitrary basis relative to which compound expressions can be interpreted – a model made up of a magazine, an apple and a paper-clip would have done as well, or indeed a one-member set containing just a bar of chocolate. The resulting inference relations that are defined are defined over all possible models, so it really doesn't matter at all how the initial model is defined. Apart from the typing of expressions as of a certain type, nothing turns on the extensions defined, because no concept of intrinsic content is defined (ultimately, this will turn out to be a weakness of the system as a basis for doing natural-language semantics).

3.3.1 Defining a model

Formally, then, a model, M is made up of:

- the domain of discourse, a set of individuals A;
- a function, F_M, the denotation assignment function, which assigns interpretations to all elementary expressions of the language selected out of the domain of discourse:

$$M = \langle A, F_M \rangle$$

The model is an ordered pair, because the function F_M depends on the articulation of the domain of discourse (not the other way round).

Our illustrative example M now might be extended and formalised as follows:

$$A \quad = \{\text{Charles, Camilla, William, Harry}\}$$

$$F_M(m_2) = \text{Charles}$$

$$F_M(m_1) = \text{Camilla}$$

$$F_M(J) \;\; = \{\text{Charles, William, Harry}\} \qquad \text{Highgrove males}$$

$$F_M(K) \;\; = \{\text{Camilla}\} \qquad\qquad\qquad\qquad \text{Highgrove females}$$

$$F_M(G) \;\; = \{\text{Charles, Camilla, William, Harry}\} \qquad \text{Highgrove Royals}$$

$$F_M(F) \;\; = \{\text{William, Harry}\} \qquad\qquad\qquad \text{sons of Charles}$$

$$F_M(H) \;\; = \{\langle\text{Charles,William}\rangle, \langle\text{William,Harry}\rangle,$$
$$\langle\text{Charles, Harry}\rangle, \langle\text{Charles, Camilla}\rangle,$$
$$\langle\text{William, Camilla}\rangle, \langle\text{Harry, Camilla}\rangle\} \quad \text{taller than}$$

$$F_M(M) \;\; = \{\langle\text{Charles, Camilla}\rangle, \langle\text{Camilla, Charles}\rangle\} \;\; \text{married to}$$

We write $F(\alpha)$ for each basic expression α because the denotation assignment function F applies to the basic expression to yield as output a given value. We write the subscript M because the function F is defined relative to the model M within which it is defined. We do not write the individuals in question in italics because it is the individuals themselves (or sets made up of those individuals) which constitute the interpretation, **not** the names of those individuals. As stressed before, the indication in the right-hand column is merely anecdotal: the content defined by the denotation assignment function F_M is **solely** given by the extensions it assigns to each basic expression.

3.3.2 Set theory: an introduction

As noted above, the model theory for predicate logic that is most usually assumed is based on *set theory*. As its name states, this theory makes use of the properties of sets, where a set is any collection of objects, whatever they may be, which are referred to as the *members* of that set. Sets are typically represented by putting their members (or their representations) within curly brackets: $\{a, b, c, d\}$ is the set consisting of the first four letters of the Roman alphabet. The membership relation is shown by the symbol $\in$ and $a \in X$, where X is some set, is true if a is a member of that set and false otherwise. So, $a \in \{a, b, c, d\}$ is true but $a \in \{b, c, d, e\}$ is false. Sets and their members must be kept distinct so the set consisting only of the element a indicated by $\{a\}$ is not a member of the set $\{a, b, c, d\}$ (from which it follows $\{a\} \in \{a, b, c, d\}$ is false). However, sets may consist of other sets so $\{a\}$ **is** a member of the set $\{\{b, c\}, \{a\}, \{a, b\}, \{b\}\}$.

We can also talk about one set A being a *subset* of another B, $(A \subseteq B)$ just in case every member of A is also a member of B. If not every member of B is in A then we say that A is a proper subset of B $(A \subset B)$. In such cases, B is called a *superset* of A. For both membership and the subset (superset) relations, we put a stroke through the symbol to signify that something is **not** a member or subset of some other set. So $\{a\} \notin \{a, b, c, d\}$ is true, as is $\{a, b, e\} \nsubseteq \{a, b, c, d\}$.

We can also refer to the set of elements that two sets share through the *intersection* operator $\cap$: $A \cap B$ is the set of elements that are members of both A and B. So, $\{a, b, c, d\} \cap \{c, d, e\} = \{c, d\}$. Of course, two sets may have no common members at all, in which case their intersection yields the *empty set* $\emptyset$, a set that has no members at all (and which, by definition, is a subset of any set). We can put two sets together and refer to all those elements that are members of either of them using the *union* operator $\cup$: $\{a, b, c, d\} \cup \{c, d, e\} = \{a, b, c, d, e\}$.

In general, the members of sets are *unordered* so it does not matter in which order the elements are written: $\{a, b, c, d\} = \{b, d, a, c\}$ is true. However, as noted earlier, sometimes it is necessary to order the members of a set in order to keep track of them. In such circumstances, the members of the set are written between angle brackets $\langle , \rangle$ and so $\langle a, b \rangle \neq \langle b, a \rangle$, as we saw in the model of the Highgrove Royals defined in section 3.3.1. As with sets, there is no (finite) limit to the number of elements that ordered sets may have so we may have ordered pairs ($\langle a, b \rangle$), ordered triples ($\langle a, b, c \rangle$) and in general ordered *n-tuples*. Since we can have sets of sets (or sets of sets of sets, ...) so we can have sets of ordered n-tuples: $\{\langle a, b \rangle, \langle b, c \rangle, \langle d, a \rangle\}$.

The following table sets out the symbols and terminology of these basic set-theoretic relations. You should try and learn these as discussions later on in the book will use the concepts and symbols freely.

Property	Symbol	Meaning	Example
Membership	$\in$	'is a member of'	$a \in \{b, h, a, z\}$
Non-membership	$\notin$	'is not a member of'	$c \notin \{h, a, z\}$
Empty (null) set	$\emptyset$	'set with no members'	
Subset	$\subseteq$	'is a subset of'	$\{h, z\} \subseteq \{h, a, z\}$
			$\{h, a, z\} \subseteq \{h, a, z\}$
			$\{h\} \subseteq \{h, a, z\}$
			$\emptyset \subseteq \{h, a, z\}$
	$\nsubseteq$	'not a subset of'	$\{h, q\} \nsubseteq \{h, a, z\}$
Proper subset	$\subset$	'a proper subset of'	$\{h, z\} \subset \{h, a, z\}$
	$\not\subset$	'not a proper subset of'	$\{h, a, z\} \not\subset \{h, a, z\}$
Superset	$\supseteq$	'a superset of'	$\{h, z, a, \} \supseteq \{h, z, a\}$
			$\{h, z, a\} \supseteq \{a\}$
	$\nsupseteq$	'not a superset of'	$\{h, z\} \nsupseteq \{h, a\}$
Proper superset	$\supset$	'a proper superset of'	$\{h, z, a\} \supset \{h, a\}$
	$\not\supset$	'not a proper superset of'	$\{h, a, z\} \not\supset \{h, a, z\}$
Set intersection	$\cap$	'members of both sets'	$\{h, a\} \cap \{a, z\} = \{a\}$
Set union	$\cup$	'members of either set'	$\{h, z\} \cup \{d, a\} = \{h, d, a, z\}$
Ordered set	$\langle \ldots \rangle$		$\langle a, b, c, d \rangle$

3.3.3 Model-theoretic semantics for predicate logic

We are now in a position to turn to the semantic content of composite expressions in predicate logic. A critical property of predicate logic, like that of its contained system propositional calculus, is that the syntactic and semantic rules are defined in parallel, so we repeat the relevant syntactic rules and then give the semantic set which is defined to reflect the modes of combination which the syntactic rules define. Formally, that is, semantics is defined to be dependent on syntax.

R5 If α is a term, and γ is a one-place predicate, then $\gamma(\alpha)$ is a wellformed formula (wff).

R6 If α, β are terms, and γ is a two-place predicate, then $\gamma(\alpha, \beta)$ is a wellformed formula (wff).

As we saw above with the rules given for propositional logic in section 3.2, semantic evaluation takes the form of a set of rules which provide a recursive characterisation of how interpretations of elements of a language L_i project via the syntax to provide interpretations of sentences of the language relative to a model. Where α is some expression of the language L_i, $[\![\alpha]\!]^M$ is to be understood as the interpretation of the syntactic expression α relative to some model M. As we shall see shortly, there has to be allowance for the fact that formulae of predicate logic may be quantified, but we ignore this at a first pass, providing only the rules for interpreting one- and two-place predicates. The rules in this section (3.3.3) rely on the set-theoretic concepts given above: a formula consisting of a one-place predicate and an argument term is defined to be true just in case the entity denoted by the term is a member of the set of things denoted by the predicate; while for two-place predicates, a formula is true just in case the ordered pair of entities denoted by the first and second arguments (in that order) are in the set of ordered pairs denoted by the predicate. (Note the standard use of *iff* to mean 'if and only if', meaning that if the first statement is true then so is the second, and vice versa, and if the first is false then so is the second, and vice versa.)

S5 If α is a term, and γ is a one-place predicate, then $[\![\gamma(\alpha)]\!]^M$ is true iff $[\![\alpha]\!]^M \in [\![\gamma]\!]^M$.

S6 If α, β are terms, and γ is a two-place predicate, then $[\![\gamma(\alpha, \beta)]\!]^M$ is true iff $\langle [\![\alpha]\!]^M, [\![\beta]\!]^M \rangle \in [\![\gamma]\!]^M$.

With these rules we can interpret the formula $\neg(K(m_2) \wedge H(m_1, m_2))$ relative to our stipulated Highgrove model. As the rules indicate, by rule S5, $K(m_2)$ is false with respect to the model because Charles, who is the assigned denotation of m_2, is not a member of the set assigned to K (the Highgrove females). More formally, we give the statement below. Note that in such statements instead of using English phrases such as 'is true' or 'is false' we write $= 1, = 0$, respectively. As noted earlier, it is usual in semantics for *true* to be associated with the numeral 1 and *false* with 0.

$$[\![K(m_2)]\!]^M = 0 \text{ since } [\![m_2]\!]^M \notin [\![K]\!]^M$$

By rule S6, $[\![H(m_2, m_1)]\!]^M$, however, is true, as the ordered pair ⟨Charles, Camilla⟩ is a member of the set of ordered pairs assigned to the predicate H in the model. With one conjunct true with respect to the model, and one false, by rule S2 the formula $K(m_2) \wedge H(m_2, m_1)$ is false with respect to the model:

$$[\![K(m_2) \wedge H(m_2, m_1)]\!]^M = 0$$

But, in consequence by rule S1:

$$[\![\neg(K(m_2) \wedge H(m_2, m_1))]\!]^M = 1$$

So from the semantic rules that operate in direct reflection of the mode of syntactic combination of elementary expressions, a semantic value for a whole formula is determined. Thus the truth conditions of the whole are determined by the meaning of the parts, their syntactic mode of combination, and nothing else – the semantics of predicate logic is by definition a rigidly compositional, denotational and truth-theoretic system. This is exactly as it should be, since predicate logic is defined to provide a basis for characterising patterns of truth-dependence which is what inference indeed consists in.

Exercise 3.2

a. Extending the given model, define a new model M_{you} to contain a new one-place predicate, P, with extension 'Highgrove member by marriage'.
b. Define also a new one-place predicate, N, with extension 'girl'.
c. Define also a new two-place predicate, R, with extension 'kinder than' (no journalistic work needed – just make it up, explaining the specification you give).
d. Take your model M_{you}, and show how, by the rules, you can establish an interpretation for:

$$N(m_1) \rightarrow R(m_1, m_2)$$

i.e.

$$[\![N(m_1) \rightarrow R(m_1, m_2)]\!]^{M_{you}}$$

3.3.4 Model-theoretic evaluation of quantified formulae

When we turn to quantified formulae, it might seem superficially as though no straightforward principle of compositionality is possible, given that the quantifiers combine with open propositional formulae to yield bound quantified formulae, yet, the variables that they bind occur at the sub-propositional level as arguments to individual predicates. Hence, we cannot directly apply the simple rules for interpreting predicate-argument structures given in the previous subsection: $[\![x]\!]^M$ is not directly defined (x is not a constant), so we cannot tell whether it belongs to some set or not. The problem is resolved by assuming an interim device, an assignment of values to variables, a *variable assignment,* which isn't part of the model itself – so not strictly part of the interpretation – but merely a fixing of an input value so that the denotational values of composite expressions can be computed in a compositional way by the rules. This stipulated assignment is an intermediate value for all *free* variables, i.e. those pending the applicability of the rule which in conjunction with the quantifier that binds them will determine the interpretation of that variable as paired by that particular quantifier. The individual quantifier rules then operate in such a way that whatever intermediate assignment of values had been given to the particular variable that a quantifier binds makes no difference in the end. In this way, the theory provides a model-theoretic analogue of the arbitrary constants that we met in Chapter 2 in using proofs with quantified variables, since the **actual** value assigned to the variable is not directly relevant for the evaluation of the truth or falsity of the quantified formula.

Because value assignments to variables are, strictly, only interim devices, they are not part of the model itself. What this then means is that all rules of semantic composition are defined relative not to some model, but to a model in conjunction with some fixed assignment of values to variables, an assignment to which the quantifier rule makes essential reference in determining the construal of the quantifier at the appropriate point in evaluating the formula. So we restate the semantic rules of predicate logic with respect to both M and g, where g is a variable assignment. The denotation of an expression α is shown as $[\![\alpha]\!]^{M,g}$, the value of α with respect to M and g. Of course, where α contains only constants, g contributes nothing to the interpretation, but it is necessary wherever variables are involved: hence all the rules are stated in these terms.

We will give the full set of revised rules at the end of this section, but we are now in a position to present the two rules needed to interpret formulae containing the existential ($\exists$) and universal ($\forall$) quantifiers.

S7 If ϕ is a wellformed formula then $[\![\forall x\phi]\!]^{M,g}$ is true iff (if, and only if) for every possible assignment of values g' exactly like g, except possibly for the value of x, $[\![\phi(x)]\!]^{M,g'}$ is true.

S8 If ϕ is a wellformed formula then $[\![\exists x\phi]\!]^{M,g}$ is true iff there is at least one assignment of values g' exactly like g, except possibly for the value assigned to x, that makes $[\![\phi(x)]\!]^{M,g'}$ true.

To see these rules in action, we return to our Highgrove model and begin with the evaluation of a very simple formula: $\forall x G(x)$. To allow a bottom-to-top compositionality, we must be able to evaluate the quantifier-free formula first, hence $G(x)$. To make this possible, we define an arbitrarily selected assignment of values to variables, assuming only two variables x, y whose values are given as Camilla and Harry, respectively:

$$g$$
$$x \rightarrow Camilla$$
$$y \rightarrow Harry$$

We then evaluate the formula $G(x)$ with respect to model M and assignment g using rule S5 with the value assigned to x given as $g(x)$, i.e. Camilla ($g(x)$ should be read as 'the result of applying the function g to the variable x'):

$$[\![G(x)]\!]^{M,g} = 1 \text{ since } g(x) \in [\![G]\!]^{M}$$

With this formula assigned a value with respect to the model and stipulated assignment, we then turn to evaluating the formula: $[\![\forall x G(x)]\!]^{M,g}$. As rule S7 tells us $[\![\forall x G(x)]\!]^{M,g}$ is true iff $[\![G(x)]\!]^{M,g'}$ is true for every possible variable assignment g' (where that includes g itself) that can be given to x. So, relative to this model M, we have to consider, in all, four assignments of values to variables, g plus the different ways in which x can vary (while keeping the values of all other variables fixed):

$$g$$
$$x \rightarrow Camilla$$
$$y \rightarrow Harry$$

$g1$	$g2$	$g3$
$x \rightarrow Harry$	$x \rightarrow Charles$	$x \rightarrow William$
$y \rightarrow Harry$	$y \rightarrow Harry$	$y \rightarrow Harry$

For each of these possibilities, $[\![G(x)]\!]^{M,g'}$ is true since $g'(x) \in [\![G]\!]^{M}$ for all possible values for x as given in the four alternatives listed above. That is, as it happens in this model, G holds of all the individuals in the domain of discourse. Hence by rule S7:

$$[\![\forall x G(x)]\!]^{M,g} = 1$$

Let us now take an example using the existential quantifier, but this time with two instances of the negation operator to show the interaction between the rules of construal for quantifiers and that for negation: $\neg \exists x \neg G(x)$. We evaluate with respect to the same model and value assignment. Taking the non-quantified formula first, we find that:

$$[\![G(x)]\!]^{M,g} = 1 \ \text{ since } \ g(x) \in [\![G]\!]^{M}$$

and so it follows by S1 that:

$$[\![\neg G(x)]\!]^{M,g} = 0$$

In the move to evaluating the quantified formula $\exists x \neg G(x)$ by rule S8, we need only have one assignment of values to variables that makes the quantified formula true. The problem is that with the initial assignment itself, we have the value false. So again, as with the universal quantifier construal, we have to consider every possible assignment of values to x, to see whether any **one** of these provides the value 1 (= 'true'):

$$g$$
$$x \rightarrow Camilla$$
$$y \rightarrow Harry$$

$g1$	$g2$	$g3$
$x \rightarrow Harry$	$x \rightarrow Charles$	$x \rightarrow William$
$y \rightarrow Harry$	$y \rightarrow Harry$	$y \rightarrow Harry$

The problem is that none of them make the formula true. On each of these g':

$$[\![\neg G(x)]\!]^{M,g'} = 0 \text{ since } g'(x) \in [\![G]\!]^M$$

(the predicate G holds of the entire domain of discourse). So with respect to the initial assignment of values to variables, there is **no** alternative which will make the formula true, and so we conclude:

$$[\![\exists x(\neg G(x))]\!]^{M,g} = 0$$

Now, given rule S1 again, we can establish:

$$[\![\neg \exists x(\neg G(x))]\!]^{M,g} = 1$$

As things have turned out, it makes no difference how we alter the initial assignment of values to variables, as both existential and universal quantifier rules require the checking in principle of all possible assignments of values for the particular variable being bound. So, once having established the value of a closed quantified formula (with no unbound variables), we can move to the conclusion that it will have the value established with respect to all other assignments since any variation not already considered can only be with respect to variables not contained in the formula, hence irrelevant to its evaluation. Hence there is a final step in the evaluation procedure: a propositional formula will be true with respect to the model if it is true for all assignments g'. We add this rule to the rules defined above:

S9 If ϕ is a wellformed formula then $[\![\phi]\!]^{M,g}$ is true iff $[\![\phi]\!]^{M,g'}$ is true for all assignments g'.

Though this derivation may have taken some getting through, with this simple pair of examples, the demonstration of compositionality for quantified formulae is relatively trivial because the formulae themselves are so simple. However, the rules apply to all more complex formulae exactly as set out here. In all more complex cases, they become a matter of very considerable complexity. The problem, as even these simple examples have shown, is that in order to establish truth of quantified formulae, all possible combinations of assignments of values to variables have to be considered as a necessary precondition of establishing the denotation of the quantified formula with respect to any given model. Nevertheless, the rules will determine algorithmically what the composite value of the whole compound formula should be, given some model and some arbitrary initial selection of values to variables from entities defined in that model.

Exercise 3.3

For each of the following expressions, provide an approximate English sentence that reflects the structure of the statement, state the truth conditions of each formula and evaluate its truth or falsity with respect to the model of the Highgrove Royals:

a. $\forall x(\exists y(M(x, y)))$
b. $\exists x(K(x) \rightarrow \exists y(M(y, x)))$
c. $\exists x(J(x) \wedge \neg\exists y(H(y, x)))$

3.4   Inferential relations semantically defined

With this formal characterisation of how the meaning of composite formulae can be built up from the interpretation of their parts, we define the various inferential relations in semantic terms, following up on their earlier proof-theoretic characterisation in Chapter 2. Earlier, we set out a relationship of entailment (more strictly inference), as a relationship between two formulae of which the formula as conclusion is deducible from just the other formula as assumption. The semantic counterpart of this proof-theoretic concept of *inference* is *entailment*. Entailment holds between some wellformed formula ϕ and some other wellformed formula ψ if in all models in which ϕ is true, ψ is also true. This, by definition, is a relation of truth-dependence: the derivability of the truth of the entailed formula from the entailing formula. It is formally expressible as:

Entailment For a pair of wff ϕ and ψ, ϕ entails ψ iff when $[\![\phi]\!]^M$ is true, $[\![\psi]\!]^M$ is true, for arbitrary M.

In short, we can show this relation as:

$$\phi \models \psi$$

where $\models$ indicates semantic derivability. This semantic dependence of ψ on ϕ matches, in all cases, that given by the proof-theoretic characterisation which, recall, was that the entailed formula ψ must be deducible ($\vdash$) from ϕ as the sole assumption.

Synonymy is the stronger variant of entailment where propositional formulae mutually entail each other. For entailments demonstrable using propositional logic formulae, both entailment and synonymy are directly computable from the truth-table algorithms.

Synonymy Two wellformed formulae ϕ and ψ are synonymous if whenever ϕ is true, ψ is true, and whenever ϕ is false, ψ is false.

That is:

$$\phi \models \psi$$

and

$$\psi \models \phi$$

For formulae whose synonymy (equivalence) derives from the logical connectives of propositional logic, all that is required to show the relation is to check this matching of truth-value assignments from the truth-table computations of the two putatively paired formulae. As illustration of this, we provide a truth-table characterisation of the two formulae $P \rightarrow Q$ and $\neg(P \wedge \neg Q)$:

$P \rightarrow Q$						$\neg(P \wedge \neg Q)$			
P	Q	$P \rightarrow Q$		P	Q	$\neg Q$	$P \wedge \neg Q$	$\neg(P \wedge \neg Q)$	
1	1	1		1	1	0	0	1	
1	0	0		1	0	1	1	0	
0	1	1		0	1	0	0	1	
0	0	1		0	0	1	0	1	

Remember, it was this pair of formulae which we demonstrated to be deducible in both directions, taking either one as the assumption to the other as conclusion. As the truth-tables display, these invariably coincide on the same truth-value assignment, whether true or false. From a denotational point of view, $P \rightarrow Q$ and $\neg(P \wedge \neg Q)$ are therefore demonstrably equivalent, hence synonymous. This is a notable result, from a linguistic perspective, as this equivalence is often disputed by linguists when applied to the putative natural-language analogue *If P, then Q*.

This result applies equally to the demonstration of equivalence of quantified formulae. Given that to be an inference relation the relation in question must hold across all possible models, the only formal way to evaluate any putative such relation is the attempt to construct a falsifying model. The model-theoretic characterisations of $\forall x G(x)$ and $\neg \exists x \neg G(x)$ already set out provide a case in point; and it was this pair of formulae which in Chapter 2 we demonstrated constituted a provable two-way inference. With this pair of formulae, it not only made no difference what initially allocated assignment of values to variables was selected (and indeed this assignment is not considered to be part of the model itself), but it won't make any difference either what extension is assigned to the predicate, that is, it won't make a difference what model is stipulated as the point of departure. What is required for $\forall x G(x)$ to be true is that every assignment to the variable makes $G(x)$ true. And for $\neg \exists x \neg G(x)$ what matters is that it be false that there even be one assignment of which $\neg G(x)$ is true: i.e. all assignments must make $G(x)$ true, exactly as in its universal counterpart. There is no possible model in which $\exists x \neg G(x)$ and $\forall x G(x)$ are both true. So in all models, the two formulae, $\forall x G(x)$ and $\neg \exists x \neg G(x)$, will always turn out to have the same truth value, whatever extension is given in the model to the predicate G: these formulae by definition are equivalent, and necessarily so. Hence, by the characterisation of content in terms of denotation, they are by definition synonymous.

Exercise 3.4

Demonstrate using proof-theoretic and model-theoretic methods (taking your model M_{you} as point of departure) that the following pairs of formulae are equivalent:

a. $(P \wedge (Q \vee R)), ((R \vee Q) \wedge P)$
b. $(\forall x((J(x) \wedge K(x)) \rightarrow G(x))), (\forall x(J(x) \rightarrow (K(x) \rightarrow G(x))))$

3.5   Evaluating syntactic and semantic characterisations of inference

Our illustrations here of both semantic and proof-theoretic character-isations of the core concepts of entailment and synonymy have been restricted to cases where both proof-theoretic and semantic characterisation are relatively straightforward. However, in general, no guarantee of the comparable complex-ity of proof-theoretic and semantic characterisations is possible. Single-premise proofs are characteristically hard to establish, especially if the assumptions made involve negation as the main operator. This particularly affects the so-called de Morgan equivalences (see section 2.5.1), whose proofs of validity are often long and complicated. On the other hand, inference relations involving arrays of quan-tifiers may be very straightforward to establish proof-theoretically by appropriate quantifier-elimination steps but will characteristically, in the semantic character-isation, involve highly complex calculations and ingenuity in the construction of models. To avoid overload, we have avoided all such cases, and provide just these minimal illustrations.

With this demonstration of proof-theoretic and model-theoretic characterisa-tions of inference and synonymy, we can now turn to the language itself in which these semantic relations have been demonstrated. What we have set out in these two chapters is a fully explicit formal system on the basis of which inference is expressible both through defined syntactic (proof) rules that operate in virtue of form, and through semantic computations on the model-theoretic interpretations of the formulae in question. Looking at predicate logic as a language with syn-tax and semantics, it is by definition a fully compositional system. The grammar of predicate logic licenses an infinite number of strings, each having a content characterisable by semantic rules applying in tandem to the application of the corresponding syntactic rule. The result is a grammar formalism for an infinite language which, with a strictly finite, indeed very small, set of rules is able to pro-vide a pairing between string and model-theoretic interpretation for each string that is licensed by the syntax. Furthermore, this grammar can be used to provide a characterisation of the core semantic relations: *entailment* and *synonymy* (*bi-directional entailment*). With its elegance, and successful characterisation of the phenomenon of inference, it is small wonder that it should have been taken as the point of departure for defining the formal study of natural language. Indeed it is very tempting to take classical logic as a model not merely of natural-language semantics but of natural-language grammars, given its clear formulation of a syntax, a semantics and a mapping from one to the other.

There is, however, a further point to bear in mind. The objective in the formal study of reasoning was, recall, to provide an explicit study of patterns of valid inference. The result is that what we might pre-theoretically see as an essentially semantic phenomenon – inference – is not merely definable semantically in terms of truth-dependence between one set of formulae and another, but is also definable syntactically, that is, in proof-theoretic terms. It is this twinned characterisation of inference provided for formal languages which lies at the heart of the psycholinguistic and linguistic debates in the characterisation of natural languages. The question can now be posed in these terms. Should we be characterising inferential relations displayed in natural languages in terms involving the denotational content of entailing and entailed sentence, following the semantic characterisation of inference for formal languages? Or should we be characterising relations between natural-language sentences in terms of deducibility in some agreed mode of representation for such sentences, as Fodor would have it, in terms of the manipulation of cognitive representations mind-internally? The dual characterisation of inference in formal languages provides the point of departure and background for this debate; but it by no means determines the outcome, as we shall see. Indeed the debate on representationalism will emerge later in this book as one of the major issues currently being re-evaluated. Unlike classical logic, where the structural and denotational characterisations of inference are co-extensive by definition, two such characterisations will diverge in capturing inferential properties of natural language. In particular, we shall see in due course that taking context into account and the issue of how that should be formally modelled will provide a new perspective within which the issue has to be re-addressed. There is also a singular lack of any notion of *concept* in formal-language semantics with which to get any handle on what the intrinsic content of a word might be, independent of the contexts in which it occurs; and this too is a problem that needs to be addressed in tandem with the exploration of context and its role in natural-language construal.

But even setting these aside, as we have already seen in passing, the relationship between predicate-logic structure and natural-language structure is far from direct. There is a conflation of linguistic distinctions in the mapping from natural language onto the more restricted set of types available in predicate logic, given the restriction in the latter to just two basic types, as we saw in the assignment of a single logical type to nouns, adjectives and intransitive verbs. And there is also the mismatch between predicate-logic quantifiers and natural-language quantifiers. Predicate-logic quantifiers are operators that bind variables in propositional-type formulae, as their syntactic and semantic rules explicitly encode. Natural-language quantifiers, on the other hand, combine with nouns to form noun phrases and thus are in some sense internal to the expressions which serve as arguments to the predicate provided by the verb. If we are to sustain compositionality of natural-language content in a way that nevertheless retains the insights that articulating a denotational semantics for predicate logic has enabled us to capture, then we shall need mechanisms for improving the match between predicate-logic types and natural-language categories. In order to make this possible, the next step, as we shall see, is to be more explicit about the logical types made use of in predicate logic, so far only characterised informally, and then to see how the set of types can be expanded to provide a richer combinatorial basis for defining natural-language compositionality.

3.6 Type theory

Deductive systems for logics are based on manipulating **formulae**, showing which other formulae are deducibly true given the assumption of the truth of the formulae that constitute the premises. The premises and conclusions of propositional logic are thus all of one semantic type: wellformed propositional formulae. This type is conventionally called type t (for 'truth-bearing expression'). We could express propositional deduction not only in terms of the formulae but also with respect to the types of those formulae. For example, we could represent $\rightarrow$ *Elimination* with formulae associated with their types (written $\alpha : \tau$ where α is a formula and τ is its type):

$$P \rightarrow Q : t, \, P : t \vdash Q : t$$

Since there are no other types used in this system of natural deduction, labelling formulae with their types is not necessary or interesting. But, when we come to logics that express the internal structure of propositional formulae, we also want to know how such expressions are built up and what constitutes a wellformed formula. Of course, we have rules that define the syntax of predicate logic in section 2.5.1, but, using a more sophisticated system of semantic types, we can use logical deduction to **prove** that some propositional formula is wellformed and thus give a simpler and more general characterisation of the syntax of our logical system. Such logics are called *type logics* and are used extensively in defining representations for the semantic structure of natural-language sentences.

We begin with two basic types:

(3.1)   Basic types:
        a. Type e, the type of an individual or term ('entity-denoting').
        b. Type t, the type of a formula ('truth-value denoting').

Complex types are derived from these using the implication sign $\rightarrow$. So from the basic types we can form the type:

$$e \rightarrow t$$

This is a conditional statement, and so, by → *Elimination*, if we put an expression of this type, say P, together with an expression of type e, say m, we get an expression of type t:

$$P : e \rightarrow t, m : e \vdash P(m) : t$$

So type $e \rightarrow t$ is the type of a one-place predicate. We can in the same way define the types of two-place predicates as $e \rightarrow (e \rightarrow t)$, since an expression of this type requires two expressions of type e to give a propositional expression of type t, through two applications of → *Elimination*. Three-place predicates then have a type $e \rightarrow (e \rightarrow (e \rightarrow t))$, and so on. In general, the rule for constructing complex types is that given in (3.2c), which is a powerful recursive rule that can in principle allow hideously complex types (and an infinite number of them). Luckily, as we shall see, only a small number of complex types are needed to analyse most expressions of a natural language.

(3.2)   a. e is a type.
           b. t is a type.
           c. If a is a type and b is a type, then $a \rightarrow b$ is a type.

Because complex types are constructed as conditional statements, the expressions they construct have *binary* internal structure, unlike expressions in pure predicate logic where individual expressions are combined all at once with an appropriate predicate. The resulting expressions are thus a bit different from those we have encountered so far and are constructed by a very general rule, the *Rule of Functional Application* (RFA). (As before, Greek letters are variables over expressions in the logical language, i.e. *metavariables*.)

(3.3)   Rule of Functional Application (RFA)
           If ϕ is an expression of type $a \rightarrow b$ and α is an expression of type a, then
           $\phi(\alpha)$ is an expression of type b.

So we say that ϕ is a *functor* and α is an *argument* and that the licit combination of two such expressions, $\phi(\alpha)$, is a *functor–argument* structure.

The simplest example of the application of RFA we have already seen is the combination of a one-place predicate P with a term m to give $P(m)$. A more complex example is shown below involving the two-place predicate *Love'* of type $e \rightarrow (e \rightarrow t)$,[2] and two individual expressions of type e, m and j. We set it out as a proof in the natural-deduction format used in Chapter 2:

1	1	*Love'* : $e \rightarrow (e \rightarrow t)$	Basic Assumption
2	2	$m : e$	Basic Assumption
1, 2	3	*Love'*$(m) : e \rightarrow t$	1, 2 → Elim(RFA)
4	4	$j : e$	Basic Assumption
1, 2, 4	5	(*Love'*$(m))(j) : t$	3, 4 → Elim(RFA)

[2] From now on we will consistently use predicates that look like English words, distinguishing them as *Love'* for example corresponding to the concept expressed by the English word *love* for ease of exposition. So we write *Word'* to express the semantic content of 'word'.

We use brackets around the formula $Love'(m)$ to show that this whole expression applies to the argument j in the last step of RFA to yield the formula as a *label* to the type t as conclusion at step 5. Now in the output of this proof, the arguments are hierarchically ordered with respect to each other and we could show the structure by a binary tree, a so-called *proof tree*:

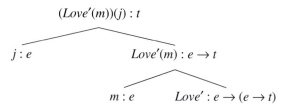

As we shall see very shortly, this coincidence of functional application in the semantics and type deduction over types as propositions is wholly systematic. In the meantime, it is impossible to miss noticing just how much this tree looks like a syntactic tree of the common sort and, like such syntactic trees, the higher the argument is in a tree, the less oblique it is, so that the highest argument is the subject, the second highest the object, and so on. Interpreting $Love'$ as the relation expressed by the word *loved*, and j and m respectively as the individuals referred to by the names *John* and *Mary*, we might construct a simple syntactic tree that fully parallels the semantic tree given above:

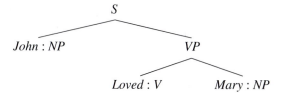

$(Love'(m))(j)$ is thus the interpretation of the string *John loved Mary* and so is equivalent to the predicate-logic expression $Love'(j, m)$, but with the arguments apparently reversed. Although the syntax of functional application is quite different from that of predicate logic, nevertheless it is possible to derive equivalences between them using what is known as the *lambda operator*, which we discuss in the next section.

3.6.1 The lambda operator

The equivalence between predicate logic and a simple subset of the type system[3] can be captured by the introduction of an operator that, like the universal and existential quantifiers, binds free variables but, unlike the quantifiers, changes the type and interpretation of any formula it combines with. The lambda operator is, as the name says, written as the Greek character λ and appears to

---

[3] Note that, as we shall see in the next chapter, type logic is far more powerful than predicate logic, so that only a restricted subpart expresses first-order predicate logic.

the left of a formula with the variable it binds. Assuming that the formula with the free variable is of propositional type (type t), then the type of the resulting expression is of predicate type (type $e \rightarrow t$). So we have a general rule of inference:

(3.4)   Lambda Deduction Rule (first version): If ϕ is a formula containing an unbound instance of a variable x of type e, then $\lambda x[\phi]$ is a wellformed one-place predicate.

$$x : e, \phi : t \vdash \lambda x[\phi] : e \rightarrow t$$

We say that λ *abstracts on* the variable x and that x is bound by the λ operator. (Hence the rule is sometimes called λ-*abstraction*.)

From a propositional formula $P(x)$ we can construct the predicate formula $\lambda x[P(x)]$. Now if P is a simple one-place predicate, the lambda expression and P have exactly the same semantic properties. But if we take a two-place predicate M and combine it with a variable x and a constant m, denoting Mary, to give $Love'(x, m)$ we can construct a lambda expression $\lambda x[Love'(x, m)]$ which is a one-place predicate. Since the lambda expression is a one-place predicate, it can be applied to an individual argument to yield a formula by RFA:

(3.5) $\lambda x[Love'(x, m)] : e \rightarrow t, j : e \vdash \lambda x[Love'(x, m)](j) : t$

By assumption, a lambda expression combined with an argument is equivalent to a formula where an instance of the argument replaces each occurrence of the bound variable within the domain of the lambda operator:

$$\lambda x[Love'(x, m)](j) \leftrightarrow Love'(j, m)$$

This is called *lambda conversion* (sometimes *beta conversion*) and is defined as follows:

(3.6)   Lambda Conversion Rule
          a. If $\lambda x[\phi]$ is a lambda expression and a is an individual constant, then $\lambda x[\phi](a)$ is a formula and is truth-conditionally equivalent to the expression $\phi*$ where $\phi*$ is derived from ϕ by replacing every occurrence of x in ϕ bound by λ by the expression a.[4]
          b. $\lambda x[\phi](a) \equiv \phi^{[a/x]}$

Given this equivalence, and the fact $\lambda x[Love'(x, m)]$ has the same type as a one-place predicate, it follows that it denotes a set. In this case, the set of all entities that love Mary. Technically this can be expressed in set-theoretic notation to give the denotation of the expression in a model M:

$$[\![\lambda x[Love'(x, m)]]\!]^M = \{a | \langle a, [\![m]\!]^M \rangle \in [\![Love']\!]^M\}$$

i.e. the set of all entities a such that the ordered pair of a and the denotation of m in M is a member of the denotation of $Love'$ in M.

---

[4] We use $\equiv$ to indicate that when $\phi \equiv \psi$, ϕ is just a synonym of ψ

The lambda operator can, however, bind free variables in any argument position. So we could take a propositional formula with a free variable in second position and abstract on that variable:

$$\lambda y[Love'(j, y)]$$

This is again an expression of type $e \rightarrow t$ and so may take an argument:

$$\lambda y[Love'(j, y)](m)$$

By the rule of *lambda conversion* this is equivalent to $Love'(j, m)$ and so, if j denotes John, $\lambda y[Love'(j, y)]$ denotes the set of entities that John loved. In other words, $\lambda y[Love'(j, y)]$ could be used to translate the passive verb phrase *was loved by John*. (Until chapter 6, we ignore tense.)

An expression may, in fact, contain more than one lambda operator, each binding a different variable. The process of lambda binding is the same as before in that an operator binds a free variable in some expression but the type of that expression may not be t. Assuming that the expression is of some type τ (read as 'tau') then the type of the abstracted expression is $e \rightarrow \tau$. So we have a more general version of lambda binding:

(3.7)   Lambda Deduction Rule (second version)
    a. If ϕ is an expression of type b containing an unbound instance of a
       variable x of type e, then $\lambda x[\phi]$ is a wellformed expression of type
       $e \rightarrow b$.

$$x : e, \phi : b \vdash \lambda x[\phi] : e \rightarrow b$$

So taking a propositional formula with two open variables like $Love'(x, y)$ we can abstract on one of the variables to give $\lambda x[Love'(x, y)]$ of type $e \rightarrow t$ and then abstract on the other variable to give $\lambda y[\lambda x[Love'(x, y)]]$ of type $e \rightarrow (e \rightarrow t)$. Since this is the type of a two-place predicate, it can be combined with two arguments in order. We repeat the proof tree from the end of the last section but this time retaining the complex lambda expression without any applications of the *Lambda Conversion Rule* (reducing brackets in lambda terms for transparency):

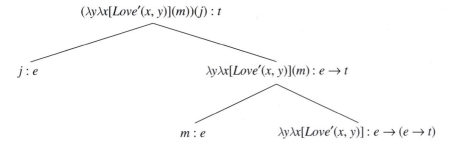

We can apply *lambda conversion* to this expression twice. First, the brackets tell us the order in which this occurs: y is the variable on the outside of the lambda expression and m is the first argument with which it combines, so we replace y with m to get:

$$\lambda x[Love'(x, m)](j)$$

This leaves x as the variable associated with j and another application of lambda conversion yields the straightforward predicate logic formula $Love'(j, m)$, as required.

Below is a slightly more complex example involving the three-place predicate $Give'$. Firstly we derive a complex lambda expression with three applications of the lambda deduction rule:

(3.8) a. $Give'(x, y, z) : t \vdash \lambda x[Give'(x, y, z)] : e \to t$
       b. $\lambda x[Give'(x, y, z)] : e \to t \vdash \lambda y[\lambda x[Give'(x, y, z)]] : e \to (e \to t)$
       c. $\lambda y[\lambda x[Give'(x, y, z)]] : e \to (e \to t) \vdash$
           $\lambda z[\lambda y[\lambda x[Give'(x, y, z)]]] : e \to (e \to (e \to t))$

Then we supply the arguments m (for *Mary*), r (for *roses*) and j (for *John*) in reverse order:

(3.9) a. $j : e, \lambda z[\lambda y[\lambda x[Give'(x, y, z)]]] : e \to (e \to (e \to t)) \vdash$
           $\lambda z[\lambda y[\lambda x[Give'(x, y, z)]]](j) : e \to (e \to t)$
       b. $r : e, \lambda z[\lambda y[\lambda x[Give'(x, y, z)]]](j) : e \to (e \to t) \vdash$
           $(\lambda z[\lambda y[\lambda x[Give'(x, y, z)]]](j))(r) : e \to t$
       c. $m : e, (\lambda z[\lambda y[\lambda x[Give'(x, y, z)]]](j))(r) : e \to t \vdash$
           $((\lambda z[\lambda y[\lambda x[Give'(x, y, z)]]](j))(r))(m) : t$

We then apply Lambda Conversion (from the inside out) to yield a predicate-logic expression that can be taken to be the translation of the English sentence *Mary gave roses to John*:

(3.10) a. $((\lambda z[\lambda y[\lambda x[Give'(x, y, z)]]](j))(r))(m) \equiv$
            $(\lambda y[\lambda x[Give'(x, y, j)]](r))(m)$
        b. $(\lambda y[\lambda x[Give'(x, y, j)]](r))(m) \equiv \lambda x[Give'(x, r, j)](m)$
        c. $\lambda x[Give'(x, r, j)](m) \equiv Give'(m, r, j)$

Notice that this technique provides a fully **compositional** account of the relation between the semantic representations of phrases and those of sentences which is not possible in standard predicate logic without the lambda operator: VPs and intransitive verbs all translate as expressions of type $e \to t$. Notice also that the order in which variables are bound by lambda operators changes the interpretation and reflects certain types of grammatical-function changing constructions such as *passivisation*. For example, reversing the order of the lambda operators over the variables in $Love'(x, y)$ gives $\lambda x \lambda y[Love'(x, y)]$. This expression combines first with an argument that is bound by λx and so is associated with the first argument, not the second. $(\lambda x[\lambda y[Love'(x, y)](j)])(m)$ is equivalent to $Love'(j, m)$, not $Love'(m, j)$, and so we have a means of representing the analysis of passive. The proof tree below thus mirrors the interpretation of *Mary was loved by John*:

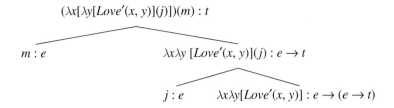

$$(\lambda x[\lambda y[Love'(x, y)](j)])(m) : t$$

$$m : e \qquad \lambda x\lambda y \,[Love'(x, y)](j) : e \rightarrow t$$

$$j : e \qquad \lambda x\lambda y[Love'(x, y)] : e \rightarrow (e \rightarrow t)$$

Notice that, in functor–argument structures, the order of application reflects *obliqueness* among grammatical functions. So the last argument to be applied corresponds to the syntactic *subject*, the second last to the *direct object* and the third last to the *indirect object*:

$$((Functor(IO))(DO))(SUBJ)$$

Within the predicate domain itself, however, the left-to-right order shows increasing semantic *obliqueness*:

$$Predicate(Agent, Theme, Goal)$$

Note that in treating predicates as more or less complex lambda expressions and equating the fixed positions in their argument array in terms of thematic roles,[5] we are in effect starting to unpack the lexical semantics of the verbs whose meaning they represent. Reference to lexical semantic properties will become increasingly frequent, and the issue is taken up in detail in Chapter 8.

Exercise 3.5

Using the proof method of type deduction, show which of the following lambda expressions are wellformed. For those that are wellformed, give their associated lambda-reduced versions:

a. $\lambda x[\exists y[Love'(y, x)]](m)$
b. $(\lambda y[\lambda z[Like'(z, y) \vee \neg(Like'(y, z))]](j))(m)$
c. $\forall x[\lambda z[Student'(x) \rightarrow Give'(x, y, z)](j)](Flowers')(m)$
d. $(\lambda x[\lambda y[\forall z[Student'(z) \rightarrow Give'(z, x, y)]]](Flowers'))(j)$

Use the following type assignments :

Type	Expression
e	$Flowers', m, j$
$e \rightarrow t$	$Student'$
$e \rightarrow (e \rightarrow t)$	$Love'$
$e \rightarrow (e \rightarrow (e \rightarrow t))$	$Give'$

Notice also that when a quantifier binds a variable in the scope of some predicate then the type of that predicate is reduced by one.

---

[5] We make no commitment to the validity of thematic roles.

3.6.2 Types reprised

As the previous discussion has demonstrated, lambda terms that combine with arguments by functional application are invariably in lock-step with type-deduction over types presented as propositional formulae. This is a famous result called the *Curry–Howard isomorphism*. It has not only played a central role in formal definitions of the combinatorial properties of the lambda calculus, but is taken as a core property in almost all definitions of the syntax–semantics interface. It is this correspondence that lies at the heart of the typing of natural-language expressions, as we shall now see.

Every λ predicate of arity *n* combines with a single argument at a time to give an expression of arity *n-1*. As we have seen, all semantic expressions (apart from lexical ones) thus have the structure:

$$functor(argument)$$

So far, arguments have only been of one type: individual constants or variables. But natural languages require greater flexibility, as some verbs take VPs or sentences as complements and so their logical counterparts must have one-place predicates or propositional formulae as arguments.

(3.11)   a. Kim believed [$_S$ that Prudence was horrible]:
                Type of $Believe' = t \rightarrow (e \rightarrow t)$
            b. Fiona may [$_{VP}$ be sick]:
                Type of $May' = (e \rightarrow t) \rightarrow (e \rightarrow t)$

Although the definition of types in (3.2), see the opening paragraph of section 3.6, is very general and potentially yields an infinite number of increasingly complex types, natural languages seem to require only a restricted set of types. Adjectives, verb phrases, common nouns and intransitive verbs all translate into expressions of type $e \rightarrow t$. The following table provides a list of types for some common syntactic categories, although we will have cause to revisit this system in the next chapter.

(3.12)   Type assignment:

Category	Type
Sentence	t
Proper name	e
Common noun	$e \rightarrow t$
Predicative adjective	$e \rightarrow t$
Verb phrase	$e \rightarrow t$
Intransitive verb	$e \rightarrow t$
Transitive verb	$e \rightarrow (e \rightarrow t)$
Ditransitive verb	$e \rightarrow (e \rightarrow (e \rightarrow t))$
Clausal verb	$t \rightarrow (e \rightarrow t)$
Auxiliary verb	$(e \rightarrow t) \rightarrow (e \rightarrow t)$

Manner adverb $(e \rightarrow t) \rightarrow (e \rightarrow t)$
Conjunction $t \rightarrow (t \rightarrow t)$
Negation $t \rightarrow t$

Note that such type assignments go well beyond the expressive power of first-order predicate logic and reflect *higher-order* logics because predicates can be arguments as well as individuals, and lambda operators may not be able to reduce expressions to an expression of predicate logic. As an illustration of this, consider a possible compositional translation of the English sentence *John didn't willingly love Mary* (ignoring many complexities). This sentence has a syntactic structure that can be roughly represented by the constituent structure:

$$[_S \text{ John } [_{VP} \text{ didn't } [_{VP} \text{ willingly } [_{VP} \text{ love Mary}]]]]$$

The following table gives a way of putting together a typed representation of the content of this sentence, showing how all the parts can be put together compositionally. (We show $\lambda y \lambda x [Love'(x, y)]$ simply as *Love'* for ease of exposition.)

(3.13)   John didn't willingly love Mary.

Constituent	Translation	Type
love	*Love'*	$e \rightarrow (e \rightarrow t)$
Mary	m	e
love Mary	$Love'(m)$	$e \rightarrow t$
willingly	*Willingly'*	$(e \rightarrow t) \rightarrow (e \rightarrow t)$
willingly love Mary	$Willingly'(Love'(m))$	$e \rightarrow t$
didn't	$\lambda P \lambda z[\neg P(z)]$	$(e \rightarrow t) \rightarrow (e \rightarrow t)$
didn't willingly love Mary	$\lambda P \lambda z[\neg P(z)](Willingly'(Love'(m)))$	$e \rightarrow t$
John	j	e
John didn't willingly love Mary	$\lambda z[\neg(Willingly'(Love'(m)))(z)](j)$	t
	$\equiv \neg(Willingly'(Love'(m)))(j)$	

$\lambda z[\neg(Willingly'\ (Love'\ (m)))(z)](j) : t$

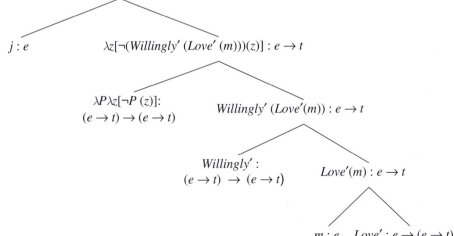

$j : e$ $\lambda z[\neg(Willingly'\ (Love'\ (m)))(z)] : e \rightarrow t$

$\lambda P \lambda z[\neg P\ (z)]:$ $Willingly'\ (Love'(m)) : e \rightarrow t$
$(e \rightarrow t) \rightarrow (e \rightarrow t)$

$Willingly' :$ $Love'(m) : e \rightarrow t$
$(e \rightarrow t) \rightarrow (e \rightarrow t)$

$m : e$ $Love' : e \rightarrow (e \rightarrow t)$

There is one thing that needs to be particularly noted here. In the first place, the translation of *didn't* is given by a lambda expression that abstracts on a predicate variable P in order to maintain $\neg$ as a propositional operator. This requires a refinement of our rule for lambda abstraction which generalises to variables of **all** types:

(3.14)   Lambda Deduction Rule (final version): If ϕ is an expression of type b containing an unbound instance of a variable u of type a, then $\lambda u[\phi]$ is a wellformed expression of type $a \to b$.

$$\phi : b, u : a \vdash \lambda u[\phi] : a \to b$$

The translation for *didn't* thus 'unpacks' the propositional argument of $\neg$ into a predicate and an argument.

Exercise 3.6

What are the types of the following expressions with their English counterparts? (Note that x, y, z are variables of type e; p, q, r are variables of type t; and P, Q are variables of type $e \to t$.)

and	$\lambda p[\lambda q[q \wedge p]]$
if	$\lambda p[\lambda q[q \to p]]$
or	$\lambda p[\lambda q[q \vee p]]$
thinks	$\lambda p[\lambda x[Think'(x, p)]]$
happy	$\lambda x[Happy'(x)]$
detest	$\lambda x[\lambda y[Detest'(x, y)]]$
isn't	$\lambda P[\lambda x[\neg P(x)]]$

Using these translations, show by type deduction how the semantic representations of the following phrases can be built up (ignore tense and associate pronouns with their obvious antecedents):

a. John thinks that if Mary detests him, she isn't happy.
b. John detests Mary or she detests him.
c. Mary is happy and she detests John; or she isn't happy and thinks he detests her.

3.7   Interpreting typed expressions

So far, we have provided a means of manipulating typed expressions to derive representations of the semantic content of natural-language expressions in a compositional manner. In this section, we discuss the model-theoretic interpretation of such expressions. Where typed expressions are equivalent to expressions in predicate logic, the model-theoretic interpretation given in section 3.3 will suffice. But, as should be obvious from the example at the end of the last section, more is needed to express the denotations of other typed expressions than simple set theory, although denotations remain essentially set-theoretic. We have already seen the denotations of three types of expression:

(3.15)   a. The denotation of an expression of type e is an entity from the domain of
            individuals (written D_e, where D_e is A, the domain of discourse).
          b. The denotation of an expression of type t is a truth value from the
            domain $\{0, 1\}$ (written D_t).
          c. The denotation of an expression of type $e \rightarrow t$ is a set of entities.
          d. The denotation of an expression of type $a \rightarrow t$ where a is a type is a set
            of objects of type a.

However, we require a slightly different way of looking at sets to express the
denotations of other typed expressions.

   Relations can be represented as a set of ordered pairs, as we have seen:

$$\{\langle a, 2\rangle, \langle b, 2\rangle, \langle b, 4\rangle, \langle b, 5\rangle, \langle d, 5\rangle\}$$

This expresses one possible relation between the first five letters of the alphabet and the first five natural whole numbers. This could also be represented
diagrammatically by linking the related elements in the two sets:

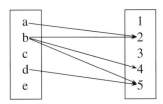

   Functions are special sorts of *relation*. A relation is a function if (and only if)
every element in the *domain* (left hand set) is assigned **one and only one** value
in the *range* (right-hand set). The diagram below represents the function:

$$\{\langle a, 1\rangle, \langle b, 2\rangle, \langle c, 2\rangle, \langle d, 4\rangle, \langle e, 4\rangle\}$$

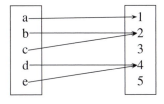

   Functions are useful because when applied to an element in the domain they
yield a single unique element in the range; i.e. they are unambiguous and (for
our purposes) fully specified. So, for example, if we think of the function given
above as F then $F(b)$ gives the value 2. Note that F as it stands only applies
to the set that is its domain, $\{a, b, c, d, e\}$. $F(4)$ yields no result, so we say that
F *maps* $\{a, b, c, d, e\}$ onto $\{1, 2, 3, 4, 5\}$ (even though not all the values in the
second set are used).

   A special type of function directly defines a set. This is a *characteristic function* which maps the elements in its domain onto the value *true* (or 1) if that
element is a member of the set or onto *false* (or 0) if it is not. The following
diagram thus represents the characteristic function of the set $\{b, d, e\}$ over the

domain of the first five letters of the roman alphabet. All sets can be associated
with a characteristic function, no matter what they contain:

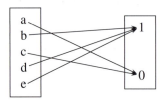

So a characteristic function is something that defines a set which we can
characterise generally with respect to the set of entities in some model, A:

(3.16)   Characteristic Function of a Set, f_Σ:

> For all $a \in A$, $f_\Sigma(a) = 1$(true), if $a \in \Sigma$, and $f_\Sigma(a) = 0$(false), otherwise.

What we say in this case that f_Σ is a function from entities (the set A in a
model) to the truth values $\{1, 0\}$ which we write as:

$$f_\Sigma \in \{1, 0\}^A$$

Now one-place predicates denote sets and are expressions of type $e \to t$, and
characteristic functions are functions from entities to truth values. This gives us
the basis for assigning denotations to expressions of all types. Just as with the
definition of types themselves, the denotations of typed expressions receive a
recursive definition based on the denotations of expressions of the basic types, e
and t. As with the earlier model theory, individual constants denote entities in the
model (i.e. are taken from A) while propositional formulae of type t denote truth
values, $\{0, 1\}$. Now an expression of type $e \to t$ denotes a characteristic function,
as we have seen, and these are defined as functions from entities in the model to
truth values. In other words, the domain of the function is the denotations of
its antecedent type (here e) and its range the denotations of its consequent type
(here t). Taking D_τ to be the denotation domain of a certain type we have the
following core case where the symbol $\mapsto$ is to be read as 'maps onto':

$$D_{e \to t} = D_e \mapsto D_t$$

This is, in fact, the general picture for working out the denotations of typed
expressions: they denote functions from the domain of things denoted by their
antecedent type onto the range of things denoted by their consequent type. The
general *denotation* of a type, τ, is symbolised as D_τ and defined recursively:

(3.17)   a. $D_e = A$ (the set of entities).
            b. $D_t = \{1, 0\}$ (the set of truth values).
            c. If **a** and **b** are types, then $D_{\mathbf{a} \to \mathbf{b}}$ is $D_\mathbf{a} \mapsto D_\mathbf{b}$, a set of functions from
               elements of type **a** to elements of type **b**.

To work out the sort of denotation an expression of a particular type will have,
you have to unpack the denotations by successively applying the rules in (3.17).

(3.18)   a. $D_{e \to (e \to t)}$ = $D_e \mapsto D_{e \to t}$ =
$D_e \mapsto (D_e \mapsto D_t)$ = $A \mapsto (A \mapsto \{1, 0\})$
(functions from entities to functions from entities to truth values).

b. $D_{(e \to t) \to (e \to t)}$ = $D_{e \to t} \mapsto D_{e \to t}$ =
$(D_e \mapsto D_t) \mapsto (D_e \mapsto D_t)$ = $(A \mapsto \{0, 1\}) \mapsto (A \mapsto \{0, 1\})$
(functions from functions from entities to truth values to functions from
entities to truth values).

Because we are using functions, we can determine the denotation of a complex expression of *functor(argument)* structure by taking the function denoted by the functor and applying that to the denotation of the argument: a determinate and fixed value is then obtained, the denotation of the expression in a particular model. This allows us to reduce the model theory for the general structured typed expressions to just two lines: the first identifies the content of a constant as whatever the denotation assignment function of the model determines (notice the significance of the word 'function' here); the second takes the denotation of the functor in the model and applies it to the denotation of the argument in the model to give the denotation of the complex expression in the model.

(3.19)   Given a model $M = \langle A, F \rangle$:
a. for any constant, c, $[\![c]\!]^M = F(c)$
b. if f is of type $a \to b$ and c is an expression of type a, then
$$[\![f(c)]\!]^M = [\![f]\!]^M([\![c]\!]^M)$$

We will not dwell further on this approach to denotation here (although we will have cause to discuss complex denotations again in the next chapter). The important point to bear in mind is that the use of a typed logic allows us to express compositionally the semantic structures associated with complex sentences in a natural language and to assign to such structures denotations with respect to given models and so provide a strong grounding for an account of natural-language semantics.

Exercise 3.7

For each of the different expressions in the exercise in section 3.6.2 say what sort of denotation these have in some model according to their type.

3.8   Summary

The advantage of predicate and propositional logic as we've seen is that the relation between syntax and semantics is fully explicitly defined, with syntactic and semantic rules defined in tandem. With expansion of the theoretical vocabulary provided by predicate logic to include the lambda calculus, we now have a formal basis for assigning types to all categories of natural-language expressions in terms of their contribution to truth conditions of the containing sentence, so that in principle we are able to define compositionality of content in such a way that the meaning of a sentence can be seen to be composed out of the elementary expressions that it contains. However, there is one major structural difference between predicate logic and natural languages within the domain of quantificational inference yet to be expressed before we can evaluate the success of this approach, and that is the logical type to be assigned to quantifying expressions. In predicate logic, these are propositional operators; in natural languages they constitute a subpart of noun phrase expressions. It is to this that we now turn.

3.9   Further reading

It is extremely rare to find a semantics textbook that sets side by side model-theoretic and proof-theoretic characterisations of inference. Notable exceptions are Gamut (1991), who provides a detailed introduction to formal specification of semantics for first-order logic, and, written for a somewhat more general audience than Gamut (1991), Barwise and Etchemendy (1992) with their user-friendly program *Tarski's World 4.0*. Both of these are logic textbooks, but invaluable for linguists also. See also Bergmann *et al.* (1980). Most logic textbooks discuss the paradoxes of material implication; for a linguistic point of view see Smith and Smith (1988). All linguistics formal-semantics textbooks introduce model-theoretic constructs, though with varying degrees of formal explicitness. See Cann (1993: chs. 2, 3, 4 and 5) for a detailed account of model theory for propositional and predicate logic as well as type theory and lambda abstraction; see also Chierchia and McConnell-Ginet (2000). These use different notations, but you can translate between them. The system normally used is Montague's ordered pair representation, $<a, b>$. This means the same as $a \rightarrow b$. As part of an introduction to formal semantics, de Swart (1998) provides a useful presentation of the grammar of first-order logic. An introduction to type theory is provided in Partee *et al.* (1990), and introduction to the Curry–Howard isomorphism in Morrill (1994). The reflection of semantic operations (e.g. applications of the lambda calculus) within a proof theory, as in the paired statements reflecting the Curry–Howard isomorphism, with semantic and syntactic operations thereby combined within a single composite syntactic system is defined as part of a general *labelled deductive system* methodology by Gabbay (1996). This co-presentation of structural and semantic aspects of compositionality is the heart of categorial grammar formalisms such as that developed by Morrill (1994). Carpenter (1997) explores in depth a whole range of issues using the lambda calculus and type theory.

4   Quantification and plurality

4.1   Generalised quantifiers

We saw in the previous two chapters how certain types of quantification (existential and universal) can be given a proof-theoretic characterisation and a model-theoretic semantics; and in the closing sections of Chapter 3, we introduced the lambda calculus and the potential it opens up for associating logical expressions of complex logical types with natural-language expressions. The turning point in using these systems for exploring a general theory of formal semantics for natural language came with Montague's account of quantification (Montague 1973), and it is to this that we now turn. Previous to Montague's setting out of a formal framework for model-theoretic semantics, linguists had faced a stumbling block: in natural languages, quantified noun phrases behave, indeed **are**, noun phrases like any other noun phrase; yet, in predicate logic, quantifiers are defined as propositional operators that take an open propositional formula (with at least one free variable) and bind it to create a propositional formula in which the variable associated with the quantifier is bound. But this means that predicate-logic quantifiers are of type $t \rightarrow t$, and not at all like the type e terms that predicate-logic names are, nor indeed like natural-language quantified noun phrases, with the NP-internal quantifying determiners. In this chapter, we introduce Montague's account of quantification, and the further extensions of so-called generalised-quantifier theory that then become definable. We explore the good and bad points of the proposed analyses and then, finally, take a look at plurality and the problems it poses for semantic theory.

4.1.1   Quantifiers, compositionality and coverage

In order to characterise noun-phrase quantification, we have seen that complex translations need to be made of sentences that contain them, involving not only the relevant quantifier but also an appropriate propositional connective: 'and' ($\wedge$) with the existential quantifier ($\exists$) and 'if' ($\rightarrow$) with the universal ($\forall$):

(4.1)   a. Every camel coughed: $\forall x[Camel'(x) \rightarrow Cough'(x)]$
             b. A dog barked: $\exists y[Dog'(y) \wedge Bark'(y)]$

Negative quantifiers such as *no* can be characterised using either the existential or universal quantifiers:

(4.2)   No buzzard mewled:
          $\neg(\exists z[Buzzard'(z) \wedge Mewl'(z)])$
          $\forall z[Buzzard'(z) \rightarrow \neg Mewl'(z)]$

Unfortunately, the logical quantifiers and their use of the propositional connectives to relate what is the *restrictor* of that quantifier (*Buzzard'* in 4.2) and the remainder of the formula are not very good tools for the analysis of natural-language quantifiers beyond the simple quantifiers *all/every, some/a* and *no*. First, there is the problem of *compositionality* (see Chapter 1 for an informal discussion): no known natural language encodes quantification using a quantifier and a clausal (or phrasal) connective. English (and other languages) can mimic the logical structures:

(4.3)   For everything, if it's a camel, then it coughed.

(4.4)   Something exists such that it's a dog and it barked.

(4.5)   It's not the case that something exists such that it's a buzzard and it mewled.
          For everything, if it is a buzzard, then it didn't mewl.

But these paraphrases are not real English, only ever appearing in discussions of logic and semantics. The question then arises as to the relation between our semantic representations (and interpretations) and the structures of natural languages: if quantification is not naturally expressed using independent quantifiers and connectives, should our concept of the meaning of quantified expressions be structured in such ways?

A related problem concerns the fact that the structure of logical quantification does not parallel the syntactic structure of quantified sentences. There is no constituent within the quantified proposition that corresponds to the quantified noun phrase (QNP) or to the quantifier itself. The representations in (4.6) are not wellformed expressions of predicate logic and so do not have any semantic interpretation and cannot constitute the meaning of the quantifier or QNP:

(4.6)   a. Every camel: $\forall x[Camel'(x) \rightarrow \ldots]$
          b. No: $\neg(\exists z[\cdots \wedge \ldots])$

Any strict interpretation of the *principle of compositionality* thus seems to be violated by this approach to quantification.

A more general problem is the apparently restrictive expressive power of predicate logic, at least at first glance. Predicate logic has only the two quantifiers $\forall, \exists$; yet natural languages typically have a rich set of quantifiers. Even with regard to numbers (predicate logic was explicitly defined as the formal language for expressing mathematical truths), while the logical quantifiers can model certain (e.g. finite numerical) quantifiers, they do so only with great difficulty and verbosity; and this again poses a problem of compositionality when applied to natural-language numerical expressions. So, for example, merely to characterise

two (meaning 'at least two'), it is necessary, not just to use two existential quantifiers, but to predicate both common-noun and verb-phrase meanings of both
bound variables and ensure that the variables are discrete (i.e. are not assigned
the same entity):

(4.7)   At least two students laughed:
           $\exists x[\exists y[Student'(x) \wedge Student'(y) \wedge x \neq y \wedge Laugh'(x) \wedge Laugh'(y)]]$

To characterise the meaning of an expression like *both* (or *exactly two*), things get
even more complicated because you have to make sure that not only are the two
bound variables necessarily discrete but also that nothing else has the properties
projected by the common noun and verb phrase. We illustrate this in (4.8) using
the $\leftrightarrow$ to represent two-way implication (iff):

(4.8)   Both students laughed:
           $\exists x \exists y \forall z[[(Student'(z) \leftrightarrow (z = y \vee z = x)] \wedge Laugh'(x) \wedge$
           $Laugh'(y) \wedge x \neq y]$

For each numeral, more quantifiers, more conjunctions of predicates, and more
statements that the variables pick out different entities, need to be added. And,
despite the fact that sentences like *Infinitely many worlds make up the multi-
verse* are meaningful, it would be impossible to characterise such meaning in
this fashion as one cannot write an infinite number of quantifiers.

   The problem is that the predicate-logic operators quantify over individuals
(of type *e*), and all assertions about sets, as with numerical expressions, have to
be reduced to quantification over individuals: it is this which renders numerical quantification so cumbersome seen from a natural-language perspective.
Moreover, this problem cannot be sidestepped, for there are a great number of
quantifiers that the logical connectives and the two predicate logic operators cannot characterise at all. These include quantifiers that refer to the number of things
that particular predicates denote, either in a rather vague way as in (4.9)–(4.11)
or in comparing the sizes of different denotations as in (4.12)–(4.13):

(4.9)   Many linguists sneezed.

(4.10)   Few philosophers sang.

(4.11)   Most babies cried.

(4.12)   More students than lecturers laughed.

(4.13)   More than half the babies cried.

At this point, it seems clear that invocation of sets and relations between sets is
ineliminable. We must go beyond classical predicate logic if we are to be able to
provide an account of the full range of quantification found in natural languages
in a compositionally acceptable way.

4.1.2   Towards compositional quantification

There are a number of ways in which our account of the semantics of quantification can be extended. In this section, we explore how a representation can be given to QNPs and quantifiers that satisfies the *principle of compositionality* (see Chapter 1 for an informal discussion). To do this, however, we need to look beyond predicate logic to a logic of a higher order: one that has variables, not just over individuals, but also over predicates. How then can we get to a compositional account of logical quantification? We begin by taking a closer look at what quantifiers do, using the pairing of logical type and expression as introduced in the previous chapter.

We have seen that quantified NPs cannot be represented as individuals because they do not denote entities, but quantify over sets of entities. In particular, quantifiers such as *more than half*, *most*, *many* quantify over sets of individuals and the semantic type of quantifiers should reflect this fact. If we are to reflect the type of a quantifier in a uniform way, the predicate-logic assignment of type $t \rightarrow t$ will not be sufficient. Types were introduced in the last chapter, with proper nouns and variables being assigned the primitive type e, propositions type t and (one-place) predicates type $e \rightarrow t$. As we have seen, combining expressions of different types is determined by $\rightarrow$ *Elimination*. So, combining expressions of types e and $e \rightarrow t$ is valid by the rule of functional application (3.3), section 3.6, repeated below in simplified form:

$$a : e, \ b : e \rightarrow t \vdash b(a) : t$$

Of course, expressions of predicate type need not combine just with individual expressions. Quantified NPs syntactically combine with VPs to yield sentences. So what we want is a type-logical inference with some type assignment to quantified expressions that will make the following a valid inference:

$$??, \ e \rightarrow t \vdash t$$

To preserve the requisite inference and so reflect the syntactic mode of combination of quantified noun phrases with VP denotations, what is needed is to translate them into semantic expressions that combine with expressions of type $e \rightarrow t$ to make expressions of type t, that is of type $(e \rightarrow t) \rightarrow t$. And indeed this does lead to the valid inference, but with the expression of type $e \rightarrow t$ now acting as argument rather than functor:

$$a : (e \rightarrow t) \rightarrow t, \ b : e \rightarrow t \vdash a(b) : t$$

Moreover, we have indeed already demonstrated in Chapter 2, the validity of:

$$P \vdash (P \rightarrow Q) \rightarrow Q$$

Now substituting the propositional variables P, Q by the terms e and t respectively, we accordingly have as a demonstrably valid inference:

$$e \vdash (e \rightarrow t) \rightarrow t$$

And what this means is that we can be sure that from some assignation of type e to expressions, for example to proper nouns such as *John*, we will be able to deduce the higher type assignment $(e \to t) \to t$. Assigning such an expression the type e will have as consequence that assigning that expression the type $(e \to t) \to t$ will also always yield valid results. And this yields the happy result that we can move to a uniform higher type assignment for all NP expressions, whether quantified or not, a result we return to very shortly. Notice that here, for the first time, we have input (argument) types that are no longer simple: the argument of a QNP is of type $e \to t$, the type of a one-place predicate, and both arguments of quantifiers are of that type. It is in this sense that the move made above brings us into the region of higher-order logics. With quantifying NPs as of type $(e \to t) \to t$, it will follow that quantifiers themselves, being expressions which combine with common nouns to give rise to QNPs, must have the complex higher type:

$$(e \to t) \to ((e \to t) \to t)$$

Given this move, how can this help us provide a compositional account of the logical quantifiers? If we maintain the interpretation of quantified NPs provided by predicate logic, we can use the *lambda operator* to provide us with a means of representing the more complex structure required by the types defined above. So we extend the use of the lambda operator from abstracting only on individual variables to other variables that range over predicates (and possibly other expressions). Take the representation for the sentence *A dog barked* (remember the symbol after the colon is the type of the logical expression):

$$\exists x[Dog'(x) \land Bark'(x)] : t$$

The predicate *Bark'* provides what is called the *nuclear scope* of the QNP, in this case the logical translation of a VP. Let us replace this content with a variable P of type $e \to t$. What we get is an expression still of type t, but one that contains an unbound variable:

$$\exists x[Student'(x) \land P(x)] : t$$

This variable, being unbound, could be abstracted upon by the lambda operator to give an expression that takes expressions of type $e \to t$ as arguments. At the end of the last chapter, we saw a generalised definition of lambda abstraction which allows the operator to bind any type of variable, type a, in any type of expression, type b, to give an expression of type $a \to b$. This is repeated below in (3.14). (Note that binding by the lambda operator is trivial if there is no occurrence of the variable u in ϕ.)

(3.14)   *Lambda Deduction Rule* (generalised): If ϕ is an expression of type b containing an unbound instance of a variable u of type a, then $\lambda u[\phi]$ is a wellformed expression of type $a \to b$.

$$\phi : b, u : a \vdash \lambda u[\phi] : a \to b$$

Using the generalised lambda to bind P, we get the representation of the semantics of *a student* (i.e. the quantified proposition without any of the VP content):

$$\lambda P[\exists x.Dog'(x) \wedge P(x)] : ((e \rightarrow t) \rightarrow t)$$

But using this very same tool, we can differentiate between what the word *student* contributes to the content of the overall formula and what the indefinite determiner *a* contributes, and thus arrive at a principled account of the concept of *restrictor* for a determiner. We replace the predicate that provides the restrictor of the variable x, here Dog', with another variable Q which we then bind to get the translation of the indefinite article *a*:

$$\lambda Q[\lambda P[\exists x.Q(x) \wedge P(x)]] : ((e \rightarrow t) \rightarrow ((e \rightarrow t) \rightarrow t))$$

This gives us derivations such as (4.14):

(4.14) $((\lambda Q[\lambda P\ [\exists x.Q(x) \wedge P(x)]])\ (Dog'))(Bark') : t$

$\lambda Q[\lambda P[\exists x.Q(x) \wedge P(x)]](Dog') :$
$((e \rightarrow t) \rightarrow t)$
                                                        $Bark' : e \rightarrow t$

$\lambda Q[\lambda P[\exists x.Q(x) \wedge P(x)]] :$ $Dog' : e \rightarrow t$
$((e \rightarrow t) \rightarrow ((e \rightarrow t) \rightarrow t))$

As with all complex lambda expressions, we can reduce them (by the rule of lambda conversion) to more simple expressions that replace bound variables by the arguments they are associated with:

$$(\lambda u.f(u))(a) \leftrightarrow f(a)$$

Assuming (as we can) that lambda conversion generalises across all wellformed instances of a lambda expression plus argument, we can reduce the formula annotating the top-node of (4.14) as follows, to get the result we expect:

$$((\lambda Q[\lambda P[\exists x.Q(x) \wedge P(x)]])(Dog'))(Bark') : t$$
$$(\lambda P[\exists x.Dog'(x) \wedge P(x)])(Bark') : t$$
$$\exists x.Dog'(x) \wedge Bark'(x) : t$$

As the unreduced characterisation of this formula shows, the status of the variables P and Q and their instantiations Dog' and $Bark'$ are identical:

$$((\lambda Q[\lambda P[\exists x.Q(x) \wedge P(x)]])(Dog'))(Bark')$$

Following standard practice within the theory of generalised quantifiers, we nevertheless are explicit about what constitutes the restrictor of the quantifier and what constitutes an appropriate concept of scope for the quantified NP as a whole. The content provided by the nominal for some quantifying determiner is the *restrictor of the quantifier*, and the predicate value associated with its accompanying VP its *nuclear scope*; indeed the nominal and VP expressions are standardly called the quantifier's *restrictor expression* and *nuclear-scope expression* respectively.

Following this pattern, the content of the universal QNP *every camel* can be represented as (4.15a) with the representation of the universal quantifier in (4.15b).

(4.15) a. $\lambda P[Camel'(x) \rightarrow P(x)] : (e \rightarrow t) \rightarrow t$
        b. $\lambda Q[\lambda P[Q(x) \rightarrow P(x)]] : (e \rightarrow t) \rightarrow ((e \rightarrow t) \rightarrow t)$

By raising the type of a noun phrase from type e to type $(e \rightarrow t) \rightarrow t$, and generalising lambda abstraction to bind higher types, it seems that we can successfully provide a compositional account of quantification defined over natural-language sentences directly, a mapping, as required, from words onto denotational contents. It allows us to provide representations for all constituents within sentences containing quantifiers: quantifier, common noun, quantified noun phrase and verb phrase. However, that's all it does. It does not solve the other problems noted above. In particular, it remains the case that the quantifiers may contain connectives that don't appear in any natural language and coverage is restricted to those expressible by the predicate logic quantifiers only. To get past this, we can eschew the complex representations for the quantifiers and treat them as if they were non-logical expressions, so given a specific denotation in the model, like all other content-bearing expressions, rather than having their semantics specified as part of the model theory. So, *a student* is given the simple semantic representation $A'(Student')$, *every dog* is $Every'(Dog')$ and *No ice-cream* is $No'(Ice-cream')$. But, of course, this doesn't help much as it doesn't transparently provide the meaning of QNPs and so we need to get to grips with the interpretation of such expressions directly.

Exercise 4.1

a. Provide a translation for the negative QNP *No student*, the quantifier *no* and a derivation of the semantics of the sentence *No student screamed*.
b. Given the new higher type for noun phrases $((e \rightarrow t) \rightarrow t)$, provide a translation for a proper name like *Hillary* in a sentence like *Hillary lost*. What do you think such a translation means?

4.1.3   Interpreting quantifiers

The study of quantification from the latter part of the twentieth century has tended to concentrate on *generalised quantifiers* which are taken to be the denotation of QNPs. The fundamental idea behind the theory of generalised quantifiers is that quantifiers themselves relate **two** sets of entities in terms of shared membership of various sorts:

- the set denoted by the restrictor (common noun denotation);
- the set denoted by the main predicate (the VP denotation).

Thus, the quantifier represented by the indefinite article *a* relates the set denoted by its common noun to that denoted by the VP with which the QNP combines, saying that those two sets must share at least one member. So *a dog barked* is true just in case there is at least one thing in the *intersection* of the set of dogs and the set of barking things. More technically, the intersection of the set of dogs and the set of barking things is non-empty. In set theoretic notation this is shown as:

$$[\![Dog']\!]^M \cap [\![Bark']\!]^M \neq \emptyset$$

This is precisely what expressions of the complex type that we have assigned to quantifiers in the previous section denote. Recall that the two primitive types *e* and *t* denote individual entities and truth values, respectively. More complex types denote *functions* over these basic denotations, as we saw in Chapter 3. An expression of type $e \rightarrow t$ denotes a function from individual entities to truth values. As we have seen, such a function actually picks out a set by mapping those entities within the set onto *true* and those not in the set onto *false*. So breaking down the type of QNPs, we see that its *domain* (i.e. its restrictor) are expressions of type $e \rightarrow t$, hence denoting sets. Its *range* are things of type *t*, i.e. truth values. Since functions that map anything onto truth values establish a set, what QNPs denote are *sets of sets of individual entities*. Such expressions are called *generalised quantifiers*. So quantifiers themselves, of type $(e \rightarrow t) \rightarrow ((e \rightarrow t) \rightarrow t)$, denote expressions that map sets onto sets of sets.

As noted above, existentially quantified expressions, given this set-theoretical perspective, relate two sets of entities which share at least one individual member, so $(A'(Lecturer'))(Laugh')$ is true with respect to some model *M* just in case the intersection of $[\![Lecturer']\!]^M$ and $[\![Laugh']\!]^M$ contains at least one entity, i.e.

$$[\![Lecturer']\!]^M \cap [\![Laugh']\!]^M \neq \emptyset$$

Now this means that the generalised quantifier $A'(Lecturer')$ denotes that set of sets X that makes $[\![Lecturer']\!]^M \cap X \neq \emptyset$ true:

$$[\![A'(Lecturer')]\!]^M = \{X | [\![Lecturer']\!]^M \cap X \neq \emptyset\}$$

What this further means is that an existential QNP denotes all the sets of entities that share at least one entity with the set denoted by the common noun it contains (its restrictor). This is shown graphically in Figure 4.1, which is usually referred to as the *existential sublimation* of the set denoted by *Lecturer'*. More

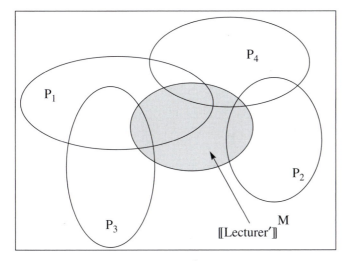

Figure 4.1: *Existential Sublimation of* $[\![Lecturer']\!]$

generally, we can define the semantics of the indefinite existentially quantifying determiner, a, ($[\![A']\!]^M$) as that function that assigns to every common noun denotation, $[\![N']\!]^M$, the family of sets:

$$\{X \mid [\![N']\!]^M \cap X \neq \emptyset\}$$

Given the analysis of existential QNPs, it is a simple matter to specify the truth conditions of a formula containing such a generalised quantifier:

(4.16) $[\![(A'(Lecturer'))(Laugh')]\!]^M$ is true iff $[\![Laugh']\!]^M \in [\![(A'(Lecturer'))]\!]^M$

More generally, the interpretation of a formula containing any QNP is given by (4.17), where α ranges over one-place predicates:

(4.17) $[\![QNP'(\alpha)]\!]^M$ is true iff $[\![\alpha]\!]^M \in [\![QNP']\!]^M$

Exactly the same can be done with respect to the universal and negative quantifiers. So $[\![(Every'(Student'))(Scream')]\!]^M$ is true iff $[\![Student']\!]^M$ is a subset of $[\![Scream']\!]^M$ i.e. $[\![Student']\!]^M \subseteq [\![Scream']\!]^M$. So, the generalised quantifier $[\![Every'(Student')]\!]^M$ denotes that set of sets X that make $[\![Student']\!]^M \subseteq X$ true, i.e.

$$[\![Every'(Student')]\!]^M = \{X \mid [\![Student']\!]^M \subseteq X\}$$

This is known as the *universal sublimation* of the set $[\![Student']\!]$ as illustrated in Figure 4.2. And from this, we can define the semantics of *every* ($[\![Every']\!]^M$) as that function that assigns to every $[\![N']\!]^M$ the family of sets:

$$\{X \mid [\![N']\!]^M \subseteq X\}$$

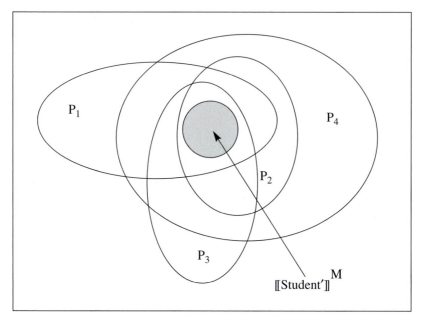

Figure 4.2: *Universal Sublimation of* $[\![Student']\!]$

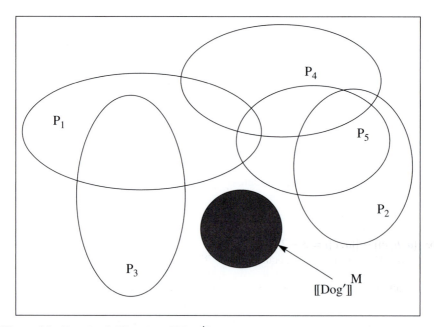

Figure 4.3: *Negative Sublimation of* $[\![Dog']\!]$

And finally to the negative quantifier, *no*: $[\![(No'(Dog'))(Bark)]\!]^M$ is true iff the intersection of $[\![Dog']\!]^M$ and $[\![Bark']\!]^M$ contains no entities at all, i.e.

$$[\![Dog']\!]^M \cap [\![Bark']\!]^M = \emptyset$$

So, $[\![No'(Dog')]\!]^M$ denotes that set of sets X that make $[\![Dog']\!]^M \cap X = \emptyset$ true, i.e.

$$[\![No'(Dog')]\!]^M = \{X | [\![Dog']\!]^M \cap X = \emptyset\}$$

and $[\![No']\!]^M$ is that function that assigns to every $[\![N']\!]^M$ the family of sets

$$\{X | [\![N']\!]^M \cap X = \emptyset\}$$

Exercise 4.2

For each of the following sentences: provide a representation of the semantic content; state the truth conditions of the representation in set-theoretical terms; and provide a set-theoretic definition of the truth-conditional content of the generalised quantifier.

a. Not every student sang.
b. Some but not every lecturer cried.
c. Not all the sweets were eaten.

4.1.4   Cardinality quantifiers

The universal and existential quantifiers state fairly general constraints on the relation between the restrictor of a quantifying NP and its nuclear scope, involving the subset relation or empty or non-empty intersection. But many quantifiers make specific reference to the **number** of elements in particular sets, i.e. to the *cardinality* of sets. The cardinality of a set A is represented as $|A|$ and gives the number of different elements that are in A:

(4.18)　　a. $|\{a, b, c\}| = 3$
　　　　　b. $|\{a, 2, c, 7, k, 2, +\}| = 6$ (not 7!)
　　　　　c. $|\{\{a\}, \{a, b\}, \{a, c\}, \{b, c\}, \{a, b, c\}\}| = 5$ (not 3!)

Since $|A|$ denotes some number, the usual arithmetical operations apply:

(4.19)　　a. $|\{a, b\}| + |\{b, c\}| = 2 + 2 = 4$
　　　　　　(N.B. $|A| + |B|$ may not be equal to $|A \cup B|$)
　　　　　b. $|\{a, b, c\}| - |\{a, c\}| = 3 - 2 = 1$
　　　　　　(N.B. $|A| - |B|$ may not be equal to $|A - B|$)

Normally, what quantifiers do is to define the specific cardinality of a set (e.g. numerals, *both*, *no*) or that the cardinality of a set is greater than or equal to ($\geq$), or less than or equal to ($\leq$) some number. By stating the semantics directly in terms of set theory, rather than reducing all such assertions to quantification over individual members of that set, we can avoid the problem, discussed earlier, that expressing the content of numerals in predicate logic requires a great deal of verbosity. All that is now required is to express the number of elements that are required to be in some set. Defining the semantics of *two* then becomes trivial. *Two students laughed* translates as $(Two'(Student'))(Laugh')$ which is true in model M iff the cardinality of the intersection of the sets denoted by $[\![Student']\!]^M$ and $[\![Laugh']\!]^M$ is greater than or equal to ($\geq$) 2:

$$|[\![Student']\!]^M \cap [\![Laugh']\!]^M| \geq 2$$

So $[\![Two'(Student')]\!]^M$ denotes that set of sets X that makes $|[\![Student']\!]^M \cap X| \geq 2$ true, i.e.

$$\{X| \; |[\![Student']\!]^M \cap X| \geq 2\}$$

And $[\![Two']\!]^M$ is that function that assigns to each $[\![N']\!]^M$ the family of sets:

$$\{X| \; |[\![N']\!]^M \cap X| \geq 2\}$$

And this approach can be extended to arbitrary other numerals:

(4.20)   A hundred and one dogs barked.
   a. $[\![(One\text{-}hundred\text{-}one'(Dog'))(Bark')]\!]^M$ is true iff the cardinality of the intersection of the sets denoted by $[\![Dog']\!]^M$ and $[\![Bark']\!]^M$ is greater than or equal to 101.

$$|[\![Dog']\!]^M \cap [\![Bark']\!]^M| \geq 101$$

   b. $[\![(One\text{-}hundred\text{-}one'(Dog'))]\!]^M$ denotes that set of sets X that make $|[\![Dog']\!]^M \cap X| \geq 101$ true, i.e.

$$\{X| |[\![Dog']\!]^M \cap X| \geq 101\}$$

   c. $[\![One\text{-}hundred\text{-}one']\!]^M$ is that function that assigns to each $[\![N']\!]^M$ the family of sets $\{X| \; |[\![N']\!]^M \cap X| \geq 101\}$.

As well as stating the semantics of numerals in a direct fashion, since cardinalities count the number of distinct elements in any given set, it is also now possible to provide the semantics of complex quantifiers which do not give a precise number but which provide cut-off points for where that number may be found. These are quantifiers such as *more than* and *fewer than*.

(4.21)   Fewer than six babies cried.
   a. $[\![(Fewer\text{-}than\text{-}six'(Baby'))(Cry')]\!]^M$ is true iff the cardinality of the intersection of the sets denoted by $[\![Baby']\!]^M$ and $[\![Cry']\!]^M$ is less than 6.

$$| \; [\![Baby']\!]^M \cap [\![Cry']\!]^M| \; < 6$$

   b. $[\![(Fewer\text{-}than\text{-}six'(Baby'))]\!]^M = \{X| \; |[\![Baby']\!]^M \cap X| < 6\}$
   c. $[\![Fewer\text{-}than\text{-}six']\!]^M$ is that function that assigns to each $[\![N']\!]^M$ the family of sets $\{X| \; |[\![N']\!]^M \cap X| < 6\}$

(4.22)   No more than six babies cried.

    a. $[\![(No\text{-}more\text{-}than\text{-}six'(Baby'))(Cry')]\!]^M$ is true iff the cardinality of the intersection of the sets denoted by $[\![Baby']\!]^M$ and $[\![Cry']\!]^M$ is less than or equal to 6.

$$|[\![Baby']\!]^M \cap [\![Cry']\!]^M| \leq 6$$

    b. $[\![No\text{-}more\text{-}than\text{-}six'(Baby')]\!]^M = \{X|\ ||Baby'||^M \cap X| \leq 6\}$

    c. $[\![No\text{-}more\text{-}than\text{-}six']\!]^M$ is that function that assigns to each $[\![N']\!]^M$ the family of sets $\{X|\ ||[\![N']\!]^M \cap X| \leq 6\}$

There are also quantifiers that compare the sizes of the sets denoted by the expression providing its restrictor and the expression providing its nuclear scope without ever specifying a particular number such as *More/fewer ... than ...* Such quantifiers might appear to quantify over three sets: the sets denoted by the two common nouns and that denoted by the VP. However, semantically this is not the case. What they really do is to compare the size of the two sets that result from taking the denotations of both common nouns and intersecting them separately with the set denoted by the VP. So the interpretation of a sentence like *More lecturers than students screamed* is taken to be equivalent to *More lecturers screamed than students screamed*:

$[\![((More'(Lecturer'))(Student'))(Scream')]\!]^M$ is true iff the cardinality of the intersection of the sets denoted by $[\![Lecturer']\!]^M$ and $[\![Scream']\!]^M$ is greater than the cardinality of the intersection of the sets denoted by $[\![Student']\!]^M$ and $[\![Scream']\!]^M$, i.e.

$$|\ [\![Lecturer']\!]^M \cap [\![Scream']\!]^M\ | > |\ [\![Student']\!]^M \cap [\![Scream']\!]^M\ |$$

So

$$[\![(More'(Lecturer'))(Student')]\!]^M$$
$$= \{X|\ |\ [\![Lecturer']\!]^M \cap X\ | > |\ [\![Student']\!]^M \cap X\ |\}$$

And $[\![(More(N_1'))(N_2')]\!]^M$ is that function that assigns to all $[\![N_1']\!]^M$, $[\![N_2']\!]^M$ the family of sets

$$\{X|\ ||[\![N_1']\!]^M \cap X| > ||[\![N_2']\!]^M \cap X|\}$$

Exercise 4.3

For each of the following sentences: provide a representation of the semantic content; state the truth conditions of the representation in set-theoretical terms; and provide a set-theoretic definition of the truth-conditional content of the generalised quantifier.

a. Fewer than twenty lecturers remained.
b. All but five students passed their exams.
c. Only one dolphin survived.

4.1.5   Contextual quantifiers

The use of generalised quantifiers to model the semantics of natural-language quantification is most illuminating when applied to quantifiers that give quite precise definitions like *exactly 4, more than half, no less than three-quarters*, etc. This is because their truth conditions can be precisely determined by the numbers of elements found in particular sets through simple arithmetic means. However, there is a class of quantifiers that do not behave in this fashion, but have a fuzzier, more apparently contextually determined meaning. Such quantifiers are exemplified in English by *few, many, most*, whose semantics are notoriously difficult to define.

The interpretation of *most*, for example, minimally requires that the majority of things in the restrictor set are involved in what is specified in the nuclear-scope set. So, for example, *most dogs barked* is true if the number of barking dogs outnumbers the non-barking dogs, as shown below (where A is the set of entities in the universe of discourse and $A - X$ is the set of all things minus those things in set X):

$$| [\![Dog']\!]^M \cap [\![Bark']\!]^M | > | [\![Dog']\!]^M \cap (A - [\![Bark']\!]^M) |$$

This yields an interpretation for *most dogs* as:

$$[\![Most'(Dog')]\!]^M = \{ X \mid |[\![Dog']\!]^M \cap X | > |[\![Dog']\!]^M \cap (A - X) | \}$$

But this can't be sufficient, as these are exactly the same truth conditions we have to assign to the **QNP** *more than half the dogs* and this predicts that *most dogs barked* means exactly the same as *more than half the dogs barked*. While some people think that this is reasonable, since the only secure thing that you can deduce from an utterance of *most (of the) dogs barked* is that *more than half the dogs barked*, most people would baulk at going from an utterance of *more than half the dogs barked* to the conclusion that *most (of the) dogs barked*. In other words, it seems that there's an entailment from *most* to *more than half* but not the other way around. It seems something more is required.

It seems that with *most* there is some large proportion of things in the restrictor set that are also in the nuclear-scope set, but this proportion is determined pragmatically according to the sorts of object and number of objects in the restrictor set and the general discourse context. So, for example, if there are six dogs and four of them barked, then *most (of the) dogs barked* is likely to be judged to be true. But if there are sixty dogs and forty of them barked, would this still be the case? Or if the restrictor set is made up of small things like beads or sand, it appears that a larger proportion of the restrictor set must be involved in whatever is contained in the nuclear-scope set. *Most (of the beads) have been stolen* is likely to be judged untrue (or at least misleading) if in fact there are lots of beads remaining. Of course, it is possible to argue for hours over the exact proportion of things that constitute grounds for using *most* (only try this at the most boring parties), but that is exactly the effect you would expect if the proportion is dependent on context, and indeed the subjective judgements of speakers and addressees. In terms of the semantics, all we can really do is to define the semantics of $Most'(N')$ as a function that assigns to all common-noun denotations the sets of sets where the number of elements in the intersection of the common-noun denotation and the VP denotation is greater than some pragmatically determined proportion of the number of things in the restrictor set (shown as c), where this is higher than 50 per cent ($\bullet$ indicates multiplication):

$$[\![Most'(N')]\!]^M = \{X| \; |X \cap [\![N']\!]^M \; | > c \bullet |[\![N']\!]^M|\} \text{ where } c \geq .5$$

For other contextual quantifiers like *many* and *few*, things are more complicated still. It has been suggested, for example, that *many* is ambiguous depending on which set the contextually derived proportion relates to. So, it is argued, the sentence *Many people live to seventy* is true just in case the number of people living to seventy is greater than the number of other things in the domain that live to seventy ('Of all the things that live to seventy, many people do').

(4.23) $[\![Many'_1(People')]\!]^M = \{X| \; |X \cap [\![People']\!]^M| > f(A)\}$
where $f(A)$ is some fixed proportion of the number of elements in A, the set of things that exist.

On the other hand, *Many students got first-class degrees* is true if, and only if, the number of students who got first-class degrees is greater than some normal proportion of students who get such results.

(4.24) $[\![Many'_2(Student')]\!]^M = \{X| \; |X \cap [\![Student']\!]^M| > c \bullet |[\![Student]\!]^M|\}$
where c is some contextually determined constant.

Yet another interpretation is said to apply to *Many women are right-handed*, which is true if, and only if, the number of women who are right-handed is greater than the normal proportion of women who are right-handed with respect to the population as a whole.

(4.25) $[\![Many'_3(Woman')]\!]^M = \{X| \; |X \cap [\![Woman']\!]^M| >$
$|X|/|A| \bullet |[\![Woman']\!]^M|\}$

And, finally, there are sentences like *Many Scandinavians have won a Nobel Prize*, which is true just in case the number of Scandinavians who have won a Nobel Prize is greater than some contextually determined proportion of people who win Nobel Prizes.

(4.26) $[\![Many'_4(Scandinavian')]\!]^M = \{X| \; |X \cap [\![Scandinavian']\!]^M| > c \bullet |X|\}$

Although homonymy clearly exists in the vocabularies of natural languages, there is a tendency among linguistic theorists to multiply ambiguity whenever there is some difference in the behaviour, semantic or otherwise, of an expression in different contexts. Treating *many* as ambiguous is part of this tendency; but the question is whether this should be characterised as ambiguity, given that it is far removed from lexical ambiguities of the form *bank* (= 'financial institution' or 'side of river'). Any analysis which posits ambiguity at this juncture in reflecting the distinctive contextually determined bases for assertions involving *many* is arguably missing a generalisation. It is possible, however, to characterise a general meaning of *many*:

(4.27) $[\![Many'(N')]\!]^M = \{X \mid |X \cap [\![N']\!]^M| > \mathbf{c} \bullet |Y|\}$ where Y is X, $[\![N']\!]^M$ or A and $\mathbf{c}$ is a pragmatically determined proportion based on these sets.

In other words, *many* may be treated as **underspecified** for its full interpretation. To interpret an utterance of the word, therefore, the hearer has to make certain choices based on context (including world knowledge), i.e. pragmatic choices must be allowed to precede semantic interpretation if we do not want to take the easy way out and say that *many* is multiply **ambiguous**. This sort of context-dependence is regarded by some as a problem, since it implies that pragmatics has to interact with semantics (i.e. the specification of truth conditions). But we will have cause as we proceed to see such context-dependence as intrinsic to the content of natural-language utterances and thus we need to allow pragmatics and semantics to interconnect much more thoroughly than is typically assumed in formal theories of semantics, going far beyond the rather restricted indexicality of words such as *I, you, this, that*, which were taken to provide the prime indicators of requiring denotations relative to the context of utterance. For the moment, we leave this as the first glimpse of the floating iceberg of a challenge for orthodox assumptions about semantics: how does one define the feeding relation between contextual parameters and denotational content? In particular, can we maintain the assumption that semantics, as a component of grammar, feeds into pragmatics, which is grammar-external (see Chapter 1), rather than the other way round?

Exercise 4.4

Provide a semantics of the quantifier *few* along the lines given above to *many*. Are there as many readings for *few* as for *many*?

4.1.6   Conservativity and monotonicity

A great deal of the interest in generalised quantifiers has been in identifying the formal properties of those quantifiers that are denoted by natural-language expressions. The most important of these is called *conservativity*. A (generalised) quantifier is conservative if (and only if) it has the conservativity property:

(4.28)   A generalised quantifier $Q(Y)$ is conservative iff

$$X \in Q(Y) \leftrightarrow (Y \cap X) \in Q(Y)$$

where Q represents the denotation of a quantifier, Y the denotation of a common noun (the restrictor set) and X (the nuclear-scope set which is often a VP) is any subset of A, the universe of discourse.

This means that whenever the set X denoted by some nuclear-scope set is in the denotation of the generalised quantifier $(Q(Y))$, then the set provided by the intersection of the sets denoted by the nuclear-scope expression and the restrictor expression $(X \cap Y)$ is also a member of the generalised quantifier. In simpler terms, conservativity gives rise to equivalence relations like those in (4.29)–(4.31). Conservativity ensures that the interpretation of a quantified noun phrase containing a common noun N is not affected by those sets of entities that are not in the extension of N. So, in assigning a truth value to some quantified formula, conservativity says that all you have to do is see if the entities that have the property indicated by the common noun bear the appropriate relation to the property expressed by the verb phrase and not lots of other things. Other entities are simply irrelevant, so that crying men have no bearing on the truth or falsity of (4.29), only crying babies do:

(4.29)   *Every baby cried* iff *Every baby is a baby who cried.*

(4.30)   *Few lecturers screamed* iff *Few lecturers are lecturers who screamed.*

(4.31)   *No lecturers laughed* iff *no lecturer is a lecturer who laughed.*

Most, but not all, natural-language quantifiers are conservative. For example, *many* in some of its interpretations is not conservative. *Many Scandinavians have won the Nobel Prize* is not semantically equivalent to *Many Scandinavians are Scandinavians who have won the Nobel Prize* but rather to *Many people who have won the Nobel Prize are Scandinavians who have won the Nobel Prize* (in other words, the interpretation of $many_4$ discussed above). Furthermore, it has been suggested that the focus word *only* combines with a noun to yield a QNP. But if this is the case, then such QNPs are not conservative, because they require not only that there is something in the intersection of the set denoted by the restrictor expression and that denoted by the nuclear-scope expression, but also that no other set intersects with the latter. So for *Only boys cry* it must be the case that there are crying boys and that there are no crying girls or adults or whatever. In fact, most linguists would not consider *only* to be a determiner in these cases. If that is so, and if we exclude the contextually dependent quantifiers (and a number of semanticists reject the idea that these are proper quantifiers in any case), then it is probably true that conservativity is a universal property of simple determiners and one, indeed, that we might expect given some general cognitive property that trades off effort of computation against interpretive effects, such as is put forward in Relevance Theory (see Chapter 1).

As well as identifying other general formal properties of quantifiers (such as their semantic independence from the identity, as opposed to the number, of entities in the extension of the common noun), there have also been attempts to characterise the properties of different subsets of quantifiers. For example, if we

know that *Every student cried* is true in some model, then adding more crying
things to the model does not affect the truth of that sentence, but adding more
students to the model **may** affect its truth, because any newly introduced student
may not be crying. On the other hand, taking away one of the students (or picking out a subset of the students) does not affect the truth value. The way truth
is maintained for quantified sentences in situations in which entities are added
or subtracted from the sets denoted by restrictor and nuclear-scope expressions
depends on the *monotonicity* of the quantifier involved.

(4.32)   If the **addition** of more entities to the extension of the restrictor
             (common-noun phrase) or the nuclear scope (verb phrase) does not affect
             the truth value of a formula with the structure $Q'(N')(V P')$, then we say
             that the quantifier, Q', is *monotone increasing*.

(4.33)   If the **subtraction** of entities from the relevant extensions/denotations fails
             to affect the truth value, then we say that Q is *monotone decreasing*.

We may make a further distinction between those quantifiers which are unaffected by increase or decrease in their common-noun extensions (restrictor)
and those unaffected by increase or decrease of their associated VP extensions
(nuclear scope). So we get the following deducibility patterns in (4.34):

(4.34)   *Monotone increasing*
             a. A quantifier Q' is *restrictor-monotone increasing* iff

             $[\![(Q'(N_1'))(V P')]\!]^M \models [\![(Q'(N_2'))(V P')]\!]^M$, where $[\![N_1']\!]^M \subseteq [\![N_2']\!]^M$

             A student with red hair is singing entails *A student is singing*.

             b. A quantifier Q is *scope-monotone increasing* iff

             $[\![(Q'(N'))(V P_1')]\!]^M \models [\![(Q'(N'))(V P_2')]\!]^M$, where
             $[\![V P_1']\!]^M \subseteq [\![V P_2']\!]^M$

             Most babies cried loudly entails *Most babies cried*.[1]

(4.35)   *Monotone decreasing*
             a. A quantifier Q is *restrictor-monotone decreasing* iff

             $[\![(Q'(N_1'))(V P')]\!]^M \models [\![(Q'(N_2'))(V P')]\!]^M$, where $[\![N_2']\!]^M \subseteq [\![N_1']\!]^M$

             No student failed their degree exams entails *No student of linguistics
             failed their degree exams*.

             b. A quantifier Q is *scope-monotone decreasing* iff

             $[\![(Q'(N'))(V P_1')]\!]^M \models [\![(Q'(N'))(V P_2')]\!]^M$, where
             $[\![V P_2']\!]^M \subseteq [\![V P_1']\!]^M$

             Few students sang entails *Few students sang well*.

---

[1] There is some interaction with other properties here such as tense: does *Most linguists read quickly*
entail *Most linguists read*?

So we see that A' is both restrictor- and scope-monotone increasing (4.36) while $Every'$ is scope-monotone increasing, but restrictor-monotone decreasing (4.37) and No is restrictor- and scope-monotone decreasing (4.38):

(4.36)   a. If a lecturer with red hair laughed, then a lecturer laughed.
            b. If a lecturer laughed loudly, then a lecturer laughed.

(4.37)   a. If every student cried a lot, then every student cried.
            b. If every student cried, then every student with a cold cried.

(4.38)   a. If no dog barked, then no scrawny dog barked.
            b. If no dog barked, then no dog barked loudly.

Other restrictor- or scope-monotone increasing quantifiers are *all, most, at least n* (for *n* a natural number) and other monotone-decreasing quantifiers are *not all, at most n*. Not all quantifiers show monotonicity properties, of course, particularly the complex ones. Examples are *exactly n, an even number of n*.[2]

Pursuing this denotational programme for natural-language expressions at the most general level, a number of linguists have tried to define linguistic universals about noun phrases according to the different sorts of monotone quantifiers that they contain. One of these is that noun phrases can be conjoined by *and* or *or* only if they contain quantifiers with the same monotone direction.

(4.39)   *Coordination constraint*: Two NPs can be coordinated by conjunction (*and*) and disjunction (*or*) iff they are both monotone increasing or both monotone decreasing.
            a. No student and every lecturer liked the book.
            b. Most students and every lecturer liked the book.
            c. *No student and most lecturers liked the book.
            d. *No student and a lecturer liked the book.

This universal has not been generally accepted – it does not hold, for example, of contrastive coordinators such as *but*. But it provides an interesting example of how the study of set-theoretic properties associated with natural-language expressions can provide explanations for certain peculiarities of natural languages that are not otherwise obvious.

Another puzzle that can be explained in terms of monotonicity is the distribution of *negative polarity items* with respect to different quantifiers. Negative polarity items (NPIs) are words like *any* and *ever* that are licensed after negation but not in positive contexts (where they have to be interpreted differently, if they can be interpreted at all):[3]

---

[2] One has to wonder to what extent such complex structures are quantifiers in the non-logical sense, i.e. are really determiners in natural languages.

[3] We use $\equiv$ to indicate that when $P \equiv Q$, P is just a synonym of Q

(4.40)   Socrates didn't write anything. ≡ Socrates wrote nothing.
              ?Socrates wrote anything. ≢ Socrates wrote nothing.

(4.41)   I don't ever want to go there again.

              *I want ever to go there again.

The puzzle is that these differences also appear with respect to quantified noun phrases, so that NPIs can appear in the scope of noun phrases containing the quantifiers *no, at most n, few* but not *every, at least n, many*.

(4.42)   a. No dogs ever barked.
              b. At most three philosophers have ever written anything about Warlpiri.
              c. Few politicians know anything about pragmatics.

(4.43)   a. *Every dog ever barked.
              b. ??At least three philosophers have ever written anything about Warlpiri.
              c. ??Many politicians know anything about pragmatics.

In what sense, however, should *few* as well as *no* be classified as 'negative' and conversely in what sense are both *every* and *many* positive? The answer lies in the fact that *no* and *few* are scope-monotone decreasing while *every* and *many* are scope-monotone increasing. But *every* is restrictor-monotone decreasing. What happens then?

(4.44)   Every politician who ever read Chomsky likes linguistics.

And *no* is restrictor-monotone decreasing as well, whereas *a* is restrictor-monotone increasing:

(4.45)   No politician who ever read Chomsky would despise linguistics.

(4.46)   *A politician who ever read Chomsky would despise linguistics.

It seems therefore that NPIs are licensed only in monotone-decreasing contexts. Notice that negation itself can be viewed as monotone decreasing, given entailments like that in (4.47), so we have the universal constraint in (4.48):

(4.47)   A dog didn't bark ⊨ A dog didn't bark loudly.
              (Cf. A dog barked ⊭ a dog barked loudly.)

(4.48)   Negative polarity items are licensed only in monotone-decreasing environments.

It is notable that such universal characterisations essentially involve reference to sets and relations between sets, as required by the generalised quantifier approach to quantification.

4.2 Plurals

So far in looking at quantifiers, we have been ignoring the fact that most quantificational determiners appear with plural noun phrases, at least in English – this is a property that varies cross-linguistically. This is typical of logical approaches to the analysis of natural-language semantics. All the information about cardinalities and, thus, number is packed into the semantics of the determiner, and the number marking on the noun is ignored. Plurality as a grammatical construct is thus marginalised and almost never mentioned in textbooks on semantics. However, plurality gives rise to a number of interesting semantic puzzles and is a proper subject of study for semantics, as well as providing a test case for explicit compositionality where all information is maintained from the syntax into the semantics.

There are different types of plural noun phrase:

| (4.49) | Some students sang. | Indefinites |
| | The lecturer told some students off. | |

| (4.50) | Children demolished the house. | Bare plurals |
| | His manner upsets children. | |

| (4.51) | The students ran away. | Definites |
| | The university failed the students. | |

| (4.52) | Many students were anxious. | Quantified NPs |
| | All lecturers were ill on Hogmanay. | |

| (4.53) | John and Mary are lovers. | Conjoined NPs |
| | Two men and three women live in that flat. | |

Plurality derives both from morphological marking on a head noun and from conjunction of singular noun phrases. In many ways, the latter are the simplest to analyse semantically, given the generalised quantifier approach to noun-phrase semantics given above. Within the standard framework, conjoined singular noun phrases can be given a representation and interpretation that does not involve plurality *per se*, simply using the lambda operator. We can use the truth-conditional equivalence between *John and Mary sang* and *John sang and Mary sang* to see how this might work. So we want to end up with a semantic expression that is truth-conditionally equivalent to:

$$Sing'(John') \land Sing'(Mary')$$

Replacing both instances of the predicate with a variable P of type $e \rightarrow t$, we get an open proposition $P(John') \wedge P(Mary')$ from which we can derive a lambda expression by abstracting on the predicate variable:

$$\lambda P[P(John') \wedge P(Mary')]$$

Because we have abstracted on a variable of type $e \rightarrow t$ over an expression of type t, this expression is of type $(e \rightarrow t) \rightarrow t$, the type of a generalised quantifier. This particular generalised quantifier denotes the set of all sets of which both John and Mary are members:

$$\{X | [\![John']\!]^M \in X \,\&\, [\![Mary']\!]^M \in X\}$$

Applying this to some predicate, as with $(\lambda P[P(John') \wedge P(Mary')])(Sing')$, yields a formula that is true in some model just in case the set denoted by the predicate contains both John and Mary, as required.

A similar approach can be taken to analysing conjoined singular quantified NPs:

(4.54)   A cat and a dog jumped.
          $\equiv \exists x \exists y [Cat'(x) \wedge Jump'(x) \wedge Dog'(y) \wedge Jump'(y)]$

Replacing the predicate $Jump'$ by a predicate variable and abstracting over this gives:

$$\lambda P[\exists x \exists y [Cat'(x) \wedge P(x) \wedge Dog'(y) \wedge P(y)]]$$

This expression denotes the set of sets that have a non-null intersection with the set of cats and the set of dogs (i.e. those sets that contain at least one dog and at least one cat). Using the representations for generalised quantifiers, we can still construct an expression that has the same type as denotation, namely:

$$\lambda P[(A'(Dog'))(P) \wedge (A'(Cat'))(P)]$$

4.2.1   Interpreting plural noun phrases

So far, we have seen how we can model simple (so called *distributive*, see 4.2.3) predication with conjoined singular noun phrases fairly easily and without having to modify any of the assumptions we have been making. However, there are problems with this approach; for example, we cannot apply the same analysis to sentences like *John and Mary met at the pub*, where the predicate derived by the VP does not seem to be amenable to a distributive reading i.e. *John met and Mary met* does not make sense. And things get a bit more tricky when we try to characterise plurality directly.

English (and most other modern Indo-European languages) makes only a morphological number distinction between *singular* and *plural*, with singular number regularly (but not exclusively, think of *sheep, duck*, etc.) meaning 'one and only one', while plural regularly (but not always, e.g. *trousers, scissors*) signifies more than one. Other languages differentiate between *dual, singular* and *plural*, with duals meaning 'exactly two' and plurals 'more than two'. And there are languages with *trials* (meaning 'exactly three') and less definable number categories such as *paucal* (meaning 'few'), and so on. We will, as we have done so far in this book, take the simplest case as exemplified in English – the distinction between 'one' and 'more than one'.

It is easy enough to define these distinctions using the cardinality of sets:

(4.55)   a. *singular:* $|X| = 1$
              b. *plural:* $|X| > 1$

It is, however, not so easy to incorporate this information directly (and compositionally) into the definitions of the truth conditions for quantified noun phrases. This is because grammatical number has as its domain a common noun (phrase), apparently restricting the number of entities to one or more than one. But, of course, a singular common noun does not specify that there can be only one entity that has the property expressed by the common noun, merely that some relevant subset of the denotation of the common noun phrase contains only one entity. Consider the truth conditions for *A student sang* in this light. Earlier in this chapter these were expressed set-theoretically as:

$$[\![(A'(Student'))(Sing')]\!]^M = 1 \text{ iff}$$
$$[\![Sing']\!]^M \in \{X | \ [\![Student']\!]^M \cap X \neq \emptyset\}$$

i.e. *A student sang* is true iff there is **at least** one entity that is both a student and sang. So another way of expressing this is to say that the cardinality of the intersection of the restrictor and scope sets is equal to or greater than 1:

$$[\![(A'(Student'))(Sing')]\!]^M = 1 \text{ iff}$$
$$[\![Sing']\!]^M \in \{X | \ |[\![Student']\!]^M \cap X| \geq 1\}$$

Now the definition of *singular* given above, if included directly, will give the wrong truth conditions:

$$[\![(A'(Student'))(Sing')]\!]^M = 1 \text{ iff}$$
$$[\![Sing']\!]^M \in \{X | \ |[\![Student']\!]^M| = 1 \ \wedge \ |[\![Student']\!]^M \cap X| \geq 1\}$$

i.e. *A student sang* is true iff there is **one and only one** entity that is a student and there is at least one singing student. But this is not what *A student sang* means, as we have already discussed several times. To get the right results we have to assume that the condition imposed by the grammatical number applies to **subsets** of the common noun denotation and that one of these subsets has a non-null intersection with the set of singers (or, equivalently, that the cardinality of the intersection is at least 1):

$$[\![(A'(Student'))(Sing')]\!]^M = 1 \text{ iff}$$
$$[\![Sing']\!]^M \in \{X | Y \subseteq [\![Student']\!]^M \ \& \ |Y| = 1 \ \& \ |Y \cap X| \geq 1\}$$

This extra level of complexity brings in the notion of *groups* which can be modelled as sets of individuals: the singular picks out all subsets of the denotation of a common noun that contain only one member, while the plural picks out those subsets that have more than one.

(4.56)   Denotation of *student*: the set of sets of all students that have a cardinality of 1: $\{Y | Y \subseteq [\![Student']\!]^M \ \& \ |Y| = 1\}$

Denotation of *students*: the set of sets of all students whose cardinality is greater than 1: $\{Y | Y \subseteq [\![Student']\!]^M \ \& \ |Y| > 1\}$

Assume that there are four students $\{a, b, c, d\}$, then we have:

(4.57) $[\![Student'_{sg}]\!]^M = \{\{a\}, \{b\}, \{c\}, \{d\}\}$

$[\![Student'_{pl}]\!]^M =$
$\{\{a, b\}, \{c, d\}, \{b, c\}, \{a, d\}, \{a, b, c\}, \{a, c, d\}, \{b, c, d\}, \{a, b, c, d\}\}$

For duals and trials etc., denotations can be given equivalently:

(4.58)   Denotation of CN_{du}: $\{X | \ |X| = 2 \ \& \ X \subseteq [\![CN']\!]^M\}$

Denotation of CN_{tri}: $\{X | \ |X| = 3 \ \& \ X \subseteq [\![CN']\!]^M\}$

Quantifiers now must relate these sets of sets in the denotation of the CN to the denotation of the nuclear-scope expression. The quantifier *two*, for example, takes the set of subsets of the restrictor set that contain more than one entity and checks that at least one of these sets has an intersection with the set denoted by the nuclear-scope expression that contains at least two elements. The difference between the universal quantifiers *all* and *every* comes down to a difference in the way they operate over the different denotations of singulars and plurals. So, *all*, which takes a plural common noun, checks that each of the non-singleton sets is a subset of the set of entities denoted by the nuclear-scope expression:

$[\![(All'(Student'_{pl}))(Sing')]\!]^M = 1$ iff for every $Y \in [\![Student'_{pl}]\!]^M$, $Y \subseteq [\![Sing']\!]^M$

Every does exactly the same thing but checks that each **singleton** set is a subset of the set denoted by the nuclear-scope expression:

$[\![(Every'(Student'_{sg}))(Sing')]\!]^M = 1$ iff for every $Y \in [\![Student'_{sg}]\!]^M$, $Y \subseteq [\![Sing']\!]^M$

Notice that the truth conditions are identical and effectively reduce to the standard generalised-quantifier definition that the set of students is a subset of the set of singers.

The introduction of groups into the model theory, while intuitively sound, presents us with a problem. This move to considering the denotation of common nouns as denoting groups raises the type of common-noun phrases to the type we have been assuming for quantified noun phrases, i.e. $(e \rightarrow t) \rightarrow t$. But if common nouns are of type $(e \rightarrow t) \rightarrow t$ then what is the type of a full noun phrase? Now the interpretations we have given to *every/all* and *a* above, although they encode the different denotations of singular and plural noun phrases, nevertheless are truth-conditionally equivalent to the generalised-quantifier denotations given above (and, indeed, the predicate-logic interpretations given in the last chapter). Given this, we could assume that noun phrases need only be of the same type: both common-noun phrases and full noun phrases will have the type

of generalised quantifiers, $(e \rightarrow t) \rightarrow t$. This will require quantifiers themselves to denote functions from sets of sets of entities to sets of sets of entities.
So we would need for (say) *all* to denote a function from the set of subsets
of the set of entities in the denotation of the common-noun phrase to a set
of sets of entities that are supersets of the set denoted by the common noun
phrase, i.e.

$$\text{Functions from } \{Y|Y \subseteq [\![N']\!]^M\} \text{ to } \{X|[\![N']\!]^M \subseteq X\}$$

But notice what happens here: the information provided by the number marking
on the common-noun phrase is simply lost in the output, and, as previously, the
truth conditions for *Every student laughs* and *All students laugh* are the same.
Now it is possible that number marking on nouns is semantically otiose in this
way, but this would make the existence of such a property entirely mysterious
and, more problematically, render anaphoric dependencies completely obscure.
In the examples in (4.59)–(4.60) given as instructions at a boys' boarding school
(thankfully no longer in existence), when the plural form is used in the first sentence, the pronoun has to be plural and, although the use of the plural pronoun
referring back to the singular universal is acceptable because of the development
of the singular reference of *they* to avoid specifying gender, in this context the
more natural pronoun is the singular *he*. This is despite the fact that both *every
boy* and *all boys* have the same semantics.

(4.59)   Every boy must rise at 7.30 a.m. He (?they) must be washed and dressed,
         ready for breakfast at 8.00 a.m.

(4.60)   All boys must rise at 7.30 a.m. They (*he) must be washed and dressed,
         ready for breakfast at 8.00 a.m.

It would seem, therefore, that the number of the common-noun phrase matters
semantically and so should not be lost when combined with a quantifier to make
a noun phrase.

   A more general objection to the suggestion above that number information is
lost is that the principle of compositionality is generally assumed to be *monotonic*. That is, no information is lost as meanings are put together. To adhere to
such a view of compositionality requires a shift in the types associated with quantified noun phrases and a concomitant shift in the type of verb phrases, which
leads to a significant increase in the complexity of the types that we need to analyse natural languages. What we need in order to maintain the number distinction
and its analysis in terms of groups is to say that the denotation of a quantified
noun phrase is a set of sets of sets, i.e. of type:

$$((e \rightarrow t) \rightarrow t) \rightarrow t$$

In this way, *all students* will denote the following, where χ is a variable over sets
of sets of sets of entities:

$$\{\chi | \{Y|Y \subseteq [\![Student']\!]^M \& |Y| > 1\} \subseteq \chi\}$$

In this formula, $\{Y|Y \subseteq [\![Student']\!]^M \& |Y| > 1\}$ is, as we have seen, the set of subsets of students with more than one member and χ is a set of sets of sets of entities: the set of all subsets denoted by the expression in the VP. This means that verb phrases themselves must be of the same type as common nouns:

$$(e \to t) \to t$$

So the VP *sang* denotes the set of all subsets of singing entities:

$$\{Y|Y \subseteq [\![Sing']\!]^M\}$$

which is called the *power set* of the set of singers. So verb phrases no longer just pick out the set of things that have the property expressed by the verb phrase but all possible groups of entities that have that property.

Such *type-raising* has further consequences. For a start, quantifiers must have a type that denotes a relation between two sets of sets (functions from sets of sets of entities to sets of sets of sets of entities):

$$((e \to t) \to t) \to (((e \to t) \to t) \to t)$$

Turning to transitive and ditransitive verbs we would be forced to raise the types of their arguments, giving transitive verbs the type:

$$(((e \to t) \to t) \to t) \to ((e \to t) \to t)$$

By itself, there is nothing technically wrong with making these moves as long as there are means of being able to reduce the complexities thus induced at some level of analysis. But the system is now very far away from the intuition that (distributive) transitive verbs denote relations between individual entities and that intransitive verbs are also about individuals. The problem is that for every apparent additional complexity in the way some denotational property of an expression is characterised, the complexity is not restricted to that expression alone, but also to every expression with which it has to combine, so that raising of types is in principle an indefinitely extendable possibility. The result is entirely contrary to the intuition that humans reason about complex entities as though they were simple, treating plural assertions, in particular, as in some way an assertion about groups directly. This has led to a suggestion to reduce the complexity of the set-theoretic structures apparently required to analyse group-denoting expressions by changing the *ontology* of the model and the nature of what we think as individuals.

Exercise 4.6

Provide model-theoretic definitions of the quantifier phrases below (including the bare plural), maintaining the plurality of the head nouns and the higher types of number-marked noun phrases:

a. Six horses neighed.
b. Some people like beans.

c. No students laughed.

d. No more students than lecturers screamed.

What problems do you encounter?

4.2.2   Extending the ontology

In natural languages, singular count terms, mass terms and plurals have common linguistic properties. They have the distribution of noun phrases (although in some languages singulars may be differentiated from plurals); they can be quantified; and they have identical internal syntactic structure. Mass terms in English can appear without a determiner just as plural ones can:

(4.61)   *Child splashed in the pond.

(4.62)   Children splashed in the pond.

(4.63)   Water splashed in the pond.

Mass terms can appear as subjects of *collective* predicates like *gather* (see 4.2.3), just as plural terms can:

(4.64)   *The child gathered around the pond.

(4.65)   The crowd gathered around the pond.

(4.66)   The children gathered around the pond.

(4.67)   The water gathered in big pools.

Mass terms show *cumulative reference*, i.e. sums of their referents are also part of the extension of such terms (see 4.2.4). Plural terms seem to have this property too:

(4.68)   If the stuff in this glass is water and the stuff in that glass is water, then the stuff in both glasses is water.

(4.69)   If the animals on one farm are (all) horses and the animals on another farm are (all) horses, then the animals on both farms are (all) horses.

From the semantic point of view, however, things are not the same. As we have seen, plural common nouns can be modelled as denoting sets of sets of cardinality greater than 1, based on a set of *atomic*, individual entities. Mass terms, however, denote things that do not contain atomic entities (at least as far as the perceptible world goes):

(4.70)   a. If X is water, then all parts of X are water.
          b. *If X are horses, then all parts of X are horses.

Since mass terms and count terms are treated similarly in natural languages, our semantics should reflect this similarity. So we need a theory that provides a unitary representation that brings out the common properties of plurals, mass terms and singular terms; and an interpretation that gives a general characterisation of the semantic structures associated with such representations.

In order to capture the similarities and differences between plurality and mass, it has been suggested (by Godehard Link) that we move away from strict set theory and extend our concept of *individual* to cover plural as well as singular entities. In other words, we treat the phrase *Mary and John* as denoting a plural individual that contains two *atomic* parts, John and Mary. If we go down this route, then it becomes possible to avoid the explosion of types noted at the end of the last section, because we can treat groups of entities as being of the same types as single individuals, i.e. of type *e*.

How can this be done? Up until now, we have been treating the universe of discourse in our models as unstructured sets, just a bundle of individual entities. However, to achieve the effect we want, we can structure our ontology in such a way that we can identify certain entities as being 'part of' other entities, technically known as a *mereology*. Consider Figure 4.4, which shows the *power set* of the set of numbers {1, 2, 3, 4} (i.e. the set of all subsets of the first four cardinal numbers). In this diagram, the sets are structured according to the elements they share, indicated by the lines that join the nodes together. Following the lines up the diagram you get the union, ∪, of the sets linked upwards to that node (more generally called the *join* ⊔) and following the lines down the diagram you get

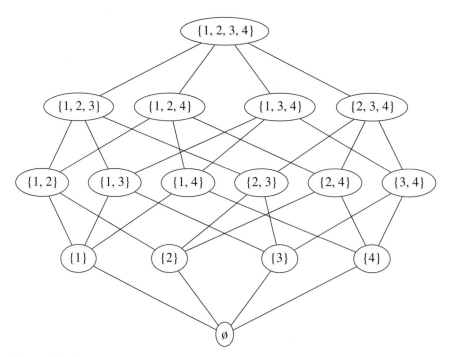

Figure 4.4: *The power set of* {1, 2, 3, 4}.

the *intersection* ∩ (or *meet* ⊓) of the sets linked downwards to that node. The top-node is known as the *supremum* (⊤) and the bottom point the *infimum* (⊥).

We can use such a structure to model the notion of *plural individuals*. In other words, we can assume that entities can be combined in the same way with entities higher up the structure having more complexity (being composed of more individuals) than those lower down. Technically this structure is a *Boolean algebra* which has well-defined logical properties with respect to the connectives ∧ 'and', ¬ 'not' and ∨ 'or' – which we will not be going into here.

We can extend this algebraic structure down to the level of *individuals*, real individuals that is, and treat the ontology of our models as a partially ordered set, a *poset*, over the set of entities. The set is partially ordered because not every individual is related by the 'part of' relation (≤) to every other individual. So, in effect, our ontology is now a set of entities *A* that is partially structured by the 'part of' relation ≤: ⟨*A*, ≤⟩. However, to model the domain of individual entities we do not want the infimum (⊥), here the empty set, because 'nothing' is not part of an individual. This has the consequence that we do not get the complete structure of a Boolean algebra as in Figure 4.4.

In this connection, consider a simple model containing just three elements, *a*, *b*, and *c* and a connective ⊕ which connects atomic elements to provide their *individual sums* (*i-sum*). We then get the structure in Figure 4.5. Notice that all the elements in Figure 4.5 (*a*, *b*, *c*, *a* ⊕ *b*, *a* ⊕ *c*, *c* ⊕ *b*, *a* ⊕ *b* ⊕ *c*) are all of denotation type *e*, i.e. entities. Groups are thus defined as i-sums and have the same status as single individual entities except that the latter, being *atomic*, have no further parts of the same sort (although, of course, they may have parts of a different sort). By allowing the ontology to be structured, we can dispense with the higher types required with sets that we saw earlier (because we know that the structured set of entities has the structure of a power set without an infimum – the empty set). We thus countenance the following new object:

a ⊕ *b* is the individual sum of *a* and *b*

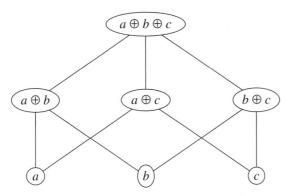

Figure 4.5: *The individual sum structure of* {*a*, *b*, *c*}.

In Figure 4.5, individual a is part of individual $a \oplus b$ ($a \leq a \oplus b$) but not of individual $b \oplus c$ and plural individual $a \oplus b$ is part of $a \oplus b \oplus c$, as is individual $b \oplus c$, and so on. Given plural objects, we actually have two *part-of* ($\leq$) relations holding between entities:

(4.71)   a. $a \leq_i b$: a is an *individual part* of b

$a \leq_i b \leftrightarrow a \oplus b = b$ (i.e. union or join)

$John \leq_i John \oplus Mary$

   b. $a \leq_a b$: a is an *atomic part* of b

$a \leq_a b \leftrightarrow (a \oplus b = b$ and a is an atom)

$Prudence \leq_a Prudence \oplus Conan \oplus Rambo$
$Prudence \oplus Rambo \not\leq_a Prudence \oplus Conan \oplus Rambo$
$Prudence \oplus Rambo \leq_i Prudence \oplus Conan \oplus Rambo$

We will here take the relations $\oplus, \leq_i, \leq_a$ as being semantic relations, i.e. things defined in the model theory,[4] and moreover assume that they are denoted by the logical predicates $\wedge_i$ (individual join), I-part (individual part) and A-part (atomic part), respectively. So we can define further notions. As already noted, single individual entities are *atomic*, expressed by the predicate At', defined as entities which have no further subparts of the same sort:

$At'(a) \leftrightarrow (\forall x[\text{I-part}(x, a) \rightarrow x = a])$ 'The only individual part of a is a itself.'

Conjoining simple individual expressions is straightforward. The semantics of the phrase *John and Mary* is represented as $j \wedge_i m$ and interpreted as $[\![j]\!]^M \oplus [\![m]\!]^M$, the individual sum of John and Mary.

Modifying the rest of the system so that it works with plural individuals is fairly straightforward. We will not go into much detail, but what we need to do is to assume that predicates can have a *group predicate* reading whereby the predicate denotes not just the set of atomic individuals that have a certain property but also the individual sums of all those atomic parts that form the denotation of the individual predicate. For any (simple) predicate, P, therefore, we take $*P$ to be the group predicate based on P denoting the set of the atoms and individual sums of atoms in P. So if the property Cat' denotes the set $\{a, b, c\}$ then $*Cat'$ denotes:

$$\{a, b, c, a \oplus b, a \oplus c, b \oplus c, a \oplus b \oplus c\}$$

'Plural' can then be defined as that set of individuals that excludes all the atomic parts. For CNs denoting *properties* like *cat*, the *plural* is simply all the non-atomic i-sums in $*P$:

$$P_{pl} = \lambda u[*P(u) \wedge \neg At'(u)]$$

---

[4] Actually, things are a bit more complicated than this (see Further reading), but what we have should be sufficient to understand the general idea.

So Cat_{pl} denotes:

$$\{a \oplus b, a \oplus c, b \oplus c, a \oplus b \oplus c\}$$

Note that the singular picks out only atomic entities:

$$P_{sg} = \lambda u[^*P(u) \wedge At'(u)]$$

So now we have a characterisation of plurality that does not involve greater type-raising: plural predicates are of type $e \to t$ just as singular ones are. So definitions of generalised quantifiers remain pretty much the same **except** that those that take plural common nouns operate only on the plural.

(4.72)   a. *Every student*: $Every'(Student'_{sg})$ denotes the set of all sets that are supersets of the set of atomic parts denoted by $^*Student'$
$\{X | [\![Student'_{sg}]\!]^M \subseteq X\}$
$\equiv \{X | [\![\lambda u[^*Student'(u) \wedge At'(u)]]\!] \subseteq X\}$
$\equiv \{X | [\![Student']\!]^M \subseteq X\}$

b. *All students*: $All'(Student'_{pl})$ denotes the set of all sets that are supersets of all the non-atomic parts of $^*Student'$
$\{X | [\![Student'_{pl}]\!]^M \subseteq X\}$
$\equiv \{X | [\![\lambda u[^*Student'(u) \wedge \neg At'(u)]]\!]^M \subseteq X\}$
$\equiv \{X | ([\![^*Student']\!]^M - [\![Student']\!]^M) \subseteq X\}$

> ### Exercise 4.7
>
> Revisit the example sentences from the end of the last section and re-define their representations and interpretations using the notion of plural individual found in this section. What problems are solved and what new problems arise, if any?

4.2.3   Collective and distributive predicates

Once we start addressing predicate denotations in terms of groups, further distinctions can be formally expressed. A distinction is traditionally made between *distributive* predicates, where the property expressed by the predicate holds of each element denoted by a plural expression (4.73), and *collective* predicates, where the expressed property holds only of a whole group (4.74). Some predicates are ambiguous between distributive and collective readings (4.75).

(4.73)   John and Mary were singing. $\vdash$ John was singing.
Some students were drunk. $\vdash$ A student was drunk.

(4.74)   John and Mary met yesterday. $\nvdash$?Mary met yesterday.
Some students gathered at the door. $\nvdash$?A student gathered at the door.

(4.75)   Three students lifted a table (together). $\nvdash$ A student lifted a table.
Three students (each) lifted a table. $\vdash$ A student lifted a table.

All the example sentences that we have been using in our discussion so far have had distributive predicates in them, so that each entity in the denotation of the subject has the property expressed by the verb phrase.

(4.76)   John and Mary sang. ≡ John sang and Mary sang.

(4.77)   Three men and one woman live at Highgrove. ≡
           Three men live at Highgrove and one woman lives at Highgrove.

For purely distributive predicates like *sing*, all we need to assume is that one can derive a group denotation from the simple set denotation, as we did above with common nouns, by using the * operator:

(4.78)   A *distributive predicate* is one whose denotation contains only atoms:

$$Distr'(P) \leftrightarrow \forall x[P(x) \rightarrow At'(x)]$$

For a distributive predicate P, the associated group predicate is *P which denotes the set of all the individual sums of atomic individuals in P (including the atoms themselves). So *Every student is singing* is semantically represented as:

$$Every'(Student'_{sg})(^*Sing')$$

which is true in a model M just in case:

$$[\![Student'_{sg}]\!]^M \subseteq [\![^*Sing']\!]^M$$

Since $[\![Student'_{sg}]\!]^M$ is defined as a set of atomic individuals and $[\![^*Sing']\!]^M$ by definition contains atomic individuals, then this is equivalent to:

$$[\![Student']\!]^M \subseteq [\![Sing']\!]^M$$

Similarly, *All students are singing* is represented as:

$$All'(Student'_{pl})(^*Sing')$$

which is true in model M just in case:

$$[\![Student'_{pl}]\!]^M \subseteq [\![^*Sing']\!]^M$$

Given that $[\![Student'_{pl}]\!]^M$ denotes the set of all non-atomic individuals constructed from $[\![Student']\!]^M$, this is true just in case: $[\![^*Sing']\!]^M$ contains such a set. Since *sing* is entirely distributive, this is equivalent to:

$$[\![Student']\!]^M \subseteq [\![Sing']\!]^M$$

In these cases the grammatical number has made no difference to the interpretation, but there are some predicates which impose a collective interpretation on their subjects, and, in these cases, number does have an effect, a fact which we are now able to reflect in the analysis:

(4.79)   John and Mary met. ≡ John met Mary and Mary met John.
           (**not** *John met and Mary met.)

(4.80)   Two drummers and three guitarists combined to form a new band.
         (**not** Two drummers combined to form a new band and three guitarists
         combined to form a new band.)

(4.81)   Those two students are a couple.
         (**not** *That student is a couple and that student is a couple.)

(4.82)   The students gathered for a party.
         (Does not entail ?*A student gathered for a party.)

In other words, some predicates are inherently group denoting. Thus, a verb like
laugh inherently denotes a set of entities and its group denotation is the set of
all i-sums of the individuals in this set. But a verb like *gather* lexically denotes a
set of i-sums and **no** atoms, i.e. the set of all groups (individual sums) of entities
that gather where each group has more than one member.

(4.83) $[\![Laugh']\!]^M = \{a, b, c\}$
         $[\![*Laugh']\!]^M = \{a, b, c, a \oplus b, b \oplus c, a \oplus c, a \oplus b \oplus c\}$

(4.84) $[\![Gather']\!]^M = \{a \oplus b, c \oplus d \oplus e\}$

A predicate P is *collective* just in case no element in the denotation of P is
atomic:

(4.85) $Coll'(P) \leftrightarrow \forall x[P(x) \rightarrow \neg At'(x)]$

Note that with a purely collective predicate you do get differences between singular and plural noun phrases. Thus, *?Every student gathered for the party* will
necessarily be false because the denotation of *every student* contains only atomic
elements, whereas that of *gather* contains only non-atomic individuals. *All (the)
students gathered for the party* will, however, be contingently true or false (i.e.
depending on the model).

   Note further that the semantics of the verb again determines whether a sentence can be interpreted distributively or not; and here we face the first glimpse of
the potential complexity involved in the semantics of individual words. Lexical
semantics for a word must, on this view, provide the basis for different types
of interpretation and can determine quite complex entailments. For example, the
transitive version of the verb *marry* denotes a relation between two individuals
(assuming a monogamous culture), the subject and the object. Its intransitive
counterpart expresses the same relation, but now the two individuals involved
are expressed by the subject.

(4.86)   *marry$_{IV}$* denotes a set of non-atomic entities, $a \oplus b$, such that 'a
         marries$_{TV}$ b':
         $[\![Marry'_{IV}]\!]^M = \{a \oplus b | \langle a, b \rangle \in [\![Marry'_{TV}]\!]^M\}$

This ensures that (in any model), if *John and Mary married* is true then so is *John
married Mary* (and by symmetry *Mary married John*) but **not** *John married*.

   As noted above, certain predicates are ambiguous between collective and
distributive readings, such as the transitive use of the verb *sing*:

(4.87)   John and Mary sang the song.

(4.88)   John and Mary together sang the song.

(4.89)   John and Mary individually and on different occasions sang the song.

Semantically ambiguous expressions are normally disambiguated at the level of representation (to allow the interpretation procedure to carry out its work straightforwardly), though such distinct but related interpretations for a single word is a matter we return to in Chapter 8. Godehard Link (and others) assume that VPs basically denote group objects (i.e. sets of sets of entities of any cardinality) and utilise a *distributive operator* ^{D} that takes scope over a verb phrase to determine distributive readings. Consider possible representations of the content of *Four students lifted the table*, which may be interpreted as depicting just one event (all four students together lifted the table) or as many as four (each individual lifted the table separately).

(4.90) $Four'(Student'_{pl})(*Lift'(The'(Table')))$ (Possibly) Collective

(4.91) $Four'(Student'_{pl})^D(*Lift'(The'(Table')))$ Distributive

The distributive operator then just picks out all atomic i-parts of an argument and asserts the predicate to be true of these:

$$^{D*}P \leftrightarrow \lambda x \forall u[\text{A-part}(u, x) \rightarrow P(u)]$$

What this says is that $^{D*}P$ denotes a set of group individuals such that if x is a member of $*P$, then all its individual parts are members of the set denoted by the *atomic* predicate P.

(4.92)   a. $[\![Four'(Student'_{pl})]\!]^M$
             $= \{X||X \cap [\![\lambda u[*Student'(u) \wedge \neg At'(u)]]\!]^M| \geq 4\}$
          b. $[\![*(Lift'(The'(Table')))]\!]^M$
             $=$ some set of sets of entities who lifted the table either individually or collectively.
          c. $^D[\![*(Lift'(The'(Table')))]\!]^M$
             $=$ some set of entities based on $[\![*(Lift'(The'(Table')))]\!]^M$ who lifted the table individually
             $(=$ the set of entities who make up the atomic members of
             $[\![*(Lift'(The'(Table')))]\!]^M$).

Notice again that the lexical semantics of the predicate will determine whether the use of the distributive operator makes any sense. Since *gather* will have no atoms in its denotation (as required by its lexical meaning), the distributive operator will always yield the null set. So $Four(Student'_{pl})^D(Gather')$ will always be false since $^D(Gather')$ will always denote the null set. Where there is more than one quantified NP in a sentence, the number of ambiguities increases according to the scope of quantifiers and the scope of the distributive operator. We will not, however, go any further into these matters.

Exercise 4.8

How many readings do the following sentences have, what are they and where does any ambiguity arise? Where ambiguities don't arise, say why not.

a. Five lawyers hired a secretary.
b. Five boys ate seven pizzas.
c. Every student met some lecturers.
d. Some students and some lecturers met in the bar.
e. All the students saw different films.
f. No lawyers hired three secretaries.

Exercise 4.9

Using the representation system that allows plural individuals, give the representations for all readings of the following sentences with a description of their truth conditions:

a. Five students attacked two lecturers.
b. Some men are anxious.
c. Lou, Kim and Sandy met in a bar.
d. Many students spoke to some lecturers.

4.2.4   Mass terms

One of the interesting things about shifting the ontological perspective in this way is that it allows us to begin modelling the semantics of *mass terms*. The only difference between the denotations of mass terms and count terms is that the former are substances which do not have atoms: i.e. all parts of the stuff denoted share the property of being that stuff (at least down to humanly relevant levels). So all parts of water are water. The 'part of' relation for substances is thus slightly different from that of countable things in that it constitutes a *material-part* relation:

(4.93) $a \leq_m b$: a is a *material part* of b

$a \leq_m b \leftrightarrow a + b = b$

'water' $\leq_m$ 'pond'

The operator that combines bits of the same substance is also slightly different. While $a \oplus b$ is the *individual sum* of a and b, $a + b$ is defined to be the *material fusion* of a and b. So, $a + b$ is not the same as $a \oplus b$ but $a + b$ may be *constitutive* of $a \oplus b$. For example, if a and b are gold rings, then $a \oplus b$ is the collection (plural object) of a and b while $a + b$ is the gold that makes up those rings. This allows us to refer to objects and the stuff that makes them up in separate ways. The sentence *The gold in these new rings is old* is obviously not contradictory: oldness is predicated of the stuff that makes up the rings whereas newness is predicated of the objects (rings) constructed from the old stuff. So we say of all the material parts of the two rings r_1 (denoting a) and r_2 (denoting b) that they are in the denotation of Old' and that the plural individual consisting of the two rings is in the denotation of New' ('m-part' stands for *material part*):

$$\exists r_1 \exists r_2 \forall m[Ring'(r_1) \wedge Ring'(r_2) \wedge {}^*New'(r_1 \wedge_i r_2) \wedge (\text{m-part}(m, r_1 \wedge_i r_2) \rightarrow Old'(m))]$$

Finally we noted above that both plurals and mass terms share the property of *cumulativity*:

(4.94)   If the liquid in this cup is tea and the liquid in that cup is tea, then the liquid in both cups is tea.

(4.95)   If the students in the semantics class are clever and the students in the syntax class are clever, then the students in both classes are clever.

If a predicate is *cumulative*, then the following postulate holds:

(4.96)   Cumulative reference:

$Cumul'(P) \leftrightarrow \forall x \forall y[P(x) \wedge P(y) \rightarrow P(x \wedge y)]$ where $\wedge$ may be individual joining ($a \oplus b$) or material joining ($a + b$).

There is, of course, more to say about the interpretation of mass terms and count terms, including whether the distinction is robust, given that mass terms can be used as count terms and vice versa (a process we might call *coercion*). For example, it is possible to use mass terms as count (4.97) and count terms as mass (4.98):

(4.97)   Barry drank three beers last night.

(4.98)   You don't get a lot of house for two hundred thousand these days.

Such examples pose serious problems for denotational semantics since they bring into focus the fact that humans are able to change the way they talk about things, according to the point of view taken. So the question arises as to whether the things mass and count terms denote vary according to the terms' use as mass or count, or whether it is the conceptualisation of the things denoted that changes. This again brings into question the relationship between what's in the mind and what's in the world. Such concerns will surface again in different domains throughout this book (see especially Chapters 6 and 8).

4.3   Coda

By extending our ontology to include mereological structures, we can provide a more wide-ranging account of the semantics of noun phrases while maintaining an analysis that does not require ever more complex semantic types.

Nonetheless, the differentiation between discrete mereological concepts is opening up a different basis of complexity. Recall from section 4.2.1 that the move to positing a more complex ontology was made in the face of the threat of spiralling levels of complexity in generalised-quantifier theory in tackling plurality. Since this complexity arises because of the commitment to expressing compositionality of content explicitly through the types, this problem threatens to arise in all new areas to which the formal-semantic tools are applied. Yet the development of mereological concepts poses its own complexity, in itself introducing a major new challenge for natural-language semantics. Again, with the various different distinctions to be drawn out, as between distributive and cumulative interpretations, we face threatening ambiguity. So it appears that whichever way we move in the formal-semantic modelling of natural-language content, the outcome involves a rich and abstract relation between expressions of the language and the denotata that we use our languages to talk about. A further problem emerged in probing the context-dependence displayed by some quantifiers. In using generalised-quantifier theory as a means of expressing context-dependent quantifier construals, it appears that all that can be provided is a characterisation of the output of any such contextual fixing of values, hence as a phenomenon of semantic ambiguity. At least this is the case if generalised-quantifier theory is to be seen as a grammar-internal component, articulating a general set of principles for establishing content for natural-language sentences in a fully compositional way. Since any such move risks not providing a general basis for explaining the systemic nature of context-dependence in natural-language construal, it is to the challenge posed by context-dependent expressions that we now turn.

4.4   Further reading

The literature on quantification in general and generalised quantifiers in particular is vast and growing (try googling on 'generalised quantifier') and we can do little more than indicate some of the introductory and seminal texts, as they relate to linguistics (rather than logic or computational modelling). There are detailed introductions to generalised quantifiers in Partee *et al.* (1990: ch. 14); Cann (1993: ch. 6); Keenan (1996); Keenan and Westerståhl (1997); Heim and Kratzer (1998); Chierchia and McConnell-Ginet (2000: ch. 9). The decomposition of quantified NPs using the λ-operator can be found in Montague (1973) and Dowty *et al.* (1981: 104–11). The primary literature on generalised quantifiers has grown steadily since the publication of Barwise and Cooper (1981). See, for example, Zwarts (1983); van Benthem (1986: chs. 1, 3); Keenan and Stavi (1986); and also the papers in Bach *et al.* (1995) and van der Does and van Eijck (1996). Some work has been done on developing proof theories for generalised quantifiers, see van Lambalgen (1996). McCawley (1981: ch. 14) discusses other

According to the standard interpretation of quantification in predicate logic there is no particular individual, a student, who is referred to in the above, it is merely asserted that the set of students is non-empty. Recall also the interpretation of indefinite noun phrases in Chapter 4 (previously and above):

(5.34) $[\![A'(Student')]\!]^M = \{X \mid [\![Student']\!]^M \cap X \neq \emptyset\}$

This point of view seems to be correct on the basis of other examples involving quantificational phrases and the pronouns they are associated with:

(5.35)   No student said he was clever.

Since *no student* cannot be said to refer to any individual student, the pronoun *he* cannot be taken to refer to any student, either. However, the use of the pronoun above is felicitous, even though there is no referent for it to be associated with. For this reason, Geach argued, pronouns occurring along with their antecedent in a single natural-language sentence can be treated instead as the bound variables of a predicate logic language. (5.35) should be translated as:

(5.36) $\neg[\exists x.Student'(x) \wedge Say'(x, Clever'(x))]$

This way of treating pronouns is also justified on the basis of universal quantification. For example, when using a quantificational noun phrase like *every student*, there is no reference to a single individual in the domain. Nevertheless, a singular pronoun can be used at least within the boundaries of a single sentence. As a result, the pronoun *he* below can best be interpreted as a non-referential term. It can be taken instead as translated as the variable x bound by the universal quantifier introduced by *every*:

(5.37)   Every student said he was clever.
          $\forall x.Student'(x) \rightarrow Say'(x, Clever'(x))$

In fact, this assumption seems also to be justified by the fact that such pronouns do not seem to behave in the same way as pronouns of laziness. Compare the sentences and their logical representations above with the following:

(5.38)   A student said a student was clever.

(5.39)   Every student said every student was clever.

The translations of the above in predicate logic are as follows:

(5.40) $\exists x.Student'(x) \wedge Say'(x, [\exists y.Student'(y) \wedge Clever'(y)])$

(5.41) $\forall x.Student'(x) \rightarrow [Say'(x, [\forall y.Student'(y) \rightarrow Clever'(y)])]$

Given the distinct truth conditions normally associated with the formulae (5.40)–(5.41) and the sentences in (5.32) and (5.37), it seems that the claim that at least some uses of pronouns correspond to bound variables, is justified.

5.2.2   E-type pronouns

If it is the case that sometimes pronouns behave as free variables (indexical uses) and sometimes as bound variables, the question arises whether there are any restrictions as to when such uses are allowed. Clearly there are differences in interpretation: compare the interpretation of *he* in (5.42), (5.43) and (5.44).

(5.42)   A student went to school and he was clever.

(5.43)   Every student went to school and he was clever.

(5.44)   No student went to school and he was clever.

It seems that we cannot get an interpretation of *he* in (5.43) and (5.44) above as a variable bound by the quantifier, i.e. within its scope: *he* can only be interpreted as referring to a male individual somehow salient in the discourse context but not necessarily a student.

This inability to interpret a pronoun as bound is sometimes attributed to the syntactic relations holding between the quantificational noun phrases and the pronouns, in particular the syntactic relation of *c-command*.[2] Whether or not the effect of scope is to be attributed to syntax or semantics (and we do not go into the issue here), there remain problems, in that certain examples of pronouns do show an apparent dependency on a quantifier, even though their syntactic structure appears to disallow treating them as bound variables. For example, consider the following:

(5.45)   A man was happy. He was going home.

(5.46)   If a man is happy, he is going home.

(5.47)   Every man who owns a donkey feeds it.

(5.48)   If a man owns a donkey, he feeds it.

In (5.45) the existential quantifier translating the indefinite cannot extend its scope to bind the variable translating the pronoun *he*, under the assumption that sentences translate into complete propositional formulae with all variables bound. The same problem appears in (5.46)–(5.48), where the quantificational expression is said to be too deeply embedded within the relative clause or the conditional antecedent to bind the pronouns *he* and *it*. Nevertheless the reference of the pronouns seems to co-vary with the choice of individuals quantified over, suggesting some kind of binding by the quantifier (these sentences are traditionally called *donkey sentences* and were introduced as puzzles for natural-language semantics in Geach 1962). Evans (1980) suggested that the above phenomena indicate yet one more use of pronouns, which he called the *E-type* use. Two types of argument were used to show that E-type pronoun uses were different

---

[2] A very simplified definition of c-command is as follows: A c-commands B if the first node above A on the syntactic tree contains B, or B is located somewhere below it, see Reinhart (1983).

from bound-variable uses. First, if the E-type pronoun was interpreted as a bound variable, some device should be used to extend the scope of the quantifier beyond its syntactic domain. However, Evans showed that, even if this non-standard avenue was taken, the truth conditions of sentences with the scope of the quantifier extended were distinct from the truth conditions of the sentences that contained the E-type pronouns. So consider for example:

(5.49)   Just one man was happy. He was going home.

The translation of the above in predicate logic with the pronoun *he* taken as a bound variable would be as follows (where $\exists!x.Man'(x)$ stands for the translation of *just one man*):

(5.50) $\exists!x.Man'(x) \wedge Happy'(x) \wedge Go\text{-}home'(x)$

However, the above logical form does not seem to express correctly the (at least most salient) truth conditions of (5.49). This is because the formula seems to require that there is a single man who both had the property of being happy and going home, without requiring that there is a single man who is happy *simpliciter*. The discourse in (5.49), though, seems to be asserting just that.

The above failure of the bound variable interpretation of the pronoun to provide satisfactory truth conditions for the sentence containing it was one of the reasons why Evans took such uses as distinct, i.e. E-type. A second (perhaps less convincing) way in which such pronouns were taken to be different was the fact that such pronouns seem to impute a certain *uniqueness*, in the case of singular pronouns, or *maximality*, in the case of plurals, to the sets of entities verifying the sentences containing the antecedent quantificational expressions. Consider the following:

(5.51)   Socrates owned a dog. It bit him.

(5.52)   Few congressmen admire Bush and they are very junior.

(5.53)   John owns three sheep and Mary vaccinates them.

Evans's point is that over and above the fact that the E-type pronouns in (5.51)–(5.53) cannot be interpreted as bound variables (at least in their most salient reading) there also seems to be an implication in (5.51)–(5.53) respectively that (a) Socrates only had one dog, (b) Bush is admired only by few congressmen and (c) John owns only three sheep.

On the basis of the assumption that in (5.51) it is implied that Socrates had a unique dog picked out by the pronoun in the second conjunct and in (5.52) and (5.53) the plural pronouns pick out the *maximal* set of individuals that verify the first conjunct (i.e. **all** the verifying individuals), Evans argued that E-type pronouns are to be taken, instead of bound variables, as *definite descriptions*. Under this view, such pronouns are not interpreted directly, but rather first replaced by a description whose content is derived from the previous sentential context. According to Bertrand Russell's analysis, definites are associated with a uniqueness requirement regarding their referent, which is what distinguishes them from indefinites. So the translation of *the dog bit Socrates* is as follows:

(5.54) $\exists x[Dog'(x) \wedge \forall y[Dog'(y) \leftrightarrow x = y] \wedge Bite'(x, Socrates')]$

This formula requires there to be only one dog that bit Socrates because of the use of the *equivalence* connective $\leftrightarrow$ and the identity requirement it imposes.[3] A dog is asserted to exist that bit Socrates and that everything that is a dog is the dog that bit Socrates.

(5.12), repeated here, shows that it is possible to give a generalised-quantifier interpretation to the definite article which conforms with the Russellian analysis:

(5.12) $[\![The'(N')]\!]^M = \{X \mid |[\![N']\!]^M \cap X| = 1\}$

The generalised-quantifier semantics of definite noun phrases is principally determined by the grammatical number of the head noun: singular noun phrases refer to a single entity whereas plural definites refer to sets of two or more entities. In addition, it seems to be implied that the unique set satisfying the semantic contribution of the common noun is the maximal collection of such entities in the model:

(5.55)   *The dogs barked* is true iff the maximal set of dogs, whose cardinality is greater than 1, barked.

This kind of semantics associated with definite descriptions is, according to Evans, what explains the *uniqueness* or *maximality* requirements on the sets of entities that constitute the interpretations of E-type pronouns. These pronouns are replaced by such descriptions during the course of interpretation. For example, in (5.51), the interpretation assigned to the whole sentence would be along the lines of what is expressed in (5.56):

(5.56)   Socrates has a dog and the dog Socrates has bit Socrates.

Similarly, in a more explicit rendering of (5.52) and (5.53), plural descriptions have to be substituted for the pronouns as in (5.57)–(5.58) respectively to get an effect equivalent to what (5.52) and (5.53) express:

(5.57)   Few congressmen admire Bush and the congressmen who admire Bush are very junior.

(5.58)   John owns three sheep and Mary vaccinates the sheep that John owns.

So the intuitions of uniqueness and maximality, associated with the sets satisfying the first conjuncts of such sentences, are attributed to the definite descriptions which replace the pronouns in the second conjunct.

---

[3] $\leftrightarrow$, which we did not discuss in detail in Chapters 2 and 3 because it does not really reflect the semantics of any simple natural-language expression, is interpreted just like mutual implication, so that $p \leftrightarrow q$ has the same meaning as $(p \rightarrow q) \wedge (q \rightarrow p)$. Truth conditionally this has the effect that $p \leftrightarrow q$ is true just in case they both have the same truth value. (Try showing this by drawing the truth-table for $(p \rightarrow q) \wedge (q \rightarrow p)$.)

It has been pointed out, however, that the requirements that the E-type analysis of pronouns places on the interpretation of sentences containing them cannot always be sustained. Consider the following:

(5.59)   Any philosopher who owns a dog feeds it vegetables.

(5.60)   Everyone who buys a sage plant in this shop gets eight others along with it.

The pronoun *it* in the sentences above must be interpreted as an E-type pronoun, since it occurs outside the scope of the quantificational expression which provides its antecedent. However, it is not necessarily the case that we should require that only philosophers who own just one dog should be quantified over, or that we must be able to distinguish a unique sage plant among the nine bought by each buyer. The same considerations apply for the next examples. Notice, for example, with (5.62), it is impossible to distinguish a unique Orthodox priest in each situation where we are able to verify the sentence:

(5.61)   If a woman shares an apartment with another woman, she shares the housework with her without negotiation (whereas if a woman shares an apartment with a man, there tends to be explicit negotiation as to who should do what).

(5.62)   If an Orthodox priest meets another Orthodox priest in church he blesses him.

Therefore, either the E-type account of such pronouns is mistaken, or the uniqueness/maximality presuppositions associated with definite descriptions must be dispensed with. The latter is the view taken by many in the literature, who would like to maintain the E-type analysis of such pronouns (see Further reading).

Evans's account, although attempting to unify uses of pronouns with referential and quantificational antecedents by reducing bound readings to sentence internal coreference,[4] in fact ends up introducing a new ambiguity in the interpretation of pronouns since, in his view, E-type pronouns cannot be assimilated to any other category. This was in addition to postulating indexical uses of pronouns, which like many other philosophers he took to be yet another distinct type. Evans clearly states that there are interpretations of pronouns that are solely governed by context-independent linguistic rules (sentence-internal coreference and E-type readings), whereas the indexical uses have to be accounted for by a separate component of the interpretive mechanisms, namely *pragmatics*. There have been many modifications of Evans's original account, which place more or less burden on the syntax, semantics or pragmatics in order to derive the requisite interpretations of E-type pronouns as definite descriptions (see e.g. Cooper 1979, Neale 1990 and Further reading).

---

[4] See Evans 1980.

Exercise 5.1

a. Explain informally your intuitions regarding whether the pronouns in (5.51)–(5.53) can or cannot be taken as variables bound by the quantifiers that are introduced by their antecedents. If you want to show the corresponding logical forms, for the purposes of this exercise, assume that *few* can be represented as the quantifier Few' and *three* as $\exists_3 x$.

b. Do you agree with Evans's interpretation of the above examples? If you disagree, construct alternative examples and contexts which refute Evans's assumption.

5.3 Discourse Representation Theory (DRT)

The solution to the problem posed by sentences which involve E-type interpretations for pronouns and the puzzle regarding the interpretation of so-called *donkey sentences* are taken to indicate the need for a distinct approach to meaning in natural languages. This approach requires taking into account, in addition to truth-conditional content, the impact of the context in which processing of discourse occurs, rather than simply providing interpretations for isolated sentences. We will explore the issues raised in section 5.2 in terms of a theory of *discourse* (utterances containing more than one sentence) called Discourse Representation Theory.

5.3.1 Introduction

The tradition in which Evans's account belongs is that of philosophers and logicians who have looked at natural languages from the point of view of the analysis of formal languages (see Chapter 3, section 3.6.2, and Chapter 4). Montague (1974) in particular, stated that, exactly as for formal languages, it was possible to define truth directly for structured natural-language strings. Even though his semantics included an intermediate translation to a formal language (his Intensional Logic) he showed that the translation could be dispensed with and is presented as merely a convenience of notation. In Montague Grammar and similar types of formal semantics, each wellformed sentence is taken to express a truth-evaluable proposition, and no level above the sentence is recognised as relevant to interpretation. The context in which each sentence is processed (textual, discourse or dialogue) is not taken into account when sentences are interpreted. The only concession is that the circumstances in which the sentence is evaluated (time, situation of utterance, etc.) are treated as just a set of alternative parameters, antecedently given in the model, in terms of which interpretations are defined (see Lewis 1970). From this point of view, if linguistic items are found to behave distinctly depending on their extra-sentential context of occurrence, then the only recourse is to characterise them as **ambiguous** and define distinct semantic rules which will derive each type of interpretation. This is why, as we saw above, E-type pronouns have to be characterised as yet another type of pronoun, given that they do not conform to the usual treatment of pronouns as variables (free or bound). One of the reasons given for this distinct treatment is that, if E-type pronouns were to be represented as regular bound variables, they would seem to require, contrary to standard assumptions, scope extensions for the quantifiers beyond the sentence in which the quantifier occurs. Take for example *indefinites*. Russell (1919) suggested that indefinite descriptions must be translated as existential quantifiers in predicate logic. This view explains the plausible translation of (5.63) as (5.64):

(5.63)   A donkey came in.

(5.64) $\exists x.Donkey'(x) \wedge Come\text{-}in'(x)$

As we saw in Chapter 4, this view is maintained in generalised-quantifier accounts of the semantics of noun phrases in natural languages. Now consider again the following sentences (as we said above these sentences are tradition-ally called *donkey sentences* and were introduced as puzzles for natural-language anaphora by Geach 1962):

(5.65)   If a farmer owns a donkey, he feeds it.

(5.66)   Every farmer who owns a donkey feeds it.

If we translate both the above into standard predicate-logic notation, in neither can the interpretation of the pronouns be taken as bound variable as in both cases they occur outside the scope of the relevant quantifiers:

(5.67) $\exists x[Farmer'(x) \wedge \exists y[Donkey'(y) \wedge Own'(x, y)]] \rightarrow Feed'(x, y)$

The formula above might seem like an appropriate translation to provide the truth conditions, but contains the free variables x and y which therefore do not allow an interpretation where all the pairs of farmers and the donkeys they own must also be pairs where the farmer feeds the donkey for the sentences to be true. It has accordingly been claimed that the truth conditions for both the above sentences should be expressed in predicate logic with the existential quantifiers translated as wide-scoping universal quantifiers as follows:

(5.68) $\forall x \forall y[[(Farmer'(x) \wedge Donkey'(y) \wedge Own'(x, y)] \rightarrow Feed'(x, y)]$

As this is not a translation that can be derived compositionally from the surface syntax of the relevant sentences, it has been assumed that the natural-language surface forms of donkey sentences are misleading. If the representation in (5.68) is taken as expressing the correct translation for (5.65) and (5.66), we have here once again an instance of the general problem of threatening ambiguity identified in sections 5.2.1–5.2.2 with respect to distinct types of pronouns; but this time it affects the interpretation of indefinites. An indefinite description like *a donkey* according to this must be ambiguous as in some cases it has to be translated as an existential quantifier (e.g. in (5.63)) and in others as a universal (e.g. in (5.65)–(5.66)). This is because if we take *a donkey* uniformly as an existential quantifier in (5.65)–(5.66) we immediately get the problem of the pronoun *it* not being able to be bound by the existential quantifier as it is outside its scope.

The problems identified above with respect to the interpretation of E-type pronouns and indefinite descriptions are not random and unconnected. Many researchers have observed that texts and discourses display internal *cohesion*, which cannot be explained by taking each sentence individually in sequence and interpreting it out of its context. Anaphoric connections among sentences is one of the ways discourses cohere. Entities introduced by names or by descriptions in one sentence can be picked up by means of pronouns subsequently, whether in the same sentence or a separate one:

(5.69)   John came in. He sat down.

(5.70)   John came in and he sat down.

(5.71)   A man came in. He sat down.

Although it has been frequently disputed (see e.g. Evans 1980), it seems that ideally one should assume that the same processes that operate intra-sententially in (5.70) for the resolution of the reference of *he* can be assumed to operate inter-sententially in (5.69) and (5.71) for the interpretation of the pronouns there. The phenomenon of *inter-sentential anaphora* displayed above seems to indicate that sentences in a discourse are not processed as independent units in a vacuum, but, instead, depend on what has been processed previously for their successful interpretation. This can be modelled by taking sentences successively to contribute to the construction of a single complex representation of the content for the whole discourse. Moreover, the contribution of each linguistic item to the construction of this representation is significant not only because of its contribution to the truth-conditional content of the whole discourse, but also for determining patterns of acceptability and successful reference. So, for example, consider the following two pieces of discourse:

(5.72)   We dropped ten marbles on the floor. We searched and we found only nine.
            It was under the sofa.

(5.73)   We dropped ten marbles on the floor. We searched and one was missing. It
            was under the sofa.

The portions consisting of the first two sentences of each discourse in (5.72)–(5.73) are truth-conditionally equivalent, in the sense that there are no situations in which one could be true and the other false. However, the anaphoric possibilities afforded by the second sentence of each discourse are distinct. This is because the way of presentation of truth-conditionally identical contents matters in coherent discourse. An account of meaning for natural languages which only accounts for truth-conditional content but does not distinguish the contribution of distinct ways of presentation (see e.g. Stalnaker 1978) cannot explain the oddity of the third sentence of (5.72) in the context provided by the previous two sentences.

The phenomenon of anaphoric resolution being dependent on the immediately preceding context relies for its explanation on the nature of how humans process linguistic inputs. Natural-language interpretation necessarily operates in a temporal-linear manner, since the linguistic signal can only be presented and perceived serially. In this respect, the processing of discourses consisting of multiple sentences in a linear sequence provides us with evidence that there are interpretational dependencies of later sentences on earlier ones. Moreover, in order to model such dependencies, we need to regard the context in which processing happens as constantly changing as more and more sentence interpretations are added to it. On the basis of the requirement to model the anaphoric phenomena we saw above, one might accordingly assume that they can best be taken to reflect the dynamic nature of processing, i.e. what speakers/hearers actually do when engaging in linguistic activities, rather than reducing their interpretations to distinct ways of interpreting linguistic items like pronouns and quantifiers taken out of their context of occurrence.

But is it a legitimate requirement to involve processing considerations in an account of meaning for natural languages? Certainly, under standard assumptions regarding the *competence/performance* distinction in linguistic analysis (Chomsky 1965), there is no necessity to enrich our notion of what meaning consists in just because processing factors seem to require it. However, the phenomena examined above (i.e. pronominal anaphora and the scope of quantifiers), as well as many other indications of context-dependency in natural languages, seem to suggest that, over and above the need to account for empirical discourse phenomena, the most theoretically sound analysis would have to involve a more comprehensive account of linguistic communication. Otherwise, one is led to postulate more and more ambiguities as explanations for phenomena that are just reflections of the way linguistic items behave depending on their context of occurrence. In this respect, the way humans process language in context and how this affects the interpretations recovered becomes a legitimate object of enquiry for natural-language semantics. From this point of view then, we would have to examine what conception of *meaning* is more appropriate to reflect how linguistic processing depends crucially on context. This should allow us to move beyond the model-theoretic semantics for single sentences we saw in Chapter 3 to an account of how whole discourses are evaluated.

According to Kamp (1981), two points of view of what meaning is have traditionally dominated the linguistic literature:

a. meaning is what determines truth conditions, the view that truth-theoretic and model-theoretic semantics take;
b. meaning is what language users **grasp** when they understand the words they hear, the view of meaning that psychologists, computer scientists and linguists are interested in, which can be called the *representationalist* approach to meaning.

The former view of what meaning is involves the definition of abstract objects like *propositions* which reflect the truth-conditional content of wellformed sentences of languages taken as systems of symbols independently of any agents' grasp. Montague Grammar and many philosophical accounts concerned with reference and truth can be taken as espousing this view (see Chapters 1 and 4). The representationalist point of view, on the other hand, involves defining formal constructs which are assumed to model the mental representations humans employ in response to linguistic processing. This is the view taken by various cognitive science and linguistic approaches, with perhaps the most prevalent the Computational Theory of Mind and the assumption of the existence of a language-of-thought (e.g. Fodor 1975) (see Chapter 1).

Hans Kamp states that Discourse Representation Theory (DRT) is a theory which aims to combine these two approaches to meaning. DRT is basically motivated by the need to give an account of how discourse processing leads to the generation of a representation of the discourse's semantic content. After formally defining how the processes of discourse interpretation operate and what output is generated, both the processes and the resulting representations can be exploited to provide solutions for context-dependency puzzles, like the phenomena of anaphora in donkey sentences we saw above. On the other hand, the representations generated in the process of interpretation can also be seen as partial models (or constraints on models) and in this respect they can be assigned orthodox truth-conditional content reflecting the intentionality of mental representations.

As DRT aims to model the incremental nature of discourse processing, it is defined as an algorithmic procedure for mapping natural-language sentences to representations of their content in context. Here we will first see informally how the construction algorithm operates and also informally define the semantics of the resulting representations. Finally we will see how this approach provides solutions for problems arising in the interpretation of natural-language discourse.

Exercise 5.2

Show the logical forms for (5.65)–(5.66) in predicate-logic notation with *a donkey* translated as an existential quantifier:

a. when it has narrow scope with respect to the universal quantifier and the conditional respectively; and
b. when it has widest scope with respect to the universal quantifier and the conditional operator.

Are these representations satisfactory in expressing the intuitive truth conditions of the sentences?

5.3.2   DRS construction

The semantic content of a discourse in DRT is represented by means of a formal construct, named a *Discourse Representation Structure* (DRS) and presented graphically in the form of a box with two levels:

(5.74)

A simplifying assumption that can be made is that discourse-initially the DRS is empty as no discourse has been processed.[5] As more and more sentences are interpreted the DRS becomes populated with content. The two sections depicted in the graph reflect the fact that DRSs formally comprise:

a. a set of variables, $x, y, z, \ldots$, taken as representations of the entities mentioned in the discourse; these variables are called *discourse referents* and such a set of variables in a DRS is called its *universe*;

b. *conditions*, inserted on the lower part of a DRS, are predications on the discourse referents denoting properties or relations that must be satisfied by the entities corresponding to those discourse referents in the model relative to which the DRS will be evaluated for truth.

Here is a schematic representation of how a DRS would look after linguistic input has been processed, with P, Q and R standing for the content derived by processing natural-language predicates like common nouns and verbs:

(5.75)

Let's see now how these DRSs are populated with discourse referents and conditions as sentences in a discourse accumulate. Kamp (1981) and Kamp and Reyle (1993) define a syntax for natural-language strings which derives tree representations for each sentence.[6] These structured natural-language strings are then taken sequentially as the input for rules, called *construction rules*, whose application results in the construction of the DRS. Construction rules operate left-to-right and top-down on the syntactic trees and indicate what to do with each type of linguistic item encountered. We will now see what kinds of representations are generated for each type of syntactic category.

---

[5] This is just a simplifying assumption for illustration purposes as it is crucial to the account that DRSs are populated not just by the processing of linguistic discourse but also other features of the cognitive environment, i.e. visual input, etc. This is essential for providing a coherent account of the indexical uses of pronouns. See also the discussion of tense and aspect in Chapter 6.

[6] It is assumed that any syntactic formalism can be taken as the basis for the operation of the construction rules, as DRT is a theory of semantics, not syntax. Currently, many diverse syntactic theories map their constructs to DRSs, hence here we do not focus on the details of the particular syntactic framework employed.

We saw earlier that an indefinite description like *a farmer* characteristically introduces some kind of entity in the discourse which can be picked up by pronominals subsequently (see e.g. (5.45) above). However, this entity cannot be taken to be necessarily some specific one, as we also saw instances where the entities vary when occurring in quantificational or conditional environments (see e.g. the donkey sentences in (5.65)–(5.66) above). Discourse referents seem the appropriate intermediate representations to capture the nature of the entities introduced by indefinites, being interpreted as neither actual individuals nor bound variables. So, in DRT, processing an indefinite NP introduces a new discourse referent into the DRS universe. The common-noun content is predicated of this referent. Then the rest of the sentence is also predicated of the discourse referent too:

(5.76)   A farmer came in.

Once a discourse referent has been introduced in the DRS universe, anaphoric reference can be made to the entity it represents by means of a pronoun. Pronouns in DRT are also taken to introduce new discourse referents in the DRS universe, as, at the point of introduction, we don't yet know how they are to be identified. However, these referents come with the requirement that they must participate in a condition of the form $\alpha = \beta$ where α is the new discourse referent introduced and β is a discourse referent already present in the DRS universe. For example, suppose that the discourse in (5.76) above is continued as in (5.77) below under the assumption that *he* refers to the farmer introduced earlier. The updated DRS is shown below the example and contains two conditions associated with the processing of the two instances of *he*: $y = x$ and $u = x$, where y is the discourse referent introduced by the first occurrence of the pronoun and u that introduced by the second.

(5.77)   He owns a donkey and he is proud.

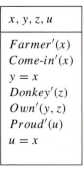

Notice that the difference between having clause concatenation by means of a full stop or a conjunction in the natural-language input is not eventually reflected in the output of the construction rules. This reflects the fact that DRT, in the version presented here, does not sharply distinguish sentence-internal from sentence-external environments (see Further reading for other versions of DRT that abandon this assumption).

Noun phrases consisting of *proper names* also introduce discourse referents with the name contributing a specification of the referent. Suppose we continue the discourse in (5.77) with:

(5.78)   John fed it.

(5.79)   is the DRS that results:

(5.79)

$$
\begin{array}{|l|}
\hline
x, y, z, u, j, w \\
\hline
Farmer'(x) \\
Come\text{-}in'(x) \\
y = x \\
Donkey'(z) \\
Own'(y, z) \\
Proud'(u) \\
u = x \\
John'(j) \\
Feed'(j, w) \\
w = z \\
\hline
\end{array}
$$

Names, unlike pronouns, do not require their discourse referents to be identified with anything else already present in the representation. They just introduce new discourse referents which become available for anaphoric use by pronouns. The name specifications accompanying the discourse referents introduced by proper names in a DRS are intended to identify the unique individual bearing that name (in that context), so that the discourse referent is taken to be associated exclusively with that particular individual.

Definite descriptions, on the other hand, behave rather like pronouns in that they are generally identified with some given antecedent, as noted in section 5.1. They differ from pronouns in adding conditions to the DRS as determined by the content of the common noun. So we might provide the DRS for (5.80) as in (5.81), where the output DRS is progressively built up (temporal information in DRT is dealt with in Chapter 6):

(5.80)   Mary saw Ronnie yesterday and the fool gave her an extension to her essay.

Mary saw Ronnie:

$$\boxed{\begin{array}{l} m, r \\ \hline Mary'(m) \\ Ronnie'(r) \\ See'(m, r) \end{array}}$$

(5.81)

and the fool gave her an extension:

$$\boxed{\begin{array}{l} m, r, u, v, x \\ \hline Mary'(m) \\ Ronnie'(r) \\ See'(m, r) \\ Fool'(u) \\ u = r \\ v = m \\ Extension'(x) \\ Give'(u, v, x) \end{array}}$$

There is much more to say about how definites and indefinites work (see references cited in the Further reading section), but the sketch given here provides the primary basis on which further refinements can be based.

> **Exercise 5.3**
>
> Provide a DRS for the following discourse, showing how it is built up sentence by sentence (ignore tense and other extraneous factors such as space deixis and treat *be* as not introducing any conditions in the DRS):
>
>   John entered the room and looked around. Mary was sitting at a desk. He looked at her and smiled. She looked at him and winced. She was unhappy.

5.3.3   Embedding

Indefinites, names and pronouns introduce what are called *atomic* or *simple* conditions in a DRS. Sentential operators like negation and conditionals introduce recursive structure in a DRS in the sense that they contribute sub-DRSs which serve as conditions inside the *main* or *principal* DRS. So consider a continuation of the discourse in (5.76)–(5.78) as follows:

(5.82)   He doesn't beat it.

The pronoun *he* above is now able to be identified either as the individual named *John* or as the farmer mentioned, hence two discourse referents are available in the DRS for identification (x and j). The choice of which referent is appropriate is not accounted for algorithmically in a deterministic way but is left open and assumed to be determined by extra-linguistic pragmatic factors. However, there are constraints, as we will see presently. Assuming that *he* above refers to John, the updated DRS that can be derived from (5.79) by processing (5.82) is as follows:

(5.83)

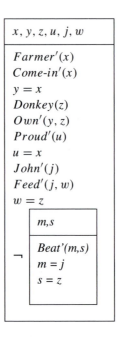

Notice that differences in processing different types of expression are evident in this DRS: the pronoun *he* introduces a discourse referent into the embedded negation box, while as we saw earlier in (5.79) the proper name *John* introduced a discourse referent into the main DRS. This is to reflect the fact that certain expressions, like pronouns, do not identify something once and for all, but only for some restricted part of a discourse. Proper names, on the other hand, introduce identifiable things that are assumed to be available throughout a discourse. They are thus treated as *rigid designators*: their associated discourse referents do not fall under the scope of operators but instead are associated uniquely and directly with their referent in the model. The effect of differences in where discourse referents are introduced is discussed below, and provides a means of handling the accessibility of referents to anaphoric expressions.

Another case where we need embedded DRSs is that of conditionals. For conditionals, two sub-DRSs are introduced related by the operator ⇒. Such sub-DRSs are called *implicative conditions*:

(5.84)   If John owns a donkey he gives it an apple.

(5.85)

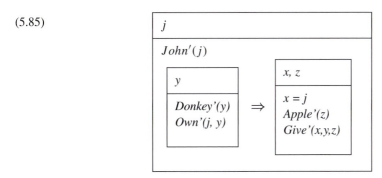

There are two things to observe here. First, there is a sense in which the need for subordinated DRSs reflects the fact that a discourse does not necessarily consist of a series of assertions about the actual world. In the case of conditionals, we postulate a hypothesis, the antecedent, and we describe what follows from it, if it **were** true, in the consequent. We assert neither the antecedent nor the consequent. This is why we cannot insert the predications and referents introduced by conditionals in the main DRS, which is supposed to reflect facts asserted as holding of the actual world. Second, we see that the discourse referent for the name *John* is inserted in the main DRS even though it has been introduced in the conditional.

It is well known that translations of natural-language universal quantification in predicate logic notation involves the → connective (see Chapters 2 and 3). In this sense, when translating natural language sentences, there is a close connection between the contents conveyed by material implication and restricted universal quantification in logic. Based on this, Kamp (1981) and Kamp and Reyle (1993) use implicative conditions for the translation of natural-language expressions involving universal quantifiers. So the sentence below, because it contains the quantifier *every*, gives rise to a condition with two parts, the *restrictor* and the *scope*, connected by the operator ⇒:

(5.86)   Every farmer owns a donkey.

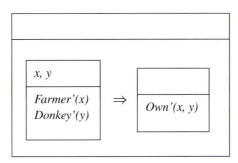

As a result of this analysis, the two donkey sentences below are assigned similar DRS representations reflecting the fact that the semantics assigned to them in predicate-logic translations seem to be identical (see (5.68) above) (because they differ in syntactic structure they are assigned slightly different representations but as we will see the eventual interpretations of these are identical):

(5.87)   If a farmer owns a donkey he feeds it.

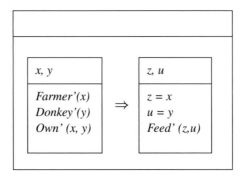

(5.88)   Every farmer who owns a donkey feeds it.

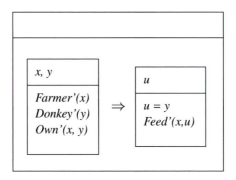

Thus, under this view, it is no accident that donkey phenomena appear in both types of structures: While indefinites in DRT are not analysed as quantificational and rely instead for their interpretation on the semantic rules or their embedding under some quantificational operator as above, universal quantifiers and conditionals introduce structure in a DRS by means of sub-DRSs and the operator $\Rightarrow$. They are then interpreted by a special rule that reflects their universal force, as we will see below. As a side-effect, the interpretation rules also assign appropriate force to the discourse referents introduced by indefinites in the sub-DRSs, hence the semantics in (5.68), which in this account does not result from any ambiguity in the meaning of the indefinites themselves but rather from the structural DRS environment they are processed in.

Exercise 5.4

What are the discourse referents associated with the pronouns in the second sentences of the discourses below? What about the definites? Draw DRSs for these discourses indicating which anaphoric links are felicitous. What additional assumptions do you need to make to construct appropriate DRSs? (Again, ignore tense specifications and treat *be* as not contributing any condition in the DRS.)

a. Mary didn't love John. She adored him. He ignored her and she moved away.
b. If Fred visits Barbara, he buys her flowers. The flowers are nice. And if he brings her chocolates, she buys him dinner$_i$. It$_i$ is very expensive.
c. Suzie hasn't invited a boy to the party. She doesn't like him.
d. Kim washed a mug. Tom broke the handle. She threw every mug away.

5.3.4   Interpreting DRSs

So we have a means of representing the things that are being talked about (the *discourse referents*) and what is being said about them (the *discourse conditions*). Before we go on to look in more detail at accessibility constraints on anaphora resolution, we need to step back and see how DRSs can be interpreted.

We said above that DRSs are taken as *partial models* (or constraints on models). To assign an interpretation in a model *M* for a DRS, one has to employ what are called *embedding functions*. These are functions mapping all and only the discourse referents in the universe of the DRS to the individuals in the domain of a model. A model *M* is thus given as a pair $\langle D, I \rangle$ where *D* is a set of individuals and *I* is an interpretation function that assigns n-tuples of individuals to predicates according to their arity, just as in the simple model theory in Chapters 3 and 4, where this is the denotation assignment function *F*. An embedding function *f* to such a model *M* *verifies* the DRS if it assigns individuals from the domain *D* to all the discourse referents of the the DRS that satisfy, according to *I*, the predications ascribed to them in the DRS conditions. For example, take the DRS above in (5.76), repeated below:

(5.76)   A farmer came in.

x
$Farmer'(x)$ $Come\text{-}in'(x)$

This DRS is verified in *M* iff the domain of *f* consists of the referent *x*, and what *f* assigns to *x* is a farmer according to *I* and that farmer came in according to *I*. So the DRS above is *true* if there is such an embedding function, that is, if we can find an individual *a* in the domain of *M* who is a farmer, i.e. $f(x) = a$ and $a \in I(Farmer')$ and $a \in I(Come\text{-}in')$ are all true. As the model may contain many individuals who are farmers who came in, there might be a set of embedding functions which all verify the DRS; but the minimum requirement is that there is at least one farmer who came in according to the model *M*. Hence we obtain the effect that although there is no specific individual referred to by the indefinite *a farmer*, a restriction is placed on the interpretation of the discourse that at least one farmer exists. So although indefinites like *a farmer, a donkey*, etc. are not taken as existential quantifiers in the traditional predicate-logic way, the existential force they convey is a consequence of the general means of interpreting DRSs by requiring that there exists at least one embedding function in the model for the DRS to be true (or verified).

There are a number of things to notice here. In the first place, the embedding function f has the effect of existentially quantifying over variables, thus guaranteeing the existence of entities if there is an embedding function that can satisfy the DRS. No existential quantifier is therefore needed in the representation system and so there is no problem with variable binding across sentential boundaries. Moreover, because of the latter property, exhaustive model-theoretic interpretation cannot occur until after the DRS of a complete discourse is constructed so that the DRS formally models the increase in information as more and more clause contents are added.

This is how the process of content accumulation is interpreted in a model: consider a possible continuation of (5.76) as *He owns a donkey. The donkey is Puck*. The DRS for the first sentence extending (5.76) is given in (5.89) and that for the whole discourse is given in (5.90).

(5.89)

x, u, y
$Farmer'(x)$ $Come\text{-}in'(x)$ $u = x$ $Own'(u, y)$ $Donkey'(y)$

(5.90)

x, u, y, v, p
$Farmer'(x)$ $Come\text{-}in'(x)$ $u = x$ $Own'(u, y)$ $Donkey'(y)$ $Donkey'(v)$ $v = y$ $Puck'(p)$ $v = p$

Consider what happens model-theoretically in the interpretation of these three DRSs. As we have seen, (5.76) is true just in case there is an embedding function f such that $f(x) \in I(Farmer')$ and $f(x) \in I(Come\text{-}in')$, i.e. there is a farmer who came in. Now, as noted above, there may be many farmers who came in, but not all of them will be donkey-owners. Thus, while f may verify (5.76), it may not verify (5.89): $f(x)$ may not be in the set of donkey-owning entities. Furthermore, f may not satisfy the other discourse referents and conditions. So for (5.89) to be true, we need another embedding function f' which satisfies the following conditions:

$$f'(x) \in I(Farmer')$$
$$f'(x) \in I(Come\text{-}in')$$

$$f'(u) = f'(x)$$
$$f'(y) \in I(Donkey')$$
$$\langle f'(u), f'(y) \rangle \in I(Own')$$

And, of course, f', while possibly satisfying (5.89), may not satisfy (5.90) because of the extra discourse referents and conditions. So the representation structures are essential in the semantic process: no final assignments of values to variables (discourse referents) can be made and no assessment of truth can be determined until the discourse is closed off. In this way, we begin to see the importance of representational semantics in being able to provide means of both resolving anaphoric relations and providing an at least partial account of context-dependent information accumulation.

How are other types of DRS interpreted, such as negation and conditional DRSs? In order to answer this we need to recognise that, as noted above, there might be new discourse referents introduced in embedded DRSs which are not included in the domain of the embedding functions f that interpret the main DRS. So we need to define a way of extending the original embedding functions interpreting the main DRS so that they can take into account the newly introduced discourse referents in the subordinate DRSs. We define an embedding function g which extends f with respect to a DRS K, just in case the domain of g, $Dom(g)$ is the domain of f plus the discourse referents in the universe of K, i.e. $Dom(g) = Dom(f) \cup U_K$, and for all discourse referents x in $Dom(f)$, f and g assign the same entities: $f(x) = g(x)$.

So now we can define truth for a negated DRS in terms of checking the extensions of the functions f that verify the main DRS. Intuitively a negated DRS will be true if we are **not** able to find such successful extensions in the model M. So we say that an embedding function f verifies a negated DRS in a model M iff f maps all the discourse referents to individuals in M that satisfy the conditions ascribed to them in the main DRS and f **cannot** be extended to a function g which verifies the DRS embedded under the negation sign. Hence, a DRS like that in (5.91) for the sentence *John doesn't own a car* is true just in case (a) $f(j) \in I(John')$ and (b) there is **no** extension g of f such that $g(x) \in I(Car')$ and $\langle g(j), g(x) \rangle \in I(Own')$ (where $g(j) = f(j)$, by the definition of the extension of an embedding given above).

(5.91)

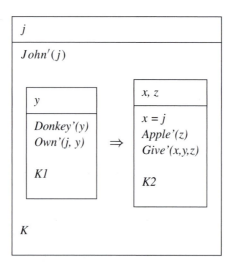

Now we can see what kind of interpretation is assigned to implicative DRSs, such as (5.85), repeated below with the DRS and its sub-DRSs named *K*, *K1*, *K2* for illustration purposes only:

(5.92)   If John owns a donkey he gives it an apple.

As always, we start with the functions that embed the main DRS in the model *M* and consider extensions of these functions for the subordinated DRSs. An embedding function *f* verifies a conditional DRS in a model *M* iff *f* maps all the discourse referents in the main DRS to individuals in *M* that satisfy the conditions ascribed to them. Moreover, for every extension *g* of *f* such that the domain of *f* is extended with the discourse referents of the sub-DRS on left-hand side of the ⇒ and verifies its conditions, we can find a function *h* which extends *g* with the universe of the sub-DRS on the right-hand side and verifies it. So to verify a conditional sub-DRS as included in *K* in (5.92), for every function *g* that verifies the box on the left-hand side, i.e. *K1* (the content of the antecedent), there must exist an extension *h* that verifies the box on the right, *K2* (the content of the consequent). In this respect, we can see that conditionals are interpreted indirectly as universal quantifications over all the discourse referents introduced by the antecedent and existential quantification over the discourse referents introduced by the consequent. Moreover, these implicit universal and existential quantifications have the property of being *unselective* in that all the discourse referents introduced in the sub-boxes are captured in their scope (see Further reading).

5.3.5   Accessibility

As we have seen, interpretation of discourse according to DRT is a process that takes place in two stages: first we construct a DRS and then we assign a model-theoretic interpretation to it, not directly to natural-language sentences. The dynamicity of interpretation resides in how the construction process updates already existing representations by adding the new information contributed by a sentence. So there are two types of explanation that can be sought for each linguistic phenomenon of interest: it can be either the result of how the construction algorithm operates or a consequence of how the eventual representation is interpreted. Here we are interested in permissible anaphoric links between pronouns and their antecedents. The fact that DRSs now have structure makes it possible to define domains in order to explain in terms of locality when anaphoric connections are felicitous or not. For example, the following anaphoric connections indicated by coindexing are not considered possible:

(5.93)   John doesn't own a car$_i$. # It$_i$ is parked.

(5.94)   # Every man$_i$ came in. He$_i$ was tired.

(5.95)   # If he$_i$ owns a donkey, a man$_i$ feeds it.

The possibility of having subordinate DRSs with their own universes promises to explain such facts in a principled way. First we need to define what are called *accessibility relations* between DRS and sub-DRSs, so that already present discourse referents can be reused for anaphoric resolution purposes only when it is permitted to do so. Accessibility relations are not arbitrary stipulations in DRT but rather reflect a notion of *scope*, if we think of discourse referents as variables bound by the quantificational force introduced by the semantic rules that interpret DRSs. The accessibility relations defined for DRSs in effect require that antecedents for discourse referents introduced by pronouns can only be found in the universes of other DRSs in case those can be reached by moving in the direction left and upwards. So a discourse referent in the sub-DRS $K2$ in the DRS in (5.92) above can be identified with any discourse referent occurring in either $K1$ or K (or in $K2$ itself, of course). However, a discourse referent in K cannot access one in $K1$ or $K2$, nor can a discourse referent in $K1$ access a referent in $K2$.

Accessibility relations among DRSs can be defined informally as follows.[7] The accessible universe U_K of a DRS K is the set of all discourse referents that occur:

- in the universe of K itself;
- in the universe of all the DRSs that graphically contain K;

---

[7] These definitions follow Kadmon (2001: 36)

5.4   Conclusion

So, to take stock, we have now introduced a theory of semantic representation that is intrinsically contextual and dynamic. The semantic representation of a discourse is progressively built up as new sentences are added to the discourse; new discourse referents may be added and new constraints may appear on new and old referents. In this way, it is possible to model how different types of noun phrase, definite, indefinite, universal and proper name, contribute to the dynamically modified discourse, determining what referents are newly introduced or identified with those previously introduced, and the scopal domains in which they appear. This allows for a unified theory of bound-variable, E-type and donkey interpretations of pronouns: the differences result from the different ways referents are embedded into the representation and their consequent accessibility relations. The resulting representations thus provide us with a tool that can be used to get a better understanding of contextual effects, something that is impossible in static theories like those discussed in previous chapters. Furthermore, the theory also shows the importance of semantic **representations** independent of their model-theoretic interpretation. As discussed above, the latter is not fully determined for sentences in isolation but only for complete discourses. Moreover, model-theoretic interpretation does not itself provide any insight into the discourse properties of noun phrases, rather, it is the **process** of constructing the representation which determines these aspects of interpretation. In the next chapter, we will see how DRT can also help us get a handle on the semantic complexities associated with the lexical meaning and grammatical properties of verbs as we turn our attention to tense and aspect, two grammatical categories that necessarily involve a notion of dynamic change.

5.5   Coda

Inevitably, in the wake of the emergence of Discourse Representation Theory, with its essential use of the DRSs as the locus of anaphoric resolution, counter-arguments have attempted to eliminate all such intervening representational constructs. It was noted relatively early on that DRT was not naturally extendible to the full range of generalised quantifiers given only the means defined above for expressing universal and existential quantification. In later variants an additional set-theoretic operator is defined for qualificational purposes (see Kamp and Reyle 1993, ch. 4). But, more seriously, it was argued that DRT is not compositional in the strict way in which the formal-semantics methodology imposes, namely, that compositionality of meaning for sentences of the language has, by definition, to hold over natural-language strings. This view of compositionality has the consequence of imposing the challenge of demonstrating the eliminability of any intervening level between natural language and model theoretic interpretation. It was in response to this that Dynamic Predicate

Logic (DPL) was developed, securing the binding of anaphoric dependencies across sentential boundaries without invoking any such level of representation. A new model theory is proposed replacing the conservative predicate-logic assumptions in which variables are bound exclusively within a domain defined by an operator. In the logic that results, the existential quantifier, conjunction and implication all allow binding beyond their traditional scope in order to deal with phenomena like cross-sentential and donkey anaphora. Under this analysis, indefinites are again translated by means of existential quantifiers similar to Russell's and other traditional treatments. The richer semantics is to formally model the intuition that sentence meaning is not just truth conditions but also involves changes in the information states of the interpreters as a result of sentence processing. This general type of approach is termed *dynamic semantics*. However, the development of DPL has largely been driven by examples with additional devices added as necessary; and each one constitutes an increase in the semantic ontology so that it edges ever closer to representationalist assumptions. Moreover, from an empirical point of view, the problem is that such accounts do not directly address the underlying challenge of anaphora in general and, in particular, how pronoun-antecedent pairings are established. To the contrary, discussions of DPL presume on syntactically determined fixed pronoun-antecedent coindexings as the input datum to be captured within a DPL account. Yet, explaining **how** antecedent-pronoun pairings are established is the heart of the DRT arguments for the necessity of such intervening representations; so the very issues which led in the direction of imposing a representationalist perspective on explanations of what is intrinsic to natural-language expressions are simply not addressed in such systems (these problems extend to the handling of presuppositions, the treatment of attitudes, etc; see Asher 1986; Kamp 1990; Geurts 1999, among others).

5.6   Further reading

The literature about definiteness and the interpretation of definite-noun phrases is already vast and still growing. See C. Lyons (1999) for an overview and, for different views, see Russell (1905) and Montague (1973), with Strawson (1950) providing the antithesis. See also Allwood *et al.* (1977: 148–55); McCawley (1981: 176–82) and the more extended discussions in Hawkins (1978); Heim (1988); Kamp (1981); Kadmon (2001) and the papers in Reuland and ter Meulen (1987). Carlson (1980) and Ojeda (1991) discuss the generic use of the definite article in English. Kaplan's account of *demonstratives* was the first serious model-theoretic characterisation of context-dependent expressions involving a distinction between *character* and *content* (see Kaplan 1977/1989). Geach (1962) introduces the treatment of pronouns as variables and the notion of *lazy pronouns* (see also Evans 1977: 467). Evans (1977, 1980) introduced the notion of E-type pronouns. Stalnaker (1974, 1978) defines a model-theoretic account of context in terms of possible worlds, but this does not address the resolution of anaphora (see also Stalnaker 1999). Lewis (1975) introduces the notion of *unselective* quantification for the so called 'adverbs of quantification' anticipating the unselective binding of discourse referents that DRT uses in interpreting DRSs. For general issues of reference, quantification and anaphora in linguistic semantics see Heusinger and Egli (2000). The notion *discourse referent* was first introduced in Karttunen (1976). Kamp (1981) is the classic paper setting out DRT, then extended by Kamp and Reyle (1993) to form an overall semantic framework. To see how model-theoretic accounts of similar data have developed over the period, see Cooper (1979); Chierchia (1992, 1995); Heim and Kratzer (1998). Heim (1988) presents a framework similar to Kamp (1981) called *File Change Semantics*; see Kadmon (2001) for comparison between the two accounts; and see Heim (1990) for a revised account introducing an E-type analysis and *situations*. Neale (1990), among others, defends a Russellian approach to definites. For accounts of Dynamic Predicate Logic, see Groenendijk and Stokhof (1990, 1991); though see Kamp (1990b), Hamm *et al.* (2006) for a rejoinder and van Eijck and Kamp (1997) for a reformulation of DRT semantics along the lines suggested by Groenendijk and Stokhof. See also Muskens (1996) for a strictly compositional version of DRT. Subsequent versions of DRT distinguish sentence-internal and sentence-external environments and assume bottom-up construction of the DRS in order to deal with presuppositions: van der Sandt (1992); Geurts (1999); Kamp (2001a, b). For an accessible, concise introduction to DRT see Geurts and Beaver (2007). For an alternative account of presuppositions within a type-theoretic framework, see Fernando (2002). For a more up-to-date and comprehensive introduction to DRT see Kamp *et al.* (2005).

6 Time, tense and events

Up to now, the semantic systems that we have been looking at have been purely *extensional*. That is to say, each element of the logic has a fixed and immutable denotation, and, reflecting this, individual words have been presumed to correspond to a fixed content. This means that no real concept of how the world changes can be expressed, as the semantics allows only for the evaluation of expressions with respect to a single, timeless situation. Thus we cannot yet handle common inferences involving changes of state:

(6.1)   'Kim went to the shops' *implies* 'Kim was not at the shops at some time t_1 and Kim was at the shops at time t_2'.

Concepts of change are expressed in natural languages through the grammatical categories of *tense* and *aspect* (among others). Although we have been writing out sentences in English with tense- and aspect-inflected verbs, in fact tense has not been reflected in the logic, so that all the sentences in (6.2)–(6.4) receive the same interpretation:

(6.2)   Rambo kicked the chair.

(6.3)   Rambo kicks the chair.

(6.4)   Rambo will kick the chair.

These are all true if and only if Rambo indeed kicks the chair, irrespective of when that event takes place with respect to the time of utterance of these sentences. But, of course, (6.2) is not true if Rambo kicks the chair two days after the sentence is uttered. In addition, given that the semantics does not handle time and changes in the world, the internal structure of the events that cause these changes cannot be referred to either. So there is no way to capture the distinct implication relations in (6.5) and (6.6):

(6.5)   'John was walking in the park' *implies* 'John was in the park'.

(6.6)   'John was walking to the park' *does not imply* 'John was in the park'.

Furthermore, we have no way of expressing the distinctions in the interpretations of sentences that present the activities they describe as ongoing (*John is building a house*) from those that typically imply a complete event (*John built a house*). In consequence, we have no way of accounting for the oddness of isolated sentences such as # *Jean is knowing the answer* and # *The dog was recognising its owner*.

For these reasons (and more), it is clear that the logical systems we have already seen are inadequate to give a full account of natural-language semantics. Therefore they need to be extended to allow at least for temporal change.[1] As will become clear very shortly, once the challenge of addressing intricacies of tense and temporal construal is taken up, there is a need to formulate word meanings in terms of a finer granularity than is possible in the semantic systems so far introduced. We will leave consideration of general issues raised by word meaning until Chapter 8, focusing here on tense and the depiction of events as a first hint of the complexities involved. We will begin by looking at a rather simple tensed logic and its interpretation. When this type of logic proves also inadequate for a satisfying treatment of natural-language interpretation, we will turn to a more sophisticated view of tense and aspect within Discourse Representation Theory.

6.1   Time and tense

The first thing we must have in order to account for tense and aspect is a theory of how to conceptualise *time*. The most suitable model of time (although not without its metaphysical and cognitive problems) is considered to be that of the *real* numbers, which constitute an infinite set, including numbers with any number of decimal points. This system has some desirable properties when it comes to the modelling of time: there is an infinite number of points (or times or *instants*) T ordered by the 'less than' $<$ (or 'greater than' $>$) relation, interpreted as 'precedes' ('follows'). The relation standardly conforms to the following:

(6.7)   Where t_i, t_j and t_k are all members of T:
   a. No time can precede itself:
      $$\forall t_i (t_i \not< t_i)$$ *irreflexivity*
   b. If one time, t, precedes another t', then t precedes all times preceded by t':
      $$\forall t_i, t_j, t_k [((t_i < t_j) \land (t_j < t_k)) \rightarrow (t_i < t_k)]$$ *transitivity*
   c. No time can both precede and follow another :
      $$\forall t_i, t_j [(t_i < t_j) \rightarrow (t_j \not< t_i)]$$ *asymmetry*
   d. There are no times that are not ordered with respect to other times:
      $$\forall t_i, t_j [(t_i < t_j) \lor (t_j < t_i) \lor (t_i = t_j)]$$ *connectedness*
   e. There is always a time between two other times:
      $$\forall t_i, t_j [(t_i < t_j) \rightarrow \exists t_k (t_i < t_k < t_j)]$$ *density*

This concept of time is often represented as an arrow pointing in one direction:

(6.8)   the timeline: ⟶ $\boxed{T}$

Of course, humans do not treat time in such a punctilious fashion. Instead, we use natural languages to talk about situations such as book-writing which

---

[1] It is also generally assumed that parameters for locations and *possible worlds* (related to *modality*) are also necessary to account for the semantics of natural languages. Be that as it may, we will only be exploring temporal change in this book.

have discernible parts and obviously express non-instantaneous events. In fact, although some verbs like *arrive* and *sneeze* do usually express instantaneous events, most verbs do not, and instead are typically associated with events that have duration beyond a moment or point of time. So we need to allow for continuous segments of time which we call *intervals* of time. *Intervals* of time are defined as a continuous set of moments of time ordered by the precedence relation, $<$. The set of all possible intervals of time, $\mathcal{I}$, is thus defined as the set of all continuous subsets, i, of a set of moments of time, T, ordered by the precedence relation, $<$:

(6.9) $\{i \subseteq T | ((t_i \in i) \wedge (t_k \in i) \wedge (t_i < t_j < t_k)) \rightarrow (t_j \in i)\}$

This definition ensures that there are no gaps in temporal intervals, reflecting the intuition that propositions mentioning events must be evaluated over a certain continuous time period, as there might be moments in that period for which it cannot be said that the event as a whole holds. For example, in *John kicked the chair*, the moment John lifts his leg must be included in the evaluation interval but on its own does not support the truth of the proposition.

Intervals of time may overlap with, be contained in or precede other intervals, defined as follows:

(6.10)   Two intervals i and j overlap (written $i \circ j$) if they share moments of time:
              $i \circ j$ iff $i \cap j \neq \emptyset$

(6.11)   One interval, i, is contained in another, j, (written $i \subseteq j$) if every moment
              in i is also in j:
              $i \subseteq j$ iff $i \cup j = j$

(6.12)   One interval, i, precedes another, j (written $i < j$), if every moment in i
              precedes every moment in j:
              $i < j$ iff $\forall t \in i[\forall t' \in j[t < t']]$

Given intervals of time i, j, k and l, one of the possible situations in which i precedes j and k precedes l, i overlaps with k and j overlaps with l and where l is a *subinterval* of j can be pictorially represented as follows:

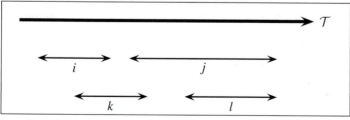

$i < j$ $i \circ k$ $l \subseteq j$
$k < l$ $j \circ l$
            $j \circ k$

Typically, closed intervals of time are written within square brackets:

$$interval\ of\ time\ \ [t_i, t_j] =_{def} \{t | t_i \leq t \leq t_j\}$$

and a moment of time is written as a single time within square brackets:.

$$moment\ of\ time\ \ [t] =_{def} \{t\}$$

An interval semantics for natural-language time references seems to be more adequate than an instant-based one. Consider what it means for a sentence like *Mary read a book* to be evaluated at an instant. Does the fact that at that particular instant Mary was drinking her tea disqualify this instant from verifying the sentence? Our intuitions seem to suggest not, but it is very difficult to define what needs to be the case for instants to verify such statements. On the other hand, evaluation at a continuous interval allows us to say that the statement is verified even though it may not strictly speaking be verifiable at each particular moment that constitutes the interval (Mary's breaking off from reading the book momentarily does not falsify the claim that she read a book at the time interval in question).

6.2   Simple tense logic

There are approaches to tense built entirely on the view of time that results from modelling natural-language tensed statements using a modal logic (rather than a classical logic) (Prior 1967). This has the effect of looking at tense reference by situating the speaker/hearer of an utterance inside the time flow and evaluating the utterance from his/her perspective. Thus tense becomes a *deictic* category that locates in time the state of affairs described by a sentence. For simple tenses, the *time of utterance*, the interval (sometimes assumed to be a moment) in which a sentence is uttered by some speaker, is the time of evaluation. At its simplest, tense as a universal linguistic category can be divided into three sorts:

(6.13)   A declarative sentence in the *present tense* can be used to assert that the event described by the sentence occurs at the time the sentence is uttered, i.e. the time of the event is located at the time of utterance.

(6.14)   A declarative sentence in the *past tense* can be used to assert that the event time occurred prior to the time of utterance

(6.15)   A declarative sentence in the *future tense* can be used to assert that the event time will occur after the time of utterance.

Natural languages typically have tense/aspectual systems that are not coincident with this simplistic view, and there is a lot of cross-linguistic variation. For example, in English, the simple present tense is used only in special circumstances such as the *historical present* used in narratives about the past to make the description more vivid or the 'sportscaster' present used to describe the immediate present in providing running commentary to sports events, *Beckham runs down the field. He kicks the ball. He SCORES!*. Unlike German, for example, in English, the present progressive may refer to present or future time: *I'm travelling on the train (now)* versus *I'm travelling to Brussels tomorrow*. Yet in common with other Germanic languages, English has only a periphrastic future (using an auxiliary verb), which may involve *modality* as well as futurity. So *I will go to the party* could indicate determination, intention as well as futurity. These uses are beyond the analytical capabilities of simple tense logics; but one might nevertheless assume that such logics provide the core of temporal reference in language, with added dimensions being provided by aspectual specifications and the types of situation conceptualisations typically associated with various verbs. So let's assume that tense is a simple deictic category determining relations between times of events or situations. And let's adopt the conception of time as modelled by the real numbers, a one-dimensional construct when combined with the *less than* relation. Then there are only three ways that two things can be related along the timeline: $<$, $>$ and $=$. In other words, 'before', 'after' and 'the same'. So we may take these as basic for tense logics.

Since tense is taken to locate the situations expressed by sentences in time, the simplest representation and interpretation of tense is in terms of *logical operators* over formulae. Thus, tense logics contain a set of tense operators which, being expressions of type $t \rightarrow t$, combine with formulae to yield tensed formulae. So we have three such operators, *Pres*, *Past*, *Fut*, and we get the logical representations of the content of English sentences as in (6.16)–(6.18).

(6.16)   A footballer runs: $Pres(\exists x[Run'(x) \wedge Footballer'(x)])$

(6.17)   Every student will graduate: $Fut(\forall y[Student'(y) \rightarrow Graduate'(y)])$

(6.18)   Mary baked a cake: $Past(\exists z[Cake'(z) \wedge Bake'(Mary', z)])$

In order to interpret such representations, it is necessary to extend the model theory of Chapter 3 to incorporate time. Thus, models are redefined as extended from:

$$M = \ll A, F \gg$$

to a temporal model:[2]

$$M = \ll A, F, <, T \gg$$

where A is a set of entities specifying the ontology of the model; T is a set of moments of time ordered by the dense linear ordering $<$, as above; and F is the function that assigns denotations to lexical items in the model at particular temporal intervals. The definition of the latter must, however, be changed to account for time. F may be defined as a function from lexical items to sets of ordered

---

[2] Here we are using $\ll \ldots \gg$ to visually distinguish *ordered sets* from temporal relations.

different temporal dependencies defined to range over the times already present in the context. It is because the times associated with tenses are dependent on each other that in interpreting a discourse such as *Mary was dancing. She fell over and twisted her ankle* we assume that all three events occur in the same time period and not that Mary was dancing earlier today, but fell over two days ago and twisted her ankle yesterday. Note that in the model theory given above, nothing prevents us from taking wildly different times for evaluating the different propositions expressed – all that matters is that the selected time interval is prior to the time of utterance.

Besides those discourse-anaphoric uses, tenses seem to display all the other uses of pronouns in natural languages. For example, pronouns can be construed *indexically*, i.e. as requiring an antecedent provided by the immediate cognitive environment:

(6.37)   (seeing Mary coming into the room A says to B:) She's not wearing a hat!

Tenses can also be used this way. Consider a variant of the famous example by Barbara Partee:

(6.38)   (getting into the car to go away A says to B:) I didn't turn off the stove!

As in the case of the pronoun above, (6.38) is not felicitously interpreted through simple existential quantification, i.e. 'there is a time t in the past such that I did not turn off the stove at t'. The intended interpretation of A's utterance seems to be that there is a specific interval of time during which no switching off of the stove by A occurred. But tense logic has no way of representing this accurately.

Tenses can also receive bound variable readings, exactly like pronouns:

(6.39)   Every student said he was ready.

(6.40)   Every time Mary cried John was upset.

(6.39) is interpreted as universal quantification over individuals with the pronoun *he* interpreted as a variable bound by the universal quantifier: for every individual, if that individual is a student then that individual said of himself that he is ready:

(6.41) $\forall x[Student'(x) \rightarrow Say'(x, Ready'(x))]$

(6.40) is interpreted in a similar way to (6.39), namely, as universal quantification over times or situations. Every situation that involves Mary crying must be also a situation of John's being upset.

(6.42) $\forall t[Cry'(Mary', t) \rightarrow Upset'(John', t)]$

E-type interpretations of tenses are also possible, as with pronouns:

(6.43)   Most students said they were ready. They were confident.

(6.44)   Usually when Mary cried John comforted her. Bill just laughed.

The pronoun *they* in (6.43) takes as its antecedent the set of students that said they were ready. Only this set of students is also said to display confidence as well. In the same way, in (6.44), it is only the occasions of Mary's crying and John's comforting her that are also said to be occasions of Bill laughing.

Seen from this point of view, the fact that tense logics express quantification over entities in the object language but quantify over times in the metalanguage is a serious disadvantage. First, there is no obvious way to express the requisite anaphor-antecedent relations that are displayed in the examples above. Each tense in such logics introduces a new operator which is interpreted anew as a quantifier over times without any reference to what has been introduced before. Second, the fact that tenses can assume all the uses of pronouns points to the conclusion that there is some fundamental symmetry in the way natural languages treat reference to entities and reference to times or situations. But this is not reflected by the distinct treatment these receive by tense logics.

A related empirical problem arises when we look at how tenses behave in more complex environments than simple clauses. Here we see that the simple tense logic analysis will not suffice. Tense in embedded clauses may be ambiguous with respect to the time taken as the point of reference:

(6.45)   Bill said that he felt happy.

(6.46)   Bill said that he felt happy at the time he said it.

(6.47)   Bill said he felt happy when he had earlier phoned Mary (but at the time of saying this he felt sad).

Bill's feeling happy clearly relates to some other time, but that time may be variously construed depending on context and other pragmatic factors. These sorts of anaphoric properties are again not expressible in this approach to tense, since this invariably merely situates a past tense in a clause with respect to an event occurring before the time of utterance. Hence (6.45) will not receive a tense-logic representation that succeeds in completely disambiguating among its possible readings. For these (and other) reasons, although we retain the concept of time as modelled by the set of real numbers, we will now abandon the operator approach to tense and pursue a more sophisticated style of analysis, one which moreover helps to bring out the anaphoric nature of tense construal: its dependence, that is, on what constructs have been set up earlier in the discourse.

Exercise 6.1

Extend the model of the Highgrove Royals in Chapter 3 into a temporal model that reflects the following scenario (Highgrove is in the west of England, Windsor Castle is just outside London, Holyrood Palace is in Scotland):

Camilla and Charles were at Highgrove, but William and Harry were not. William was flying a helicopter around Windsor Castle and Harry was in Afghanistan. Charles went to Holyrood

Palace the next day and William flew back to Highgrove in his helicopter. Charles returned two days later, kissed Camilla and shouted at William. The next day Harry also returned to Highgrove for a party that was to be held the day after. The party was a great success.

(Hint: treat each day as a fixed time period.)

Exercise 6.2

Translate the following sentences into (first-order) tense logical formulae, state their truth conditions, and evaluate their truth or falsity with respect to the model you have just constructed and the times of utterance given in brackets after each example.

a. Camilla will be at Highgrove (uttered on day 2).
b. William flew to Highgrove and was shouted at by Charles (uttered on day 5).
c. Harry, William and Charles are not at Highgrove, but Camilla is (uttered on day 3).
d. If Harry is in Afghanistan, then William is flying around Windsor Castle (uttered on day 4).
e. Charles kissed Camilla and the party is a great success (uttered on day 4).

6.3   Event theory

Since the latter decades of the twentieth century, the idea that verbs and verb phrases have as the basis of their denotation just sets of ordered n-tuples of individuals, as envisaged within standard model theory (Chapter 3), has increasingly lost favour. Instead, following work by the philosopher Donald Davidson which has been subsequently developed by both philosophers and linguists, many linguists, both in semantics and syntax, adopt the view that the interpretation of verbs requires a change in the ontology in order to recognise the existence of *events* in addition to the existence of individual entities. So events become part of the ontology just as individual entities are part of the ontology. Consequently, in any model there is a subset, E, of elements in A such that $Event'(e)$ is true of all events $e \in E$. We say that our ontology is now *sorted* into two sorts, events and individuals.

Verbs (and potentially adjectives and nouns) thus have included in their denotation the events that they describe, as well as the participants in those events that they require. For example, the verb *cut* denotes a set of cutting events involving two participants, an *agent* and a *patient*. There are two ways of characterising such denotations: either (a) by taking verbs to denote sets of events and treating participants as being related to those events by primitive participant roles (an account which may be called the 'separation' approach to reflect the way thematic roles are separately specified in the representation) or (b) by taking verbs to denote ordered n-tuples consisting of an event and the participants in that event. The sentence *Mary cut the cake* could then have the two representations in (6.48):

(6.48) a. $\exists e \exists x [Cutting'(e) \wedge Agent'(e, Mary') \wedge Patient'(e, x) \wedge Cake'(x)]$
  b. $\exists e \exists x [Cut'(e, Mary', x) \wedge Cake'(x)]$

One of the advantages of such event-based approaches is that *entailments* are easy to read off the representations by simple rules of natural deduction such as conjunction and existential elimination. (6.49) gives some of the entailments from (6.48a), and (6.50) those derivable from (6.48b) (tense ignored for the moment).

(6.49) a. $\exists e [Cutting'(e)]$
   There was a cutting event.
  b. $\exists e \exists x [Cutting'(e) \wedge Patient'(e, x) \wedge Cake'(x)]$
   A cake was cut.
  c. $\exists e \exists x [Cutting'(e) \wedge Agent'(e, Mary') \wedge Patient'(e, x)]$
   Mary cut something.

(6.50) a. $\exists e \exists x \exists y [Cut'(e, y, x)]$
   There was a cutting event.
  b. $\exists e \exists x \exists y [Cut'(e, y, x) \wedge Cake'(x)]$
   A cake was cut.
  c. $\exists e \exists x [Cut'(e, Mary', x)]$
   Mary cut something.

There are advantages and disadvantages to both types of representation and concomitant view of their denotations. We will not go into any detail here, but the main problem for the 'separation' approach in (6.48a), as we see it, is the assumption that there are primitive relations such as *Agent'*, *Patient'*, etc. which are necessary to link participants to some event. No such assumption needs to be made for the approach in (6.48b), where inferences of agentivity and affectedness are matters for lexical semantics and not the semantics of propositions. We will therefore adopt this latter event-based approach in what follows.

One of the real advantages of adopting event theory is that adverbials and adpositional phrases are much easier to analyse. In the type theory presented in Chapter 3, verb phrases are assigned the type $e \rightarrow t$, which means that any VP modifier like *slowly* or *with a knife* must be assigned a type that takes VP denotations into VP denotations, i.e. $(e \rightarrow t) \rightarrow (e \rightarrow t)$. In event theory, such expressions can be treated as predicates over events, i.e. as expressions of type $(e \rightarrow t)$:

(6.51) $\exists e [Walk'(e, John') \wedge Slow'(e)]$
  John walked slowly.

(6.52) $\exists e \exists x \exists z [Cut'(e, Mary', x) \wedge Cake'(x) \wedge With'(e, z) \wedge Knife'(z)]$
  Mary cut a cake with a knife.

6.3.1   Types of eventualities

Different construals of states of affairs can be distinguished by look-ing at how these states of affairs are conceptualised in terms of *part–whole* relations, i.e. whether they are presented as having parts and what is the rela-tion of the parts to the whole. *Events* or actions like cutting, walking, building and so on are usually contrasted with *states* like knowing, loving, being tall, etc. We will use the general term *eventualities* when we do not wish to distinguish between them. Construals of eventualities as states differ from event construals in the same way as mass nouns are typically interpreted distinctly from count nouns: events are countable, individuable and have atomic parts, whereas states do not seem to have any of these properties. Hence, if it is true that Mary is tall at some time, then at any slice of that time Mary is still tall, no matter how finely the temporal interval is divided (in parallel a mass noun like *water* denotes a substance any part of which, however tiny, retains the property of being water, at least within human perceptual capacities). If Mary painted a picture, however, then there are points of time during the relevant interval at which she was in the process of painting a picture but she cannot be said to have painted a picture (since she might not have finished it yet). In parallel, consider an NP involving a count noun, e.g. *a chair*: the denotation of such an NP can be seen as having parts, namely legs, a seat, a back, etc. which cannot be characterised as chairs.

Events may be further divided into *achievements*, which are typically instan-taneous changes of state; *accomplishments*, which involve a process that leads to a natural terminus, like e.g. creation or destruction of something; and *processes* (or *activities*), which are events which are ongoing but do not involve any sort of significant change of state.

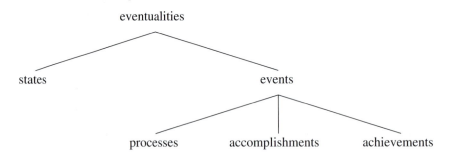

(6.53)   Hilary reached the summit.   *achievement*

(6.54)   Bob built a house.   *accomplishment*

(6.55)   Mary walked in the garden.   *process/activity*

This classification is based on Vendler (1967) and there are other more or less complex variations. We will stick to this basic classification for the purposes of this book, and will return to other properties of these eventuality types in the next section.

Note that there is a question here as to whether these distinctions (distinctions in terms of *Aktionsart*, see 6.5) pertain to the **ontology**; i.e. whether the eventualities themselves exist and can be differentiated in virtue of distinct qualities; or whether it is the **predicates** that refer to such eventualities which present events/states in distinct ways; and whether these distinctions are linguistic or conceptual. While many philosophers take the former ontological view, in favour of the latter consider that the same eventuality can be conceptualised or described by distinct types of predicate:

(6.56)   John drank beer last night at 11 o'clock.   (activity)

(6.57)   John drank a pint of beer last night at 11 o'clock.   (accomplishment)

Moreover, tests which supposedly distinguish between various types of eventualities can give variable results depending on the context of the utterance (see the discussion of (6.88–6.91) below). For example, statives like *know* are not supposed to occur in the imperative because it involves some notion of agentive causation:

(6.58)   B: John already knows the answer to this question. Kim, know the answer
                    by tomorrow or there will be trouble.
               K: But I know the answer already.

A related concern that arises here is whether the eventuality type of a predicate can be determined once and for all in the lexical entry associated with a verb (or noun). It has been pointed out repeatedly that this is not the case, as the **syntactic** context, i.e. the combination of verbs and their arguments and adjuncts, can shift the type of the eventuality. For example, consider the distinct qualities and classification of sentences with the same verb but distinct objects or subjects:

(6.59)   John pushed the cart for three hours.   (activity)

(6.60)   John pushed the cart to the shed.   (accomplishment)

(6.61)   John built a castle in ten minutes.   (accomplishment)

(6.62)   John built castles for ten minutes.   (activity)

This seems to indicate that eventuality distinctions like the ones noted above are properties of situations associated with whole clauses, not just verbs, and such properties can only be determined by taking into account the particular linguistic and non-linguistic context of an utterance involving such predicates. But how such properties are derived from the compositional structure of the clause in conjunction with pragmatic inferencing is beyond the scope of this short introduction (see Chapter 8 and Further reading for some hints). With these reservations we will turn now to a discussion of an account of tense in English that combines event theory with times.

Exercise 6.3

What types of event do the following verbs and verb phrases normally express? Note any problems you may encounter in your classification.

dream; love; drink orange juice; drink a coffee; arrive; die; sneeze; laugh; be ill; concentrate; move; run; run to the shops; perform a task; eat; eat an ice cream; eat apples.

6.4   Tense in English

6.4.1   Reichenbach's analysis of tenses in English

The philosopher and logician Hans Reichenbach suggested (1947) that tenses may be more perspicuously analysed in terms of three *reference times*. These three temporal intervals are: E, the time at which the event occurs (the *event time*); U the time of utterance (the *utterance time*, often written S); and a third time, R, which is a time to which other times make reference (the *reference time*). Previously, in effect, we only used two of these, the event time and the utterance time. Using these three times, Reichenbach was able to provide characterisations of tenses in terms of the relative ordering between the three intervals (in (6.63), a comma means 'unordered' and $<$ means 'precedes'):[4]

(6.63)   a. Simple present: U, R, E *Mary sees John (suddenly)*
                 (All times coincide.)
             b. Simple past: $E, R < U$ *Mary saw John*
                 (Event and reference times coincide, preceding time of utterance.)
             c. Simple future: $U < E, R$ *Mary will see John*
                 (Event and reference times coincide, following time of utterance.)
             d. Present perfect: $E < U, R$ *Mary has seen John*
                 (Utterance and reference times coincide but follow the event time.)
             e. Past perfect: $E < R < U$ *Mary had seen John*
                 (Event time precedes the reference time which precedes the utterance time.)
             f. Future perfect: $U, E < R$ *Mary will have seen John*
                 (Event time and utterance time precede reference time.)

The first three tenses are essentially equivalent to those defined above, but the last three differ in crucial ways. In the *present perfect*, the utterance and reference times coincide to give the structure whereby the result of the preceding event has 'present relevance'. The other perfect tenses differ in respect to the relative orders of pairs of the times. So in the *past perfect* (*pluperfect*) the three times are fully ordered with respect to each other so the result of the event is relevant to some time before the time of utterance, while in the *future perfect* the

---

[4] Reichenbach used '_' for the *precedes* relation.

temporal relationship between utterance and event times is left unspecified (both are merely required to precede the reference time).

We will not go further into the Reichenbach analysis of tense (although it will appear in a slightly altered form below), but it is clear that the use of a reference time provides more scope to account for the temporal contours of tensed sentences. Furthermore, it shows that tense can be perspicuously modelled without the use of tense operators. Indeed, the use of temporal reference points, rather than logical operators, to define tense, and the fact, noted earlier, that tenses may provide anaphoric anchors for situations allows for the possibility of using DRT as the representation language for modelling tense (and aspect). This is because the reference time can provide the necessary connection between the time of a reported eventuality and others that have already been introduced in the representation of the discourse content. We will provide some indication of how this result can be achieved below without going into great detail (for which consult Further reading).

6.4.2   Tense in DRT

The way that event theory can be made to work with times is to specify the relations that eventualities may have with respect to temporal intervals directly, rather than in terms of indices on the model. This requires intervals as well as eventualities to be represented in our logical language. First of all, we treat temporal intervals as *discourse referents* in the way we have already seen in the last chapter. Distinct sortal construals of eventualities as states or events will be represented in the DRSs directly (but we will not go into how these construals are derived, which we take to be a function of the interaction between the intrinsic semantics of different sentence components and the context of construal). We use the following notational conventions to distinguish types of discourse referents that stand for eventualities and times:

(6.64) e: event (process, achievement, accomplishment)
s: state
t: temporal interval (event time)
n: now (utterance time)
r: reference time

Following Kamp and Reyle (1993), we treat *events* (processes, accomplishments, achievements) as differing from *states* in the way they relate to the event time: events are *included* in the event time so that the event time provides the temporal boundary within which a particular event is included, as shown in (6.65a); states may *overlap* with the event time and so may have occurred prior to that time or may exist after it, as shown in (6.65b):

(6.65)   a. $e \subseteq t$: event is included in event time
Mary walked to work yesterday.

b. $s \bigcirc t$: state overlaps with event time[5]

John was sick yesterday (and still is today).

For the *simple past tense* in English, we adopt Reichenbach's analysis and take the event time as coinciding with the reference time, with both preceding the time of utterance:

(6.66)   *simple past*

$t < n$ event time precedes utterance time

$r = t$ reference time is event time

Analysing a sentence like *Mary baked a cake* is fairly straightforward. We assume that every new utterance adds a time of utterance n to an empty DRS. Parsing *Mary* adds a new discourse referent m. The transitive verb *bake* is usually associated with an accomplishment, so the event e that it introduces is taken to be contained within the event time. The latter is specified by the past tense morphology to be coincident with the reference time and to precede the utterance time. Finally, *a cake* introduces a new discourse referent, x, into the DRS with a condition that it be a cake. This is represented in developing DRSs in (6.67):[6]

(6.67)   Mary baked a cake

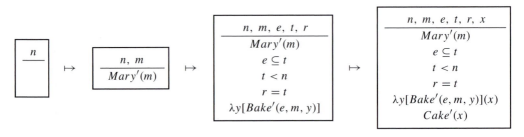

Analysing the simple past of a stative verb like *love* is similar except for the relation of overlap, rather than inclusion, between the state and the event time. The final DRS for a sentence like *John loved Mary* is:

---

[5] We use the symbol $\bigcirc$ for representing the overlap relation. For current purposes it can be taken to be like the semantic, o, relation of temporal overlap given in section 6.1, but see Kamp and Reyle (1993: 664ff.) for possible semantics of the sorts of DRSs we present here.

[6] In order to show how the DRS might be progressively built up on a word-by-word basis the example shows an intermediate step where there is a one place predicate $\lambda y[Bake'(e, m, y)]$ which applies to the discourse referent introduced by the direct object. This is for expository purposes only and is not intended as a serious account of a way to make DRT incremental.

(6.68)

$$\begin{array}{|c|}
\hline
n,\ j,\ s,\ t,\ r,\ m \\
\hline
John'(j) \\
s \bigcirc t \\
t < n \\
r = t \\
Love'(s, j, m) \\
Mary'(m) \\
\hline
\end{array}$$

In the simple present tense in English, because it allows future time reference (*I go to London next week*), we need only specify that the event time does not precede the time of utterance, allowing the former to be coincident or follow the latter.[7]

(6.69)   *simple present*

$t \not< n$ event time does not precede utterance time

$r = n$ reference time is utterance time n

Analysing *The students are asleep*, gives the development shown in (6.70). We assume that the initial DRS represents a context in which there is a group, G, that the definite noun phrase *the students* can pick out. Note here that the copula just introduces the state which is identified by the predicative adjective and is not represented as having any other content. The identification of event time with utterance time shown in the final DRS is an inferential update of $t \not< n$, induced by the semantics of the stative predicate *Asleep'*.

(6.70)   The students are asleep.

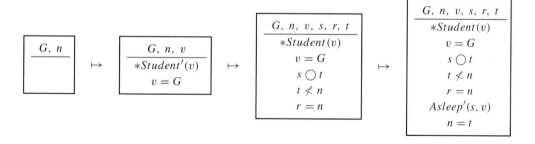

The future-time reference of a sentence like *Bill goes to Aberdeen tomorrow* is determined by the temporal adverbial *tomorrow*, which entails the update that the event time follows the time of utterance:

(6.71)   Bill goes to Aberdeen tomorrow.

---

[7] Given the past construals of the present tense in the use we called *historical present* earlier, this is of course a simplification and is supposed to be taken more as a typical interpretation of the present tense not an invariable one.

(6.76)   John entered the room. He smiled and sat down.

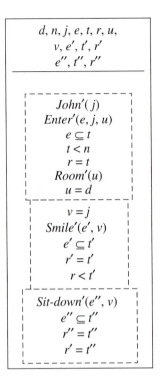

Exercise 6.4

Provide DRSs for the following discourses. Identify any problems you encounter (simplify predicates where necessary):

a. Mary liked Hillary and baked a cake for her, but Hillary didn't like it.
b. John will go to Edinburgh tomorrow. He takes the 6:15 train and has a meeting at 11:00.
c. A politician took a bribe, but denied it when he was accused of the crime.
d. Sue was ill yesterday. She didn't come to work and I now have three reports to write.

6.5   Aspect and Aktionsart

As we saw, tense is a category whose construal is essentially anaphoric with the role of relating eventualities to the time of utterance and reference time(s). However, in most languages, tense morphology encodes much more than such temporal location properties. In addition, the perceived internal consistency of the eventuality described may be presented through the aspectual distinctions each language makes available. The category of *aspect* may present an event as ongoing, or completed or as habitual or generic. Besides inflectional morphology, aspectual distinctions are also expressed in interaction with lexicalised properties of the predicates describing eventualities, what is called *lexical aspect* or *Aktionsart*. The interaction of these two types of aspect and temporal location information given by tense is important in determining the exact semantic properties of assertions. Given the reservations noted in section 6.3.1, regarding the importance of both the syntactic context and the context of utterance for such distinctions, we will examine next how these are related and how they combine to produce variable interpretations. We start with grammatical aspect.

6.5.1   Grammatical aspect

Within the tense systems of natural languages, what is typically referred to as *grammatical aspect* is often very difficult to separate out from tense *per se*. The *present perfect* tense in English, for example, is more aspectual than tense-like since it conveys primarily aspects of the internal structure of an event, i.e. its completion and present relevance; nevertheless it also indicates the pastness of the event with reference to the utterance time as a necessary part of its interpretation.[8]

We can distinguish two basic types of *grammatical aspect*. An eventuality can be presented as continuing at some interval of time without indicating how long it has lasted or will last in relation to that time, yielding *imperfective* aspect. In English this is typically indicated by *be V+ing* forms (6.77)–(6.78) or, for *habituals, used to V* (6.79) or just the simple present tense (6.80).

(6.77)	Mary is singing a song.	*present progressive*
(6.78)	John was baking a cake.	*past progressive*
(6.79)	Bill used to smoke.	*habitual past*
(6.80)	Bill smokes.	*simple present*

Alternatively, an eventuality may be presented as a whole, complete or undifferentiated, giving the *perfective* aspect (not to be confused with the morphological perfect construction). It is usually assumed that the simple past and future constructions in English are typically associated with perfective aspect and so convey the concept of completedness of the eventuality mentioned. The morphological perfect construction also intrinsically conveys perfective aspect, although it also, as noted above, has a stative aspect component that is non-complete in the sense that the result state of the completed event is not specified to have ended (see below, in 6.5.2–6.5.3):

(6.81)	John ran to the park.	*simple past*

---

[8] What is morphologically encoded relative to aspectual categories differs from language to language. For example, the English morphological perfect construction differs in its aspectual interpretation from what may be called *perfects* in Greek, German or French, making aspectual distinctions in language among the hardest of tasks for the second-language learner.

(6.82)   The train will arrive at 1 p.m.   *simple future*

(6.83)   Mary has baked a cake.   *present perfect*

However, note that although the simple tenses in English typically convey perfective aspect, nevertheless there are sentences where the notion of completedness for the eventuality described is denied without contradiction. For example, the following are acceptable in the appropriate contexts:

(6.84)   A: How did Mary spend the morning?
          B: Oh, she read her new book all morning. I suppose she's still at it.[9]

(6.85)   A: What did you do yesterday?
          B: The usual, I read *War and Peace*: I fear I'll never finish it.

(6.86)   A: What did you do yesterday?
          B: I painted the drawing room. It's such a big job, I don't know when I am going to finish. Hopefully tomorrow.

(6.87)   A: I heard Mary is ill, how is that possible, she's so health conscious.
          B: Remember Mary smoked for twenty years. In fact, as far as I know, she still does.

So, unlike in languages where there is an inflectional marking of the perfective–imperfective distinction, it might be argued that, in English, the simple tenses do not encode perfectivity but are only interpreted as perfective through inferential means, again indicating the all-pervading importance of context on utterance interpretation. For the purposes of the rest of this chapter, however, we will make the simplifying assumption that *simple present* and *past* in English are interpreted as perfective in terms of their aspectual properties whether this is the result of inference or an encoded default or optional association. This is because the interaction of the perfective–imperfective distinction with lexical aspect is important in characterising semantic properties of sentences and therefore in deciding how to represent contents. We turn to these interactions and their representation next.

6.5.2   Lexical aspect

As already noted, grammatically marked aspect interacts with lexical aspect, which has to do with idiosyncratic semantic properties expressed by verbs, such as whether they are typically associated with states, processes, achievements or accomplishments.

States and events

As we have seen above, a basic distinction that can be made between predicates in terms of what is conveyed by lexical aspect is that between *states*

---

[9] Example from Zegarac (1993).

(or stative predicates) and *events*. This basic distinction is one that must be determined, inferentially or otherwise, for each predicate, as we have seen that states and events relate distinctly to reference times in the discourse representation structure (see (6.65) in section 6.4.2). Syntactically, in English, these two classes have been claimed to be distinguished according to their compatibility with certain constructions. For example, states cannot be naturally expressed by the progressive construction, at least not without a rich context:

(6.88)   # Ethel is knowing the answer.   (state)

(6.89)   Ethel is playing golf.   (event)

The primary semantic property of state predicates is that the extensions of a state at one interval remain the same for all subintervals of that interval, including moments; and all substates of that state are states of the same sort. Thus, if Ethel knew the answer all day yesterday, then she knew the answer yesterday afternoon. States are thus like mass terms with no real internal structure, in other words, they do not involve change and are not dynamic, in contrast to events. This goes some way to explaining the restriction noted above. The progressive construction in English may be said to express some sort of *continuative* grammatical aspect, a subtype of the imperfective, which specifically defines some form of activity/process interpretation for the predicate involved.[10] Assuming that the progressive form expresses continuative aspect, uses of stative verbs in the progressive form will only be pragmatically acceptable if the apparent state can be *coerced* into a dynamic process interpretation. This *coercion* mechanism requires that an inference can be associated with what is normally a state predicate, so that some process can be derived as related to, or leading to, that state. So *know* is quite difficult to coerce (although not impossible) but something like *be intelligent*, although clearly stative in most contexts, can be coerced: *John was being intelligent* is thus interpreted as 'John was behaving in an intelligent fashion'. These coerced predicates are characteristically interpreted as dynamic and temporary, unlike genuine state interpretations (this concept of coercion is a central problem in lexical semantics, that we will return to in Chapter 8).

Similarly, stative verbs are often peculiar in the perfect constructions of English (the forms involving the auxiliary *have* plus the perfect participle). The perfect form encodes a complex aspectual situation which focuses on some state that results from an immediately preceding event; but if states have no internal structure this is difficult to interpret, unless some sort of coercion takes place or if there is an implied resulting state that differs from an earlier one. For example, *Ethel has known the answer* may become acceptable in a particular context

---

[10] Terminology here is very varied and often muddled. The term *progressive* is often used interchangeably for the syntactic *-ing* forms in English and the aspectual properties they express. We will from now on use *progressive* for the morphological form and *continuative* for its aspectual interpretation.

if it is known that Ethel is forgetful, and *Mary has loved John* may be interpreted involving a physical activity of loving or with an implication that Mary
no longer does love John. In such cases, pragmatic inference is required to allow
the typically stative predicate to express an eventuality with the internal structure
necessary to convey the more fine-grained information specific to the perfect.

There are other properties of states which need to be differentiated, since they
play a role in the availability of stative construal for different sentence types:
states hold as properties of entities rather than being initiated by them. In other
words, they are non-*agentive*. Although a state might come about as the result
of some event, the agentivity, if any, is a property of the causing event, not the
resulting state. This gives us an explanation of why depiction of states is not
naturally expressed with an imperative form:

(6.90)   # Know the answer!   (state)

(6.91)   Play golf!   (event)

Since imperatives ask for some situation to be brought about, the agentivity that
this implies is in contradiction to the non-agentivity of a state. Again, however,
states may be coerced into conveying an interpretation in which that state is
initiated. Thus, the Delphic exhortation to *Know yourself!* is to be interpreted
as more like 'Seek to understand yourself'. This raises substantial issues about
what the meaning of a word amounts to, in allowing such flexibility and apparent
extendability, which we turn to in Chapter 8.

Event types

Turning now to events, as we have seen, they are subdivided by
Vendler into three categories:

(6.92)   *activities/processes*: run, walk, drive a car, sing;

(6.93)   *accomplishments*: sing a song, paint a picture, write a book;

(6.94)   *achievements*: recognise, find, lose, die.

To understand the differences between these types, one can provide a general
characterisation of event predicates as referring to a temporal structure in which
potentially there is a *preparatory phase*, a *culmination point* and a *result state*:

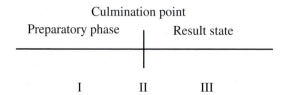

When a verb is associated with different grammatical aspects (perfective or
imperfective, etc.) we get the effect of focusing on different parts of this structure. Different types of predicate result in different effects according to whether

these are construable as depicting an event with a preparatory phase, culmination point or result state. As an illustration, we will focus mainly on the effect of the typical perfective construal of the *simple past* in English with different types of predicate.

Accomplishments

Accomplishments are complex events that imply a preparatory phase, I (an activity of some sort), a result state, III, and a culmination point at which the result state comes into being, II. The content conveyed by a sentence like *Mary wrote a letter*, for example, involves a preparatory phase of writing which at some point culminates, leading to there being a letter that Mary wrote:

Accomplishment: *preparatory phase* and *culmination point*

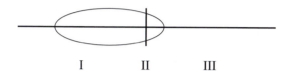

Some achievements may be construed as involving a preparatory phase as well

Achievements

Achievements, on the other hand, typically involve an instantaneous transition between states. An assertion of the sentence *John recognised the dog* seems to imply that there was a transition from a state of John's not recognising the dog to one in which his recognition of the dog is achieved:

Achievement: *culmination point*

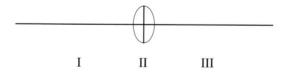

Some achievements may be construed as involving a preparatory phase as well as an instantaneous change of state. The content conveyed by the verb *die* is like this in that the *simple past* in its completed (perfective) interpretation, as in *The plant died*, simply provides the information that the plant underwent a change of state from alive to dead. However, the lead-up to this change of state may be conceived of as a process that leads up to such a change of state as shown by the acceptable use of the progressive form in the sentence *The plant is dying* to express continuative aspect. In such uses, normally achievement predicates behave like accomplishments, in that a preparatory phase must be assumed so that they become compatible with the progressive. Typically though, such interpretations do not involve any notion of agency on the part of the subject (unlike typical accomplishments). Not all achievement verbs can be easily construed as compatible with a preparatory phase. Although *The train to London is arriving at platform 19* is fine, *John is recognising the dog* is peculiar and requires a rich context to make it acceptable (such as that John has Alzheimer's disease and does not always recognise his dog).

Activities

Finally, *activities* (or *processes*) are not complex in structure in the way that achievements and accomplishments are. A sentence like *John sang* in the simple past merely expresses that some process of John's singing occurred without focusing on any of its constituent parts:

Activity: *no structure*

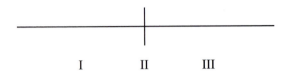

I   II   III

Activities are thus like states in that they typically express lack of significant internal structure. However, unlike states, we may consider activities, like the denotations of count nouns, to consist of *atomic parts*. We need to differentiate atomic from other parts of activities because there are subparts of these events that cannot themselves be considered to have the characteristics of that activity. Thus, walking events have subparts that may be considered walking events, but bits of these 'atomic' walking events (snapshots) cannot be walking, since, for example, lifting a leg from the ground does not by itself indicate walking. We can therefore treat activities like walking as groups of atomic walking events.

In sum, characterising events such as accomplishments and achievements as complex events allows us to reduce the number of primitive sorts of eventualities to just two: *states* and *activities/processes*. So accomplishments can be characterised as involving a process (or set of processes) leading to a result state, while achievements can be characterised as a transition between two states or an activity plus a transition between two states. Not all linguists agree that achievements and accomplishments should be treated as complex events in this way, but, as we shall see below, this view of the structure of such events allows us to account fairly straightforwardly for their behaviour in relation to grammatical aspect, to which we now turn.

6.5.3   Representing aspect

In this section, we give, using DRT, a representational characterisation of the interaction of grammatical aspect with lexical aspect. The discussion will show how the primary aspectual distinction between perfective and imperfective construal of events may give rise to variable interpretations for different event types.

Perfective aspect and event type

As noted above, there are two basic types of aspect: perfective and imperfective. Perfective aspect (remember, not to be confused with **morphological** perfect forms) presents a situation as temporally undifferentiated, but **complete**, and ignores any internal structure it may have. The sentence *Jo kicked Chester* thus presents the event of Jo kicking Chester as a complete unit, without indicating how long or how often it occurred. Hence, to know the truth value of the formula that reflects the content for this sentence, all we need to know is whether the event occurred or not (at some time in the past). The perfective may be (and often is) treated in English as the semantically neutral aspect, so the representations of normal tensed sentences give essentially perfective interpretations. So simple past, present and future tenses are all considered perfective.[11]

Because activities may be construed as denoting groups of atomic, individual events, as suggested above, and so are without an inherent culmination point, when in combination with the perfective aspect, their construal indicates nothing but that some event has occurred, without giving any rise to any entailment that the activity has ceased. So the sentence *The dog barked all night and is still barking* is not contradictory. Using the DRT style of analysis and combining this with the analysis of simple tenses earlier, we get the following representation of the perfective construal of an activity, which is just the equivalent of the past tense representations given in section 6.4.2:

(6.95)   A dog barked.

$$
\begin{array}{|l|}
\hline
n,\ x,\ e,\ t,\ r,\ u \\
\hline
e \subseteq t \\
t < n \\
r = t \\
Dog'(x) \\
Bark'(e, x) \\
\hline
\end{array}
$$

With achievements, on the other hand, perfective aspect presents an event which consists of a transition between states and therefore focuses on the culmination point. The result state might persist, but the event itself has necessarily finished. Thus, *Mary reached the summit at midday* entails that at any time after midday the specific event of Mary's reaching the summit does not hold any more (it only holds as having happened in the past), although the result state of Mary's being at the summit may be true. So for an achievement we have the follow-

---

[11] Although with the caveat noted earlier that such construals are context-dependent, cf. the construal of present tense forms of English as either the perfective historical or narrative present *Beckham scores a goal* or the imperfective generic *Beckham scores goals*.

ing representation, where f is the discourse referent for some contextually given summit:

(6.96)   Mary reached the summit.

$$
\begin{array}{|c|}
\hline
f,\ n,\ m,\ e,\ t,\ r,\ u \\
\hline
e \subseteq t \\
t < n \\
r = t \\
Mary'(m) \\
Reach'(e, m, u) \\
Summit'(u) \\
u = f \\
\hline
\end{array}
$$

If the verb *reach* is treated as denoting an event with internal structure indicating a change of state from not being somewhere (here the summit) to being somewhere (at the summit), then there is a straightforward update of (6.96) to (6.97), which makes explicit which change of state has occurred.

(6.97)   Mary reached the summit.

$$
\begin{array}{|c|}
\hline
f,\ n,\ m,\ e,\ t,\ r,\ u,\ s \\
\hline
e \subseteq t \\
t < n \\
r = t \\
Mary'(m) \\
Reach'(e, m, u) \\
Summit'(u) \\
u = f \\
\neg \begin{array}{|c|} \hline s' \\ \hline Be\text{-}at'(s', m, f) \\ s' < s \\ \hline \end{array} \\
Be\text{-}at'(s, m, f) \\
s \bigcirc t \\
\hline
\end{array}
$$

For accomplishments, the perfective aspect functions as with achievements to present the complex event of preparatory activity plus result state as a single element, so again the event must have culminated at the relevant time and the result state must hold. So if *John baked a cake* involves an internal structure of the process of John's baking the cake, plus the coming into existence of a cake, then we can conclude that there existed a cake at the event time that John had baked. This is given straightforwardly by the DRS in (6.98):

(6.98)   John baked a cake.

$$
\begin{array}{|c|}
\hline
n,\ j,\ e,\ t,\ r,\ x \\
\hline
e \subseteq t \\
t < n \\
r = t \\
John'(j) \\
Bake'(e, j, x) \\
Cake'(x) \\
\hline
\end{array}
$$

Things are a bit different for *states*, as we've already seen. Because states are temporally undifferentiated, without inherent beginning and endpoints and without atomic parts, the perfective simply picks out some relevant sub-state. *The student knew the answer* is true at time t just in case there is a state of the student's knowing the answer which is true of an interval of time that includes t. It does not preclude the student's knowing the answer at any time later. The tense of such sentences, however, may give rise to *implicatures*, these being implications that are derivable relative to particular contexts without corresponding to an intrinsic property of the words in question.[12] Thus, the past perfective construal of a verb may give rise to an implicature that the state described has ended, as in, for example, an utterance of *John knew the answer*, while some future perfective construal such as *John will know the answer* may give rise to an implicature that the state does not obtain now. However, these implicatures may often be cancelled (cancellability being diagnostic of an implicature) depending on the specific semantic properties of the state expressed by some verb.

The English perfect construction, as we have seen, expresses perfective aspect in that it requires an accomplishment or achievement to have culminated, but additionally focuses on some state resulting from the culmination. This state is construed as having relevance with respect to the reference time, which for the *present perfect* is the time of utterance, but for the *past perfect* is some time before the utterance time.[13] We may characterise the semantic effect of *present perfect* therefore as in (6.99), where we use a predicate $Result\text{-}from'(e, s)$ to indicate that the state s results from some event e, without going into detail about the semantics of such a predicate.[14]

(6.99)   English *present perfect*:

$e \subseteq t$	event is contained in event time
$t < n$	event time precedes time of utterance
$r = n$	reference time is utterance time

---

[12] *Implicature* is a concept central to pragmatic theories: see Chapter 1.

[13] The semantics of the *past perfect* differs minimally from that of the *present perfect* in that the reference time r precedes the the utterance time n.

[14] Kamp and Reyle (1993) use a symbol $\supset\subset$ interpreted as 'abut' so that the state starts immediately as the event ends. The analysis of the temporal and event structure also differs slightly from the one proposed there.

Result-from'(e, s)	some state immediately follows on from event
$s \bigcirc r$	state overlaps with reference time

If a verb like *die* includes a final state of being dead, then the perfect gives rise to representations such as (6.100).

(6.100)   The plant has died.

$$
\begin{array}{|c|}
\hline
a,\ e,\ t,\ n,\ r,\ s,\ u \\
\hline
e \subseteq t \\
t < n \\
r = n \\
Result\text{-}from'(e, s) \\
s \bigcirc r \\
Die'(e, u) \\
u = a \\
Plant'(u) \\
Dead'(s, u) \\
\hline
\end{array}
$$

Notice what is happening here. Some basic temporal and event structure is associated with particular morphological forms, such as *simple present* and morphological *perfect*, but exactly what can be inferred about the situation expressed by sentences containing them depends on the lexical semantics of the verbs themselves and (possibly) the grammatical or semantic properties of their complements. Trying to account fully for aspectual interpretation thus relies on inference not just over what is explicitly given in some sentence, but also over the unexpressed semantic properties of the words it contains, a much more complex view of meaning than what we saw in Chapters 2, 3 and 4. This complexity becomes even more explicit when we consider imperfective aspect which we now turn to.

Imperfective aspect and event type

While an assertion of perfectivity is an assertion that an event is complete, the imperfective aspect focuses on an on-going or incomplete activity. There are different types of imperfective, the most commonly discussed ones being *habitual*, where a series of events are construed as being one larger event (e.g. *Jo used to kick the chair*) and *continuative*, where a single event is presented as continuing (e.g. *Jo was kicking the chair*). Finer-grained distinctions than these may be made but in all such construals what is happening is that it is the internal structure of an event that is being highlighted: for *habitual aspect*, it is the ongoing series of events, and for continuative aspect, it is some ongoing (continuous) activity/process. We can represent the latter type of aspect using the overlap relation, indicating that some event overlaps with the event time, $e \bigcirc t$, a property normally associated with states, and stipulating that e is an activity:

(6.101)   Continuative aspect:

$e \bigcirc t$ event overlaps with event time

$Activity'(e)$ event is an activity

Assuming, as we have done, that the progressive morphological form in English expresses continuative aspect, we get example DRSs such as that in (6.102):

(6.102)   Bill is running.

$$\begin{array}{|c|}
\hline
n,\ b,\ e,\ t,\ r \\
\hline
t = n \\
r = t \\
e \bigcirc t \\
Bill'(b) \\
Activity'(e) \\
Run'(e, b) \\
\hline
\end{array}$$

Notice that this has no entailment of completion, because the semantics of the intransitive verb *run* indicates no inherent culmination point. So the inference is that Bill may continue to run after t or have run before t.

For verbs that normally indicate events construed as achievements or accomplishments, the progressive form focuses on the **preparatory** stage of the event, itself necessarily an activity/process. It follows that an achievement verb, like *die*, is acceptable in the progressive form because it can be characterised as denoting an event which has a preparatory stage that is an activity: the process of dying.

(6.103)   The plant was dying.

$$\begin{array}{|c|}
\hline
p,\ n,\ u,\ t,\ r,\ e \\
\hline
t < n \\
r = t \\
e \bigcirc t \\
Plant'(u) \\
u = p \\
Activity'(e) \\
Process\text{-}of\text{-}dying'(e, u) \\
\hline
\end{array}$$

Notice here that there is no condition within the DRS $Die'(e, u)$ as this would necessarily include the result stage of the dying process, i.e. being dead, but there is no such entailment from an utterance of *The plant was dying* to *The plant is dead*. Similarly, an accomplishment verb in the progressive form focuses on the activity part of the event and excludes the result state as in (6.104), where the activity of running is shown as Run'_j (as distinct from its accomplishment interpretation shown as Run'_k):

(6.104)   Bill was running a marathon.

$$
\begin{array}{|c|}
\hline
n,\ b,\ t,\ e,\ r,\ x \\
\hline
t < n \\
r = t \\
e \bigcirc t \\
Bill'(b) \\
Activity'(e) \\
Run'_j(e, b) \\
Marathon'(x) \\
\hline
\end{array}
$$

There is a problem with such a characterisation, however, and that is that there is no representation of the fact that Bill isn't just running but he's running a marathon. As with achievements, we cannot directly include a condition of this sort since $Run'_k(e, b, x)$ will necessarily yield the result state of Bill's having finished running the marathon, even though no such entailment exists from (6.104) itself. This problem has long been known and is often referred to as the *imperfective paradox* (Dowty 1979). The progressive focuses on some subpart of an event that is an activity and so does not include any inherent culmination point. In consequence, a sentence containing a verb in the progressive also does not guarantee that any expected result state is ever achieved. We can see this because of the acceptability of sentences like:

(6.105)   Mary was building a new house but went bankrupt and the house was never finished.

It is clear that there must be no entailment from an assertion involving the progressive form of an accomplishment verb to a perfective construal: no complete event may have been accomplished.

This problem is difficult to solve as it appears to involve *modality*. That is to say, the accomplishment event does not necessarily get completed but could be completed if all 'goes according to plan'. It is this last concept, however, that is really problematic, as the characterisation of what it means for something to go according to plan is very difficult to formalise. In order to solve this problem

Dowty (1979) employs what he calls *inertia worlds*, possible worlds (i.e. varying states of affairs) that are exactly like the current world in every way up to the relevant moment, but may diverge from it thereafter. These worlds all develop in a fashion most consistent with whatever has gone before, i.e. nothing unexpected happens and the event in question is completed. These are the worlds relevant for assessing the truth of the existence of the completed event denoted by the sentence in the non-progressive form. Hamm and van Lambalgen (2005), on the other hand, within a theory of logic programming, talk of plans that may not come to fruition. Many other solutions to the problem have been suggested, but we will sidestep the issue here. We will analyse the progressive form of accomplishment verbs as involving modality, like Dowty, but merely weakly say that such progressive forms involve only a process characterising the preparatory phase but nevertheless allowing that this process **could** be extended into an event that is characteristic of the completed accomplishment. So we analyse *Bill was running a marathon* not as in (6.104), but as (6.106), noting in passing that problems remain with such an analysis.[15]

(6.106)   Bill was running a marathon.

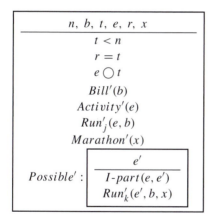

Given this type of representation, no contradiction results if the activity is interrupted and the accomplishment is never culminated. Hence, we can continue the development of the DRS in (6.106) as in (6.107), where we can infer that the running of the marathon was never completed:

(6.107)   when he had a heart attack.

---

[15] Note that the the relation *I-part* is to be interpreted just as the individual-part relation for count nouns. If we were to analyse all events as complex ordered sets, then this could be replaced simply by the membership sign $\in$.

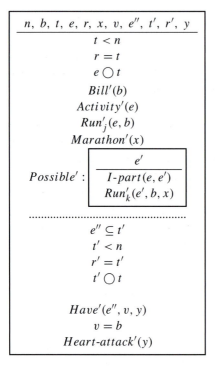

$$n, b, t, e, r, x, v, e'', t', r', y$$
$$t < n$$
$$r = t$$
$$e \bigcirc t$$
$$Bill'(b)$$
$$Activity'(e)$$
$$Run'_j(e, b)$$
$$Marathon'(x)$$

$$Possible' : \begin{array}{|l|} \hline e' \\ \hline I\text{-}part(e, e') \\ Run'_k(e', b, x) \\ \hline \end{array}$$

$$e'' \subseteq t'$$
$$t' < n$$
$$r' = t'$$
$$t' \bigcirc t$$

$$Have'(e'', v, y)$$
$$v = b$$
$$Heart\text{-}attack'(y)$$

There is much, much more to say about aspect, both grammatical and lexical, a topic which continues to provide fruitful ground for research. We have barely scratched the surface here, but what is very important to notice at this juncture is the increasing reliance on pragmatic inference to obtain the intended interpretations. Particular grammatical forms, such as the progressive, provide a fairly weak semantic characterisation of the aspectual properties that they convey, such as being an activity that overlaps with the event time. All the rest is derived by some, partially pragmatic, negotiation of the meaning involved in the understanding of words in context, particularly verbs. This means that combinations of grammatical aspectual properties with the meanings of individual verbs will give rise to quite different types of interpretation, and thus we get considerable variation in the acceptability of particular forms depending on context. This is a matter we return to in Chapter 8.

Exercise 6.5

Draw DRSs for the following discourses:

a. Mary is very upset. Every plant has died.
b. John was washing his hair when he remembered his dentist appointment.
c. Hillary has been arguing about the economy for weeks. Now she is just bored and has decided that she will go on holiday.
d. When John entered the room, Mary was crying. He ignored her and she ran out, still sobbing uncontrollably.

6.6   Conclusion

In this chapter we saw first how tense systems in language provide a basis for presenting assertions about how events are envisaged as taking place across a flow of time. We also saw how this open-ended potential for complex conceptualisation about the temporal flow can in part be dependent on context, with the interpretation of tense forms being relative to what has preceded in the discourse, paralleling pronominal dependencies. We then went on to give a glimpse of possible interactions between lexical content (*Aktionsart*) and tense/aspect construal. With this sketch of the intricacies of how even one language encodes reference to time and the way in which, based on such encodings, events can be described as holding across intervals of time, it has become abundantly clear that the relation of a word or phrase to the different modes of its construal is highly complex. Indeed it threatens to open up an indefinite and open-ended complexity, a topic which we take up in the final chapter.

But a second property also has inexorably emerged during the course of this chapter. In order to keep track of how some interval of time is envisaged, characteristically with distinctions between sub-intervals, any one such interval being itself construable as divisible to an indefinite depth of complexity, a level of representation at some level of abstraction from the flow of time itself is completely indispensable. In this discussion, the use of DRT provided essential vocabulary for talking about the subtle relations between concepts made available by words, and their interactions with the intervals of time they are taken to describe. Indeed, it is in this area that the Janus-faced nature of DRT comes into its own, with its representational flavour enabling structures to be constructed and inter-related, yet its grounding in a model-theoretic basis enabling such representations to constitute semantic explication of the natural-language expressions themselves. Without such representational constructs, all the semantics can provide is an unstructured sequence of time points, a construct far too minimal to explore the rich array of dependencies that are expressible. But with representational constructs such as those provided by DRT, we have a means, at least, of addressing the complexity of temporal inference that natural languages make available in a relatively tractable form.

We turn, in the following chapter, to another area of natural language where there is abundant evidence of the need for representationalism in semantic explication, both in the characterisation of content and in the characterisation of context.

6.7   Further reading

For basic information about the linguistic analysis of tense and aspect, see Comrie (1976, 1985); Lyons (1977: 677–90); Dahl (1985). The suggestion that temporal intervals are more useful for the analysis of natural languages was proposed by Bennett and Partee (1972/2004), and developed in Dowty (1979: ch. 3); Cresswell (1985: ch. 3), and many others. The basic tense logic was proposed in Prior (1967) and there are good introductions in Dowty *et al.* (1981: 112–21); Cann (1993: 233–51); Steedman (1997); Chierchia and McConnell-Ginet (2000). Kearns (2000: ch. 7) gives a good overview of tense and aspect and an introduction to Reichenbach's approach, for which also see Reichenbach (1947) and Michaelis (2006). Event theory owes its increasing popularity to Davidson (1967) (and see also the other articles in Davidson 2001). Examples of this approach are legion and can be found in Parsons (1989); Dowty (1991); Kamp and Reyle (1993); Tenny and Pustejovsky (2000); Rothstein (2004); and many more. Lasersohn (1995) and Schein (1993) discuss events in detail with reference also to plurality. For a symmetric model-theoretic treatment of individuals, times and possibilities, see Schlenker (2006). The DRS account sketched here is based on Kamp and Reyle (1993: 483–521, 556–93) (albeit simplified in places); see also Kamp and Schiehlen (2001). Different approaches to tense and aspect which nevertheless use event theory can be found in Moens and Steedman (1988); Hamm and van Lambalgen (2005); Fernando (2007). See also Bittner (2008). For the general problems raised by intensionality for model-theoretic semantics see Fox and Lappin (2005). For the issue of representationalism in relation to tense and aspect interpretation see Hamm *et al.* (2006).

7   Ellipsis as a window on context

7.1   Puzzles at the syntax–semantics interface

As the last three chapters have demonstrated, formal-semantic methodologies have now an expressive power and flexibility well beyond that of predicate logic, with its flat syntax and propositional quantifier-binding operators. Use of the lambda calculus, with the attendant concepts of type-lifting and generalised quantifiers that this makes available, in conjunction with tense (and general modal) logic, led to a rich array of analyses across a very wide range of natural-language phenomena, while preserving a concept of compositionality of meaning defined over natural-language sentences. Indeed, it was the evident applicability to natural language of the lambda calculus in combination with constructs of tense and modal logic that was at the heart of Montague's claim that natural languages were essentially like formal languages. Yet, as we have already seen, the assumptions on which these formal tools are grounded are not problem-free, suggesting that something intrinsic to natural language is somehow missed, despite the sophistication of the tools. And the heart of this problem is the systemic context-dependence of natural-language expressions, as work in DRT has brought out so vividly.

It became evident of course from the outset that the context-dependence of natural language required resources over and above the model-theoretic devices appropriate for formal languages (see Chapter 3). However, within early formulations of formal semantics (Lewis 1970), the phenomenon of context-dependence was treated as essentially peripheral, as if merely needing some stipulation of a speaker-index, a hearer-index and some limited set of further indices as additional parameters in the formal models for the truth-theoretic evaluation of strings.[1]

The significance of the work on DRT, led by Kamp (1981) and swiftly followed by others, was that it brought into sharp focus the problem of capturing properties of those expressions of natural language, specifically anaphoric devices, whose intrinsic contribution to content is to signal a dependence on context for their interpretation. Moreover, as we saw in Chapter 6, patterns of dependence displayed by pronominal anaphora are paralleled in the tense/aspect

---

[1] This issue remains controversial. See Chapter 8 for a recent defence of the assumptions underpinning the Davidsonian programme by Cappelen and Lepore (2005).

domain; but there arise further complexities associated specifically with the sortal distinctiveness of the concepts of eventualities and times that are variously depicted by tense and aspect specifications.

In probing such context-dependency, two further properties emerged. First, as we've seen, explanations of context-dependence invariably seem to require essential reference to structural notions, for example, *discourse representations* and *discourse referents*, that may not correspond directly to structural properties of the surface sentential string or the more coarse-grained model-theoretic constructs. Though the phenomenon of pronominal anaphora is perhaps the best known among linguists, it is arguably the complexity of event reference that provides the most striking evidence of the need for rich granularity of structure in natural-language interpretation. The intermediate structural constructs that we saw as essential components of tense and aspect interpretation, i.e. event discourse referents, are characteristically not reflected in argument terms by the morpho-syntax of many of the world's languages, making them a special challenge. Indeed, as noted in Kamp *et al.* (2005), it was the observation of intricate cross-sentential dependencies of French tense/aspect construal which triggered the development of what became Discourse Representation Theory (DRT). Second, the requisite relations between anaphoric expression and its antecedent may well extend beyond a single sentence boundary; however, in any account in which structural representations are delimited in defining properties for isolated sentence-strings, all such cases will be excluded and set aside as completely separate phenomena to be dealt with by another module of the interpretation system. In both these respects, DRT constitutes a radical departure from formal-language assumptions of content as definable directly over natural-language sentences. And as further work has emerged, it has become evident that dependence on some structural concept of context transcending the confines of isolated sentence construals lies at the heart of the flexibility of natural-language interpretation. So, at the very least, the phenomenon of context-dependence raises challenges for strictly model-theoretic explanations of natural-language content.

Nevertheless, there is one striking respect in which DRT does not diverge from formal-semantic assumptions, despite all subsequent developments, and this is the presumed independence of syntax and semantics. Following the formal-language methodology, semantic interpretation operates on whatever structures inhabited by words have been defined by the syntactic component, prior to any semantic consideration. The consequence of this commitment is that all cases where anaphora construal interacts with syntactic properties of sentences will get classified as solely within the remit of syntax and explicable by those syntax-internal principles. But such interplay between construal of anaphoric expressions and syntax occurs in all natural languages, whether by *resumptive* pronouns serving to identify the site of construal of a left-dislocated expression (in some cases called *intrusive* pronouns), *crossover* effects which involve interaction between left-dislocated expressions and pronominals which do **not** constitute the site of their construal, so-called *hanging topic* structures, *left* and *right dislocation* structures, *expletive* pronouns, etc. If you turn to any textbook, you find that examples are legion. In all syntactic textbooks, such phenomena are invariably taken as strictly syntactic and completely independent of semantic or discourse-anaphoric uses of the same morphological expressions. Indeed such syntactic phenomena are said to be subject to sui generis structural restrictions, so-called *island constraints*, all these restrictions being taken as evidence that the phenomenon in question is syntactic and, hence, grammar-internal. The inevitable consequence of this stance is postulating multiple ambiguities for a single pronominal form even though the phenomena are constant for pronominals across the spectrum of natural languages.

Retention of the syntax-semantics interface to reflect sentence-internal as opposed to discourse anaphoric phenomena has the disappointing consequence that a unitary concept of anaphora remains elusive. Indeed the very terminology of *expletive pronoun, resumptive pronoun, intrusive pronoun, E-type pronoun,* etc., captures vividly just how deeply ingrained is the assumption that there is no unitary basis to pronouns in language. Unexpectedly, given the huge impetus the development of DRT gave to the need to explore a unitary basis to anaphora, the DRT methodology is silent at this juncture, and is content just to articulate anaphoric dependencies that uncontentiously fall within the proper remit of (discourse) semantics. Only these sub-types of anaphoric dependency are then used as evidence of the essential representational structure to be articulated over and above that defined by syntactic principles. So, relative to DRT assumptions, we indeed face at least two levels of representation: (a) representation of structure in syntax reflecting structural properties of strings, and (b) representations of structure in semantics, reflecting structural aspects of assigned content. The puzzle of what phenomena should be classified as syntactic and what as semantic which then artificially ensues threatens to leave unexplained the more fundamental concept of context itself. All that the account provides is an analysis whereby some phenomena displaying anaphoric dependence are classified as context-dependent (the ones pertaining to semantics), others not (the ones that are classified as syntactic). The challenge of whether there is any unitary concept of context-dependence relative to which a phenomenon like anaphora can be explained in at least an integrated way remains wide open.

It might seem that anaphoric dependencies between pronouns and their antecedents is just one puzzle among others, perhaps a minor one, so that its satisfactory resolution should not be seen as foundational for natural-language models. However, as will become clear in this and the next chapter, context-dependence, the defining property of anaphoric elements, occurs with any type of linguistic expression, not just pronouns. We now turn to look at another phenomenon, or set of phenomena, that can be seen in these terms and which can be taken as diagnostic in probing the concept of context. This phenomenon is *ellipsis* and, as we shall see, its pervasiveness in natural languages makes it an important factor in any modelling of human linguistic abilities and performance.

7.2   Ellipsis: preliminaries

As we saw at the very outset of this book, *ellipsis* is the quintessential context-dependency phenomenon, since the interpretation of elliptical fragments, by definition, depends on what context provides. As (7.1) illustrates, ellipsis comes in several forms. In English, propositional interpretations can be recovered from context both from the trigger of a bare noun phrase, or from a presented subject plus bare auxiliary, or from a sequence of such fragments:

(7.1)   John is coming to the house on the 17th with Harry; and Tom on the 20th with Sue. You too? I also heard Mary was, with Bill, but on the 22nd.

So, as with anaphora, there is the immediate question of whether ellipsis itself constitutes a single phenomenon. Intuitively, it should provide a window on what constitutes context: things can get left out because in context it is obvious what is meant – the context provides all the information that is necessary, and no more needs to be said. This simple observation, however, leaves the problem wide open. What does the context make obvious, and what form does it take? Is it words that the speaker doesn't need to utter because they are given in the context, with the phenomenon therefore falling within the remit of syntax? Or is it word meanings that the hearer can recover, so a semantic puzzle? Or is it the content attributed to words, as uttered in the specific context, that the hearer can recover, so in some sense pragmatic? Or what? Different elliptical forms suggest different answers to these questions, but all share the property of allowing some minimal form to be a trigger for the construction of some much richer, generally clausal, form of interpretation. Intuitively, it is the context as it unfolds in the utterance of (7.1) which is determining the interpretation of each of *Tom on the 20th with Sue, You too?, Mary was, with Bill* and *on the 22nd*. If we were to say, to the contrary, that **different** concepts of context determine the varying forms of interpretation for different types of fragment, we would be forced to analyse the construal of (7.1) as imposing on speakers a shift from one type of context-dependence to another. This might be justifiable, but it would hardly be an analysis to be preferred a priori, given the naturalness of shift from one form of ellipsis to another. Thus the challenge is whether a single answer to this set of questions is even possible.

The further significance of ellipsis is the way it conflicts with the standard methodological assumption that language can be studied as a single monologue-style phenomenon. Whatever forms of ellipsis can be expressed by one speaker can be expressed across more than one speaker, as the similarity between (7.1) and the alternative replies in (7.2) makes plain:

(7.2)   A: John is coming to the party with Harry.
     (i) B: And Tom with Sue.
     (ii) B: You too?
     (iii) B: And I heard Mary was.
     (iv) B: Not with Bill?
     (v) B: On the 19th?

Furthermore, there are elliptical forms which are specific to dialogue (at least as a simplification), in particular, the pairing of question and answer sequences:

(7.3)   A: Who did every husband visit?
           B: His wife.

As (7.3) also illustrates, dependencies of a familiar anaphoric sort can be seamlessly continued across from one speaker to another, even involving the binding of a pronoun by a quantifying expression.

  This might of course be taken to buttress the view that sentences can be studied independently of use, with fragmentary answers as a peripheral mimicking of complete sentences. But the presumption that sentence wellformedness, the purview of the grammar, can be defined only for single-speaker utterances is very far from the truth. As (7.4)–(7.6) show, linguistic dependencies of all types can be split across more than one speaker, whether in a question–answer exchange or more generally:

(7.4)   A: We are going
           B: to our mother
           C: to keep her company.

(7.5)   A: What did you give
           B: Eliot? A teddy bear.

(7.6)   A: It's Mothering Sunday. What are you planning?
           B: For myself? Nothing much. For my mother, a visit to the nearby park.

(7.4) involves a split between a given verb and required or optional adjuncts, whereas (7.5) involves a split between a verb and its complement. (7.6) can be seen as a split between the antecedent for a reflexive anaphor and the anaphor itself, and notice that in this case the shift in morphological form between first and second person apparently does not disturb the successful construal of the question as addressed to B about B's plans for herself. In each of these cases, the fragment follow-on is interpreted, as all elliptical fragments are, relative to the context in which the fragment occurs, here, context being the immediately previous dialogue turn.

  These examples display a further phenomenon characteristic of many forms of ellipsis. Ellipsis across conjuncts and/or across speakers displays an essential *parallelism* between the antecedent form of construal and the elliptical form, a parallelism which, as B's reply in (7.6) shows, may be reflected also in the form of the expressions chosen, so that there is both semantic and syntactic parallelism. This parallelism of interpretation and syntactic form is displayed also in coordination structures:

(7.7)   Clinton, the *Times* guy interviewed; and I think Obama, the *Telegraph*
           woman.

(7.8)   Which of his pictures is Tom submitting to the competition, and which is
           Harry?

Here too, the division of explanation as between sentence-internal, hence context-independent forms of explanation, (7.1), (7.7)–(7.8), and cross-speaker-based hence context-dependent forms of explanation, (7.4)–(7.6), seems artificial and misplaced. To the contrary, what each of these fragmentary uses (7.1)–(7.8) share is the presumption of being interpretable entirely unremarkably in the dialogue context.

The challenge then that ellipsis presents is (i) whether an integrated account of ellipsis is possible, and if so, (ii), what concept of context should be articulated to provide the basis for such an account, given all these divergent types of use. Ellipsis, that is, presents the same sort of challenge as pronominal anaphora, but even more sharply. In many cases, the lack of any morphological form corresponding to the interpretation to be assigned means that, in some sense to be explained, it is context itself which has to determine all these divergent forms of interpretation. The fall-back of course is that such elliptical fragments do not present a unitary phenomenon to be explained; but this would leave the concept of context-dependence itself lacking any general explanation. In short, the challenge posed by ellipsis is not a challenge to turn away from lightly.

7.3   Ellipsis: linguistic debates

Seen from a history-of-linguistics perspective, ellipsis might be taken as a barometer of the way linguistic argumentation has developed over the past years. Ellipsis data were originally used as evidence for deletion operations as part of syntax, then for LF-indexing mechanisms at the syntax–semantics interface, then as a purely semantic phenomenon involving higher-order abstraction and even by some (arguably most) as a mixture of the two. At the turn of the twenty-first century, there emerged arguments that at least some subpart of the phenomenon must be analysed as squarely pragmatic, hence outside the remit of the grammar. And finally, there are arguments that address the way fragments are used in dialogue, broadening the debate to include data often not even considered to be within the remit of a purely linguistic model.

The problem, as recognised from very early on, has been that, though the phenomenon is indubitably one of construal, apparently triggered by the morphological expression at the ellipsis site being so minimal, the range of variation depends on the particular form of antecedent. Elliptical forms give rise to different interpretations, even when the antecedent is taken upon just one interpretation. For example, the alternative answers (i) and (ii) in (7.9) are both ambiguous:

(7.9)   A: John is coming to the party with Harry.
        (i) B: And Tom with Sue.
        (ii) B: And I heard Sue was.

Sue in (i) can be construed either as subject of the predicate to be reconstructed or as indication that Harry is part of a group containing Sue and Tom; and the ellipsis site in (ii) can be understood either as 'coming to the party' or as 'coming to the party with Harry'.

To add to the puzzle, as we shall see, the limits on the construal available may display hallmarks of a syntactic phenomenon such as sensitivity to island constraints, generally taken to be diagnostic of the need for a syntactic explanation; but this isn't true for all types of ellipsis. Consider the following:

(7.10)   John hasn't travelled with Mary, but I know a woman who has.

(7.11)   *John was travelling with a woman that Bill stayed with the man who also had.

(7.10)–(7.11) involve classic island violations since the ellipsis sites indicated by the auxiliaries *had/has* occur inside a relative clause. Nevertheless, (7.10) is grammatical but (7.11) is not. Notice that if an island violation does **not** occur in constructions such as (7.11), called *antecedent contained ellipsis*, of which more below, these are grammatical (e.g. *John travelled with a woman Bill suggested he should*).

In consequence, the phenomenon looks at least superficially heterogeneous, and this is generally taken to justify the different explanations linguists might propose for even a single elliptical form. As part of this methodology, ellipsis has been taken as an argument for syntactic constituency. VP-ellipsis, for example, is generally taken as an argument that, even in languages where the order may be very free, a verb plus its object NP constitute a VP constituent even when the surface ordering fails to reflect this, so that the relationship between the form of the ellipsis site and the basis from which its interpretation is projected is indirect.

(7.12)   John, Mary dislikes; and Sue does too.

The disparity between the surface structure constituting the antecedent and the ellipsis site indicates that assigning distinct underlying structures for every possible interpretation is little more than a blind multiplication of ambiguities. Those taking this stance turn, rather, to a semantic form of explanation, though, as we shall see, this too is not without its problems.

In this chapter, we set out some of the many arguments that have been put forward as contributions to the ongoing controversy over whether ellipsis is a syntactic phenomenon or merely of semantic significance. What will finally emerge is that the most promising way to get an appropriately integrated account of ellipsis is to give a procedural slant to the concept of context so that what is preserved in context is a record not merely of what information has been processed but also the way such information has been built up. We shall present a potential resolution to the debate as to whether construal involves **representations** of content or merely those contents themselves. In this account, the concept of a procedure for building up content, on which this type of resolution for ellipsis turns, is essentially representational, intermediate between linguistic elements and their denotations. If this account can be sustained, then the intrinsic representational properties of context and content alike will emerge as ineliminable.

7.3.1   Ellipsis: syntactic puzzles

Ever since the early hey-days of transformational grammar ellipsis has been seen by many as syntactically heterogeneous, without a uniform basis. Indicative are the putative distinct structures assigned graphically iconic names (Ross 1967) – *sluicing* (7.13), *stripping* (7.14), *gapping* (7.15) – others more mundanely labelled – *VP-deletion/VP-ellipsis* (7.16) and *antecedent-contained deletion/ellipsis* (7.17):

(7.13)   We are reading an article by Chomsky, but I can't remember which ~~article we are reading~~.

(7.14)   Everyone is preparing a review article, ?not ~~is preparing~~ an independent paper.

(7.15)   John is preparing a review article, Sue ~~is preparing~~ a joint paper.

(7.16)   John is preparing a review article, and Sue is ~~preparing a review article~~ too.

(7.17)   John is reviewing everything that Sue is ?~~reviewing everything that Sue is reviewing everything that . . .~~

As these labels indicate, ellipsis was not seen as a phenomenon of context-dependence at all, but as a set of grammar-internal syntactic processes involving deletion of sequences of expressions under some suitable notion of identity (the question-marks above show that this is not a simple issue).

This assumption led to an immediate puzzle: as can already be seen above in (7.14) and (7.17) the notion of identity required cannot be invariably defined by taking into account the surface sequence of words – some parts of the morphological specification of the antecedent clause have to be suitably suppressed in the reconstruction of the second conjunct (Fiengo and May 1994). Consider also the following:

(7.18)   I am handing in my assignment late, and so is John.

(7.19)   I am handing in my assignment late. John ~~is handing in his/my assignment late~~ too.

(7.20)   Sue has defended herself much better than her solicitor was able to ~~*defended herself~~.

(7.18) is not naturally interpreted as 'John is handing in **my** assignment late'. In (7.20) a simple-minded deletion or copying mechanism will give ungrammatical results, either because of the verbal form required or because of the unsuccessful binding of the reflexive in the desired interpretation. Indeed, the phenomenon cannot involve trivial deletion of some initially fully articulated expression, because in the so-called antecedent-contained deletion (7.17), the ellipsis site is contained within its antecedent *reviewing everything that Sue is*, so any such assumption leads to infinite regress.

This might seem to suggest that the requirement that elliptical expressions involve in some sense identity with their antecedents can be met only by a semantic notion of identity. However, some types of ellipsis are clearly subject to constraints normally taken to be indicative of the need for a syntactic explanation. In particular, as we've already seen, the island sensitivity of antecedent-contained deletion is incontrovertible:

(7.21)   John interviewed every student Bill had.

(7.22)   *John interviewed every student that Bill ignored the teacher who had.

With this display of so-called *strong-island* sensitivity (which is widely agreed to be diagnostic of syntactic movement or its feature-passing analogue), there is general agreement within the community that at least some cases have to be given a structural form of explanation defined over the syntactic structure assigned to the linguistic string. Accordingly, rather than abandon syntactic solutions in the face of evidence that morphological properties of words may have to be ignored (see above (7.18)–(7.20)) some concept of reindexing of expressions was explored to salvage the deletion approach. This involved deletion at the ellipsis site relative to matching of only a subset of morphological features, ignoring what are called *phi-features*, hence waiving the necessity of identity of morphological specification (Fiengo and May 1994).[2] In (7.18), this involves suppressing first-person features to yield some pronominal at the ellipsis site which then allows binding by the local subject, and therefore licensed deletion. However, such a move is far from unproblematic, as it is not merely suppression of features that is required, but replacement. Consider the following dialogue-based example:

(7.23)   A: You're sitting on my chair.
            B: No, I'm not ~~sitting on your/my chair~~.

What A and B are arguing about is whether B is sitting on A's chair, not, as B says, whether B is 'sitting on my chair', i.e. his own. So retaining morphological specifications would give quite the wrong interpretation, but suppressing the first-person features for some general pronominal element wouldn't be sufficiently restrictive either: what is required is the replacement of first-person by second-person features. It is notable that the problems that arise on such accounts do so solely because of the grounding of the account in syntactic trees, trees, that is, that are inhabited by lexical items of the language like *my* and *your*.

---

[2] *Phi-* or *φ-features* are features that often take part in syntactic agreement and the identity of reference such as person, number and gender.

A further problem is that a single string under a single interpretation can function as antecedent in two distinct ways to yield discrete interpretations, as in:

(7.24)   John thinks he's clever. Bill does ~~think Bill is clever~~ too. John's wife however certainly does not ~~think John/Bill is clever~~.

(7.24) allows the second clause to be construed as 'Bill thinks that Bill is clever' on the basis of the first clause as antecedent, the so-called *sloppy* reading (the term *sloppy* was coined because the predicate content is **not** denotationally identical to the content of the antecedent VP from which it is established). But the third clause may take that very same first clause as antecedent, although this time construing the elliptical form not sloppily, but *strictly*, as 'John's wife does not think that John is clever' (conversely, the term *strict* was coined for such readings because the denotational content of both the ellipsis site and its antecedent are identical). But, if ellipsis is analysed as involving identity of structure assigned to the string modulo minor variation of morphological features, then it would seem that the first conjunct in (7.24) has to be assigned more than one syntactic structure even under a single interpretation ('John thinks John is clever') of that first conjunct (see also (7.37) below).

Exercise 7.1

Fixing the interpretation of *his* in (a) as picking out John, how many interpretations do you think (a) has? What sort of analysis would you set up for each interpretation?
   (a) John voted for his mother on the basis of her popularity; and so did Bill.
Does (b) have the same range of interpretations as (a)? If so why; if not why not? (Clue: in (b) the modification is a clausal adjunct.)
   (b) John voted for his mother, because she is popular; and so did Bill.

7.3.2   Ellipsis: semantic challenges

These and other problems have seemed to some to favour looking for an explanation in terms of semantic operations defined over the natural-language strings directly, presuming on a syntactic analysis that matches the surface sequence of expressions. Debates about ellipsis were indeed transformed by the detailed specification of such a semantic account by Dalrymple *et al.* (1991). Dalrymple *et al.* defined a mechanism of construal which applied directly to syntactic structures as a semantic rule for the fragment expression itself, on the basis of the denotational content of the previous conjunct in a paired coordinate structure. Consider the following example:

(7.25)   John sneezed and Bill did too.

The above sentence has a structure which involves a *parallelism* between the two conjuncts: whatever property P is predicated of John in the first conjunct is also predicated of Bill in the second. The core of the idea is that ellipsis involves a semantic equation involving unification. The interpretation of an elliptical element like *did (too)* as occurs in *John sneezed and Bill did too* is that some identical property P holds both of Bill and of John, and to resolve the ellipsis we must determine the value of P. To determine the value of P, we need to look at what is predicated of John in the first conjunct. This can be expressed as the following equation:

(7.26) $P(John') = Sneeze'(John')$

Resolving P then involves applying an abstraction operation to the content of the antecedent conjunct, *John sneezed*, to yield a predicate abstract that could be applied to the parallel subject, *Bill*, in the second ellipsis-containing conjunct. So, a possible solution of the equation above giving the value for P would be as follows:

(7.27) $P = \lambda x.Sneeze'(x)$

The abstract $\lambda x.Sneeze'(x)$ is then what must be predicated of Bill as well, to resolve the ellipsis in the second conjunct. So:

(7.28) $[\lambda x.Sneeze'(x)](Bill')$

This then reduces to:

(7.29) $Sneeze'(Bill')$

which is exactly the content resolving the ellipsis in the second conjunct.

This process is not unrestricted: all selected abstracts must involve a presumption of parallelism between first and second conjuncts, and must involve one *primary* argument – the subject. Accordingly, (7.30) is ambiguous according to whether Bill is thinking of taking John's mother to John's sister (the *strict* reading) or whether he is thinking of taking his own mother to see his own sister (the *sloppy* reading):

(7.30)   John is thinking of taking his mother to see his sister, and so is Bill.

  [=] 'John is thinking of taking John's mother to see John's sister and Bill is thinking of taking John's mother to see John's sister.'

  OR

  [=] 'John is thinking of taking John's mother to see John's sister and Bill is thinking of taking Bill's mother to see Bill's sister.'

But we cannot get a reading like the following, in which the parallelism of construals across the conjuncts is not sustained:

(7.31) $\neq$ 'John is thinking of taking John's mother to see John's sister and Bill is thinking of taking John's mother to see Bill's sister.'

Both the parallelism between conjuncts and the specification that the subject must be involved are independent stipulations in this account. In particular, nothing prevents the property P from being created by abstracting out any one or more arguments in the first conjunct. In (7.32) then, where two subjects are present in the matrix and subordinate clauses of the first conjunct, nothing prevents a predicate being constructed by abstracting out the embedded subject. This would yield a predicate which we might informally present as λx[NEG John said yesterday that x fainted] which can then be taken as the value for P to be applied to the parallel subject *Bill*. This will give us the reading in (7.33):

(7.32)   John said yesterday that Tom had fainted but it's certainly not the case that Bill did.

(7.33) $\neq$ John said yesterday that Tom had fainted but it's certainly not the case that John said yesterday that Bill fainted.

However, (7.32) does not have the reading indicated in (7.33), in which such an abstract is applied to the subject in the second conjunct, even though this is an appropriate way to resolve P. Equally (7.34) below does not have the reading indicated in (7.35):

(7.34)   The mayor of London stumbled and New York did too.

(7.35) $\neq$ 'The mayor of London stumbled and the mayor of New York stumbled too'

even though, equally, there is a way to resolve P so that it gives us the appropriate property, namely:

(7.36) $P = \lambda x.\lambda y.Stumble'(x) \wedge Mayor'(x, y)$

Nevertheless, if we grant these stipulations, the result, as can be seen in the strict–sloppy interpretations, is that we can derive non-identical resolutions for ellipsis from a single semantic content, a clear advantage over any syntactic account (and some semantic ones), for which ambiguity of source structure had to be invoked. This is especially significant because alternation of strict–sloppy readings can occur in sequence even though there is a single antecedent that has to provide the resolution:

(7.37)   John thinks he's a fool. Harry does too, although his wife doesn't.

So a possible reading of (7.37) is (7.38):

(7.38)   = 'John thinks John is a fool. Harry thinks Harry is a fool, although Harry's wife doesn't think Harry is a fool.'

To resolve the first ellipsis we need the kind of structure or interpretation that is appropriate for a sloppy interpretation, namely, $\lambda x.Think'(x, Fool'(x))$. But if we try to use the same abstract for the resolution of the second ellipsis we get only the reading 'Harry's wife doesn't think that Harry's wife is a fool'. In order to get the reading (7.38), we need an abstract like $\lambda x.Think'(x, Fool'(Harry'))$, which is a structure or interpretation for the first resolved ellipsis site that is appropriate to what generates a strict reading. But this has not been derived. So there are conflicting requirements on the structure/interpretation of the second sentence which cannot be resolved unless we assume, in an ad hoc way, that it can be assigned two distinct simultaneous analyses (see also (7.24) above). On the other hand, the Dalrymple *et al.* semantic account gets the facts right without assuming such ambiguity, because there is no requirement that the abstract resolving P has already appeared in any way in the antecedent structure and it is created anew when the equation is solved. But as we saw and will now see further, this is a property of the account that has the undesirable consequence that it is not restrictive enough.

Problems with syntax–semantics interaction

With the stipulation of the subject as a so-called primary argument, this pattern of replicating the mode of interpretation of the first conjunct in construing the second conjunct can be seen to extend to quantified expressions; this yields additional problems. Whatever pattern is applied in the fixing of scope of quantifiers in the first conjunct must be replicated in the second elliptical conjunct too:

(7.39)   Each journalist interviewed a friend of mine, and each student did too.

For example, in the above, if the indefinite *a friend of mine* takes wide scope with respect to the universal derived by *each journalist* then, at the ellipsis site, the indefinite must be assigned wide scope too, this time with respect to the universal *each student* (this does not necessitate that the indefinite has widest scope, there can be two separate friends involved). This parallelism restriction is remarkable in that it does not seem naturally amenable to either syntactic or semantic explanations without introducing complexities of either interpretation or structure. Several semantic solutions have been proposed in the literature and all involve type-lifting to a higher-type mode of quantification. But, even if this was successful, other examples show that this is not the only source of complexity.

The syntactic subject at the ellipsis site isn't always the sole or even the primary basis for calculating the requisite abstract: in (7.40), it is the expression inside the relative clause modifying the subject NP which provides the term that has to be abstracted over to set the right predicate (an example from Michael Wescoat):

(7.40)   The policeman who arrested Bill failed to read him his rights, and so did the policeman who arrested Tom.

(7.41)   = 'The policeman who arrested Bill failed to read Bill Bill's rights and the policeman who arrested Tom failed to read Tom Tom's rights.'

In order to get the sloppy reading in (7.41), the type of abstract to be defined has to be able to isolate any term within the subject *the policeman who arrested*

Tom as a possible binder of the pronouns *him* and *his* within the VP antecedent *failed to read him his rights* and not merely the subject as a whole. And in the following examples, it is rather the containing structure which provides the basis for the sloppy readings of the pronoun *him*, and not the subject at the ellipsis site itself (this type of example is due to Hardt 1993):

(7.42)   A: Who was hit by Mary?
           B: John said Mary hit him, Bill also said she did, and only Harry said she hadn't.

(7.43)   = 'John said Mary hit John, Bill said Mary hit Bill and only Harry said that Mary hadn't hit Harry.'

(7.44)   If Tom was having trouble in school, I would help him. On the other hand, if Harry was having trouble, I doubt that I would.

(7.45)   = 'If Tom was having trouble in school, I would help Tom. On the other hand, if Harry was having trouble I doubt that I would help Harry.'

The above cannot be handled unproblematically on the semantic account, as in these examples the sloppy readings do not rely on simultaneous abstraction of multiple occurrences of the same variable to be bound by the syntactic subject **at** the ellipsis site (Hardt 1993). For the semantic account to be made empirically adequate with respect to all the counterexamples to the parallel subject stipulation, it will appear that we require yet a further increase in the complexity of the type specification to assign to the ellipsis site. This is because we seem to be required to derive ad-hoc relations and properties of arbitrary types which, moreover, are not ever part of the original interpretation of the first conjunct in order to resolve such ellipses. This approach then appears too powerful and unconstrained if it is to handle the data successfully and nevertheless has no principled basis for deriving the parallelism constraint that seems to lie at the heart of how the required readings are derived. And the pretheoretic intuition that it is context itself that determines ellipsis construal has vanished: it is only the result of applying some appropriate abstraction operation to some previous conjunct that provides the appropriate construal for the elliptical form.

The problem is analogous to the problem faced in addressing plurals and quantification. Within the Montague formal-semantics methodology, there is always the potential of lifting the types to increasingly high levels of complexity, defining related and distinct lexical specifications, and then seeing whether appropriately richer modes of combination can express the requisite content. There is reason however to doubt whether such a solution is worth pursuing, for, with ellipsis, there are phenomena for which solely the search for appropriate higher types will not provide any sufficient account. These are the data that demonstrate the imposition of syntactic restrictions on ellipsis construal. The strong-island sensitivity of antecedent-contained deletion (antecedent-contained ellipsis on the semantic form of explanation) as in (7.22), repeated below as (7.46), for example, is inexpressible:

(7.46)   *John interviewed every student that Bill ignored the teacher who had.

The account will predict these to be wellformed. There is also no basis for reconstructing case sensitivities displayed by fragments, in any language with rich case morphology. For example, German elliptical fragments bear the case appropriate to the verb and syntactic position that has to be reconstructed in order to resolve the ellipsis (the difference between the wellformed English and German responses can be attributed to the impoverished case system of English):

(7.47)   *Hat er   nicht den Brief   geschrieben?*
          has he$_{NOM}$ not   the$_{ACC}$ letter written
          'Didn't he write the letter?'

          *Nein. Ich/*Mich.*
          no   I$_{NOM}$/I$_{ACC}$
          'No. I did.'

(7.48)   A: Hat   Kim   nicht   den Brief   geschrieben?
               Did   Kim   not   the letter write?
               'Didn't Kim write the letter?'

          B: Nein   Ich/*Mich
               No   I$_{NOM}$/*Me$_{ACC}$
               'No, I did.'

Moreover, as the indicated answers show, such case-marking is essential in question–answer fragments in German. So despite the richness of higher-order unification accounts, they remain at best incomplete, having to appeal to independent syntactic constraints in order to account for the facts.

The upshot in the issue of whether to promote syntactic or semantic bases for explaining ellipsis is that on neither style of analysis is the phenomenon treated in a unified way.

7.3.3   Ellipsis as pragmatic reconstruction

Even this is not the end of the matter. There are cases which appear to resist either syntactic or semantic accounts of ellipsis, requiring rather a pragmatic form of explanation. These are fragment expressions which do not fall into the pattern of using some clausal antecedent from which to build up interpretation (as both syntactic and semantic accounts require) but are freely interpreted from the utterance scenario directly:

(7.49)   A (coming out of the lift): McWhirters?
          B: Second on the left.

(7.50)   A (seeing a woman enter): Sue's mother.

(7.51)   A to B (standing together checking the stock market, as regular joint
              activity): Rising again, I see.

On the basis of evidence such as this, it has been argued by Robert Stainton in a
number of papers that fragments of this type have to be seen as sub-sentential
assertions. In consequence, these cannot be taken as either syntactically or
semantically of the type that corresponds to propositions, therefore the grammar
itself is not sufficient to license them: some form of pragmatic module has to
be involved. This has been denied by, e.g. Stanley (2000) and Merchant (2004),
who argue that such fragments indeed form part of a clausal string, with some
invisible remainder.

    One problem with these pragmatically construed fragments is that even if
some abstract content could be invoked, it would seem that the remainder structure into which the fragment has to be construed as nesting may not itself be
a constituent. Faced with such data, Jason Merchant argues that nonetheless,
contrary to appearances, all such cases involve covert movement to some left-
dislocated position adjoined to a containing sentential node, so that what the
fragment is adjoined to is some covert expression of propositional type to be
indexically construed, which is by definition a constituent. An analogous semantic account makes a similar move, in proposing that such fragments are semantically a sentence, with propositional content, hence of propositional type. But,
as Stainton points out, a syntactic account along such lines makes empirically
wrong predictions. Answer fragments to questions, for example, on this account
would be wrongly expected to be as sensitive to island constraints as though
there had been overt movement, but this signally isn't true, as indicated by:

(7.52)   A: You have been seeing Tom and who?
              B: Sue.

(7.53)   A: *Who have you been seeing Tom and?
              B: Sue.

Stainton also argues against a semantic style of analysis for these fragments
where they are also assigned a propositional type (i.e. are taken to express a
full proposition), because this leads to unwarranted assumptions of ambiguity of
the expressions themselves. These are being analysed sometimes of type individual, sometimes of type proposition, all with no distinctiveness in the expression
itself, merely in the context within which it occurs.

    The disparate nature of ellipsis construal has been graphically labelled its
'fractal heterogeneity' by Ginzburg and Cooper (2004), ellipsis apparently making use of whatever information the grammar may provide, with morphological,
syntactic, semantic, even phonological information yielding different bases for
ellipsis, a phenomenon suggestive of the need to employ a rich, multi-level form
of analysis. With its multi-modular approach to grammar formalisms, Head-
Driven Phrase Structure Grammar (HPSG) might seem the most appropriate
framework to adopt, for its feature-matrix format which includes information

about phonology, morphology, syntax, semantics and pragmatics can in principle express generalisations across the various modules while nevertheless articulating distinct phonological, morphological, syntactic, semantic and pragmatic constraints between the different levels of generalisation (see Ginzburg and Cooper 2004; Ginzburg forthcoming).

The challenge posed by ellipsis construal remains however. How is it that a phenomenon of context-dependence, upon which speakers and hearers can draw so freely, and with such certainty of success, can apparently require such complex cross-module constraints? The problem for all these accounts is that there is no commitment to an integrated explanation of the phenomenon of ellipsis itself. To the contrary, there is a plethora of ambiguities, apparently discrete structures, and failure to characterise just how context might be seen as providing input in each case of ellipsis construal. Even the pragmatic stance (adopted by Carston 2002; Elugardo and Stainton 2004; and Stainton 2004) presumes that the pragmatic explanation is peripheral, with most ellipses being the effect of heterogeneous syntactic processes. The HPSG move to articulate yet a further pragmatic module as part of a sign-based grammar, though a technical device with increased expressive power over other accounts, does not address the heart of the problem, since the invocation of a pragmatic context module within a sentence-based grammar is far from unproblematic. There is good reason to want to retain a concept of pragmatics as external to any grammar formalism. A solution which simply conflates a model of linguistic capacity with a model of performance in general cannot be more than an interim account. Pragmatic explanations seek to address how it is that entirely general cognitive constraints determine the richness of language construal in context, given some encoded specification as input to that process; for that we need a concept of context which is broader than that provided by some sub-component of grammar. The alternative, more radical view is to take ellipsis as the datum from which we can induce the richness of information that context provides, and on the basis of that, to define the requisite concept of context which will enable an integrated account to be provided despite the diversity of content expressible via elliptical fragments. So we turn back to a descriptive classification of the types of ellipsis construal to see what challenge has to be met by any putative integration of the different sorts.

7.4   Ellipsis: towards a unitary account

It is uncontroversial that, in part, ellipsis allows reiteration of content directly, as in strict interpretations of VP-ellipsis, where the construal of the antecedent VP and that of the ellipsis site are identical:

(7.54)   John saw Mary, and Tom did too.

In such cases, the immediate context for the construal of the fragment provides a predicate content for reuse without modification. For these cases, an account in terms of copying/reconstructing representations of content is possible (but not essential).

Then there are cases where the fragment is an add-on to what is in the context, building on what has been started in the context. Question–answer pairs might be seen in this light:

(7.55)   A: Where are you going?
           B: To London.

The interpretation of the answer in (7.55) requires the entire interpretation structure of the question, modulo the replacement of the *wh* term by what is proffered as its answer. But the phenomenon is much more widespread than this, since all of the fragment extensions of previous utterances fall into this category, whether or not what is provided in context is a complete sentence in its own right, as in (7.56), or not, as in (7.57):

(7.56)   A: We're going to Casa Plana.
           B: To show my mother what we've done there.
           C: I am coming too.

(7.57)   A: We're going to ...
           B: Casa Plana.
           C: I am coming too then.

Explanation of these involves essential use of representations, since the construal to be provided can only be characterised structurally: the full structure isn't yet available over which to define compositionally some content. The fragment in such sub-sentential cases has to be seen as a development of the structure made available in the immediately previous context.

The essential use of representations in ellipsis construal goes further than this. There are also cases where it appears to be only the **process** of building up interpretation that is replicated from context, leading to a different content, but established in the same manner. These are the sloppy construals of VP-ellipsis:

(7.58)   John washed himself. Sue refused to, until I told her she must.

To add to the complications, these strategies can be put together, so that a fragment to be interpreted from context can take up a parallel strategy with which to build up interpretation from the point at which the context is interrupted (in each of (7.59)–(7.64) we italicise what is reconstructed):

(7.59)   A: They haven't managed to get their project finished though we've
              certainly been told we must.
           B: So they no doubt have also.

(7.60)   = B: 'So they no doubt have *been told to get their project finished* also.'

(7.61)   Which of his paintings has John sold, and which of his sculptures?

(7.62)   = 'Which of John's paintings has John sold and which of John's sculptures
           has John sold?'

(7.63)   Which of his paintings has John sold, and which has Bill?

(7.64)   = 'Which of John's paintings has John sold and which *of Bill's paintings has Bill sold*?'

For example, the interpretation of the elliptical fragment in (7.63) involves identifying the subject of the second conjunct as part of the fragment construal and then interpreting the pronoun in the fragment relative to this subject in an echo of the strategies used in interpreting the first conjunct. Since the nominal inside the fragment is also elliptical, the nominal has first to be built up as though it contained a pronominal *his*, so that the predicate derived from *sold which of his paintings* can then be construed in the same manner as the first conjunct which involves a binding by the subject.

    If we are to make sense of these, and yet retain an integrated perspective on context as providing the wherewithal in each case to establish the content of the fragment, we have to have a concept of context which is rich enough to encompass all of these as an integral part. And for this, we turn to Dynamic Syntax, a model of natural-language content which, like DRT, posits a level of structural representation that reflects what is needed for semantic interpretation. The advantage of Dynamic Syntax, as we shall see, is that the concept of context provided by the theory is not just a complex of content and structure, for, in addition, *actions* used to build up interpretation are part of the context too. Any one of these three is accordingly available for reuse.

7.5   Dynamic Syntax

       Dynamic Syntax is a model of how interpretation is built up relative to context, reflecting how hearers (and speakers) build up interpretations for strings incrementally using information from context as it becomes available. So Dynamic Syntax (henceforth, DS) is like DRT in spirit in that local predicate-argument structures are induced from the left–right processing of words. But it goes considerably further than DRT in three major ways. Firstly, the mechanisms for building up such structures are presumed to apply in a strictly incremental way, with both representations of content and representations of context being built up on a word by word basis following the dynamics of on-line processing, rather than as in DRT sentence by sentence. Second, this **process** of building up structure is taken to be what constitutes the syntactic component of the grammar, so that the articulation of natural-language syntax is nothing more than articulation of constraints on growth of interpretation. Accordingly, predicate-argument structures are defined as binary-branching trees; and associated with such trees are *procedures/actions* that define how parts of trees can be incrementally introduced and updated. Third, context is defined to be just as structural and just as dynamic as the concept of content is: so *context* constitutes a record not merely of the (potentially partial) structures built up, but also the procedures used in constructing them (Cann *et al.* 2007). In short, the general methodology is a representationalist stance vis-à-vis natural-language construal (Fodor 1983), with the further assumption that concepts of underspecification and update should be extended from semantics/pragmatics into syntax.

7.5.1   The tree-logic and tree-growth processes

The general process of parsing is building as **output** a tree whose nodes reflect the content of some propositional formula. The **input** to this task is a tree that does nothing more than state at the root-node the goal of the interpretation process to be achieved, namely, to establish some propositional formula. For example, in the parse of the string *John upset Mary*, the output tree to the right of the $\mapsto$ in (7.65) constitutes some final end result: it is a tree in which the propositional formula itself annotates the top-node, and its various subterms appear on the dominated nodes in that tree rather like a proof tree in which all the nodes are labelled with a formula and a type (see Chapter 3, section 3.6). The input to that process is an initial one-node tree (as in the tree representation to the left of the $\mapsto$ in (7.65)) which simply states the goal as the *requirement* (shown by $?Ty(t)$) to establish some content, a formula of appropriate propositional type t (there is also a *pointer*, $\diamondsuit$, see below):

(7.65)   John upset Mary.

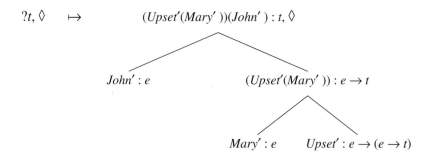

The parsing task, using both lexical input and information from context, is to progressively enrich the input tree to yield such a complete output using general tree-growth actions, lexical tree-growth actions, and, when triggered by some lexical item, pragmatic tree-growth actions. As all types of action are defined in the same terms, i.e. as *actions* that map one partial tree to another, different types of action can interact to yield as output some appropriate tree with a propositional formula of type t at the top-node, and with all sub-nodes in the tree appropriately annotated with subterms of that formula. The node annotations, called *decorations*, include concept formulae (we use *Fo* for *Formula*); type specifications (*Ty* for *Type*); and also a tree-node indicator (with one distinguished as the root-node, $Tn(0)$). The primitive types are types e and t as in formal semantics but construed syntactically,[3] and, as in the Curry–Howard isomorphism, labelled type-deduction is used to determine the decorations on non-terminal nodes (see Chapter 3), with pairing of formula and type specifications written as $\phi : \tau$ (ϕ the formula labelling τ the type). In all cases, the output is a fully annotated (*decorated*) tree whose top-node is a formula value representing a proposition derived by the string of words processed relative to that particular context (the proposition expressed by the utterance).[4] Notice how, in both trees of (7.65), there is a $\diamond$ at the type-t-indicated node. This is a *pointer* which keeps track of where the parse process has got to.

Despite the assumption that this progressive build-up of a semantic representation is a basis for doing syntax, syntax in this model is **not** taken to include a level of representation where there is structure over a string of words. Indeed the trees are not taken to be inhabited by words, and there is no notion of linear ordering expressed on the tree: the annotations on the tree are solely representations of conceptual content. Linear order is treated by restrictions on how the parse progresses. In particular, all lexically induced actions can take place only if the condition triggering these actions matches the decorations on the node at which the pointer has got to in the parse. Indeed, this aspect of DS is a response to the question that arises when it becomes obvious that semantic **representations** are necessary for interpretation: if semantic representations **are** necessary, is it necessary also to have an intermediate representation of apparent syntactic properties of hierarchically structured strings of words? The DS answer is a definitive 'No'.

To articulate growth of representation following the order in which the words are given, trees in the DS system need to be defined as formal objects so that one can talk explicitly about both their structural properties and the attendant notion of tree growth. To this end, DS adopts a (modal) logic of finite trees (LOFT: Blackburn and Meyer-Viol 1994). There are two basic modalities, ways of describing node relations: $\langle\downarrow\rangle$ and $\langle\uparrow\rangle$. $\langle\downarrow\rangle\alpha$ holds at a node if α holds at its daughter, and the inverse, $\langle\uparrow\rangle\alpha$, holds at a node if α holds at its mother. There are sub-types: $\langle\downarrow_0\rangle$ indicating an argument daughter and $\langle\downarrow_1\rangle$ indicating a functor daughter (and similarly for the up modality). DS trees are binary, with the argument always appearing on the left and the functor on the right by convention. To achieve a mechanism of tree growth, *partial trees*, i.e. not yet fully decorated and not yet binary trees, have to be defined, and this involves two further concepts. The first is to incorporate a means of defining structural underspecification, trees in which a relation between nodes may be less than fully determined.

---

[3] There are other types, but the list is highly restricted. Unlike in categorial grammar formalisms (see e.g. Steedman 2000), there is no recursive definition of types, no type-lifting or composition of functions.

[4] We simplify the exposition here for illustration purposes: the full presentation of DS includes the assumption that the proposition expressed is relative to a time point given by a term denoting some temporal/modal relation to the time of utterance (Gregoromichelaki 2006). A further simplification is that names and words with conceptual content are simply assumed to stand in one-to-one correspondence with concepts, with no attempt to address the substantial issues in addressing the context-sensitivity of either (see Chapter 8).

For example, early on in a task of language processing it is commonplace for there to be indication that something must be the case in a future development of the tree. In particular, when first encountering a left-dislocated phrase in long-distance dependencies, as in (7.66), we know that the relative position of the construal of that phrase will become fully identifiable at some later point in the parse, even though its exact location is not obvious at the outset:

(7.66)   John, Mary knows Sue dislikes.

This is the long-distance dependency phenomenon standardly taken as evidence of movement, though here analysed in terms of the corresponding parsing actions. Such underspecification is straightforwardly expressible in a modal-tree logic using Kleene star, $*$, operators. These are operators that allow successive iteration, and are here defined over mother and daughter relations, indicating some possible sequence of mother relations, or conversely a possible sequence of daughter relations, allowing concepts of *dominate* and *be dominated by* to be defined, even before the fixed number of such mother or daughter relations is fixed. For example, $\langle \uparrow_* \rangle Tn(a)$ is a decoration on a node, indicating that somewhere dominating it is the node $Tn(a)$.[5] All that is determined is that the node in question must always be dominated by the $Tn(a)$ in any future developments of the tree. The second, corollary, concept is that of requirement for update. This is essential to get appropriate reflection of the time-linearity involved in building up trees in stages (partial trees): for every node, in every tree, all aspects of underspecification are twinned with a concept of *requirement*, $?X$, for any annotation X on a node; and these are constraints on how the subsequent parsing steps must progress. Such requirements apply to all types of decoration, so that there may be type requirements, $?Ty(t)$ (or $?t$), $?Ty(e)$ (or $?e$), $?Ty(e \rightarrow t)$ (or $?e \rightarrow t$), etc; tree-node requirements, $?\exists x Tn(\mathbf{x})$ (associated with underspecified tree-relations); and also formula requirements $?\exists x Fo(\mathbf{x})$ (associated with pronouns and other anaphoric expressions). These requirements drive the subsequent tree-construction process, because unless they are eventually satisfied the parse will be unsuccessful.

Just as the concept of tree growth is central, so too is the concept of *procedure* or *action* for mapping one partial tree to another. Individual transitions from partial tree to partial tree are all defined as procedures for tree growth. The general dynamics that is defined using the LOFT language of tree descriptions is a set of actions whose effect is to gradually unfold tree structure, with some actions imposing requirements and others resolving them. The actions are defined in a programing-like language involving such commands as IF ... THEN ... ELSE ... make($\langle \downarrow \rangle$), go($\langle \downarrow \rangle$), put($\langle \alpha \rangle$), make($\langle \downarrow_* \rangle$), etc. The details of these actions are not necessary here, but sets of such actions incorporated in individual units can be either general *computational rules* for tree growth or *lexical actions* associated with words contributing concepts and other

---

[5] This is a standard tree-theoretic characterisation of *dominate*, used in LFG to express *functional uncertainty*; see Kaplan and Maxwell (1988)

aspects of structure. For example, verbs in English are parsed when the pointer resides at a node previously constructed by a general computational rule. The verb itself contributes not only a concept formula (e.g. $Upset'$) but also creates a new node and moves the pointer there to await the parsing of the object immediately afterwards. Note that in the following trees each node in the tree is labelled with a formula ϕ and type τ ($\phi : \tau$); with perhaps some other labels, such as tree-node ($Tn(n)$); the *pointer* $\diamond$ which indicates the node under construction; or requirements, which are symbolised as $?\alpha$, where α may be a type or an existentially quantified expression requiring to construct an appropriate label such as $?\exists \mathbf{x}.Tn(\mathbf{x})$ 'a tree-node address is required' or $?\exists \mathbf{x}.Fo(\mathbf{x})$ 'a formula value is required'.

(7.67)   Parsing *John upset*:

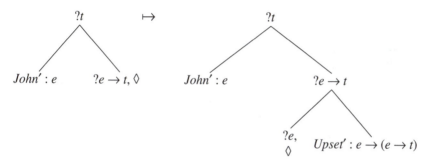

Parsing of an object will then provide the appropriate formula value for this node and then computational rules can take over, compositionally determining the combination of those concepts to satisfy the requirements remaining in a strictly bottom-up fashion:

(7.68)   Parsing *John upset Mary*:

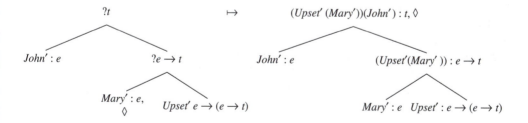

Underspecification and constraints on update

With structural underspecification defined within the tree logic, this concept is used to define long-distance dependency effects in a way that follows the time-linear dimension of processing in real time. When first processing the word *Mary* in (7.69) below it is construed as providing a term whose role isn't yet identified. So its parse is taken to involve the application of a computational action which introduces from the initial root node decorated with $?t$, a relation to that top-node which is **underspecified** at this juncture, identifiable solely as dominated by the top-node. The exact specification of this relation must then be provided either from context or the construction process (in line with Stainton's claim; see section 7.3.1). In (7.69), for example, application of such a rule is the opening strategy, leading to the introduction of an *unfixed* node requiring type e, i.e. with requirement $?e$:

(7.69)   Mary, John upset.

This enables the expression *Mary* to be taken to decorate this node: this is step (i) of (7.70). Accompanying the underspecified tree relation is a requirement for a fixed tree-node position: $?\exists \mathbf{x}.Tn(\mathbf{x})$. The update to this relatively weak tree-relation becomes possible only after processing the verb. This is the *unification* step (ii) of (7.70), an action which satisfies both type and structure update requirements:

(7.70)   Parsing *Mary, John upset*:

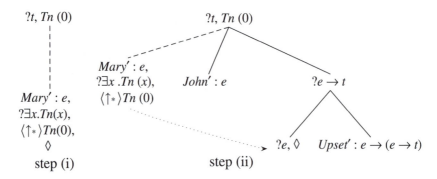

This process feeds into the ongoing development, leading to the creation of some completed tree, in this case by subsequent steps of labelled type deduction. What is innovatory in DS is this incorporation into the grammar-mechanics of a concept normally associated only with parsing algorithms. This is furthermore combined with different locality effects to yield a family of operations for building and updating relatively weak structural relations. Defining a concept (or family of concepts) of **structural** underspecification is far from being the only concept of underspecification: to the contrary, for each type of decoration, there are underspecified variants. Of these, that associated with anaphora is arguably the most familiar, given its introduction independently in DRT. In DRT, this involved construction of a discourse referent from a pronoun that is to be updated by its identifiability with some suitably accessible antecedent discourse referent (see Chapter 5). The DS account is very like that of DRT. Pronouns are assumed to be associated with an interim value that is updated by some contextually provided value. Anaphoric expressions are lexically defined as inducing tree-growth actions that annotate a node in a tree with a temporary formula value (a *metavariable*) of a given type (e.g. **U**, **V**, etc.). The update for such a metavariable is driven by an accompanying requirement $?\exists x. Fo(\mathbf{x})$, a requirement which has to be satisfied either by selection of a proper value from context or from the construction process (e.g. reflexive pronouns require the provision of such an update from within a minimal predicate-argument domain, other pronouns require a value to be provided from outside that domain). In consequence, though anaphoric expressions contribute to the monotonic tree growth process like all other words, they do not introduce a fully specified concept. The system thus licenses underspecification and its update both for decorations of nodes in the tree, and for structural relations involved in the construction of the tree.

With the concept of requirement as a general mechanism for guiding tree growth, requirements for modal statements are defined as a means of articulating constraints on **future** tree developments. For example, $?\langle\uparrow\rangle e \rightarrow t$ is the requirement associated with the accusative case, determining that the node being decorated by the case-marked expression must, eventually, be immediately dominated by a mother node whose formula is of predicate type. With this combination of (i) formulae able to be underspecified lexically, (ii) nodes able to have underspecified relations to some dominating node, and (iii) constraints on future developments in the tree, the effect is a basic concept of tree growth defined to cover the emergent growth of predicate-argument structures in individual trees.

To achieve the basis for characterising the full array of compound structures displayed in natural language, DS defines in addition the licence to build paired trees, so-called *linked* trees, linked together solely by the sharing of terms, established, for example, by encoded anaphoric devices such as relative pronouns. Consider the structure derived by processing the string *John, who smokes, left*:

(7.71)   Result of parsing *John, who smokes, left*:

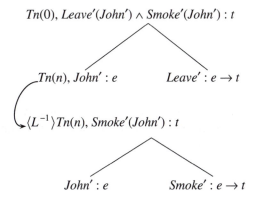

The arrow linking the two trees depicts the *link* relation. The tree whose node is pointed by the arrow is the *linked* tree (read $\langle L^{-1}\rangle$ as 'linked to'). Within any one such linked tree, the full range of computational, lexical and pragmatic actions remain available; with this flexibility to allow the incremental projection of arbitrarily rich compound structures, the result is a formal system combining lexical, structural and semantic specifications, all as constraints on the growth of trees. Along lines similar to those sketched here to account for case specifications and discontinuity effects, all assumed syntactic phenomena can be reformulated in tree-growth terms, leading to the comprehensive DS claim that the syntax of natural languages does not involve a separate level of representation besides what is needed for semantics (Cann *et al.* 2005, and elsewhere). So, in DS, like categorial grammar but unlike DRT, there are explicit syntactic claims associated with the use made of a broadly proof-theoretic methodology.

One caveat before proceeding: DS is a grammar formalism and as such it includes **no** reflection of **how** choices among alternative grammatical possibilities are made in the development of interpretation, even though this is indeed central to the task of on-line parsing and production. The articulation of general cognitive constraints on processing and how these might, in conjunction with whatever the grammar makes available, determine **which** interpretation is picked out relative to a particular context and a particular intended effect (i.e. disambiguation) is taken to be the purview of a pragmatic theory. All that the DS framework provides is the space of grammatical possibilities, which is modelled as licensed tree growth. The shift is to depart from seeing the grammar as totally independent of all dynamics of language performance into seeing a grammar formalism as providing that space of possibilities within which such representations of content can be built up; furthermore, to define, at any arbitrary point in that process, what subsequent options are licensed.

7.5.2   Quantification dynamics and the epsilon calculus ▬▬▬▬▬

Despite the departure from DRT into developing a more strident representationalist commitment, there is a respect in which DS structures remain very close in conception to at least early variants of DRT. The argument nodes in the structures projected are invariably filled by formulae of type e; and there is no type-lifting mechanism, unlike in generalised-quantifier theory. More specifically, quantifying expressions are analysed in terms grounded in a proof-theoretic labelled-deduction methodology; quantified noun phrases are taken to contribute *arbitrary names* of a sort familiar from natural-deduction predicate-logic proofs (see Chapter 2). These names are defined as denoting the arbitrary witness of their containing assertion. The logic within which these names are defined is the *epsilon calculus*, a logic which was developed by David Hilbert as constituting the formal study of these arbitrary names. This logic is a conservative extension of predicate logic, which means that exactly the same theorems are provable, though in making explicit the properties of these names that are only implicit in predicate logic it is more expressive. With this extra expressivity, the defined names (so-called *epsilon terms*) carry a record of the propositional formula within which they occur. Consider the following equivalence between a plain predicate logic formula and its equivalent in the epsilon calculus:

(7.72) $\exists x.F(x) \equiv F(\,\epsilon x.F(x)\,)$

The schematic formula on the right-hand side of the equivalence sign, an epsilon calculus formula, is an ordinary predicate-argument expression, like e.g. $F(a)$. However, within the argument of this expression, there is a required second token of the predicate F as the *restrictor* for that argument term (ϵ is the variable-binding term operator that is the analogue of the existential quantifier, here binding the variable x). The effect is that the term $\epsilon x.F(x)$, as indicated by the underbracket in example (7.72), replicates inside it the content of the overall formula that is predicated of it (notice the replication of F both as predicate, and as restrictor in (7.72)). As it turns out, this internal complexity to the epsilon terms corresponds directly to what is required as the antecedents of the E-type pronouns (see Chapter 5), for the puzzle of these is precisely that they appear to require some computation of the whole content of the sentence containing the antecedent with which the pronoun is identified; and this is the property by definition of epsilon terms, as we shall now see.

In the interpretation of sentence sequences where the interpretation of the first sentence provides the context for interpreting the second, it is well known that in some sense the whole content of the first sentence is carried over as part of the construal of a pronoun in the second (in (7.73), affecting the construal of the pronoun *it*):

(7.73)   Ruth: Are you writing an essay?
            Sue: I have already submitted it.

What Sue has already submitted is the essay she has been writing (as asked about by Ruth). Parsing and compiling the tree for the parse of the question (leaving the Q annotation and tense complexities on one side), involves building the tree given below in (7.74) as the context. DS then defines formal evaluation rules which when applied to the formula on the top-node eventually yield a completed epsilon term, the name abbreviated below as **a**:

(7.74)   CONTEXT:

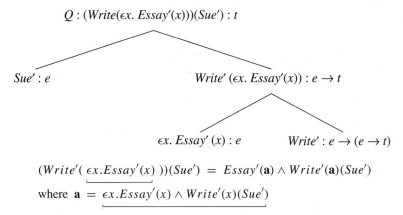

$$Q : (Write(\epsilon x.\ Essay'(x)))(Sue') : t$$

$$Sue' : e \qquad\qquad Write'\ (\epsilon x.\ Essay'(x)) : e \rightarrow t$$

$$\epsilon x.\ Essay'\ (x) : e \qquad Write' : e \rightarrow (e \rightarrow t)$$

$$(Write'(\ \epsilon x.Essay'(x)\ ))(Sue') \ = \ Essay'(\mathbf{a}) \wedge Write'(\mathbf{a})(Sue')$$

$$\text{where } \mathbf{a} \ = \ \epsilon x.Essay'(x) \wedge Write'(x)(Sue')$$

Notice how the content of the entire first conjunct becomes the restrictor of the resulting epsilon term.

Next, the answer to the question is processed in the context created by application of the above rules. So, when the term **a** is taken as providing the object-argument of *submit*, replacing the metavariable **V** contributed by *it*, it will accordingly be the complete term $(\epsilon x.Essay'(x) \wedge Write'(x)(Sue'))$, abbreviated as **a**) which becomes that object argument (the tree here displays both metavariable and formula assigned for both arguments nodes). So, in the tree below, there are two instances of substitution (shown by the upwards-pointing double arrow): the first replacing the metavariable **U** projected by *she* with the content *Sue'*, and the second replacing the metavariable **V** projected by *it* with the epsilon term abbreviated by **a**:

(7.75)   TREE UNDER CONSTRUCTION

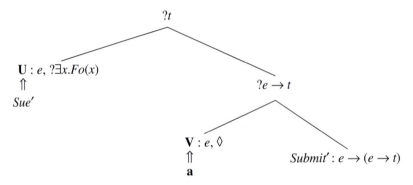

And once the propositional formula is constructed out of the second sentence it is also subject to evaluation rules for the constructed term. What we then get is an accumulation of information, all recorded within the new epsilon term (now abbreviated as **a'**) that was copied over from the tree in the context. This is because exactly the same procedure for evaluating the term takes place a second time in the evaluation of the content of the answer, this time with the composite epsilon term being extended further by adding the new information in its restrictor:

$$Submit'(\,\epsilon x.\ Essay(x) \wedge Write'(x)(Sue)\,)(Sue) \qquad =$$

$$Essay(\mathbf{a'}) \wedge Write(\mathbf{a'})(Sue) \wedge Submit'(\mathbf{a'})(Sue)$$

$$\text{where } \mathbf{a'} = \epsilon x.\ Essay'(x) \wedge Write'(x)(Sue) \wedge Submit'(x)(Sue)$$

The formal mechanisms for evaluating epsilon terms as they are incrementally reused from one structure to the next thus reflect the incremental compilation of information as it is processed in the on-going dynamics of natural-language interpretation, notably incorporating E-type effects as a mere sub-case of anaphoric dependency without special stipulation. The more general dynamics is that scope dependencies are not reflected structurally in the tree by some analogue of quantifier-movement/storage, but constitute constraints on how the arguments in the result tree should be severally evaluated. The reason for looking this way at quantification is to implement a direct correspondence between the types assigned to quantifying expressions and their syntactic behaviour. Unlike formalisms that allow separation between syntactic and semantic generalisations, and then have to invoke type-lifting to resynchronise syntax and semantics (see Chapter 4), taking quantifying expressions as contributing context-dependent names of witnesses means that their assigned structure directly reflects the way in which their construal is built up.

7.6   Ellipsis and context

The reason for emphasis on DS at this juncture has been its applicability in the explication of ellipsis. The problem about ellipsis, recall, is that model-theoretic accounts were too weak to handle syntactic or morphological constraints, and that syntactic accounts posited unlimited ambiguity without any attempt at even seeing ellipsis as a context-relative phenomenon. In DS though, unlike DRT and HPSG, syntax and semantics are not two distinct sub-systems: syntax just **is** the growth of semantic representation. Furthermore, the concept of context for utterance interpretation is characterised in essentially similar terms as the grammar formalism, with procedures driving the process of building up representations of content as a process of incremental context update: content and context have indeed to be developed in tandem to preserve the incremental and local nature of the progressive context-update dynamics. Growth of content through anaphoric construal across clausal boundaries illustrates this, as the characterisation of E-type effects demonstrates how subparts of the context may become components of what is constructed as the representation of content for some subsequent utterance. With this perspective, DS aims to provide a basis for directly expressing how semantic content can be established not only by interaction with context but also with sensitivity to structural patterns. From this point of view, in the domain of elliptical phenomena, as we shall see, what DS aims to reflect is the robust but folk concept of the pairing between context and ellipsis. *Context*, in general, will be defined as a composite record of what has just taken place: some content that has been established, represented as formulae in a logical language; the constituent structure of these formulae in the form of trees; the words that induced it; and the parsing actions that have been used to gradually build it up. Given this notion of context, any aspect of it can be reused as a basis for construal of ellipsis. We can now see what this amounts to when applied to the ellipsis data.

7.6.1   Use of context-provided formulae

First, according to DS, elliptical phenomena demonstrate the ability by language-users to pick up on content annotations as made available in some context tree, reusing a formula just established by a simple substitution operation. Ellipsis can take several forms; but this direct reuse of a formula from context is illustrated by the strict readings of VP-ellipsis. In these cases, what is required as the antecedent of the ellipsis site can be modelled as identified with some predicate representation provided in the immediate context, exactly analogous to discourse coreference of the sort familiar from pronoun construal. The only difference between pronoun and ellipsis construal on this account is their logical type assignment (e vs. $e \rightarrow t$). To express the appropriate conditions for ellipsis construal, triggering elements like auxiliares are assumed to contribute place-holding metavariables on the tree, which can be substituted by re-use of some formula expression built up in the previous context (below, **DO** is a metavariable of type $e \rightarrow t$ whose substituends are restricted to denoting action predicates):[6]

(7.76)   A: Who upset Mary?
         B: John did.

         Parsing *John did*:

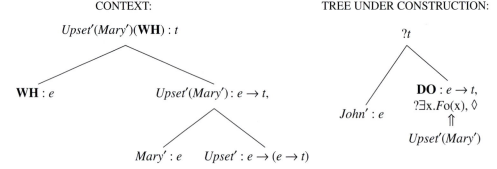

The answer first provides an update to the term provided by the *wh* expression, and the VP pro-predicate is then interpreted by substitution of the predicate formula $Upset'(Mary')$, taken from the context of the immediately previous parse.

This account incidentally involves the commitment that indexical interpretations of VP-ellipsis are available, contrary to what was claimed by Hankamer and Sag (1976). This is because metavariables by definition can be provided values from contextually provided representations of content, whether or not these are constructed by processing linguistic input; for example, such representations might be constructed by processing other aspects of the cognitive environment such as visual signals. Consider the case of a mother and teenage son standing at the shore's edge looking at the size of the waves, with the mother deciding how best to dissuade her son from surfing. A mere

---

[6] The DS account of *wh* expressions posits a particularised metavariable **WH** that acts as a temporary place-holder for the upcoming answer.

command 'Don't go now' would surely risk the very action she is hoping to dissuade him from. A much less confrontation-risking comment might take the form:

(7.77)   I wouldn't if I were you. There are severe rip tides round here.

All that is required for the success of this utterance, on this view, is that the context for utterance interpretation can be presumed to contain representations of predicate-argument content inferrable by reasoning over information culled from any form of processing, in this case information provided by anxiously scanning the shore-line. Incidentally, all such cases are problematic for the higher-order unification account of ellipsis, which presumes on some source conjunct whose content provides an appropriate abstract which can be taken as the content of the elliptical verb phrase. In cases like the above, there is no such antecedent available; and it is far from obvious in what sense the action of scanning the shore-line can be said to lead to some propositional content to provide input to the requisite abstraction process.

7.6.2   Context-provided structure

Other types of ellipsis can be seen from this perspective as instances where the context is providing structure. As we have already seen, in question–answer pairs, the expression which provides the answer provides the means of updating the very structure provided by the parse of the question.

(7.78)   A: Who did John upset?
          B: Himself.

There are many fragment forms in dialogue which similarly build up structure from the point reached in the utterance process: question–answer pairs are a proto-typical instance of this mechanism. From a DS perspective, this phenomenon can be analysed in exactly these terms, i.e. by taking up the output of the parse of the question as the input to the processing of the fragment. In (7.78), the problem that presents itself is that the interpretability of the elliptical answer, *himself*, depends on the structure which provides the antecedent for the reflexive being available; otherwise the reflexive cannot be locally identified. The structure set up in parsing the question can be seen as providing the very structure needed and the parse of the fragment on this assumption takes that very structure as input (the TREE AS CONTEXT in (7.79)). Processing the fragment updates this contextual tree to a structure in which the object argument has a fixed value (the TREE UNDER CONSTRUCTION in (7.79)):

(7.79)   Parsing *himself*:

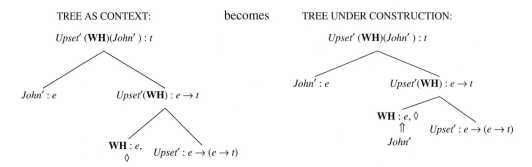

With the **WH** metavariable substituted by the formula $John'$, the two terminal nodes combine to yield a new non-terminal formula $Upset'(John')$, and so progressively up the tree, occurrences of **WH** are substituted by the replacement $John'$ to yield a full proposition as answer:

(7.80)   Parsing *himself*:

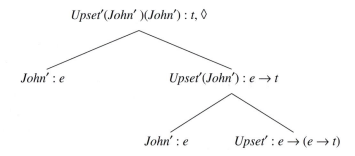

Note here the pattern of a single fragment construed as an enrichment of structure independently provided. This pattern extends to the sub-sentential fragments interpreted directly from some utterance scenario, with only the assumption that the scenario in which an utterance is made may be such as to make salient an open proposition in anticipation of some value to be provided for one of its arguments. Generally these are sanctioned when there is some routine to be followed in processing such fragments; requests at ticket-offices, orders in restaurants, requests for directions and so on. This is no more than the indexical construal of VP-ellipsis already referred to, where the situation itself can induce the construction of a structured representation which is then taken as point of departure for construal of the presented fragment. With the assumption that the concept of context is a cognitive one – some set of possibly incomplete structured representations as point of departure for the interpretation process – these examples are unproblematic, and fall within the general case. They differ only in that, in these, there is no previous uttered string from which to build up interpretation of the fragment.

7.6.3   Context as a record of parsing actions

Finally, there are the cases where the construal of ellipsis leads to a different interpretation from that of its antecedent. Here, as there is no direct copying or substitution involved, these involve a licence to reuse the actions invoked for the processing of some immediately previous clause. In other words, the parsing process used to construct a preceding tree may be rerun at the ellipsis site. This provides possibilities for certain changes in the information conveyed by the elliptical expression vis-à-vis the contextually provided input allowing the sloppy ellipsis construal. In these cases, we want to be able to reflect the way in which linguistic input is in some sense reused to yield a modified interpretation but without having to commit the account to literal reuse of the words themselves (which we saw above in 7.3.1 leads to problems):

(7.81)   A: Who hurt himself?
           B: John did.

Informally, the DS processing for the question in (7.81) involves the following actions after parsing of the subject *who*: constructing a two-place predicate as indicated by the verb; the construction of an object argument; and then, because this object contains a reflexive pronoun, it is obligatorily identified with the argument provided as subject. Now, if we assume that these actions themselves are stored as a sequence in context, they will then be accessible in that sequence for reuse in the next stages of the parse. When it comes to processing the elliptical *did* in the answer, this sequence of actions which is recorded in the context can be invoked and rerun, as *did* contributes a metavariable whose required substitution from context gives licence to do exactly that. Reapplying these very same actions in the new tree whose subject node has been decorated by the expression *John* of the elliptical fragment then gives rise to the construal of the answer as involving a rebinding of the object argument to the provided new subject. The effect achieved is the same as the higher-order unification account but without anything beyond what has already been used for the processing of the previous linguistic input and, consequently, without any need to assign some distinct type to the elliptical element *did* or the subject *John*. All that has to be assumed is that the metavariable contributed by the anaphoric *did* can be updated by some suitable selection of some action-sequence taken from the context.

The DS style of analysis, with its emphasis on incremental procedures for interpretation, can now be seen to have advantages over both semantic and syntactic accounts of ellipsis. The first is that parallelism effects in ellipsis construal are directly predicted:

(7.82)   A student had interviewed every professor; and so had a journalist.

(7.83)   Mary washed herself in front of Sue; and so did her mother.

To recapitulate, whatever way the first conjunct is taken to be construed, the second must be construed in that manner also, whether this be scope construal, the way the reflexive anaphor is construed and so on. This parallelism, which in all semantic and syntactic accounts has to be stipulated as an independent constraint, is straightforwardly ensured by the assumption that an already used set of actions is being rerun. On the account of sloppy construal of elliptical forms, in particular, there remains a concept of identity between context and form despite the non-identical resulting interpretation: the identity is in the selected subsequence of actions that is applied to different effect in the construal of the ellipsis site.

A second advantage is the prediction that sloppy construals of VP-ellipsis are derived in the presence of an antecedent linguistic expression, without this having to imply any bifurcation of elliptical phenomena into grammar-internal vs. grammar-external. Actions stored in context will be available only as a record of previously parsed/produced utterances. This is because the context keeps a record of the sequence of computational and lexical actions that were actually associated with linguistic expressions, plus any pragmatic actions that gave rise to the interpretation of the antecedent. So the report that at least some forms of ellipsis construal involve just what a previous linguistic expression induces is matched in the analysis, without having to posit a type of ellipsis that makes reference to the linguistic string itself: it is merely that when actions have been used in processing linguistic expressions, these are available for reuse as a regular part of the context itself.

A third result of this analysis is that it strengthens the parallelism between anaphoric expressions and ellipsis. There is no need for reshuffling of syntactic or morphological features specific to ellipsis construal to preserve some requisite concept of linguistic identity, as is posited on syntactic accounts for such examples as:

(7.84)   John has washed his socks and so has Sue.

(7.85)   A: You're sitting on my chair.
            B: No, I'm not.

On this account of ellipsis, fragments are simply parsed using whatever structure or action sequences the context provides and is compatible with the encoded features of the fragment.

In this connection, it is notable also that though marginal, pronoun construal may also be modelled as involving reuse of actions provided by context, yielding non-identical assignments for antecedent and pronominal. These are the *paycheque pronouns* first identified by Karttunen (1969):

(7.86)   John puts his paycheque in the bank, but Bill keeps it under his bed.

Under this type of construal, the pronoun *it* is interpreted in the same manner as *his paycheque* was in the first conjunct: that is, as the set of procedures for constructing a term with a metavariable as one of its internal arguments, an interim place-holder, which is identified relative to the subject but within its own local structure. This local subject will be *Bill'*, hence the construal of *it* as 'Bill's paycheqe'. The account thus directly reflects the intuition that ellipsis involves reconstruction from context in direct analogy with anaphora, indeed differing only in type assignment, despite the apparently tighter association of ellipsis construal with what is traditionally thought to be a grammar-internal process of syntax.

7.6.4   Context defined

Bringing these sub-types together, *context* for a partial tree is defined as a composite record of previous actions, words and decorated structure that has been established up to that point in parsing. This necessarily includes the local structure currently being built (and its associated actions), and also may include previous complete trees (and their associated actions). In virtue of DS being a grammar formalism and not itself imposing a choice mechanism, there are no restrictions on the size of the context: this is taken to be a relevance-constrained issue (see Chapter 1). Accordingly, unless particular inferential effects are to be achieved, the context is expected to be no more than either that contributed by processing the immediately previous utterance (as in the majority of ellipsis types), or even the partial structure currently under construction (as in the *antecedent-contained ellipsis* cases). In particular, given that in ellipsis there is no linguistic content associated with the trigger to narrow down the content to be selected from context to determine some larger than minimal context, there is normally no motivation for selecting anything other than the smallest context.

With this characterisation of context, problems that apply to other accounts of ellipsis do not apply to a DS form of analysis. The ambiguity in simple cases arises simply because the immediate context makes available more than one form of resolution – both formulae and actions are available (italicised material reflects what is reconstructed):

(7.83)   Mary washed herself in front of her mother, and so did Sue.

(7.87)   = 'Mary washed herself in front of Mary's mother and Sue *washed herself in front of Sue's mother.*'

           OR

(7.88)   = 'Mary washed herself in front of Mary's mother and Sue *washed herself in front of Mary's mother.*'

The parallelism effects associated with ellipsis immediately follow, as indeed (7.83) illustrates, and are expected to be part of a broader phenomenon. Quantifier construal, and the parallelism effects that apply there, follow the same lines (see section 7.3.2):

(7.82)   A student had interviewed every professor, and so had a journalist.

In general, actions from the immediate context will constitute a natural choice, any such selection always constituting an optimal economy measure, the replication of what is in the immediate context by definition minimising the effort of context search. For example, the complexity which examples such as (7.40) create for a semantic account gives rise to no increase in complexity in the DS-style of account: the appropriate sequence of actions already used in context simply has to be replicated in the process of construal for the ellipsis site:

(7.40)   The policeman who arrested Bill failed to read him his rights, and so did the policeman who arrested Tom.

Moreover, because **all** information from words has to be used, and used incrementally, the richer the information that precedes the ellipsis site within the clause to be built up, the less flexibility there will be in the selection of actions with which to resolve the ellipsis site. In antecedent-contained ellipsis, we have the limit case:

(7.21)   John interviewed every student Bill had.

(7.17)   John is reviewing everything that Sue is.

Both arguments for the predicate to be reconstructed are determined by what precedes: the relative pronoun provides one argument for the predicate, the subject expression the other. So at least in the simple cases as in (7.21)–(7.17), the only actions that can be selected from the context are those associated with the verb of the matrix clause. Indeed, given the fact that both context and ellipsis site are within a domain for which the construal of a quantifying term has to be resolved (see section 7.5.2), this is the only context that can be selected. The notorious structural restrictions associated with antecedent-contained ellipsis also immediately follow. It is the positioning of the relative pronoun at the left periphery of its clause that determines the strong-island restrictions associated with this structure. Appearing at the left periphery of its clause, the relative pronoun is independently taken to decorate an unfixed node that has to be resolved in its local domain (Kempson *et al.* 2001; Cann *et al.* 2005), and it is this that determines that the unfixed node must be eventually fixed within the bounds of an individual tree, hence within an 'island'.

Finally, as long as case specifications can be seen as constraints on tree growth update (see section 7.5.1), the German data in (7.47)–(7.48) in which fragments seem to require reconstruction with appropriately case-selecting verb forms (section 7.3.2) are also unproblematic, as whatever constraints the case specifications impose, these are by definition constraints on tree growth. Such constraints will apply just as much on partial structures constructed by actions culled from the record stored in context, as on a structure directly induced by a full clausal sequence of words. This is a problem we leave for the keen reader (see the exercise below).

So, in general, apparent problems for other analyses are resolved in the DS style of explanation in ways that sustain the intuition that the interpretation to be assigned to an elliptical fragment is given by the context in which it is uttered.

Exercise 7.2

What kind of DS analyses do you think might be posited to reflect the following data?

a. Consider a situation in which A and B play a game in which they point to objects reminding them of different people.
(A says pointing out some object, say a tree, as reminding him of his father:)

*Mein   Vater/*Meinen   Vater*
my   father$_{NOM}$/*my   father$_{ACC}$
'My father.'

Consider also that in German the full utterance expressing the same content would be something like the following:

Der Hund   erinnert   mich   an   meinen Vater
the dog$_{NOM}$ reminds   me   of   my father$_{ACC}$
'The dog reminds me of my father.'

b. Consider a situation in which A and B go into a room and see a man on the floor bleeding profusely.

*Einen   Doktor,   schnell/*Ein   Doktor,   schnell*
a   doctor$_{ACC}$,   quick/*a   doctor$_{NOM}$,   quick
'A doctor, quick.'

c. In German, fragmentary answers to questions involve case restrictions:

A: *Hat   Hans   nicht   den Brief   geschrieben?*
   Did   Hans$_{NOM}$ not   the letter$_{ACC}$ write
   'Didn't Hans write the letter?'

B: *Nein   Ich/*Mich*
   No   I$_{NOM}$/*me$_{ACC}$
   'No. I did.'
   What does this indicate?

Exercise 7.3

Consider (a):

(a) John told Bill to vote for his mother, because Jim had; so Tom then did.

Does (a) have the interpretation:

'John told Bill to vote for John's mother because Jim had *told Bill to vote for Jim's mother*; so Tom then *told Bill to vote for John's mother because Jim had told Bill to vote for Jim's mother.*'

If so, why? If not why not? If it isn't clear, why should this be the case?

7.7   Summary reflections

If we look back now across the development of ellipsis explanations over the last half-century, we see exactly the same shift in types of analysis as has pervaded semantic analysis in general. In attempting to model ellipsis, a first presumption was simply to assume that syntax and its representations of hierarchical structure for strings of words should be used to address the problem. With emergent evidence that it is the interpretation of the antecedent string which in some sense is made use of, linguists then turned to model-theoretic characterisations of content to provide a basis for capturing ellipsis phenomena, with the aim of sustaining the view that no representationalist basis was needed for the projection of the requisite content. However, representational constructs seem in the end to have turned out to be essential, if the broad array of ellipsis phenomena are to be captured. And it is the very types of interpretation for which the semantic account was defined – the sloppy construals of VP-ellipsis – which appear to shift the balance in favour of representationalist assumptions about the systematic nature of content to be associated with words of the language.

In this connection, we have seen how, in DS, the presumption that records of actions are stored in context yields the potential to provide a uniform characterisation of elliptical phenomena. It promises to provide a simpler and less powerful basis than the higher-order unification account. It reflects the parallelism that is otherwise a stipulated primitive, external to either syntactic or model-theoretic explanations. It reinstates the parallelism between anaphora and ellipsis as equally devices whose interpretation is determined directly by what context provides. And finally, it leads us to an essentially representationalist conclusion. Elliptical fragments are correctly predicted to be subject to very divergent forms of interpretation, possibly departing from those of their antecedent; but this is nothing more than the result of procedures being reapplied in a novel environment, hence to different effect. There is a consequence to this emerging conclusion that ellipsis does indeed provide a window on the constitution of the context. The procedures for establishing content for such elliptical fragments are constructive devices rebuilding structure relative to a newly provided context, and thus essentially representationalist in nature. So study of ellipsis leads to the conclusion that interpretations for natural-language expressions qua expressions have to be in terms of the construction of representations rather than in terms of the content assigned relative to context, for it is only by this assumption that an integrated characterisation of ellipsis is made possible.

7.8   Further reading

Ellipsis has been the subject of a large body of research since the seventies, when it was used as a criterion for constituent identity (Ross 1967), with the problematic interface with pragmatics noted from early on (Morgan 1973,

1989). Analyses fall into four broad categories: syntactic, semantic, pragmatic and some mixture of these. Analyses developed within the movement-based frameworks took off in the 1990s with Fiengo and May (1994); see also Fox (2002) for a characterisation of parallelism. Largely, however, syntactic accounts of ellipsis have been specific to individual construction-types: VP-deletion accounts other than Fiengo and May include Stanley (2000), Merchant (2004); stripping, Merchant (2002); sluicing, Chung *et al.* (1995); antecedent-contained deletion (ACD), Hornstein (1994) and many others. Within HPSG, there have been accounts by Lappin (1999); Ginzburg and Cooper (2004); Purver (2004); Fernandez (2006). The formal semantics characterisation of ellipsis was given a kick-start by Dalrymple *et al.* (1991); Shieber *et al.* (1996). The challenge for these accounts is whether appropriate syntactic constraints are expressible: see Lappin (1996, 1999); Hardt (2008) for debate. Pragmatic accounts include Stainton (2004); Stainton and Elugardo (2004): this view is disputed in Stanley (2000); Merchant (2004); and Ludlow (2004). See arguments and counter-arguments presented in Elugardo and Stainton (2004); Progovac *et al.* (2006); Bezuidenhout (2006b). Ellipsis is regularly used as a diagnostic for semantic identity: see in this connection Cappelen and Lepore (2005). Problems of quantification and ellipsis are confronted by Shieber *et al.* (1996); Steedman (2000), Kempson *et al.* (1999); Purver *et al.* (2006). Some accounts cross disciplinary boundaries: Kehler (2002); Purver *et al.* (2006); Cann *et al.* (2007). Work on such cross-module interaction has also taken place within an extension of DRT, with formal modelling of ellipsis and cross-sentential rhetorical relations, hence formal pragmatic modelling: Asher and Lascarides (2003); Schlangen (2003); Schlangen and Lascarides (2003).

In the turn into this century, work on dialogue has been expanding rapidly, with ellipsis as a major sub-domain, occurring commonly in dialogue: Schlangen (2003); Purver (2004, 2006); Cann *et al.* (2005); Fernandez (2006); Purver *et al.* (2006); Cann *et al.* (2007); Ginzburg (forthcoming). As argued in Purver *et al.* (2006); Cann *et al.* (2007), Dynamic Syntax is a framework argued to be well suited to modelling ellipsis in dialogue. Proof-theoretic concepts defined in Dynamic Syntax have much in common with a number of categorial grammar frameworks: in particular these frameworks all make notable use of labelled natural deduction tools, see Morrill (1994); Steedman (1996, 2000); Fernando (2002); Piwek (2007); and also, within LFG, Crouch (1999). For the use of the epsilon operator in the analysis of E-type pronouns see Slater (1986); Egli and von Heusinger (1995).

8   What a word can mean

At this juncture, we need to bring back into the picture the background to the representationalism debate that was set out in Chapter 2. In classical logic (both propositional and predicate logic), there is strict correspondence between proof-theoretic and model-theoretic characterisations of the core semantic concepts of inference, entailment and synonymy; and it was in virtue of this equivalence that we said there that study of formal languages provided an essential back-ground to the issue of representationalism in semantic theorising about natural languages. However, with the explosion of context-relativity that the discussion of tense, aspect, anaphora and ellipsis has opened up, it might seem that the issue of representationalism is independent of the question of whether inference can be expressed syntactically, as in proof theory, or model-theoretically, as in model-theoretic semantics. It is certainly the case that with proof systems for logic having been developed systematically only for formal languages, if we want a fully general formal characterisation of some concept of language–world relation for natural languages, then the characterisation has to be in model-theoretic (or some equivalent) terms. Nevertheless, it doesn't follow that no characterisation of inference entailment and synonymy can be provided for natural languages. For any interpretation of a natural-language sentence that is expressible using a predicate- or propositional-logic formula, these core semantic concepts as defined in logic can still be taken as grounding such interpretations. But the essential modification is that the properties of inference, entailment and syn-onymy, will apply as characterisations of sentences **as taken in some context,** in effect then, sentence **contents**. So, for example, the trio of sentences *John is fractious. If he is, then he is tired. Therefore he is tired* indeed illustrate a valid inference as long as the sentences are understood as picking out the same indi-vidual j at the same point in time t_i and predicating of him that he is fractious; and such an interpretation could be modelled as:

(8.1) $$Fractious'(j, t_i) \rightarrow Tired'(j, t_i), Fractious'(j, t_i) \vdash Tired'(j, t_i)$$

Yet, as a relation between natural-language strings disembodied from any con-textual fixing of the anaphoric elements, this inference cannot be claimed to hold: this is because (i) the pronouns could be picking out someone quite different in each sentence, (ii) the ellipsis site could be differently construed, and (iii) there is no logical reason why the present tense should pick out the same time. The problem will apply to all sentences containing context-dependent elements; so the problem is an entirely general one. It is utterance contents which stand in semantic relations such as entailment, not sentences. But we saw in Chapter 1 that making appropriate predictions of entailment and synonymy is very generally agreed to be a core criterion of adequacy for any putative account of natural-language semantics. If, then, we are to get at what semantic relations there might be between sentences, independent of any such context input, the only possible remaining source will be that of meanings associated with words. And so, finally, we turn to the topic that many textbooks on semantics begin with: the topic of word meaning.

In all that we have looked at so far, apart from the brief foray into event semantics in Chapter 6, words have either been assigned mere stipulations as to what they might denote in some model or some unanalysed term as a primitive concept; and the only point of interest has been getting compositionality of compound expressions right. Yet, as hinted in Chapter 6, there are problems in addressing word meaning of an entirely different order of complexity. Moreover, it is with respect to this area of meaning that people happily spend an evening arguing; so there is a robust intuition that this aspect of meaning is central to any explanation of natural-language content. In a sense, as we shall see, the discussion of tense and aspect of Chapter 6 showed the core properties of this level of content attribution. What we saw there was that tense and aspect construal display very great flexibility, allowing processes of so-called *coercion* that enable a linguistic form to allow a construal manipulated way beyond what it might seem, canonically, to convey. This process is, like other areas of natural-language interpretation, triggered by individual contexts; but it gives every appearance of being richer and more creative than the mere picking up from context of some already established content or pattern as is in anaphora and ellipsis. This flexibility is endemic to lexical content in general; and, finally, we now turn to setting this problem against a historical narrative, showing how research on the lexicon has evolved over the period in which formal models of semantics have changed.

From the very beginnings of formal-semantic modelling, word meanings have been the poor relative in the family of formal semantic analyses, the elderly member of the family who doesn't fit in to some new style of life the family may have adopted, and about whom the family try not to talk too much in the hope that no one will notice this embarrassing lapse from their newly adopted way of life. The awkwardness of traditional assumptions about lexical semantics for linguists came to the fore in the late sixties and early seventies. It was shortly after the methodology which Chomsky was finding so fruitful in developing criteria of adequacy for syntax was extended to the challenge of defining analogous criteria of adequacy to provide a benchmark for evaluating theories of natural-language semantics. The criteria set out were: succeeding in expressing the relation between word meaning and sentence meaning; modelling ambiguity for expressions only as appropriate; and modelling synonymy and entailment relations between sentences and between words. The methodology was to devise rule specifications that get the right results in just the same spirit as that which Chomsky had set out for syntacticians. Katz, Fodor and Postal presumed that such rules should be defined as applying to yield semantic representations capable of expressing the appropriate relations, enabling entailment or synonymy relations such as that between *John killed Bill* and *Bill died*, or between *John is a bachelor* and *John is an unmarried man* to be expressed. These representations involved the articulation, within the semantic component of the grammar, of a supposedly universal set of *semantic markers* – **adult**, **human**, **cause**, **become**, etc. – and a set of *projection* rules. These rules applied to the *deep structure* of a sentence and the semantic markers associated with the words of the sentence in question, and yielded as output a semantic representation that constitutes the sentence's meaning. There was no attempt to address issues of context-dependence, since the specific goal was to characterise context-independent properties of sentences as displayed in a grammar. This system of semantic markers and attendant rules was presumed to require justification only according to their success in predicting relations matching speakers' judgements of sentence/word relatedness of meaning, following the parallel methodology for syntax.

This methodology, however, caused outrage among the philosophically inclined community, for whom semantics, by definition, constitutes a modelling of the relation between expressions of the system under study and the denotations to which these expressions correspond (following the formal-language concept of semantics; see Chapters 2–3). It was the setting out of this programme for linguistic semantics (see Katz 1972) that gave rise to Lewis's savage criticism in the early 1970s that all semantics that lacked a formal characterisation of the language-denotation mapping was worthless, simply not constitutive of semantics, with the claim that became the mantra of formal semantics that 'Semantics with no treatment of truth conditions is not semantics' (Lewis 1970). As we saw in Chapter 1, this criticism was taken at the time to be so devastating, and the point so well taken, that the attempt to articulate a vocabulary of concepts relative to which words might be defined and sentence-meanings accordingly characterised was abandoned. Formal semanticists then, with very few exceptions (see Dowty 1979, 1988), set aside all attempts to capture any basis for lexical definitions, articulating, at most, constraints on denotational assignments that would assure co-extensiveness in cases of demonstrable synonymy relations (though many were argued to be spurious, involving subtle distinctiveness between supposed synonymy pairs). Buttressing this vacuum despite his own commitment to representationalism and cognitive forms of explanation, Fodor subsequently argued for the next twenty years (Fodor 1981; Fodor and Lepore 1998; Fodor 2000) that attempts to define words in terms of any other constructs, whether definitions, prototypes or stereotypes, are all equally doomed to failure.

The puzzle which the pairing of a word and some notion of meaning poses is that despite long and very rich traditions of dictionary-making, there are really very few words for which we can successfully provide definitions at all (see Fodor 1998, an extensive argument to the effect that words express primitive unanalysable concepts). We might perhaps be able to provide definitions for verbs of causation such as *kill, blacken, paint* or kinship terms such as *bachelor* or *mother*; but the list stops almost at that point. But, as we saw in Chapter 1, it's worse than that; for even within this list, such verbs have their interpretation very largely determined by context. The Fodor example was that of the word *paint*, with the various concepts that it can be associated with (*Michelangelo painted a picture, Michelangelo painted the ceiling of the Sistine Chapel (because the paint was chipping), Michelangelo painted the walls of his studio and his house*, etc.) and the impossibility of finding a definition that covers all the essential components of even a single use. But the extendability and context-dependence of word meaning is an entirely general phenomenon. Take almost any word at random, and the phenomenon is replicable in kind. For example, consider whether you think that the meaning of the word *create* is identical in the following sentences:

(8.2)   John created a scene.

(8.3)   John created such a din we couldn't hear ourselves speak.

(8.4)   John created a sandcastle as big as his little brother.

(8.5)   John's sandcastle created a very good impression.

If not, one will be invoking some variant of an account that assigns multiple ambiguity to the word according to each and every use; and unless we are content to invoke lexical ambiguity for a word each time its interpretation in some use is at all distinct from that of previous uses, this flexibility suggests that there is something else going on between the words themselves and the actions/events/objects in the world which they describe. And there are worse problems than this. A single word can be used on one occasion to mean more than one thing. Food can be delicious, the process of eating it can take hours; books can be fascinating in content, yet heavy in physical weight. Nonetheless, we can talk about objects in terms of such different attributes in one breath as it were, as though the concepts in question were the very same:

(8.6)   The meal was delicious, but lasted three hours.

(8.7)   Your book was fascinating, but too heavy to carry around.

The problem notoriously extends to plurals, with assertions both about a class of objects as a kind, and arbitrary instances of that kind:

(8.8)   Pheasants, which are rapidly becoming a major pest in south-west Scotland, ate all my new plants last night.

This is the phenomenon we have already seen a glimpse of, with such sentences as *John is being intelligent*, which involves the conversion of an attribution of a state into the process of a state holding at a time (see Chapter 6). The problems posed by lexical meaning are far from new; the more difficult question is what to do about the issues such apparently uncontrollable flexibility can raise.

This problem has been taken to be so problematic that until very recently it has been presumed by those working in formal semantics that issues raised by lexical relations between words have simply to be set aside as intransigent. Content words have been, accordingly, assumed to have some fixed denotation, contrary to fact, with rules of syntax and semantics together determining the meaning of the whole; and this pattern extends to Dynamic Syntax and to much of the work on DRT (though in DRT, there is now intensive work probing appropriate formulations of internal structure for word content, following the lead DRT has taken in temporal semantics: Kamp and Reyle 1993; Kamp and Rossdeutscher 1994; Kamp *et al.* 2005). Where there are expressions whose interpretation genuinely does vary independently of the language, such as in anaphora and ellipsis, these are treated as variables or, in some sense, underspecified, with a semantics that isn't part of the model at all. Relative to this programme, the concept of word meaning itself remains, undeniably, a mystery, with no exploration at all of what *concept* a word might express in virtue of which it can have the (range of) denotations it displays in each particular use. At best, words are associated with so-called *meaning postulates* which express constraints on denotations for words so that synonymous words or phrases, by stipulation, can be modelled as having the same extension. *Kill*, for example, is defined in such a way as to ensure that a sentence such as *John caused Bill to die* will be true in all worlds in which *John killed Bill* is true. In Montague semantics in particular, the intuition that words express concepts is not captured at all. As indicated in Chapters 4 and 6, words are simply assigned, by stipulation, some fixed extension at an index in a model enabling the syntax–semantics correlation to be computed. But even when this is extended to incorporate possible worlds as a formal reflection of multiple contingent circumstances relative to which a sentence might be judged true or false, the approach is still rigidly extensional. The interpretation of a word is the set of possible extensions, a function from a possible world to an extension. Nothing is defined to capture why such extensions hold – to capture, for example, what it is about *kill* that determines the particular set of extensions assigned in the model, or why there might be any correspondence with extensions assigned to *die*. The question is, what more there should be to say?

The question, moreover, is an important one. If the *principle of compositionality*, which we might now reiterate as the constraint that the meaning of a sentence is a (monotonic) function of the meanings of all the words it contains together with constructions used to put the words in order, is valid (at least as a guiding principle for research into meaning, even if it cannot be absolute) then lexical meaning must be seen as forming the basis for all (linguistic) meaning.

8.1   The Generative Lexicon

Some linguists have been brave enough to consider how to make the problem of word meaning at least computationally tractable. In particular James Pustejovsky set out a theory of the Generative Lexicon (Pustejovsky 1995) in which information is associated with a *lexeme*, a unit associated with a word form for which different types of specification are set out:

(i) *argument structure*: dictating number and semantic type of logical arguments.

(ii) *event structure*: specifying the event type of lexeme (or phrase) – for verbs, whether activity or state.

(iii) *qualia structure*: specifying default argument assignments that may get over-ridden by other forms of information, and the listing of any other forms of encyclopaedic information.

(iv) *lexical inheritance structure*: displaying the relations between the concept determined by the word and its hierarchical relation to other semantic constructs, displayed in the form of lattices of feature values or word association sets. All such structures are set out as lattices, networks with individual nodes labelled with primitive classificatory concepts of various sorts.

Of these, *qualia structure* is the most novel, encompassing as it does contingent, hence default, information, contrary to standard assumptions of monotonicity of content accumulation (hence requiring revision of the *compositionality principle*). These may cover:

a. formal properties of some object (orientation, magnitude, shape, etc.);

b. telic information, the purpose and function of the described object;

c. agentive information, i.e. factors involved in the origin or bringing about of an object (creator, natural kind, causality).

As this list indicates, the range of information expressible as part of the lexical specification associated with the word is essentially limitless. Yet this information is, by claim, stored in the lexicon, hence a subpart of the grammar formalism.

The goal of the theory is, furthermore, to provide a generative lexicon-internal mechanism for combining attributes of the entity described, leading to a non-monotonic form of interpretation; and the theory accordingly provides an explicit model for how meaning shifts can take place. In particular, the qualia structure provides the structural template over which *semantic transformations* (generative devices such as *co-composition*, *type coercion* and *subselection*) may apply to alter the meaning of a lexical item or phrase. So, for example, the verb *use* is semantically underspecified. The factors that allow us to determine which sense is appropriate for any use of the verb are the qualia structures for each phrase in the construction in which the verb occurs and a rich mode of composition, which is able to take advantage of this qualia information:

(8.9)   a. John used the knife on the turkey.
           b. Mary used soft contact lenses since college.
           c. This car uses diesel.

Overall, Pustejovsky's theory presents the hypothesis that the human conceptual apparatus is generative and compositional. It is defined as able to build complex meanings out of less complex ones, with complex concepts being derived from others over structured configurations specific to the lexicon (i.e. not reducible to independent principles of the syntax of the language). Furthermore, the attributes assigned to words may change in context, without these necessarily constituting a change in meaning of the term itself as in (8.9). (8.6)–(8.8) are said to be cases of *coercion* unifying distinct attributes of a single lexeme by a specifically defined coercion operation. But this means that the more context-sensitive the meanings of heads of phrases are supposed to be, the richer must be the lexical entries for all the elements they combine with. At least in principle, every time a verb takes a new meaning in combination with a noun phrase, the complexity of the noun's lexical entry must increase, and not merely that of the verb itself.

Despite the breadth of empirical domain to which the Pustejovsky system of annotations can apply, the challenge as to how the structures advocated are grounded in any familiar semantics (with mapping onto semantically or syntactically defined forms of inference) remains substantive. Without any such grounding, and with a very rich vocabulary of features, it is unclear what substance is attributable to the claims being made. Faced with this lack of restrictiveness, and the self-evident context-dependence of information defined as part of an item's qualia structure, one might rather wonder whether the intrinsic content of the word itself shouldn't be treated as more radically underspecified, analogous to pronoun and ellipsis construals. With this form of critique, from model theorists on the one hand, and from Fodor on the other, the force of a Pustejovsky style of explanation remained in doubt, at least for many working in semantics; and the status of lexical meaning within the overall characterisation of natural-language semantics became stuck in a theoretical stalemate.

Recently, however, the research outlook for lexical semantics has begun to shift; and a number of research strands are probing the parallelisms between word-meaning flexibility and other aspects of context-dependence. One is the conservative claim (Cappelen and Lepore 2005) that the folk intuition that words in general have a single meaning across contexts is the core to the explanation of why human communication is so successful. Other projects (Cooper 2007; Larsson 2008) take on the challenge for the Pustejovsky paradigm of probing what is necessary to provide the grounding for the coercion data which the Pustejovsky model brought to the fore, but within a formal-semantics paradigm. These separate strands of research are developing independently of each other, and largely within different research communities, one at the philosophy/pragmatics interface, the other at the semantics/computational-linguistics interface. Put together with emergent work on DRT and Dynamic Syntax, they bring out just how radical the shift in perspective has been in semantic research since those early days in the seventies. As we shall now see, issues of context-dependence have moved firmly centre stage, transforming the debate over the status of semantics and its relation to grammar formalisms for natural language. Perhaps surprisingly, however, despite the early rejection of representationalism by the formal-semantics community, it is this which is inexorably becoming the core methodology for semantic theorising, as such intermediate constructs are now being provided the formal grounding which they so signally lacked in those early days. Furthermore, these intermediate representations are now seen to offer the added bonus of being grounded in the empirical findings of cognitive psychology, an essential prerequisite for any cognitively plausible model of language.

8.2   Semantic Minimalism

The first claim we turn to is in stark contrast to the Pustejovsky view of lexical meaning, as it promotes the view that the vast array of lexical (i.e. content) words, namely, those with intrinsic predicative content, are context insensitive. The account is aptly termed Semantic Minimalism (Capellen and Lepore 2005). According to this view, utterance interpretation enjoys the resounding success it does in most circumstances because by far the majority of words are unitary in meaning across contexts. Natural-language expressions are said to divide between a relatively restricted, basic set of *indexical* terms that are intrinsically context-dependent, and some remainder, which are not. There is a clear division to be made between some basic set of indexicals, viz. *I*, *you*, *now*, *here*, *this*, *that*, *he*, *she*, *it* ..., which are irreducibly context-dependent (in the case of pronouns at least in their indexical use), and the remainder (see also Kaplan 1977/1989). In setting out what they take to be a debate probing what utterance content amounts to, apart from such explicit context-dependency indicators, Cappelen and Lepore set aside any cases of variability which could be argued to be system-internal (such as lexical ambiguity). They then focus their attention on words that have been argued by pragmatists to involve some aspect of context-dependence. These include colour terms such as *red*, gradable adjectives such as *tall*, *heavy*, the item *know* under various construals, and the predicate *ready* supposedly defined as having some syntactically covert argument ('ready for what?'). For these they argue that all criteria of identity and truth-evaluability indicate that they display no context-sensitivity. They then generalise from these to the claim that no lexical content words display any context-sensitivity at the level of minimal propositional content (with the possible exception of any words for whom an added covert indexical can be justified, e.g. the word *local* might be taken to require a (covert) argument indicating local to what, see Partee 1989). To the contrary, they argue, their univocal nature is what enables interlocutors to establish a firm concept of shared content despite having no access to each other's mental states. On their view, content sharing is the foundation-stone of communication and any utterance of, e.g. *Rudolf has a red nose* is true just in case Rudolf has a red nose and expresses the minimal proposition 'Rudolf has a red nose' (Cappelen and Lepore 2005: 3). This is not, however, the simplistic claim that such content items display no context-sensitivity. To the contrary, Cappelen and Lepore simultaneously advocate that an utterance may involve the assertion of indefinitely many propositions depending on 'a potentially indefinite number of features of the context of utterance and of the context of those who report on or think about what was said by the utterance' (Cappelen and Lepore 2005: 4). Nonetheless, they claim that minimal utterance contents, as opposed to *speech act contents*, are clearly delimitable on any occasion of use as identifiable without any enrichment, unless there is encoded indication of the expression requiring interpretation from context (the basic set of indexical expressions aside); and this minimal content then is what both speaker and hearer can agree on, get reported as agreeing on, etc. Implicit in their claim is the assumption that interlocutors are able to distinguish shared and private attributes of content in a systematic and straightforward way, with the language system being set up to reflect this distinction.

It is notable that having made a delimitation between the basic set of indexical expressions and the remainder, they then exclude all discussion of cases where any variation in interpretation could be said to result from the effects of system-internal processes, e.g. lexical homonymy; and on these same grounds they also exclude all discussion of ellipsis, presuming that ellipsis too is a phenomenon where diversity of construal is grounded in grammar-internal operations, hence not context-dependent. While this stance with respect to ellipsis is a widespread view, at least among syntacticians, we have already seen reason to believe, to the contrary, that ellipsis constitutes a clear window on what kind of notion of context is required for utterance interpretation. This is a matter we take up immediately below. However, the first consequence to note in the debate Cappelen and Lepore have triggered is that the core phenomena of context-dependence, i.e. anaphora and ellipsis (and tense too: see below), are excluded by fiat from the supposed attempt to probe what context-sensitivity in utterance interpretation amounts to.

8.2.1   Ellipsis and criteria for identity of content

With ellipsis and anaphora set aside, Cappelen and Lepore proceed to argue that the definition of content for utterances has to be liberal enough to allow variable construals across discrete contexts while sustaining a notion of identical content. For example, they argue that the sentence *John is ready* can be appropriately used as part of a report that in two quite separate contexts, Nina had said that John was ready, both, that is, in relation to a discussion of John's being prepared for an exam and in relation to John being prepared to go out in heavy rain:

(8.10)   In both contexts, Nina said that John was ready.

Accordingly, they argue, the requisite notion of content for an expression such as *ready* is indifferent to whatever differences there might be between interlocutors, their private goals, the purpose of the conversation, etc. This, they suggest, is obvious evidence of a core cross-context notion of content for words such as *ready*. Such examples, they argue, show that expressions like *ready* should not be assigned some hidden argument to be identified from context providing the specification of what John might be ready for. Quantification over groups of individuals is also used to provide apparent evidence of such commonality of content. As they point out, a predicate expression attributed to some quantified conjoined subject expression may apparently allow different construals of the predicate applied to that compound argument:

(8.11)   Both John and Bill are ready: one for his exam, the other to get off on holiday.

(8.12)   Both John and Bill are tall: John is tall for an adult, Bill for a nine-year-old.

   In this connection, they observe in passing that VP-ellipsis is supposedly a well-established test for identity of content. In their view, genuine context-sensitive expressions have fixed interpretations under VP-ellipsis. For example, below in (8.13) Bob can only be said to like the speaker's mother, not his own or somebody else's:

(8.13)   John likes my mother and Bob does too.

This is not the case for other uses of pronouns like the following where the interpretation can shift according to the subject of the second conjunct (the sloppy reading, see Chapter 7):

(8.14)   John likes his mother and Bob does too.

Hence, they argue that, because VP-ellipsis construal preserves strict identity of content only when the VP in question contains a speaker-specific or hearer-specific pronoun, but not when other non-indexical construals of pronouns are involved, the VP-ellipsis test appears to distinguish only the 'utterance-scenario' concept of context. They go on to correctly observe that this criterion is problematic for any claim that the domain restriction for a quantified expression is context-sensitive, since, they suggest, the following does not require identical construal for *a store* across the two conjuncts:

(8.15)   John went to a store and so did Bill.

The above, they observe, may be taken to correctly describe a situation in which John may have gone to a store in New York, and Bill to any store whatsoever. The data are not, however, as problematic as Cappelen and Lepore think for what they call *radical contextualism*, the view that utterance interpretation systematically displays context-dependence. What is at issue is not the circumstances which would validate the truth of some utterance, but rather whether the two conjuncts can be construed in the two different ways. And relative to this, the felicity of (8.16) seems moot:

(8.16)   John went to a store and so did Bill, though only John took a five-hour train ride first to get to New York.

What is at issue is whether the first conjunct *John went to a store*, on its own, can be taken to convey the information that John went to a store in New York. But it is very unclear whether that conjunct *simpliciter* could be said to have conveyed that information. Rather, it might be that both conjuncts have a domain specification that is general with respect to stores, with the subsequent add-on being genuinely informative. Nonetheless, other examples can be constructed as evidence of the point Cappelen and Lepore were hoping to demonstrate. (8.17), for example, could be taken to constitute an example displaying the requisite flexibility of construal under VP-ellipsis to make their point:

(8.17)   John is sick because he really is. Mary is, because she is whenever anyone else is.

Even within a single sentence, the predicate to be constructed from *sick* does not have a constant value across the different reconstructions in (8.17) despite successive use of VP-ellipsis (as we saw, the VP-ellipsis test supposedly shows that only interpretations of context-sensitive expressions **must** remain constant). One might accordingly argue that it can only be some relatively weak concept of what it means to be 'sick' that is reconstructed at the various ellipsis sites ((8.17) is constructed by us).

However, using data such as (8.17) to buttress the Cappelen and Lepore conclusion would not be warranted. As we have already seen in the previous chapter, ellipsis does not always reflect identity of **content**: regularly it allows other aspects of the interpretation process to be what is retrieved from context. Therefore, the VP-ellipsis test cannot be used to isolate some privileged notion of context-dependence. According to the Dynamic Syntax modelling of this, rather than merely picking up some antecedent denotational content, divergent effects under VP-ellipsis can be induced by picking up on **actions** which immediately previously have been used in building up interpretation. Moreover (8.17), far from showing the context-insensitivity of construal of the term *sick*, might contrarily be said to demonstrate this term's sensitivity to an extremely local concept of context. The word *sick* is first construed relative to *really*; then it is interpreted relative to the local context provided by the assertion of John's being sick, but now attributed to Mary. Finally, it is construed relative to the adjunct clause with the quantification over times that *whenever anyone else is* provides, hence the bound-variable effect of the assertion about Mary made by the *because* clause. In each case, the elliptical form leads to repeated construction of a concept $Sick'$, $Sick''$, etc. relative to the most immediate local context as provided by the words as they unfold, and the contents these give rise to. Indeed, as (8.17) shows, the context is able to shift even within sub-sentential units in an essentially anaphoric way. It was this form of explanation, turning on the intricacies of different contexts, that provided us with an integrated basis for explaining ellipsis effects, ranging across sloppy construals of VP-ellipsis, antecedent-contained ellipsis and more. But the relevance of such examples here to the lexical-meaning debate is that phenomena such as VP-ellipsis cannot be used as a definitive test of the relative thinness of lexical content. From the present perspective, to the contrary, it would rather lead us to expect that content can be derived by rerunning some context-provided set of actions to yield different effects. Instead of leading us to conclude that lexical content words have to be analysed as relatively thin in content and constant across contexts, this would therefore suggest that the concept of content associated with lexical expressions is rather a *procedure* for constructing concepts in context. It is the pattern of these actions of concept-construction which is what remains constant, giving rise to the different construals of the item in question.

In the light of this alternative account of the interaction between lexically defined specifications and VP-ellipsis effects, we can now see the quantificational cases of (8.11)–(8.12) in a similar vein. What would seem to be required to get a handle on the examples (8.11)–(8.12) is that the procedures associated with some predicate like *be ready* can be sequentially triggered as applying to each conjunct in some phrasal coordination of NPs in order to yield the necessary conjoint propositions as the appropriate output propositional content, with this allowing possibly distinct construals. Though an account of phrasal coordination and quantifiers such as *both* has not been properly formulated here, there are obvious grounds for exploring this style of analysis: it allows not only a unified story of ellipsis but also an account of fine-grained context-dependency effects without having to invoke the notion of a separate level of 'minimal' content.

There is in addition an independent reason why (8.10) might be explicable without invoking any weak notion of minimal propositional content, as such. As Wedgwood (2007) points out, it is far from clear that predicates associated with verbs such as *say* take only propositions as complements, a core assumption for Cappelen and Lepore. Rather, such verbs take whatever construct might be associated with interpreting a sentence sequence, whether this be an incomplete logical form, a report of some (incomplete) proposition, or, according to present assumptions, procedures used in building up such propositional content. And this would lead us to expect an array of cases such as the following:

(8.18)   Both yesterday and today Nina said she was ready, but in both cases she turned out to be ill-prepared, yesterday for the cookery competition, today for the physics test.

(8.19)   Both John and Bill said that they were annoyed with themselves, one moaning that he was cross he had done so little, the other that he hadn't made better choices.

(8.20)   Both from a design and a content perspective, I'd say this poster is excellent.

(8.18) involves the predicate *ill-prepared*, which is construed as a two-place predicate even if its complement PP (prepositional phrase) headed by *for* is not overtly expressed, so covertness in itself is clearly no indication of some attribute not being part of the context-dependent content. And the expansion notably involves ellipsis requiring reconstruction of that predicate with both the additional argument implicit in the form itself and a temporal specification. The plural reflexive in (8.19) is clearly not the form of what John and Bill had severally said, so though the plural reflexive form indicates what is needed to build up the several propositional contents, these have to be built from the words without replicating them. And (8.20) provides phrasal coordination of adjuncts providing the precise parameter relative to which two distinct propositions have to be built up, each making reference to just one of these. From a perspective of context in which a record of procedures used in building up interpretation is retained, it is then a sequence of content-inducing actions which could be said to constitute the complement of the predicate expressed by *say*, reiterated relative to each conjunct in the compound expression as before.

In connection with the general Cappelen and Lepore stance that, once having dismissed indexicals, all other aspects of natural-language content are context-insensitive, there is one critical sleight of hand that invariably creeps in. In discussing sentences with no such self-evident indexicals, Cappelen and Lepore turn to discuss in detail sentences such as *Rudolf has a red nose*, as they say 'if we keep tense fixed [footnoted:] as we will do throughout this book' (p. 3). With this caveat slipped in, they go on to argue that the sentence as uttered has no context-relative aspects to its content. But this is another by-fiat move. Tense is as context-dependent for its construal as anaphora, as we've already seen in Chapter 6. This is a phenomenon that has been well documented ever since Partee (1973), Kamp (1978) and many others since. (8.21)–(8.23) illustrate indexical, bound-variable and E-type effects respectively:

(8.21)   I left the stove on (said at the airport leaving for holiday).

(8.22)   Whenever I left the stove on, the smoke alarm went off.

(8.23)   I left the stove on; the smoke alarm went off; the neighbours had to call the fire brigade; and I was in meetings throughout, and missed the whole drama.

Any move to ignore tense or distinguish it as exceptional and nevertheless deem that utterance interpretation in general is a context-independent phenomenon is a simple refusal to attend to aspects of utterance interpretation that happen not to confirm their claim. Unlike pronouns and ellipsis, tense cannot be treated as peripheral: every sentence involves some temporal specification indicating the placement of the propositional content being articulated within the flow of time (even when these involve universal quantification over time as in universal truths, or in apparently tenseless languages like Chinese, where tense information is inferred from particular aspect markers or the linguistic context). And this, more than anything, is why the challenge of addressing the intricacies of lexical, and as we now know aspectual, content cannot simply be put aside into the 'pragmatics waste-basket' as someone else's problem, as pragmatics used to be envisaged in the 1980s (see Kamp 1978 for a clear statement of the prevalent methodology at the time that pragmatics was no more than the residue of natural-language content left over as intransigent to any potential for semantic modelling). And, as with anaphora and ellipsis, this dependency of construal on some antecedent term transparently straddles sentence boundaries and may also straddle different interlocutors' utterances. It is only by assuming that the construal of each of anaphora, tense and ellipsis is a unitary phenomenon spanning both sub-sentential and cross-sentential domains that we have any hope of providing a unitary explanation of any one of these phenomena.

But with ellipsis, anaphora and tense construal now brought together, we see that each of them involves analyses in terms of a progressive building up of context and content across a process of utterance construal, either within or across utterance sequences. But in this unification, we see that Cappelen and Lepore have not isolated the right concept of context-dependence upon which natural language so heavily depends. They invariably open discussion as though the relevant concept of context is that of the context of utterance as situated act, the indexical specifications of *I* and *you* fixed by the utterance scenario itself, with other basic terms added only as necessary (this is the Kaplan concept of *context*, see Kaplan 1977/1989). But this is not the concept of context appropriate to ellipsis, anaphora and tense construal. For these, as for utterance interpretation in general, it is rather the concept of cognitive context relative to the process of building up interpretation that is required, with associated concepts of minimal cognitive context relative to which content decisions are progressively made. And once we grant that natural-language construal is relative to an evolving and cognitive concept of context, then both ellipsis and anaphora construal provide independent evidence of the richness of information to be recorded as part of context. Context-dependent construal may involve identity of some content to be copied over, but it may also involve no more than identity of the procedures for processing the items in question, preserving the patterns of how interpretation is set up; this richer concept of context then gives us the diversity of effects.

But once having granted this richer and more procedural concept of context, word meaning seems quite as context-dependent as other more self-evidently context-dependent expressions. There may be words whose intrinsic content involves a concept of context restricted only to the utterance-event, *I*, *you*, *now*, *here*, but these are exceptional among context-dependent expressions, notably learned late in first-language acquisition, quite unlike the regular anaphoric expressions such as the personal pronouns, the demonstratives, the anaphoric verbal forms, locative/temporal pronominals *there*, *then*, and tense, all of which are construed relative to the cognitive concept of context, and learned early by the language-acquiring child. This is not to deny that there may be some basis for distinguishing the context-sensitivity both of pronouns, demonstratives and ellipsis, and also of full-content lexical items such as *red*, *paint*, etc.; to the contrary, the former are distinctive in that their sole, and encoded, function is as a pointer to some interpretation to be provided by context. For full content words, context-sensitivity involves some much less tangible additional narrowing down of the concept to be expressed, in a sense that needs to be made precise.

The debate which Cappelen and Lepore (2005) triggered has indeed brought to the fore the challenge of how to ground the context-relativity of such content words without simply asserting their reducibility to the very same phenomenon as anaphoric expressions. But, in the meantime, with the recognition that the relevant concept of context-dependence is that shared by core anaphoric expressions, the issue of how context-sensitive their construal actually is remains open.

8.3   Variability in word meaning: new avenues of research

The sceptic's response to this disagreement between Cappelen and Lepore and pragmatists might be to conclude that word meaning is doomed to remain either a mere classificatory discipline, with over-rich and poorly grounded feature specifications, or an indeterminate bog within which pragmatists and philosophers can continue to disagree without either type of research constrained by the desideratum of leading to results which are amenable to formal analysis, hence to substantive progress in our understanding (recall our commitment in Chapter 1 to seeking to pursue formal models as a way of imposing criteria of adequacy on substantive semantic research). However, recent work is exploring novel ways of addressing the phenomenon of word meaning in ways that seem much more amenable to formal analysis, while preserving the grounding in accounts which have cognitive plausibility, and which suggest an intermediate stance that directly reflects ongoing change of word meaning. Two avenues of research in particular stand out.

8.3.1   Word meaning as concept-clusters

In exploring grounds for formal modelling of semantic change, Larsson (2008) suggests ways in which concept-items can be characterised in semantic terms as clusters of context-particular construals. On the one hand, a word will characteristically be subject to subtly distinct forms of use as triggered by individual contexts. On the other hand, each such use may, by repeated occasions of its employment, come to achieve a routinised association of word–interpretation correspondence. Indeed psycholinguistic evidence suggests that such routinisation of word–interpretation correspondences takes place extremely fast, even within individual exchanges between participants, with swift buttressing upon repeated occasions of interaction (Garrod and Anderson 1987; Garrod and Doherty 1994). Thus the view that Larsson seeks to formulate is the view that any established content word in the lexicon will be associated with a structured cluster of such correspondences. In consequence, what is unitary about the concept of meaning for a word may be little more than a cluster of the concepts it is used to name (though of course it may be considerably more, for example, one would expect family-resemblance relations to hold among the elements of the cluster since words are borrowed from domain to domain). Nonetheless, because, relative to any such cluster, it is a single word for which this set of correspondences holds, this word is perceived as having a pluralistic but nevertheless quasi-stable content within the vocabulary, stable in that the cluster, though individually shifting, forms a word-cluster pair that persists over time within the vocabulary of the language.

Larsson's starting point for providing a formal vocabulary for talking about this phenomenon is to assume that upon an individual utterance, an agent may set up a novel word-construal correspondence. The data Larsson considers are of two sorts. There are novel word–meaning correspondences of the sort reported in Clark and Clark (1979), when a cyclist delivering newspapers is referred to as having *porched* the newspaper, meaning 'having thrown it in such a way that it landed in the porch'. Also there are quasi-novel but nevertheless regularised usages such as use of the clock arms as a means of describing directions:

(8.24)   You're going diagonally sort of north-east, a sort of two o'clock direction, almost three o'clock, from the allotments.

Larsson defines the concept of a *usage set* for an agent A with respect to some expression c, $[S]_c^A$, which is the set of all the situations where A has observed a use of c. Agents generalise over these situations with the result of developing a *usage pattern* with respect to c, $[c]^A$, a function of A's usage set for c. With respect to any individual novel use of c in some situation s, c is said to involve setting up some utterance-specific meaning $[c]_s$ for Agent A. So for example, in coming to process *porch the newspaper* as conveying the information 'getting the newspaper to be on the porch while on the bicycle', the processor will have to add to their already established word–content correspondence:

$$[porch]_{building\text{-}entrance}$$

a novel pairing:

$$[porch]_{action\text{-}of\text{-}securing\text{-}delivery\text{-}of\text{-}newspaper}$$

Each listing in this cluster indicates a pairing between the word and the situation-type it reflects. The second item, being, by assumption, an addition to A's set of entries for *porch* will have associated with it some indication as to whether or not the novel $[c]_s$ is consistent with A's overall usage pattern $[c]^A$. If it is, it may be taken to constitute positive evidence reinforcing the already established $[c]^A$. If not, it may be taken to constitute negative evidence for other already established usages. Here, since it is logically independent, it simply constitutes a novel addition to the cluster. (The formal notation Larsson provides for representing how such evidence accumulates is not given here.)

Turning now to the semi-regularised usage of a clock-face for direction-giving, the dynamic, shifting meaning of the expression *two o'clock* might include at least two components depending on the appropriate contexts of use, shown below as the pair of correspondences:

$$[2 \ o'clock]_{clock}$$

$$[2 \ o'clock]_{direction\text{-}giving}$$

The task for the hearer here, where there is more than one established possibility, is to determine whether the situation in question is such as to trigger the direction-giving construal or the time-indicating construal. If the hearer is not able to find an appropriate correlation, they might create a new association which might or might not be retained beyond this use. Any usage of the expression *two o'clock* then leads to an update operation on the word–correspondence pairs with which it is associated. Either the current usage buttresses one such pairing (as indeed (8.24) would buttress the direction-giving form of construal), or it would correspond to no such pair and so would lead to the construction of a new pair. If, furthermore, the constructed pairing is inconsistent with any already established pairing, it will provide negative evidence with respect to that pairing, which might in some cases lead to revision. The accumulation for an individual speaker A over time is then taken to involve shifting values for each of the construals A has associated with c, some being progressively buttressed by continued reusage, others atrophying by lack of usage, with shifting membership of the cluster as novel word-construal pairings are set up.

Though Larsson presents his notation in a model-theoretic (or rather situation-theoretic) formulation, as he himself notes, there is no particular commitment in the claims he is making to the form of semantic modelling to be adopted, and it is clear that either denotational or representationalist assumptions are commensurate with this type of formulation. We should note, in passing, that there is no commitment here to defining concepts, but only to the weaker enterprise of creating appropriate pairings between words and some associated usage pattern, or, equivalently, some usage-specific construal; so the problem associated with definitions (as raised in different forms by Fodor, Lewis before him and Quine before him) is not raising its ugly head here. Whatever more specific form of modelling is taken to instantiate this claim, context-dependence for lexically contentful words is, on this view, taken to at least include the task of disambiguation or further specification for an intrinsically polysemous word, the word corresponding to a single concept of content only in so far as it names a cluster of word–construal correspondences. Larsson goes on to set out a model of semantic change based on the way in which dialogue moves like clarifications/corrections/extensions, etc. may or may not buttress any one such individual pairing in the cluster of paired item-correspondences assigned to the expression. Hence word meaning is constantly shifting as a result of language use, establishing an intrinsically dynamical system with the word never having to be taken as having an immutable, fully defined content.

The interest of this programme of research from the perspective of lexical meaning and the requisite concept of context-dependence underpinning natural language is that it provides an intermediate position between the *radical contextualism* stance (according to which the content of the individual expression would be presumed to be radically underspecified as to its intrinsic specification, with only general cognitive principles determining the occasion-specific construal), and the *minimal semantics* stance (according to which expressions simply lack context-dependence altogether). It also provides a bridge between what are taken to be regular uses of a word and creative occasion-specific uses. This is urgently needed, as, for far too long, metaphorical usages have simply been taken to be recalcitrant and therefore to be ignored by all formal semantic models; and the novel perspective opening up following Larsson's account suggests that these can now be seen to be part of the general extreme flexibility which word construal allows, in this closely allied to the concept of an *ad-hoc concept* advocated by Carston (2002) and Wilson and Carston (2007). Indeed, with these new formulations, we now reach a point of contact between formal-semantic methodologies and explorations of pragmatics and philosophy of language which address the cognitive basis for **how** speakers are able to use words with attributed contents ranging from minor extensions of some presumed content through to fully creative use of metaphor.

There is a further consequence of this view, stemming from its grounding in a formal-semantics methodology. Despite defining a fully determined form of construal relative to a particular situation of usage for a word, from the perspective of the contribution of that word within the language system it inhabits, the word will only be seen as contributing a set of available procedures for pairing word and content. There is therefore a retreat from the assumptions of the formal semantics paradigm as defined for formal languages: natural-language expressions are not on this view directly interpreted in the formal-language sense.

Exercise 8.1

Look up the words *go*, *chase*, and *run* in the dictionary and establish how many discrete senses should be posited as a grammar-internal fact for each word. Is there a difference in kind between your characterisations (for instance that one sense is able to act quasi-anaphorically)? If so, formulate a characterisation of this in terms that enable this aspect of its interpretation to be expressed.

Exercise 8.2

Take the words *brother* and *save* as in the following examples and distinguish as many sub-senses as you think are warranted. Is there a difference in kind between your characterisations in virtue of their distinct semantic type? If so, attempt to formulate how you would reflect this in your account.

(a) John saved his brother.
(b) John saved the day.
(c) John saved all his life.
(d) My brother is clever.
(e) My brother is 250 kilos.
(f) My brother is outside.
(g) My brother is on tenterhooks waiting for his results.
(h) The brothers were always poor.

8.3.2   Language as a tool-box

The same basic insight is expressed in work by Robin Cooper and Aarne Ranta. Seeking to preserve model-theoretic insights while nevertheless coming to grips with the variability of word meaning and grammar, Cooper and Ranta are exploring a programme of research in which natural languages are seen as a toolkit for constructing formal languages, procedures for constructing representations of content, rather than merely a static body of correspondences between expressions and assigned contents. Cooper's Type Theory with Records (TTR) in particular explores this new research perspective to model such data as *The lunch, which was delicious, took for ever*, reformulating Pustejovsky's observations to address the issue of how words can obtain extended meanings that can then be used for entirely novel combinations. The general dynamics is to articulate concepts of underspecification as types (equivalently content-type specifications) within a proof-theoretic perspective, with generalisations over such types as representations of content. Procedures for constructing information types are defined using labels to keep track of how such representation types are constructed. The emphasis on procedures then allows the formulation of both stored, encoded representations of content and also novel constructed types as part of a natural language characterisation.

A *record* is a set of fields consisting of a label and an object, e.g. schematically below where $l_1, \ldots, l_n$ stand for labels and $a_1, \ldots, a_n$ for some objects:

(8.25)
$$
\begin{bmatrix}
l_1 & = & a_1 \\
l_2 & = & a_2 \\
\ldots & & \\
l_n & = & a_n \\
\ldots & &
\end{bmatrix}
$$

The concept of underspecification comes in with the reflection that objects belong to types and that types are objects in their own right. Several objects may be of the same type, i.e. stand in the 'of-type' relation to the type. Therefore the type itself can be seen as an underspecified representation of the collection of objects of that type. For instance, to take a concrete example, a record can be used to model a situation where John smiles:

(8.26)
$$\begin{bmatrix} x & = & John' \\ c & = & p \end{bmatrix}$$

where p is a proof that John smiles.

Here p is a proof (e.g. an observation) that John smiles. Thus a record is a collection of ordered pairs of labels (such as x and c) and objects such as individuals and proofs. For any label there is at most one ordered pair whose first member is that label (i.e. a record is a function from labels to objects). Now a record *type* is like a record except that in place of objects we have types (of objects):

(8.27)
$$\begin{bmatrix} x & : & Individual \\ c & : & Smile'(x) \end{bmatrix}$$

The above is a type which includes records in which there is an individual labelled x and a proof (labelled c) that that individual smiles. Notice that the proof type $Smile'(x)$ depends on the choice of individual, the choice of x. This type can thus be seen as an underspecified representation of situations in which some individual smiles. The record in (8.26) will be of that type as it specifies appropriate fields matching the ones in the record type (8.27), and the objects assigned to the labels in the record are of the types specified in the record type, i.e., $John'$ is of type $Individual$ and p is a proof (observation) that John smiles.

This relation between record and record type provides an analogue to the DRT formulation of content, bringing out the representationalist flavour which the labelling methodology imposes. So *A man owns a donkey* might take the form of the record type:

(8.28)
$$\begin{bmatrix} x & : & Individual \\ c_1 & : & Man'(x) \\ y & : & Individual \\ c_2 & : & Donkey'(y) \\ c_3 & : & Own'(x, y) \end{bmatrix}$$

where x, y are variables of type individual;
c_1 is of the type of proof that x is a man
(hence a proof that is dependent on some choice of x);
c_2 is of the type of proof that y is a donkey, and
c_3 is of the type of proof that x owns y
(notice the dependency of this type on previous types above).

A record of that type of records would be some instantiation of the variables e.g.:

(8.29)
$$\begin{bmatrix} x & = & a \\ c_1 & = & p_1 \\ y & = & b \\ c_2 & = & p_2 \\ c_3 & = & p_3 \end{bmatrix}$$

p_1 is a proof of $Man'(a)$;
p_2 is a proof of $Donkey'(b)$;
p_3 is a proof of $Own'(a, b)$.

In using abstraction from particular records onto record types, or even abstraction from those, Cooper provides a means of expressing various degrees of partiality of natural-language content vis-à-vis an expression's construal relative to context. Such abstractions from records, hence from proofs, allows explicit modelling of context as records and also abstractions over contexts, making it possible to express what it means for an expression to have a context-dependent construal, even though its own intrinsic contribution is context-independent: such expressions can be analysed as functions from contexts (modelled as records) to record types (Cooper 2005). We can see this in the representation of *Sam wrote a program*, in which the representation of the record constituting Sam's writing a program depends on having already set up a record introducing a representation of that individual. Even in this simple case, we can see meaning as a function from records to record types (note that variables are annotated relative to the record within which they are introduced, so that $r.x$ indicates the value of x in the record r which is bound by the lambda operator).

(8.30)   *Sam wrote a program*

$$\lambda r: \begin{bmatrix} x & : & \textit{Individual} \\ c_1 & : & \textit{Named}'(x, \text{`Sam'}) \end{bmatrix} \left(\begin{bmatrix} y & : & \textit{Individual} \\ c_2 & : & \textit{Program}'(y) \\ c_3 & : & \textit{Write}'(r.x, y) \end{bmatrix} \right)$$

In plain English, to formally represent an assertion pertaining to some individual named 'Sam', there has to be a record introducing the necessary representation of that individual and the property of having established that he bears the name 'Sam'. Relative to that, there can then be an assertion of there being some individual program and the assertion that Sam wrote it. What this then gives us is a means of stating dependencies of record types on records, indeed with indefinitely rich nesting of such dependencies.

So far, this is little more than the familiar working assumption in formal semantics that words stand in one-to-one correspondence with unanalysed concepts. However, the theoretical vocabulary is now rich enough to express constructive use of this mechanism for presenting background assumptions. Cooper uses this move, for example, as a general basis for the expression of dependencies intrinsic to restricted quantification. For example, the interpretations of common nouns like *lunch* can be seen as functions from records r to record types with a dependency on r. Additional restrictions in the kinds of things that can be specified by these nouns (*presuppositions*), can be introduced as constraints in the record r that specifies the domain of the function. In the case of *lunch* we can specify that whatever is characterised as such can be both food and an event:

(8.31)

$$\lambda r: \begin{bmatrix} x & : & \textit{Individual} \\ c_1 & : & \textit{Food}'(x) \\ c_2 & : & \textit{Event}'(x) \end{bmatrix} \left(\begin{bmatrix} c_3 & : & \textit{Lunch}'(r.x) \end{bmatrix} \right)$$

This mechanism extends naturally to allow the construction of innovative arbitrarily complex dependencies that are not part of the regular routinised lexical repertoire.

Turning to the challenge of capturing the novel combinations observed by Pustejovsky as in *The blancmange took for ever*, Cooper (2007) shows how the system can model *coercion* by combining what might otherwise be complementary attributes of an individual, as more normally represented in distinct record types. For example, *The lunch took for ever*, which seems so standard a mode of expression that it barely involves an extension of the base concept, can be formulated as a dependency on typings involving food and temporal events, not involving any innovative use in combination with *took for ever*, as the domain restriction for *lunch* includes the specification that it can refer to events:

$$(8.32) \quad The'\ (\lambda\, r: \begin{bmatrix} x & : & Individual \\ c_1 & : & Food'(x) \\ c_2 & : & Event'(x) \end{bmatrix} \left(\begin{bmatrix} c_3 & : & Lunch'(r.x) \end{bmatrix} \right),$$

$$\lambda\, r: \begin{bmatrix} x & : & Individual \\ c_1 & : & Food'(x) \\ c_2 & : & Event'(x) \\ c_3 & : & Lunch'(x) \end{bmatrix} \left(\begin{bmatrix} c_4 & : & \textit{Took-for-ever}'(r.x) \end{bmatrix} \right))$$

The above reflects the implementation of a (dynamic) generalised quantifier analysis within the type-record framework. The determiner *the* is interpreted as a predicate (shown as The' above) holding between two functions: one introduced by the common noun and one by the VP. Common nouns are treated as functions from records r of a type that introduces a variable as one of its labels (x above) to a record type which is dependent on r (notice the annotation $r.x$ above which indicates the value for x in record r). The same treatment is given to VPs, the second argument of the predicate The'. In this account, these functions correspond to the type $< e, t >$, only here in place of entities we have records (introducing an individual as the value for x) and record types (the equivalent of a proposition in this framework). This analysis exploits a dependency between the types of the two records for common noun and VP to introduce constraints restricting the domain of the common noun (e.g. being food and being an event), which are then passed on through the dependency to the function representing the VP (notice that the same variable x is used in both functions so that constraints can accumulate both from the common noun and the VP). Thus, in a sense, the common noun is interpreted as introducing a context with presuppositions which must be satisfied before the function introduced by the VP can apply.

Such a procedure for recursive building up of dependent record types can apply equally to innovative types, as would be involved in *The blancmange took for ever*. Cooper argues that (8.33) below is **not** the most suitable representation of such strings:

(8.33) $The'(\lambda r: \begin{bmatrix} x & : & Individual \\ c_1 & : & Food'(x) \end{bmatrix} (\begin{bmatrix} c_2 & : & Blancmange'(r.x) \end{bmatrix}),$

$\lambda r: \begin{bmatrix} x & : & Individual \\ c_1 & : & Food'(x) \\ c_2 & : & Blancmange'(x) \end{bmatrix} (\begin{bmatrix} c_3 & : & Took\text{-}for\text{-}ever'(r.x) \end{bmatrix})$

Instead, the reading that is derived involves some aspect of the fact that blanc-mange is of type food which requires preparation and this preparation can take time (*Blancmg-prep'* to be read as the concept of blancmange preparation):

(8.34) $The'(\lambda r: \begin{bmatrix} x & : & Individual \\ c_1 & : & Event'(x) \end{bmatrix} (\begin{bmatrix} c_2 & : & Blancmg\text{-}prep'(r.x) \end{bmatrix}),$

$\lambda r: \begin{bmatrix} x & : & Individual \\ c_1 & : & Event'(x) \\ c_2 & : & Blancmg\text{-}prep'(x) \end{bmatrix} (\begin{bmatrix} c_3 & : & Took\text{-}for\text{-}ever'(r.x) \end{bmatrix})$

And it is in making this move to innovative typings, with the word used to create a context-particular concept, that the conceptualisation of language shifts inexorably into being a set of procedures for defining record types and their instances, that is, records, rather than merely a reflection of generalisations over records as independently given.

As on the Larsson view, with whose development it is closely aligned, such word–interpretation pairings may be highly context-specific. Indeed the Cooper and Ranta framework is one possible formal framework within which the Larsson insight can be grounded. As on that view, record-type specifications of arbitrary complexity may, over time, become stabilised and routinised to be called up by some individual look-up (word or phrase), with multiple possible pairings for any one such natural-language item. In consequence, for any one word (or less commonly phrase), there may be a multiple set of pairings, each a specific expression–interpretation pairing but nevertheless not fixed as the one single word–interpretation pairing that is constant across contexts. Generalising from this flexibility to the level of the grammar of a natural language, natural languages can be seen as a mechanism for constructing formal languages. Each word or routinised phrase contributes a set of formal-language-like item-denotation pairings, any one such pairing freely generatable by procedures which are formally defined within the system, itself a fully explicit formal device. Thus the system provides a formal articulation of flexibility of content for natural-language expressions despite its grounding in formal-semantics methodologies. The aim in this research paradigm is indeed to preserve the advantages to be achieved by a formalist methodology within an overall framework that enables the analyst not merely to be precise about compositionality of content for compound expressions, but also to make tractable the much more elusive and flexible concept of word meaning. And, in grappling with the challenge of attempting to model the flexibility intrinsic to natural-language construal, Cooper and Ranta argue, it is essential to take a step back from the model-theoretic stance that semantics is solely given by single word–denotation pairings, not by abandoning it, but by generalising across different such pairings. Rather, words and the combinatorial apparatus that combines them are seen as a set of procedures for constructing the types of structure–content pairings which formal semantics made tractable in the 1970s and 80s. The Cooper and Ranta claim is, thus, that extending model-theoretic tools to the systemic context-dependency of natural-language expressions involves seeing the natural language itself as one step of abstraction up from the formal-language methodology that those early results were grounded in. From the present point of view, this can be interpreted as showing that, even within solidly grounded formal semantic assumptions, the representationalist nature of the TTR constructs is what allows its success in accounting for the flexibility of language use.

8.4   New directions in semantics

At this point, we need to take stock of where we've got to, and look back to see how far we have come from the system underpinning formal languages that constituted the starting point for formal modelling of the semantics of natural language. In these formal languages, recall, content was by definition denotational; and the issue of representationalism, in so far as it was an issue at all, was only whether a syntactic (proof-theoretic) or semantic (model-theoretic) characterisation of inference is to be preferred, given that both are available. Yet in taking on board the commitment to modelling the underspecification which is systemic to natural-language construal, given the pervasive interaction between encoded content and context-particular parameters, we have found over and over again that representationalist assumptions become inevitable.

First, with the development of DRT, it became established that any integrated account of anaphora would require a representationalist stance. Furthermore, as a separate branch of research, the representationalism intrinsic to the DRT methodology provided a welcome entrée into the threatening opacities of lexical semantics, providing a means of formulating procedures for manipulating lexical content. This representationalist perspective, as we saw, is buttressed by ellipsis. Just as with anaphora, debates have raged as to whether construal can be simply model-theoretic or involves essential attributes of structure; but the evidence shows that structural factors in ellipsis construal are essential to its explanation. In other areas of natural-language investigation, however, the issue is somewhat less clear. Those working in areas of quantification in particular continue to explore model-theoretic characterisations in the absence of any appropriate proof system, though there is recognition of the problematic context-dependence of quantifiers, such as *many, most*. In the areas of tense and aspect construal, too, the research community continues to explore denotational characterisations of content, though the biggest advances in this area have been in DRT, whose assumptions provide a bridge between model-theoretic and structuralist assumptions.

Finally, we have come to current emergent work on lexical meaning, and here we have found the same conclusion emerging via consideration of recent developments in Type Theory with Records: if the content of expressions of natural language is to be explained, the explanation has to involve characterisations which eschew the direct mapping of expressions onto denotational content. Natural language has to be seen, rather, as providing a set of procedures for interpretation. In so far as these new proposals are representationalist in spirit, they are, however, not subject to the types of criticism that bedevilled the early Katz programme. To the contrary, current work has developed out of a formal semantics methodology and is committed to grounding the explanations to be provided in formal paradigms of appropriate explicitness. Nevertheless, it remains a matter for debate whether the ultimate basis for explication should be model-theoretic or more in the spirit of proof-theory, giving core status to the mappings from representation to representation as an expression of content.

8.4.1   Semantics and pragmatics

In the flurry to adopt current new methodologies, it should not be forgotten that the claim that natural-language content involves positing an essential level of representation is not a novel claim. Such representationalist assumptions, and, furthermore, recognition of the systematic gap between encoded linguistic specifications and context-relative interpretation have been twin assumptions championed informally ever since the 1980s by those working in the sister discipline of *pragmatics*. Within at least one sub-branch of pragmatics, there has been emphasis on the systematic underspecification of content for some proposition expressed, and Sperber and Wilson (among others) have claimed that encoded linguistic content underdetermines any such occasion-specific content. However, in these pragmatic characterisations, what has been the primary focus of attention is not so much the form in which the information is represented but **how** underspecified encoded linguistic content gets enriched. Moreover, a concern for explaining supposedly nonstandard forms of usage has long been central to such research paradigms; indeed, this is in an area where pragmatics research has always led the exploration of the extendability of supposed conventional bases for language construal. For example, Carston (2002) and Wilson and Carston (2007) have explored what is involved in the process of interpretation of an assertion such as *Robert is a bulldozer*. This, they claim, involves either narrowing or broadening some schema for construal that the word itself provides, necessitating the construction of some *ad-hoc concept* as the basis for interpretation.

This provides another emergent point of contact between pragmatic and semantic research paradigms, for the exploration of ad-hoc concepts is tantalisingly close to the Larsson and Cooper formulations of how occasion-specific interpretations of a word or phrase are constructible, despite the former having emerged from a cognitivist framework of assumptions and the latter from a formal semantic methodology. And this is by no means the end of the list of converging trends. In pursuing optimal ways for modelling fragment construal in dialogue, with the goal of reflecting the easy exchange between speaker/hearer roles in informal conversation, both representationalist and denotationalist frameworks share a commitment to capturing the dynamics of how anaphoric and elliptical fragments are progressively built up to ensure cross-party coordination (Ginzburg and Cooper 2004; Purver *et al.* 2006; Cann *et al.* 2007; Ginzburg (forthcoming)). These various rapprochements suggest that what brings these apparently conflicting background assumptions together is more important than what separates them.

In this drawing together of representationalist and denotationalist assumptions, there is one question which cries out for exploration of a new answer. This is the question of what *sentence meaning* amounts to, so that compositionality of content can be defined over the words in the sentence sequence. This question is one which we have spent the entire book trying to find an answer to, only to find putative answers perpetually slipping away. So perhaps we should confront the possibility that there may after all be no concept of *sentence meaning* in virtue of which strings of the language can be said to have a fixed content corresponding to what a speaker who successfully acquires that language knows. The question as to what compositionality of meaning for sentences amounts to has transformed itself into a further, somewhat different question. When seen against the backdrop of the general consensus that natural-language expressions are intrinsically underspecified with regard to the denotational content they can be used to express, with dependence on context for values both at the level of word construal and at the level of phrasal construal the new question is: does the concept of sentence meaning have any role to play in determining the systematic compositionality of content as expressed by natural languages?

The orthodox answer to this question, still commonly aired by both formal semanticists and pragmatists alike, affirms that semantics is a component of the grammar whose output, namely sentence-strings with assigned structure and meaning, feeds into whatever general module or device is associated with pragmatic reasoning (recall the discussion in Chapter 1, section 1.5). This grammar-external system or module (see Sperber 2002 for the proposal of *massive modularity*) has the burden of explaining phenomena attributable to application of pragmatic principles such as the principle of relevance (the weighting of cognitive effort considerations against inferential or other cognitive effect: see Chapter 1). The workings of this module are assumed to explain how such general cognitive principles determine the specific interpretation assigned to linguistic stimuli in context over and above what is encoded in the grammar.

This process involves the enrichment of some weak specification of sentence meaning to yield some propositional content (and its *implicatures*) as dictated by the specific context within which the sentence is uttered. Yet what we have seen in the chapters setting out DRT, Dynamic Syntax and the Cooper and Larsson approaches is that the hook-up with context is progressive and relevant to the determination of construal at both the level of word and phrase, well before any composite content for the sentence as a whole is established, with even quantifier-scope construal showing effects of context-dependence, despite being a supposedly strictly global, non-incremental process (see 7.3.2).

What is generally recognised is that encoded constraints on interpretation imposed by the presence of pronouns, elliptical constructions, tense, quantifer-nominal pairing, etc. are merely strategies/instructions for interpretation-construction. These yield a particular interpretation only as a consequence of reasoning that reflects a real-time dynamics conducted in a particular context, sentential or otherwise. But if context-relative fixing of content has to be defined as input to the process of building up interpretation, then a notion of sentence meaning independent of context is not isolatable at all, on any basis, for com-positionality of content for the natural-language expressions has to be defined relative to such fixing of context-dependent parameters. From this perspective the concept of meaning for a sentence that is in some way disembodied from context is a chimera, simply evaporating once our understanding of context and the corresponding concept of word meanings become appropriately refined. The ramifications of granting the centrality of context in natural-language construal are thus very considerable and the issues surrounding this urgently need to be explored.

8.5   Coda

This short introduction to the way semantics has evolved over the last fifty years is inevitably far from comprehensive. Perhaps the most serious omission is the lack of discussion of the issues raised by *intensionality* (except in the domain of tense), an area where the formal semantics community granted the limitations of their adopted methodology from very early on (*intensional-ity*, broadly construed, is the universal human ability to imagine scenarios and have beliefs that lack any grounding in real events). Nonetheless, the emerging consensus is that language should be seen as an intrinsically dynamical system, a system whose parts are available for use in ways that allow open-ended but not unlimited modes of construal. Getting a formal handle on the language capacity seen in these terms thus now constitutes the major challenge facing natural-language semantic research.

There is good reason to conclude that what we have seen gives a good prognosis for the fruitfulness of future research into semantics. On the one hand, as we've seen, it is an established fact among pragmatists that utterance interpretation is essentially context-dependent, a point agreed even by Cappelen and Lepore (though there is a terminological question as to whether to treat this phenomenon as variation in the *speech act content* instead). On the other hand, in psycholinguistics, it is now a familiar and thoroughly established fact that decisions made in connection with human parsing are on-line and incremental; evidence is also emerging that language production decisions are made incrementally, despite the fact that production is a planning task. So, representationalist and denotationalist assumptions come together in modelling the dependence of interpretation on what the immediate cognitive context provides. This means that, without having to surrender its commitment to the rigour of formalist assumptions, formal semantic research is now able to articulate accounts of natural-language interpretation in tandem with pragmatic and psycholinguistic insights. After a long theoretical night struggling with apparent conflicts between functionalist and formalist methodologies, we can at last work in harmony together, surely a very good sign indeed.

8.6   Further reading

The range of material on lexical meaning is vast. The issue of what a word can mean is raised within almost every philosophical tradition, well beyond the confines of European philosophical and philological traditions. In this textbook, we have only addressed those developed within the recent linguistics tradition at the philosophy/linguistics interface. Even within this narrow time-span, the variation in types of analysis is very broad, ranging from early lexical field semantics Lyons (1977: ch. 13); Cruse (1986: ch. 1); componential analyses, whether feature-based (Cruse 1986) or structure-based (Jackendoff 2002; Levin and Rappaport 2005); computational-linguistic analyses (Pustejovsky 1995 and others following him); formulations in terms of meaning postulates within formal semantics (Cresswell 1985; Dowty 1988; Cann 1993). These views all have their adherents and detractors: see for example Fodor and Lepore's (1998) critique of Pustejovsky and his reply (Pustejovsky 1998). Fodor's own views in this area, that the concept a word expresses is an unanalysable primitive, have been aired over a broad time-span (Fodor 1981, 1998; Fodor and Lepore 1998). Some have argued for a pragmatics component within the grammar formalism, broadly construed (Pustejovsky 1995; Chierchia 2005), others that meaning systematically underspecifies contextually assigned content (Bezuidenhout 2006a; Carston 2002; Cann *et al.* 2005; Wilson and Carston 2007). For discussions of *aspect* that relate to lexical modelling, see the Further reading section, Chapter 6. Relevant philosophical debate on whether words could be said to be decomposable into more primitive concepts at all was raised initially by Quine (1960). From very early in the generativist framework, there has been psycholinguistic evidence tending to disconfirm the status of decompositional analysis below the word level: see Fodor *et al.* (1975), and subsequent arrays of psycholinguistic experimentation buttressing this. Nonetheless some work in psycholinguistics persists with such methodology: Levin and Pinker (1991); Rosch (1983). Discussions of the semantics/pragmatics interface are covered in depth both within pragmatics, Sperber and Wilson (1995, 1998); Carston (2002); Wilson and Carston (2007), and within formal semantics, Kamp (1978); Kamp *et al.* (2005); von Heusinger and Turner (2003); Lascarides and Stone (2006). The Sperber proposal of *massive modularity*, associated with the relevance-theoretic concept of a pragmatics module, remains highly controversial: see Sperber (2002); Carruthers (2006); Samuels (2006). The generally accepted 'semantics-as-truth-conditions' view was encapsulated by Gazdar as the equation 'pragmatics = meaning − truth conditions' (Gazdar 1979). This stance has also been the backbone of the Davidsonian account of the semantics of natural language as the articulation of the T-sentences of the language (see Chapter 1), a view which Cappelen and Lepore (2005) explicitly defend. Evaluation of Cappelen and Lepore (2005) is the focus of Bezuidenhout *et al.* (2006); see also Recanati (2004); Wedgwood (2007). Characterisations of the variability of lexical meaning within current formal semantics explorations include Cooper (2007); Larsson (2008); with Cooper using these insights as a basis for applying the Grammar-Formalism framework of Ranta (1994) in a new departure in which each natural language is seen as a collection of resources for formal grammar construction: see Cooper and Ranta (2008).

Bibliography

Allan, K. 1980. 'Nouns and countability', *Language* 56, 541–67.

Allwood, J., Andersen, L. and Dahl, O. 1977. *Logic in Linguistics*. Cambridge University Press.

Asher, N. 1986. 'Belief in Discourse Representation Theory', *Journal of Philosophical Logic* 15, 127–89.

Asher, N. and Lascarides, A. 2003. *Logics of Conversation*. Cambridge University Press.

Bach, E. 1986. 'The algebra of events', *Linguistics and Philosophy* 9, 5–16.

Bach, E., Jelinek, E., Kratzer, A. and Partee, B.H. (eds.) 1995. *Quantification in Natural Languages*. Dordrecht: Kluwer.

Barwise, J. and Cooper, R. 1981. 'Generalized quantifiers and natural language', *Linguistics and Philosophy* 4, 159–209 (reprinted in Portner and Partee, eds., 2002).

Barwise, J. and Etchemendy, J. 1992. *The Language of First-Order Logic*, 3rd edn. Stanford: CSLI Publications.

Bäuerle, R. 1979. 'Tense logics and natural language', *Synthese* 40, 225–30.

Bäuerle, R., Schwarze, C. and von Stechow, A. 1981. *Meaning, Use and Interpretation of Language*. Berlin: Walter de Gruyter.

Bennett, M. and Partee, B. 1972. *Toward the Logic of Tense and Aspect in English'*. Bloomington: Indiana University Linguistics Club (reprinted as 'Toward the logic of tense and aspect in English', in Partee, B. (2004) *Compositionality in Formal Semantics*. Oxford: Blackwell).

Benthem, J. van 1986. *Essays in Logical Semantics*. Dordrecht: Reidel.

Bergmann, M., Moor, J., and Nelson, J. 1980. *The Logic Book*. New York: Random House.

Bezuidenhout, A. 2006a. 'The coherence of contextualism: a reply to Cappelen and Lepore', *Mind and Language* 21, 1–10.

Bezuidenhout, A. 2006b. 'VP ellipsis and the case for representationalism', *ProtoSociology* 22.

Bezuidenhout, A., Gross, S., Recanati, F., Gendler-Szabo, Z., Travis, C., Cappelen, H. and Lepore, E. (2006). Multiple review of *Insensitive Semantics: A Defense of Semantic Minimalism and Speech Act Pluralism*, by Herman Cappelen and Ernie Lepore, *Mind and Language* 21, 1, 1–73.

Bittner, M. 2008. 'Aspectual universals of temporal anaphora', in Rothstein, S. (ed.), *Theoretical and Crosslinguistics Approaches to the Semantics of Aspect*, 349–85. Amsterdam: John Benjamins.

Blackburn, P. and Meyer-Viol, W. 1994. 'Linguistics, logic and finite trees', *Bulletin of the IGPL* 2, 3–31.

Bunt, C. 1985. *Mass Terms and Model Theoretic Semantics*. Cambridge University Press.

Burton-Roberts, N. (ed.) 2007. *Advances in Pragmatics*. London: Palgrave Macmillan.

Cann, R. 1993. *Formal Semantics: An Introduction*. Cambridge University Press.

Cann, R. 2002. 'Sense relations: formal approaches' in Cruse, Hundsnurcher and Lutzeier (eds.), *Handbuch der Lexicologie*, 529–35. Berlin: Walter de Gruyter.

Cann, R., Kempson, R. and Marten, L. 2005. *The Dynamics of Language: An Introduction*. Amsterdam: Elsevier.

Cann, R., Kempson, R. and Purver, M. 2007. 'Context-dependent wellformedness: the dynamics of ellipsis', *Research on Language and Computation* 5, 333–58.

Cappelen, H. and Lepore, E. 2005. *Insensitive Semantics: A Defence of Minimal Semantics and Speech Act Pluralism*. Oxford: Blackwell.

Carlson, G. 1980. *Reference to Kinds in English*. New York: Garland Publishing.

Carpenter, R. 1997. *Type-Logical Semantics*. Cambridge, MA: MIT Press.

Carruthers, P. 2006. *The Architecture of the Mind: Massive Modularity and the Flexibility of Thought*. Oxford University Press.

Carston, R. 2002. *Thoughts and Utterances: The Pragmatics of Utterance Interpretation and Cognition*. Oxford: Blackwell.

Chierchia, G. 1992. 'Anaphora and dynamic binding', *Linguistics and Philosophy* 15, 111–83.

Chierchia, G. 1995. *Dynamics of Meaning: Anaphora, Presupposition, and the Theory of Grammar*. University of Chicago Press.

Chierchia, G. 2005. 'Scalar implicatures, polarity phenomena, and the syntax/pragmatics interface', in Belletti, A. (ed.), *Structures and Beyond*, 39–103. Oxford University Press.

Chierchia, G. and McConnell-Ginet, S. 2000. *Meaning and Grammar: An Introduction to Semantics*, 2nd edn. Cambridge, MA: MIT Press.

Chomsky, N. 1965. *Aspects of the Theory of Syntax*. Cambridge, MA: MIT Press.

Chung, S., McCloskey, J. and Ladusaw, W. 1995. 'Sluicing and logical form', *Natural Language Semantics* 3, 239–82.

Clark, E. V. and Clark, H. H. 1979. 'When nouns surface as verbs', *Language* 55, 767–811.

Comrie, B. 1976. *Aspect: An Introduction to the Study of Verbal Aspect and Related Problems*. Cambridge University Press.

Comrie, B. 1985. *Tense*. Cambridge University Press.

Cooper, R. 1979. 'The interpretation of pronouns', in Heny, F. and Schnelle, H. (eds.), *Syntax and Semantics 10: Selections from the Third Groningen Round Table*, 61–122. New York: Academic Press.

Cooper, R. 1983. *Quantification and Syntactic Theory*. Dordrecht: Reidel.

Cooper, R. 2005. 'Do delicious lunches take a long time, presentation to GSLT internal conference, 28–29 October. Revised as 'A record-type theoretic account of copredication and generalized quantification', in *Kvantifi Rator för en Tag: Essays Dedicated to Dag Westerståhl on His Sixtieth Birthday*, www.phil.gu.se/posters/festskrift3/.

Cooper, R. 2007. 'Copredication, dynamic generalized quantification and lexical innovation by coercion', in *Proceedings of GL2007, Fourth International Workshop on Generative Approaches to the Lexicon*.

Cooper, R. and Ranta, A. 2008. 'Natural languages as collections of resources', in Cooper, R. and Kempson, R. (eds.), *Language in Flux: Relating Dialogue Coordination to Language Variation, Change and Evolution*. London: College Publications.

Cresswell, M. 1985. *Structured Meanings. The Semantics of Propositional Attitudes.* Cambridge, MA: MIT Press.

Crick, F. 1994. *The Astonishing Hypothesis.* London: Macmillan.

Crouch, R. 1999. 'LFG and labelled deduction', in Dalrymple, M. (ed.), *Semantics and Syntax in Lexical Functional Grammar*, 319–58. Cambridge, MA: MIT Press.

Cruse, D. 1986. *Lexical Semantics.* Cambridge University Press.

Dahl, O. 1985. *Tense and Aspect Systems.* Oxford: Blackwell.

Dalrymple, M., Shieber, S. and Pereira, F. 1991. 'Ellipsis and higher-order unification', *Linguistics and Philosophy* 14, 399–452.

Davidson, D. 1967. 'The logical form of action sentences', in Rescher, N. (ed.), *The Logic of Decision and Action*, 81–120. University of Pittsburgh Press (reprinted in Davidson 2001).

Davidson, D. 2001. *Essays on Actions and Events*, 2nd edn. Oxford University Press.

Davidson, D. and Harman, G. (eds.) 1972. *Semantics of Natural Language.* Dordrecht: Reidel.

Davis, S. (ed.) 1991. *Pragmatics: A Reader.* Oxford University Press.

Does, J. van der and Eijk, J. van (eds.) 1996. *Quantifiers, Logic, and Language.* Stanford: CSLI Publications.

Dowty, D. 1979. *Word Meaning and Montague Grammar: The Semantics of Verbs and Times and Generative Semantics and Montague's PTQ.* Dordrecht: Reidel.

Dowty, D. 1981. 'Thematic proto-roles and argument selection', *Language* 67, 547–619.

Dowty, D. 1988. 'Type-raising, functional composition and non-constituent coordination', in Oehrle, R. T., Bach, E. and Wheeler, D. (eds.), *Categorial Grammars and Natural-Language Structures*, 153–98. Dordrecht: Reidel.

Dowty, D., Wall, R. and Peters, S. 1981. *Introduction to Montague Semantics.* Dordrecht: Reidel.

Egli, U. and von Heusinger, K. 1995. 'The epsilon operator and E-type pronouns', in Egli, U. et al. (eds), *Lexical Knowledge in the Organization of Language*, 121–41. Amsterdam: Benjamins (Current Issues in Linguistic Theory 114).

Eijck, J. van and Kamp, H. 1997. 'Representing discourse in context', in Benthem, J. van and Meulen, A. ter (eds.), *Handbook of Logic and Language*, 179–237. Amsterdam: Elsevier.

Elugardo, R. and Stainton, R. (eds.) 2004. *Ellipsis and Nonsentential Speech.* New York: Springer-Verlag.

Evans, G. 1977. 'Pronouns, quantifiers and relative clauses', *Canadian Journal of Philosophy* 7, 467–536 (reprinted in Evans 1985, 76–175).

Evans, G. 1980. 'Pronouns', *Linguistic Inquiry* 11, 337–62.

Evans, G. 1985. *Collected Papers: Gareth Evans.* Oxford University Press.

Fernandez, R. 2006. 'Nonsentential utterances in dialogue: classification, resolution and use.' Unpublished PhD thesis, London University.

Fernando, T. 2002. 'Three processes in natural language interpretation', in Sieg, W., Sommer, R. and Talcott, C. (eds.), *Reflections on the Foundations of Mathematics: Essays in Honor of Solomon Feferman* (Association for Symbolic Logic, LNIL 15), 208–27. Wellesley: A K Peters.

Fernando, T. 2007. 'Observing events and situations in time', *Linguistics and Philosophy* 30, 527–50.

Fiengo, R. and May, R. 1994. *Indices and Identity.* Cambridge, MA: MIT Press.

Fodor, J.A. 1975. *The Language of Thought*. Cambridge, MA: Harvard University Press.

Fodor, J.A. 1981. *Representations: Philosophical Essays on the Foundations of Cognitive Science*. Cambridge, MA: MIT Press.

Fodor, J.A. 1983. *The Modularity of Mind*. Cambridge, MA: MIT Press.

Fodor, J.A. 1989. 'Review essay: *Remnants of Meaning* by Stephen Schiffer', *Philosophy and Phenomenological Research* 50, 409–23.

Fodor, J.A. 1990. *A Theory of Content and Other Essays*. Cambridge, MA: MIT Press.

Fodor, J.A. 1998. *Concepts: Where Cognitive Science Went Wrong*. Oxford University Press.

Fodor, J.A. 2000. *The Mind Doesn't Work That Way: The Scope and Limits of Computational Psychology*. Cambridge, MA: MIT Press.

Fodor, J.A., Fodor, J.D. and Garrett, S. 1975. 'On the psychological unreality of lexical definitions', *Linguistic Inquiry* 4, 515–31.

Fodor, J.A. and Lepore, E. 1998. 'The emptiness of the lexicon', *Linguistic Inquiry* 29, 269–88.

Fox, C. and Lappin, S. 2005 *Foundations of Intensional Semantics*. Oxford: Blackwell.

Fox, D. 2002. *Economy and Semantic Interpretation*. Cambridge, MA: MIT Press.

Gabbay, D. 1996. *Labelled Deductive Systems*. Oxford University Press.

Gamut, L.T.F. 1991. *Logic, Language, and Information*. University of Chicago Press.

Garrod, S. and Anderson, A. 1987. 'Saying what you mean in dialogue: a study in conceptual and semantic co-ordination', *Cognition* 27, 181–218.

Garrod, S. and Doherty, G. 1994. 'Conversation, co-ordination and convention: an empirical investigation of how groups establish linguistic conventions', *Cognition* 53, 181–215.

Gazdar, G. 1979. *Pragmatics: Implicature, Presupposition, and Logical Form*. New York: Academic Press.

Geach, P. 1962. *Reference and Generality*. Cornell University Press.

Geurts, B. 1999. *Presuppositions and Pronouns*. Amsterdam: Elsevier.

Geurts, B. and Beaver, D. 2007. 'Discourse Representation Theory', in Zalta, E. (ed.), *The Stanford Encyclopedia of Philosophy* (summer 2007 edn),
http://plato.stanford.edu/archives/sum2007/entries/discourse-representation-theory/.

Gillon, B.S. 1992. 'Common semantics for English count and mass nouns', *Linguistics and Philosophy* 15, 597–639.

Gillon, B.S. 1999. 'The lexical semantics of English count and mass nouns', in Viegas, E. (ed.), *The Breadth and Depth of Semantic Lexicons*, 19–37. Dordrecht: Kluwer.

Ginzburg, J. forthcoming. *Semantics and Conversation*. Stanford: CSLI Publications.

Ginzburg, J. and Cooper, R. 2004. 'Clarification, ellipsis, and the nature of contextual updates', *Linguistics and Philosophy* 27, 297–366.

Gregoromichelaki, E. 2006. 'Conditionals in Dynamic Syntax.' Unpublished PhD thesis, London University.

Grice, H.P. 1989. *Studies in the Way of Words*. Cambridge, MA: Harvard University Press.

Groenendijk, J. and Stokhof, M. 1990. 'Dynamic Montague Grammar', in Kalman, J. and Polos, L. (eds.), *Proceedings of the Second Symposon on Logic and Language*, 3–48. Budapest: Eotros Lorand University Press.

Groenendijk, J. and Stokhof, M. 1991. 'Dynamic predicate logic', *Linguistics and Philosophy* 14, 39–100.

Guttenplan, S. 1997. *The Languages of Logic: An Introduction to Formal Logic*, 2nd edn. Oxford: Blackwell.

Hamm, F., Kamp, H. and van Lambalgen, M. 2006. 'There is no opposition between formal and cognitive semantics', *Theoretical Linguistics* 32, 1–40.

Hamm, F. and van Lambalgen, M. 2005. *The Proper Treatment of Events*. Oxford: Blackwell.

Hankamer, J. and Sag, I.A. 1976. 'Deep and surface anaphora', *Linguistic Inquiry* 7, 391–428.

Hardt, D. 1993. 'Verb phrase ellipsis: form, meaning, and processing.' Unpublished PhD thesis, University of Pennsylvania.

Hardt, D. 2008. 'VP ellipsis and constraints on interpretation', in Johnson, K. (ed.) *Topics in Ellipsis*, 15–29. Cambridge University Press.

Hawkins, J.A. 1978. *Definiteness and Indefiniteness*. London: Croom Helm.

Heim, I. 1988. *The Semantics of Definite and Indefinite Noun Phrases*. New York: Garland Publishing.

Heim, I. 1990. 'E-type pronouns and donkey anaphora', *Linguistics and Philosophy* 13, 137–77.

Heim, I. and Kratzer, A. 1998. *Semantics in Generative Grammar*. Oxford: Blackwell.

von Heusinger, K. and Egli, U. (eds.) 2000. *Reference and Anaphoric Relations*. Dordrecht: Kluwer (Studies in Linguistics and Philosophy 72).

von Heusinger, K. and Turner, K. (eds.) 2003. *Where Semantics meets Pragmatics*. Amsterdam: Elsevier (Current Research in the Semantics/Pragmatics Interface 16).

Hodges, W. 2001. *Logic*, 2nd edn. London: Penguin.

Hoeksema, J. 1983. 'Plurality and conjunction', in ter Meulen, A. (ed.), *Studies in Model-theoretic Semantics*, 63–83. Dordrecht: Foris.

Horn, L. 1989. *A Natural History of Negation*. Chicago University Press.

Horn, L. and Kato, Y. (eds.) 2000. *Negation and Polarity: Syntactic and Semantic Perspectives*. Oxford University Press.

Hornstein, N. 1994. 'An argument for minimalism: the case of antecedent-contained deletion', *Linguistic Inquiry* 25, 455–80.

Jackendoff, R. 2002. *Foundations of Language: Brain, Meaning, Grammar, Evolution*. Oxford: Blackwell.

Joosten, F. 2003. 'Accounts of the count-mass distinction: a critical survey', *Linguisticae Investigationes* 36, 159–73.

Kadmon, N. 2001. *Formal Pragmatics: Semantics, Pragmatics, Presupposition and Focus*. Oxford: Blackwell.

Kamp, H. 1978. 'Semantics versus pragmatics', in Guenthner, F. and Schmidt, H. (eds.), *Formal Semantics and Pragmatics for Natural Language*, 255–87. Dordrecht: Reidel.

Kamp, H. 1981. 'A theory of truth and semantic representation', in Groenendijk, J., Janssen, T. and Stokhof, M. (eds.), *Truth, Interpretation and Information*, 1–32. Dordrecht: Foris (reprinted in Portner and Partee 2002, 189–222).

Kamp, H. 1990a. 'Prolegomena to a structural account of belief and other attitudes', in Anderson, C. and Owens, J. (eds.), *Propositional Attitudes: The Role of Content in Logic, Language, and Mind*, 27–90. Stanford: CSLI Publications.

Kamp, H. 1990b. 'Comments on: J. Groenendijk and M. Stokhof "Dynamic predicate logic"', in van Benthem, J. and Kamp, H. (eds.), *Partial and Dynamic Semantics I*, 109–31. Edinburgh: DYANA Deliverable, R2.1.A.

Kamp, H. 2001a. 'Presupposition, computation, and presupposition justification: one aspect of the interpretation of multi-sentence discourse', in Bras, M. and Vieu, L. (eds.), *Semantics and Pragmatics of Discourse and Dialogue: Experimenting with Current Theories*, 57–84. Amsterdam: Elsevier.

Kamp, H. 2001b. 'The importance of presupposition', in Rohrer, C., Rossdeutscher, A. and Kamp, H. (eds.), *Linguistic Form and Its Computation*, 207–54. Stanford: CSLI Publications.

Kamp, H., van Genabith, J. and Reyle, U. 2005. 'Discourse Representation Theory', in Gabbay, D. and Guenthner, F. (eds.) *Handbook of Philosophical Logic*. Dordrecht: Kluwer.

Kamp, H. and Reyle, U. 1993. *From Discourse to Logic*. Dordrecht: Kluwer.

Kamp, H. and Rossdeutscher, A. 1994. 'DRS-construction and lexically driven inference', *Theoretical Linguistics* 20, 165–235.

Kamp, H. and Schiehlen, M. 2001. 'Temporal location in natural language', in Kamp, H. and Reyle, U. (eds.), *How We Say WHEN It Happens: Contributions to the Theory of Temporal Reference in Natural Language*, 181–232. Berlin: Max Niemeyer Verlag.

Kaplan, D. 1977/1989. 'Demonstratives', in Almog, J., Perry, J. and Wettstein, H. (eds.), *Themes from Kaplan*, 481–564. Oxford University Press.

Kaplan, R. M. and Maxwell, J. T. 1988. 'An algorithm for functional uncertainty', in *Proceedings of the Twelfth International Conference on Computational Linguistics*, vol. I, 297–302. Morristown, NJ: Association for Computational Linguistics.

Karttunen, L. 1969. 'Pronouns and variables', in Binnick, R. *et al.* (eds.), *Papers from the Fifth Regional Meeting of the Chicago Linguistic Society*, 108–16. Chicago Linguistic Society.

Karttunen, L. 1976. 'Discourse referents', in McCawley, J. (ed.), *Syntax and Semantics* 7, 363–85. New York: Academic Press.

Katz, J.J. 1972. Semantic Theory. New York: Harber & Rous.

Kearns, K. 2000. *Semantics*. London: Palgrave Macmillan.

Keenan, E. 1996. 'The semantics of determiners', in Lappin, S. (ed.), *The Handbook of Contemporary Semantic Theory*, 41–63. Oxford: Blackwell.

Keenan, E. and Stavi, J. 1986. 'A semantic characterization of natural language determiners', *Linguistics and Philosophy* 9, 253–326.

Keenan, E. and Westerståhl, D. 1997. 'Generalized quantifiers in linguistics and logic', in van Benthem, J. and ter Meulen, A. (eds.), *Handbook of Logic and Language*, 837–93. Amsterdam: Elsevier.

Kehler, A. 2002. *Coherence, Reference, and the Theory of Grammar*. Stanford: CSLI Publications.

Kempson, R. 1977. *Semantic Theory: An Introduction*. Cambridge University Press.

Kempson, R., Meyer-Viol, W. and Gabbay, D. 1999. 'VP ellipsis: towards a dynamic structural account', in Lappin, S. and Benmamoun, E. (eds.), *Fragments: Studies in Ellipsis and Gapping*, 227–90. Oxford University Press.

Kempson, R., Meyer-Viol, W. and Gabbay, D. 2001. *Dynamic Syntax: The Flow of Language Understanding*. Oxford: Blackwell.

Kuhn, T. 1962. *The Structure of Scientific Revolutions*. University of Chicago Press.

Ladusaw, W. 1996. 'Negation and polarity items', in Lappin, S. (ed.), *Handbook of Contemporary Semantic Theory*, 241–61. Oxford: Blackwell.

Lakatos, I. and Musgrave. A. 1972. *Criticism and the Growth of Knowledge*. Cambridge University Press.

Lambalgen, M. van 1996. 'Natural deduction for generalized quantifiers', in van der Does, J. and van Eijck, J. (eds.), *Generalized Quantifiers: Theory and Applications*, 225–36. Stanford: CSLI Publications.

Lappin, S. 1996. 'The interpretation of ellipsis', in Lappin, S. (ed.), *Handbook of Contemporary Semantic Theory*, 145–175. Oxford: Blackwell.

Lappin, S. 1999. 'An HPSG account of antecedent-contained ellipsis', in Lappin, S. and Benmamoun, E. (eds.), *Fragments: Studies in Ellipsis and Gapping*, 68–97. Oxford University Press.

Larson, R. and Segal, G. 1995. *Knowledge of Meaning: an Introduction to Semantic Theory*. Cambridge, MA: MIT Press.

Larsson, S. 2008. 'Formalising the dynamics of semantic systems in dialogue', in Cooper, R. and Kempson, R. (eds.), *Language in Flux: Relating Dialogue Coordination to Language Variation, Change and Evolution*, 121–42. London: College Publications.

Lascarides, A. and Stone, M. 2006. 'Formal semantics of iconic gesture', in Schlangen, D. and Fernández, R. (eds.), *Proceedings of the Tenth Workshop on the Semantics and Pragmatics of Dialogue (BRANDIAL)*, 64–71. Universitätsverlag Potsdam.

Lasersohn, P. 1995. *Plurality, Conjunction and Events*. Dordrecht: Kluwer.

Lemmon, E. J. 1965. *Beginning Logic*. London: Thomas Nelson and Sons.

Lepore, E. and Ludwig, K. (eds.) 2005. *Donald Davidson: Meaning, Truth, Language and Reality*. Oxford University Press.

Lepore, E. and Smith, B. (eds.) 2006. *Oxford Handbook of Philosophy of Language*. Oxford University Press.

Levin, B. and Pinker, S. (eds). 1991. *Lexical and Conceptual Semantics*. Oxford: Blackwell.

Levin, B. and Rappaport, M. 2005. *Argument Realization*. Cambridge University Press.

Lewis, D. 1970. 'General semantics'. *Synthese* 22, 18–67 (reprinted in Davidson and Harman 1972, 169–218).

Lewis, D. 1975. 'Adverbs of quantification', in Keenan, E. (ed.), *Formal Semantics of Natural Language*, 3–15. Cambridge University Press.

Link, G. 1983. 'The logical analysis of plurals and mass terms: a lattice-theoretical approach', in Bäuerle, Schwarze and von Stechow 1981: 302–23 (reprinted in Portner and Partee 2002).

Link, G. 1998. *Algebraic Semantics for Language and Philosophy*. Stanford: CSLI Publications.

Ludlow, P. 2004. 'A note on alleged cases of nonsentential assertion', in Elugardo, R. and Stainton, R. (eds.), *Ellipsis and Nonsentential Speech*, 95–108. Dordrecht: Kluwer.

Lyons, C. 1999. *Definiteness*. Cambridge University Press.

Lyons, J. 1977. *Semantics*. Cambridge University Press.

Lyons, J. 1981. *Linguistic Semantics: An Introduction*. Cambridge University Press.

McCawley, J. 1981. *Everything That Linguists Have Always Wanted to Know about Logic (But Were Afraid to Ask)*. University of Chicago Press.

Merchant, J. 2002. *The Syntax of Silence*. Cambridge, MA: MIT Press.

Merchant, J. 2004. 'Fragments and ellipsis', *Linguistics and Philosophy* 27, 661–738.

Michaelis, L. 2006. 'Time and tense', in Aarts, B. and MacMahon, A. (eds.), *The Handbook of English Linguistics*, 220–34. Oxford: Blackwell.

Moens, M. and Steedman, M. 1988. 'Temporal ontology and temporal reference', *Computational Linguistics* 14, 15–28.

Montague, R. 1973. 'The proper treatment of quantification in ordinary English', in Hintikka, J., Moravcsik, J.M.E and Suppes, P. (eds.), *Approaches to Natural Language*, 221–42. New York: Springer (reprinted in Montague 1974: 247–70).

Montague, R. 1974. *Formal Philosophy. Selected Papers of Richard Montague*, ed. Thomason, R. New Haven: Yale University Press.

Morgan, J. 1973. 'Sentence fragments and the notion *sentence*', in Kachru, B., Lees, R.B. and Malkiel, Y. (eds.), *Issues in Linguistics: Papers in Honor of Henry and Renee Kahane*, 719–51. Urbana: University of Illinois Press.

Morgan, J. 1989. 'Sentence fragments revisited', in Music, B., Graczyk, R. and Wiltshire, C. (eds.), *CLS: Parasession on Language in Context*, 228–41. Chicago Linguistics Society.

Morrill, G. 1994. *Type-Logical Grammar*. Dordrecht: Kluwer.

Muskens, R. 1996. 'Combining Montague Semantics and Discourse Representation Theory', *Linguistics and Philosophy* 19, 143–86.

Neale, S. 1990. *Descriptions*. Cambridge, MA: MIT Press.

Ojeda, A. 1991. 'Definite descriptions and definite generics', *Linguistics and Philosophy* 14, 367–98.

Parsons, T. 1989. 'The progressive in English: events, states and processes', *Linguistics and Philosophy* 12, 213–41.

Parsons, T. 1990. *Events in the Semantics of English: A Study in Subatomic Semantics*. Cambridge, MA: MIT Press.

Partee, B.H. 1973. 'Some structural analogies between tenses and pronouns in English', *Journal of Philosophy* 70, 601–9.

Partee, B.H. 1984. 'Nominal and temporal anaphora', *Linguistics and Philosophy* 7, 243–86.

Partee, B.H. 1989. 'Binding implicit variables in quantified contexts', in Wiltshire, C., Music, B. and Graczyk, R. (eds.), *Papers from CLS 25*, 342–65. Chicago Linguistic Society.

Partee, B. H., ter Meulen, A. and Wall, R. 1990. *Mathematical Methods in Linguistics*. Dordrecht: Kluwer.

Pelletier, F. 1979. 'Non-Singular reference: some preliminaries', in Pelletier, F. (ed.), *Mass Terms: Some Philosophical Problems*, 1–14. Dordrecht: Reidel.

Pelletier, F. (ed.) 1979. *Mass Terms: Some Philosophical Problems*. Dordrecht: Reidel.

Pickering, M. and Garrod, S. 2004. 'Toward a mechanistic psychology of dialogue', *Behavioral and Brain Sciences* 27, 169–226.

Piwek, P. 2007. 'Meaning and dialogue coherence: a proof-theoretic investigation', *Journal of Logic, Language and Information* 16, 403–21.

Popper, K. 1965. *Conjectures and Refutations: The Growth of Scientific Knowledge*. London: Routledge.

Portner, P. and Partee, B. (eds.) 2002. *Formal Semantics: The Essential Readings*. Oxford: Blackwell.

Prior, A. 1967. *Past, Present and Future*. Oxford: Clarendon Press.

Progovac, L., Paesani, K., Casielles, E. and Barton, E. (eds.) 2006. *The Syntax of Non-Sententials*. Amsterdam: John Benjamins.

Purver, M. 2004. 'The theory and use of clarification requests in dialogue.' Unpublished PhD thesis, London University.

Purver, M. 2006. 'CLARIE: Handling clarification requests in a dialogue system', *Research on Language and Computation* 4, 259–88.

Purver, M., Cann, R. and Kempson, R. 2006. 'Grammars as parsers: meeting the dialogue challenge', *Research on Language and Computation* 4, 289–326.

Pustejovsky, J. 1995. *The Generative Lexicon.* Cambridge, MA: MIT Press.

Pustejovksy J. 1998. 'Generativity and explanation in semantics: a reply to Fodor and Lepore', *Linguistic Inquiry* 29, 289–311.

Quine, W.V.O. 1960. *Word and Object.* Cambridge, MA: MIT Press.

Ranta, A. 1994. *Type-Theoretical Grammar.* Oxford University Press.

Recanati, F. 2004. *Literal Meaning.* Cambridge University Press.

Reichenbach, H. 1947. *Elements of Symbolic Logic.* London: Macmillan.

Reinhart, T. 1983. *Anaphora and Semantic Interpretation.* London: Croom Helm.

Reuland, E. and ter Meulen, A. (eds.) 1987. *The Representation of (In)definiteness.* Cambridge, MA: MIT Press.

Rosch, E. 1983. 'Prototype classification and logical classification: the two systems', in Scholnick, E. (ed.), *New Trends in Cognitive Representation: Challenges to Piaget's Theory*, 73–86. New York: Lawrence Erlbaum.

Ross. H. 1967. 'Constraints on variables in syntax.' Unpublished PhD thesis, MIT.

Rothstein, S. 2004. *Structuring Events: A Study in the Semantics of Lexical Aspect.* Oxford: Blackwell.

Rothstein, S. 2008. *Theoretical and Crosslinguistics Approaches to the Semantics of Aspect.* Amsterdam: John Benjamins.

Russell, B. 1905. 'On denoting', *Mind* 14, 479–93.

Russell, B. 1919. *Introduction to Mathematical Philosophy.* London: George Allen and Unwin.

Samuels, R. 2006. 'Is the mind massively modular?', in Stainton 2006: 37–56.

Sandt, R. van der 1992. 'Presupposition projection as anaphora resolution', *Journal of Semantics* 9, 333–77.

Schein, B. 1993. *Plurals and Events.* Cambridge, MA: MIT Press.

Schlangen, D. 2003. 'A coherence-based approach to the interpretation of non-sentential utterances in dialogue'. Unpublished PhD thesis, Edinburgh University.

Schlangen, D. and Lascarides, A. 2003. 'A compositional and constraint-based approach to non-sentential utterances', in Muller, S. (ed.), *The Proceedings of the 10th International Conference on Head-Driven Phrase Structure Grammar*, 380–90. Stanford: CSLI Publications.

Schlenker, P. 2006. 'Ontological symmetry in language: a brief manifesto', *Mind and Language* 21, 504–39.

Shieber, S., Dalrymple, M. and Pereira, F. 1996. 'Interactions of scope and ellipsis', *Linguistics and Philosophy* 19, 527–52.

Slater, B. H. 1986. 'E-type pronouns and e-terms', *Canadian Journal of Philosophy* 16, 27–38.

Smith, N.V. and Smith, A. 1988. 'A relevance-theoretic account of conditionals', in Hyman, L. and Li, C. (eds.), *Language, Speech and Mind: Essays in Honour of Victoria Fromkin*, 1322–52. London: Routledge.

Sperber, D. 2002. 'In defence of massive modularity', in Dupoux, E. (ed.), *Language, Brain and Cognitive Development: Essays in Honor of Jacques Mehler*, 47–57. Cambridge, MA: MIT Press.

Sperber, D. and Wilson, D. 1995. *Relevance: Communication and Cognition*, 2nd edn. Oxford: Blackwell.

Sperber, D. and Wilson, D. 1998. 'The mapping between the mental and the public lexicon', in Carruthers, P. and Boucher, J. (eds.), *Language and Thought*, 184–200. Cambridge University Press.

Stainton, R. 2004. 'In defense of nonsentential assertion', in Szabo, Z. (ed.), *Semantics versus Pragmatics*, 383–457. Oxford University Press.

Stainton, R. (ed.). 2006. *Contemporary Debates in Cognitive Science*. Oxford: Blackwell.

Stainton, R. and Elugardo, R. 2004. 'Shorthand, syntactic ellipsis, and the pragmatic determinants of what is said', *Mind and Language* 19, 442–71.

Stalnaker, R. 1974. 'Pragmatic presuppositions', in Munitz, M. and Unger, P. (eds.), *Semantics and Philosophy*, 197–213. New York University Press.

Stalnaker, R. 1978. 'Assertion', in Cole, P. (ed.), *Syntax and Semantics 9*, 315–32. New York: Academic Press (reprinted in Davis 1991).

Stalnaker, R. 1999. *Context and Content*. Oxford: Clarendon Press.

Stanley, J. 2000. 'Context and logical form', *Linguistics and Philosophy* 23, 391–434.

Steedman, M. 1996. *Surface Structure and Interpretation*. Cambridge, MA: MIT Press.

Steedman, M. 1997. 'Temporality', in Benthem, J. van and Meulen, A. ter (eds.), *Handbook of Logic and Language*, 895–935. Amsterdam: Elsevier North Holland.

Steedman, M. 2000. *The Syntactic Process*. Cambridge, MA: MIT Press.

Strawson, P. 1950. 'On referring', *Mind* 59, 320–44.

Swart, H. de 1998. *Introduction to Natural Language Semantics*. Stanford: CSLI Publications.

Tenny, C. and Pustejovsky, J. 2000. *Events as Grammatical Objects: The Converging Perspectives of Lexical Semantics and Syntax*. Stanford: CSLI Publications.

Vendler, Z. 1967. *Linguistics in Philosophy*. Ithaca: Cornell University Press.

Wedgwood, D. 2007. 'Shared assumptions: semantic minimalism and Relevance Theory', *Journal of Linguistics* 43, 647–81.

Wilson, D. and Carston, R. 2007. 'A unitary approach to lexical pragmatics: relevance, inference and ad hoc concepts', in Burton-Roberts, N. (ed.), *Advances in Pragmatics*, 230–60. London: Palgrave Macmillan.

Wilson, D. and Sperber, D. 2004. 'Relevance theory', in Hom, L. and Ward, G. (eds.), *The Handbook of Pragmatics*, 607–32. Oxford: Blackwell.

Zegarac, V. 1993. 'Some observations on the pragmatics of the progressive', *Lingua* 90, 201–20.

Zwarts, F. 1983. 'Determiners: a relational perspective', in ter Meulen, A. (ed.), *Studies in Modeltheoretic Semantics*, 37–62. Dordrecht: Fons.

Index